The Working Class in American History

A list of books in the series appears at the end of this volume.

Workingmen's Democracy

Workingmen's Democracy

The Knights of Labor and American Politics

Leon Fink

University of Illinois Press   *Urbana and Chicago*

Illini Books edition, 1985

© 1983 by the Board of Trustees of the University of Illinois
Manufactured in the United States of America
P 5 4

This book is printed on acid-free paper.

I thank the editors of *Radical History Review, Labor History,*
and *Social History* for permission to adapt essays that were
originally published in their journals.

Library of Congress Cataloging in Publication Data

Fink, Leon, 1948–
    Workingmen's democracy.

    (The Working class in American history)
    Bibliography: p.
    Includes index.
    1. Knights of Labor—History. 2. Labor and laboring
classes—United States—Political activity—History.
I Title. II. Series.
HD8055.K7F56   322'.2'0973   82-6902
ISBN 0-252-01256-9   AACR2

To Irving and Beatrice Borman Fink,
who taught me first principles

Contents

Preface   xi

1   Working-Class Radicalism in the Gilded Age: Defining a
Political Culture   3

2   The Uses of Political Power: The Knights of Labor
and the State   18

3   When Cleon Comes to Rule: Popular Organization and
Political Development. Part I: Rochester, New Hampshire   38

4   When Cleon Comes to Rule: Popular Organization and
Political Development. Part II: Rutland, Vermont   66

5   City-Building and Social Reform: Urban Workers within the
Two-Party System, Kansas City, Kansas   112

6   Together but Unequal: Southern Knights and the Dilemmas of
Race and Politics, Richmond, Virginia   149

7   Bullets and Ballots: Worker Mobilization and the Path to
Municipal Socialism, Milwaukee, Wisconsin   178

8   Labor, Party Politics, and American Exceptionalism   219

Selected Bibliography: Primary Sources   234

Index   239

Preface

TWO WELL-TRAVELED ROUTES into the Gilded Age are likely to leave the present-day visitor with the same puzzled and unsatisfied feeling. One itinerary pursuing the political history of the era begins in 1876 with the official end of Reconstruction and winds through the election of William McKinley in 1896. The other route, this one taking a social prospectus, departs with the great railroad strikes of 1877 and picks its way through the drama and debris of an industrializing society. The problem is that the two paths never seem to meet. Compartmentalization of subject matter in most textbooks into "politics," "economic change," "social movements," and so on only papers over the obvious unanswered question—what impact did an industrial revolution of unprecedented magnitude have on the world's most democratic nation?

The question, of course, permits no simple answer. By most accounts the political era inaugurated in 1876 appears, except for the Populist outburst of the mid-1890s, as a conservative, comparatively uneventful time sandwiched between the end of Radical Reconstruction and the new complexities of the twentieth century. With the Civil War's financial and social settlement out of the way, a society desperately wanting to believe that it had removed its last barriers to social harmony by and large lapsed into a period of ideological torpor and narrow-minded partisanship. Political contests, while still the national pastime (national elections regularly drew 80 percent, state and local elections 60–80 percent of eligible voters, 1876–96), seem to have dwelt less on major social issues than on simple party fealty. Fierce rivalries engendered by the sectional, ethnocultural, and economic interest group divisions among the American people increasingly were presided over and manipulated by party professionals. To be sure, genuine policy differences—e.g., over how best to encourage both industry and trade, the degree of danger posed by the saloon, honesty in government—fueled a venomous political rhetoric. As echoed by both national parties from the late 1870s through the early 1890s, however, a complacent political consensus had emerged, stressing individual opportunity, rights in property, and economic freedom from constraints. The welfare of the American Dream, in the minds of both Democrats and Repub-

licans, required no significant governmental tinkering or popular mobilization. Acknowledging the parties' avoidance of changing social and economic
realities, a most compelling recent commentary on the late nineteenth-century
polity suggests that the "distinct, social need" of the time was in part filled
by heightened partisanship and the act of political participation itself.[1]

In contrast to the ritualistic quality of politics, the contemporary social
world seems positively explosive. Consolidation of America's industrial revolution touched off an era of unexampled change and turmoil. As work shifted
decisively away from agriculture between 1870 and 1890, the manufacturing
sector, with a spectacular increase in the amount of capital invested, the
monetary value of product, and the number employed, sparked a great economic leap forward. By 1880 Carroll D. Wright, U.S. Commissioner of
Labor Statistics, found that the application of steam and water power to
production had so expanded that "at least four-fifths" of the "nearly 3 millions of people employed in the mechanical industries of this country" were
working under the factory system. It was not just the places of production but
the people working within them that represented a dramatic departure from
preindustrial America. While only 13 percent of the total population was
classified as foreign-born in 1880, 42 percent of those engaged in manufacturing and extractive industries were immigrants. If one adds to this figure
workers of foreign parentage and of Afro-American descent, the resulting
nonnative/nonwhite population clearly encompassed the great majority of
America's industrial work force. Not only, therefore, had the industrial revolution turned a small minority in America's towns and cities into the direct
employers of their fellow citizens, but the owners of industry also differed
from their employees in national and cultural background. This sudden transformation of American communities, accompanied as it was by a period of
intense price competition and unregulated swings in the business cycle, provided plentiful ingredients for social unrest, first manifest on a national scale
in the railroad strike of 1877.[2]

The quintessential expression of the labor movement in the Gilded Age
was the Noble and Holy Order of the Knights of Labor, the first mass organization of the American working class. Launched as one of several secret
societies among Philadelphia artisans in the late 1860s, the Knights grew in
spurts by the accretion of miners (1874–79) and skilled urban tradesmen
(1879–85). While the movement formally concentrated on moral and political
education, cooperative enterprise, and land settlement, members found it a
convenient vehicle for trade union action, particularly in the auspicious economic climate following the depression of the 1870s. Beginning in 1883,
local skirmishes escalated into highly publicized confrontations with railroad
financier Jay Gould, a national symbol of new corporate power. Strikes by
Knights of Labor telegraphers and railroad shopmen touched off an unprecedented wave of strikes and boycotts that carried on into the renewed depres-

sion in 1884–85 and spread to thousands of previously unorganized semiskilled and unskilled laborers, both urban and rural. The Southwest Strike on Gould's Missouri and Texas-Pacific railroad lines together with massive urban eight-hour campaigns in 1886 swelled a tide of unrest that has become known as the "Great Upheaval." The turbulence aided the efforts of organized labor, and the Knights exploded in size, reaching more than three-quarters of a million members. Although membership dropped off drastically in the late 1880s, the Knights remained a powerful force in many areas through the mid-1890s. Not until the Congress of Industrial Organizations revival of the 1930s would the organized labor movement again lay claim to such influence within the working population.[3]

At its zenith the movement around the Knights helped to sustain a national debate over the social implications of industrial capitalism. Newspaper editors, lecturers, and clergymen everywhere addressed the Social Question. John Swinton, the leading labor journalist of the day, counted Karl Marx, Hawaii's King Kalakaua, and the Republican party's chief orator, Robert G. Ingersoll, among the enlightened commentators on the subject. Even the U.S. Senate in 1883 formally investigated "Relations between Labor and Capital." Nor was the debate conducted only from on high. In laboring communities across the nation the local press as well as private correspondence bore witness to no shortage of eloquence from the so-called inarticulate. One of the busiest terminals of communications was the Philadelphia office of Terence Vincent Powderly, General Master Workman of the Knights of Labor. Unsolicited personal letters expressing the private hopes and desperations of ordinary American citizens daily poured in upon the labor leader: an indigent southern mother prayed that her four young girls would grow up to find an honorable living, an unemployed New York cakemaker applied for a charter as an organizer, a Cheyenne chief sought protection for his people's land, an inventor offered to share a new idea for the cotton gin on condition that it be used cooperatively.[4]

Amidst spreading agitation, massed strength, and growing public awareness, the labor issues ultimately took tangible political form. Wherever the Knights of Labor had organized by the mid-1880s, it seemed, contests over power and rights at the workplace evolved into a community-wide fissure over control of public policy as well. Indeed, in some 200 towns and cities from 1885 to 1888 the labor movement actively fielded its own political slates. Adopting "Workingmen's," "United Labor," "Union Labor," "People's Party," and "Independent" labels for their tickets, or alternatively taking over one of the standing two-party organizations in town, those local political efforts revealed deep divisions within the contemporary political culture and evoked sharp reactions from traditional centers of power. Even as manufacturers' associations met labor's challenge at the industrial level, business response at the political level was felt in the dissolution of party structures, creation of antilabor citizens' coalitions, new restrictive legislation, and ex-tralegal law and order leagues. In their ensemble, therefore, the political confrontations of the 1880s offer a most dramatic point of convergence be-tween the world leading out of 1876 and that stretching from 1877. As a phenomenon simultaneously entwined in the political and industrial history of the Gilded Age the subject offers an opportunity to redefine the main issues of the period.

Both for reasons of theme and research method, this study, like other recent work on nineteenth-century America, concentrates on events in specific, local communities. One author has articulated the prevailing wisdom among social historians in asserting that "the local community constituted the main arena of intellectual, social, and political life."[5] Five distinct but related studies here explore the meaning and impact of the workingmen's political movement in communities which differed in size and geographical location as well as in economic and social character. Each study concentrates on the confrontation of new political forces with established authority, pursuing events until the movement around the Knights of Labor had dissolved or been absorbed into something else. The initial source and developing composition of the work-ingmen's movement, its aims, ambitions, and achievements, the strength and strategy of its opposition, and the impact of these contemporary contests upon subsequent labor and political traditions provide a common thread of con-cerns. The diverse situations, reflecting the uneven experience of the country as a whole, encourage a shifting conceptual emphasis from chapter to chapter.

Two synthesizing essays introduce the community studies and place them within a wider frame of reference. Chapter 1 offers a character study of the labor movement in the Gilded Age, an examination of basic values and ideological assumptions underlying the formal activity of the Knights of Labor. The social critique of the labor radicals is shown here as a *bricolage* of widely shared attitudes toward work, family, community, and citizenship in America. Chapter 2 focuses more specifically on attitudes toward politics and the state evident in the workingmen's movement. While reluctantly engaging in direct political involvement, the Knights of Labor in practice extended Republican-ism's traditional commitment to limited government and equal rights to its ideological limits.

The case studies begin with a two-part examination of the New England towns of Rochester, New Hampshire (chapter 3), and Rutland, Vermont (chap-ter 4), emphasizing the impact of a changing social balance of power on political development. In both towns a basically nonpartisan town-meeting tradition reflected the authority, both formal and informal, of a Republican, merchant-industrialist elite, active in Protestant churches, voluntary organizations, and private philanthropy as well as public service. In an increasingly industrial age, however, such control excluded rather than incorporated a growing wage-earning population. Such exclusion became most dramatic, as in Rutland, where the labor force was overwhelmingly composed of Catholic ethnic minorities. In both towns the fact of labor organization in the mid-1880s upset the traditional town rulers, politicizing a cultural divide that had already developed. A moment of stark, class-based polarization at the height of Knights of Labor influence soon faded before the unmistakably superior organization of capital over labor. An enduring testament to the local impact of a democratic social movement, nevertheless, survived in the entry of labor representatives into competitive party politics.

If the two New England towns captured the entry of the organized working class into political life, the western boom town of Kansas City, Kansas, witnessed the impact of labor revolt upon groups already integrated into the two-party system (chapter 5). Empowered by the Great Southwest Strike and perched on a coalition of ethnic and racial groups, a labor-Republican regime under Mayor Thomas Hannan laid claim to a particular labor perspective on issues of town-building and municipal reform. Like other political machines, however, the Hannan regime soon demonstrated a commitment, above all else, to its own survival. The capacity of urban boss politics at once to represent and to absorb worker interests is highlighted in the Kansas City case by the frustration of Kansas Populists in trying to reach out from their agrarian base to this laboring town.

A detailed examination of events in Richmond, Virginia, in 1886, chapter 6 explores the tensions between race and class identities affecting southern workers. As in other major cities, Richmond Knights of Labor demonstrated not only considerable economic clout but also real political influence, sweeping municipal elections in May 1886 and preparing to extend their victory in federal elections the next fall. The social geography of the South, however, imposed a special dilemma on labor reform efforts. While the two-party system posed insuperable barriers to a black-white labor political unity, the alternative, third-party option risked the most severe censure from authorities in both the white and black communities. The failure of District Master Workman William Mullen's race for Congress placed the complex and tragic forces operating in the workers' world in bold relief.

By focusing on the labor stronghold of Milwaukee, Wisconsin, chapter 7 allows us to pursue the implications of a politicized labor movement beyond the point normally experienced in the United States. As in Kansas City the strike wave of 1886 — and its repressive aftermath — galvanized a powerful and united working-class political response. Exceptional to Milwaukee, however, was the organizational autonomy of a German-American labor culture that first through the Knights of Labor and later through the Socialist party became the basis of a majority electoral coalition. The changing components of that coalition from the era of the Knights of Labor to the era of the Socialist party highlight the larger question of the relation of mass mobilization and workplace action to electoral strategies of social change.

In conclusion we reflect on the rise and fall of the movement of the 1880s and the impact of this historical moment for developments in the twentieth century (chapter 8). Born in the locally bounded world of the nineteenth century, the Knights of Labor struggled to come to grips with a dynamic corporate capitalism that transcended local community authority and its sanctions. If ideologically unoriginal, the Knights of Labor nevertheless broke important new ground — primarily by identifying a common struggle for a remarkably diverse body of working people. Politically, the Knights' impact was uneven, showing the greatest capacity for independent action where governing structures proved brittle and unyielding before the new social movement. That their success was short-lived did not mean that working-class politics in the United States was "absent" or irrelevant. A subtler look at the social roots of American politics and state interventions is required before we can be so cavalier. These essays, it is hoped, represent a step in that direction.

One cannot write history without an awareness of the complex levels of influence upon a single activity. This consideration becomes a ticklish predicament in trying to assign gratitude, and I have therefore decided to concentrate on only the most direct and formal of intellectual acknowledgments. An older generation of British historians first whetted my appetite for the discipline of history when I arrived at Harvard College as an undergraduate in 1966. I have in some sense studied the political culture of nineteenth-century workers since 1968–69, when I took part in the Comparative Labour History program of the Centre for Social History at Warwick University, England. Contact there with Edward Thompson, David Montgomery, Fred Reid, James Hinton, and an engaging group of graduate students spun me into a world of intellectual and political commitments from which I have not yet recovered. I received my first real grounding in American history at the University of Rochester, 1970–72, where the seminars of Christopher Lasch, Eugene Genovese, and Herbert Gutman emphasized, respectively, the importance of thought, power, and the unknown as objects of historical curiosity.

It was with Herbert Gutman that I worked most closely, particularly after joining him at the City College of New York in 1972. My permanent debt to the sympathy and insight he brings to the study of working-class historical experience is, doubtlessly, readily apparent; his personal encouragement and shrewd editorial judgment throughout the writing of my dissertation, however, were equally significant. Besides Gutman, Gregory Kealey, Stephen Hahn, David Montgomery, and Eugene Genovese gave an earlier draft of the manuscript a most helpful critical reading. In addition, Eric Foner, Brian

Greenberg, Lawrence Goodwyn, Joan Wallach Scott, Donald M. Scott, Michael Frisch, Daniel Walkowitz, Karen Kearns, Neil Basen, Peter Rachleff, Michael Fitzsimmons, Nick Builder, and Scott Ware made useful suggestions concerning specific sections of the work; Ingrid Lehmann and Caroline Orzelska Wong generously contributed their linguistic skills to the Milwaukee material; and my father-in-law, Harry Levine, offered helpful suggestions regarding presentation of the tables. While approaching final revisions I have also benefited from the general historical counsel of North Carolina colleagues Roger Lotchin, Nell Painter, Gil Joseph, and Harry Watson. Ceci M. Long did an excellent job in typing the manuscript, and the editorial skill of Susan L. Patterson enhanced the final copy.

I received vital research assistance in the course of their normal responsibilities from the staffs of the New York Public Library, Columbia University Library, Schomburg Center for Research in Black Culture, Catholic University archives, Duke University archives, Vermont State Historical Society, Proctor Free Library, Rochester Free Library, Wisconsin State Historical Society, Virginia Historical Society, and the Kansas State Historical Society. I owe special thanks to Robert Richmond, Kansas state archivist, Virginia librarian Howson W. Cole, Henry Miller of the Wisconsin State Historical Society, and the Reverend Peter Beckman of Benedictine College, Atchison, Kansas. In the same spirit I would like to propose a general toast to an uncelebrated group of historians—those proud local chroniclers who took down names, dates, and events in a town or county and so preserved a record for future analysis. For providing me the means to carry out my research, I am grateful for the National Defense Education Act and for the Manpower Administration of the Department of Labor, whose 1974–75 dissertation grant enabled me to travel to the local archival collections. I also thank Samuel R. Williamson, Dean of College Arts and Sciences, University of North Carolina at Chapel Hill, for use of his discretionary funds. Finally, I would like to pay tribute to the patience of Moe Foner, Executive Secretary, District 1199 National Union of Hospital and Health Care Employees, for allowing me to complete old business first.

My greatest debt in the writing of this book is to Susan Levine. Throughout the process she has been my most demanding, persistent, and insightful critic. More important still, she has turned a lengthy immersion into the world of the Knights of Labor from what might have been a wintry isolation into a buoyant subculture. I had better add that the title to this work reflects the reality of the political culture of the day, not my ignorance of the part women played in the Knights of Labor as a whole.

NOTES

1. Richard Hofstadter, *The American Political Tradition and the Men Who Made It* (New York, 1948), 164–85; Morton Keller, *Affairs of State: Public Life in Late Nineteenth-Century America* (Cambridge, Mass., 1977), 532–33.

2. U.S. Tenth Census, 1880, *Report on Manufactures of the United States* (Washington, D.C., n.d.), 17, 36; U.S. Thirteenth Census, 1910, Pt. 4, *Population, Occupation Statistics* (Washington, D.C., 1914), 41; U.S. Eleventh Census, 1890, *Compendium of the Eleventh Census,* Pt. 3 (Washington, D.C., 1897), 68; Ira Berlin and Herbert G. Gutman, "The Structure of the American Urban Working Class in the Mid-Nineteenth Century: The South, the North," paper presented at the Annual Meeting of the Organization of American Historians, Apr. 3, 1981, Detroit, Mich.; Philip S. Foner, *The Great Labor Uprising of 1877* (New York, 1977).

3. Jonathan Garlock, "A Structural Analysis of the Knights of Labor" (Ph.D. diss., University of Rochester, 1974), 194–210.

4. Mary J. Lockett to Powderly, Apr. 14, 1886, David Davidson to Powderly, Apr. 14, 1886, Powderly to D. W. Bushyhead, July 12, 1886, C. H. Merry to Powderly, Mar. 14, 1886, Terence V. Powderly Papers, Catholic University, Washington, D.C.

5. Daniel J. Walkowitz, *Worker City, Company Town: Iron and Cotton-Worker Protest in Troy and Cohoes, New York, 1855–84* (Urbana, Ill., 1978), 13. On the meaning of community studies, see Kenneth L. Kusmer, "The Concept of Community in American History," *Reviews in American History,* 7 (Spring 1977), 380–87, and C. J. Calhoun, "Community: Toward a Variable Conceptualization for Comparative Research," *Social History,* 5 (Jan. 1980), 105–29.

During the previous winter, arrangements had been made for widespread strikes to take place on the first of May [1887], the object of which was of course to secure to those who worked with their hands an increased pay, combined with shorter hours of labor. . . . And it was understood some sort of organized demonstration would be made at the annual [Quincy] town meeting. It of course does not need to be added that demonstrations of this character, organized privately and outside, are the greatest element of danger to which popular government, and especially town-meeting government, can be subjected. It was so in the days of Athens and of Rome, and it will continue to be so as long as human nature and human institutions remain as they are. Cleon and Claudius are recurring characters.*

—Charles Francis Adams,
Three Episodes of Massachusetts History

Of course every citizen has the legal right to express his views on all questions brought before town meeting, but there are many ways of depriving him of his right; by violence, by noisy and disorderly conduct on the part of others, by ridiculing his peculiarities of speech or lack of oratorical ability or wealth, by preconcerted action on the part of any set, by the use of parliamentary rules which are not well understood by the many, etc. . . . All these means [except for violence] have been used by the real managers of our town meetings, the "Wisdom's Corner," to prevent a free expression of the people's will.

—Quincy *Monitor,* Irish Catholic
and pro–Knights of Labor newspaper

*Cleon, the son of a tanner and one of the first of humble origin to achieve power in the Athenian democracy, was immortalized as a vulgar demagogue by Thucydides and Aristophanes. The reign of the Roman Emperor Claudius witnessed the first emergence of freedmen in public life as well as other signs of loss of authority by a decadent patriciate.
(Courtesy of Marylin Arthur and Henry Boren.)

1

Working-Class Radicalism
in the Gilded Age:
Defining a Political Culture

THE LABOR MOVEMENT of the Gilded Age, not unlike its nineteenth-century British counterpart, spoke a "language of class" that was "as much political as economic." In important ways an eighteenth-century republican political inheritance still provided the basic vocabulary. The emphasis within the movement on equal rights, on the identity of work and self-worth, and on secure, family-centered households had informed American political radicalism for decades. A republican outlook lay at the heart of the protests of journeymen-mechanics and women millworkers during the Jacksonian period; it likewise inspired abolitionist and the women's suffrage and temperance movements and even contributed to the common school crusade. Within the nineteenth-century political mainstream this tradition reached its height of influence in the free labor assault of the Radical Republicans against slavery. The fracture of the Radical Republican bloc, as David Montgomery has demonstrated, signaled a break in the tradition itself. The more conspicuous and politically dominant side of the schism reflected the growing ideological conservatism of America's industrialists and their steady merger into older socioeconomic elites. A less complacent message, however, also percolated through the age of Hayes, Harrison, and Hanna. Taking place largely outside the party system, this renewed radicalism found a home within an invigorated labor movement.[1]

Working-class radicalism in the Gilded Age derived its principles—as grouped around economic, national-political, and cultural themes—from the period of the early revolutionary-democratic bourgeoisie. Implicitly, labor radicals embraced a unifying conception of work and culture that Norman Birnbaum has labeled the *Homo faber* ideal: "an artisanal conception of activity, a visible, limited, and directed relationship to nature." The *Homo faber* ethic found its political embodiment in Enlightenment liberalism. "From that source," notes Trygve R. Tholfson in a recent commentary on mid-Victorian English labor radicalism, "came a trenchant rationalism, a vision of human emancipation, the expectation of progress based on reason, and an inclination to take the action necessary to bring society into conformity with rationally demonstrable principles." In the late nineteenth century Enlightenment liberalism was harnessed to a historical understanding of American nationalism, confirmed by both the American Revolution and the Civil War. Together these political, economic, and moral conceptions coalesced around a twin commitment to the citizen-as-producer and the producer-as-citizen. For nearly a century Americans had been proud that their country, more than anywhere else in the world, made republican principles real. In this respect the bloody war over slavery served only to confirm the ultimate power of the ideal.[2]

Certain tendencies of the Gilded Age, however, heralded for some an alarming social regression. The permanency of wage labor, the physical and mental exhaustion inflicted by the factory system, and the arrogant exercise of power by the owners of capital threatened the rational and progressive march of history. "Republican institutions," the preamble to the constitution of the Knights of Labor declared simply, "are not safe under such conditions." "We have openly arrayed against us," a Chicago radical despaired in 1883, "the powers of the world, most of the intelligence, all the wealth, and even law itself." The lament of a Connecticut man that "factoryism, bankism, collegism, capitalism, insuranceism and the presence of such lump-headed malignants as Professor William Graham Sumner" were stultifying "the native genius of this state" framed the evil in more homespun terms. In 1883 cigar-makers' leader Samuel Gompers, not yet accepting the inevitability of capitalist industry, bemoaned the passing of the day of "partners at the work bench" that had given way to "the tendency . . . which makes man, the worker, a part of the machine." The British-born journalist Richard J. Hinton, an old Chartist who had commanded black troops during the Civil War, also reflected on the sudden darkening of the social horizon. The "average, middle-class American," he complained, simply could not appreciate the contemporary position of American workers: "They all look back to the days when they were born in some little American village. . . . They have seen their time and opportunity of getting on in the world, and they think that is the condition of society today, when it is totally a different condition."[3]

In response the labor movement in the Gilded Age turned the plowshares of a consensual political past into a sword of class conflict. "We declare," went the Knights' manifesto, "an inevitable and irresistible conflict between the wage-system of labor and republican system of government." To some extent older demons seemed simply to have reappeared in new garb, and, as such, older struggles beckoned with renewed urgency. A Greenback editor in Rochester, New Hampshire, thus proclaimed that "patriots" who overturn the "lords of labor" would be remembered next to "the immortal heroes of the revolution and emancipation." Labor rhetoric in the period rings with a variety of appeals to an extended republican heritage. "If you lose this fight," Michigan Knights' leader Thomas B. Barry exhorted striking lumbermen in 1885, "you have nothing to do but get a collar and chain and hammer and staple, and tell your employers to fasten you to a block." Others similarly denounced unorganized railroad workers as "Corbin's chattel" or assailed Pinkerton agents as "Hessians." After the deployment of Pinkertons by Chicago meatpacking firms in 1886, a pro-labor Catholic newspaper pointedly warned that "the Roman republic was free until the patricians gathered around them their armed clients." Knights' national officer Ralph Beaumont's description of New York corporation directors who "walk around with pug dogs, while their offspring follow behind in their nurses' arms" and a Michigan labor orator's denunciation of Congressmen as "pot-bellied millionaires, who live on porterhouse steaks, drink champagne, smoke 15 cent cigars . . . who will ride out with their wives, or more likely other peoples' wives" represented the invective of latter-day Tom Paines.[4]

Unlike Tom Paine, however, late nineteenth-century American radicals had the advantage of being able to rely on rather than abandon historical experience. A philosophical Ohio farmer, Donn Piatt, thus offered the contrast that "in Europe labor is accustomed to oppression, and it is a hard part of God's destiny for them, to be borne patiently as long as they can get enough to hold body and soul together." Americans, however, were different: "Our people have been carefully educated to consider themselves the best on earth, and they will not patiently submit to privation such as this system is leading to. They not only feel that they are the best of the earth, but there is no power, no standing army, no organized iron rule to hold them down."[5]

Piatt was not alone in his nationalistic pride. To many other outside observers in the 1880s, the American working class—in terms of organization, militancy, and collective self-consciousness—appeared more advanced than its European counterparts. A leader of the French Union des Chambres Syndicales Ouvrières compared the self-regarding, individualist instincts of the French workers to those of the Americans enrolled in the Knights of Labor (Ordre des Chevaliers du Travail):

> Unfortunately, the French worker, erratic as he is enthusiastic, of an almost discouraging indolence when it is a question of his own interests, does not much lend himself to organization into a great order like yours. He understands nevertheless their usefulness, even cites them as an example each time that he has the occasion to prove the possibility of the solidarity of workers; but when it comes to passing from the domain of theory to that of practice, he retreats or disappears. Thirsty for freedom he is always afraid of alienating any one party while contracting commitments toward a collectivity; mistrustful, he is afraid of affiliating with a group whose positions might not correspond exactly to those inscribed on his own flag; undisci-

plined, he conforms with difficulty to rules which he has given to himself.
. . . He wants to play it safe and especially will not consent to any sacrifice
without having first calculated the advantages it will bring to him.

Eleanor Marx and Edward Aveling returned from an 1886 American tour with
a glowing assessment of the workers' mood. Friedrich Engels, too, in the
aftermath of the eight-hour strikes and the Henry George campaign, attached
a special preface to the 1887 American edition of *The Condition of the
Working Class in England in 1844:*

> In European countries, it took the working class years and years before
> they fully realized the fact that they formed a distinct and, under the
> existing social conditions, a permanent class of modern society; and it took
> years again until this class-consciousness led them to form themselves into
> a distinct political party, independent of, and opposed to, all the old politi-
> cal parties, formed by the various sections of the ruling classes. On the
> more favored soil of America, where no medieval ruins bar the way, where
> history begins with the elements of the modern bourgeois society as evolved
> in the seventeenth century, the working class passed through these two
> stages of its development within ten months.[6]

Nor was it only in the eyes of eager well-wishers that the developments of
the 1880s seemed to take on a larger significance. Surveying the map of labor
upheaval, the conservative Richmond *Whig* wrote in 1886 of "socialistic and
agrarian elements" threatening "the genius of our free institutions." The
Chicago *Times* went so far in its fear of impending revolution as to counsel
the use of hand grenades against strikers.[7]

Revolutionary anticipations, pro or con, proved premature. That was true
at least partly because both the movement's distant boosters as well as its
domestic detractors sometimes misrepresented its intentions. Gilded Age labor radicals did not self-consciously place themselves in opposition to a
prevailing economic system but displayed a sincere ideological ambivalence
toward the capitalist marketplace. On the one hand, they frequently invoked
a call for the "abolition of the wage system." On the other hand, like the
classical economists, they sometimes spoke of the operation of "natural law"
in the marketplace, acknowledged the need for a "fair return" on invested
capital, and did not oppose profit per se. Employing a distinctly pre-Marxist
economic critique that lacked a theory of capital accumulation or of surplus
value, labor leaders from Ira Steward to Terence Powderly tried nevertheless
to update and sharpen the force of received wisdom. The Knights thus modified an earlier radical interpretation of the labor-cost theory of value, wherein
labor, being the source of all wealth, should individually be vested with the
value of its product, and demanded for workers only an intentionally vague
"proper share of the wealth they create." In so doing they were able to shift
the weight of the analysis (not unlike Marx) to the general, collective plight

of the laboring classes. In their eyes aggregation of capital together with cutthroat price competition had destroyed any semblance of marketplace balance between employer and employee. Under the prevailing economic calculus labor had been demoted into just another factor of production whose remuneration was determined not by custom or human character but by market price. In such a situation they concluded, as Samuel Walker has noted, that "the contract was not and could not be entered into freely. . . . The process of wage determination was a moral affront because it degraded the personal dignity of the workingman." This subservient position to the iron law of the market constituted "wage slavery," and like other forms of involuntary servitude it had to be "abolished."[8]

Labor's emancipation did not, ipso facto, imply the overthrow of capitalism, a system of productive relations that the Knights in any case never defined. To escape wage slavery workers needed the strength to redefine the social balance of power with employers and their allies—and the will and intelligence to use that strength. One after another the Knights harnessed the various means at their disposal—education, organization, cooperation, economic sanction, and political influence—to this broad end: "To secure to the workers the full enjoyment [note, not the full return] of the wealth they create, sufficient leisure in which to develop their intellectual, moral and social faculties, all of the benefits of recreation, and pleasures of association; in a word to enable them to share in the gains and honors of advancing civilization."[9]

A wide range of strategic options was represented within the counsels of the labor movement. One tendency sought to check the rampant concentration of wealth and power with specific correctives on the operation of the free market. Radical Greenbackism (with roots in Kelloggism and related monetary theories), Henry George's single tax, and land nationalization, each of which commanded considerable influence among the Knights of Labor, fit this category. Another important tendency, cooperation, offered a more self-reliant strategy of alternative institution-building, or, as one advocate put it, "the organization of production without the intervention of the capitalist." Socialism, generally understood at the time as a system of state as opposed to private ownership of production, offered a third alternative to wage slavery. Except for a few influential worker-intellectuals and strong pockets of support among German-Americans, however, Socialism (for reasons which will become clearer in the next chapter) carried comparatively little influence in the 1880s. The argument of veteran abolitionist and labor reformer Joseph Labadie—"To say that state socialism is the rival of co-operation is to say that Jesus Christ was opposed to Christianity"—met a generally skeptical reception. Particularly in the far West, self-identified anarchists also agitated from within the ranks of the Order.[10]

If Gilded Age labor representatives tended to stop short of a frontal rejection of the political-economic order, there was nevertheless no mistaking their philosophic radicalism. Notwithstanding differences in emphasis, the labor movement's political sentiments encompassed both a sharp critique of social inequality and a broad-based prescription for a more humane future. Indeed, the labor representative who shrugged off larger philosophical and political commitments in favor of a narrow incrementalism was likely to meet with incredulity. One of the first, and most classic, enunciations of business union-ism, for example, received just this response from the Senate Committee on Labor and Capital in 1883. After taking testimony from workers and labor reformers across the country for six months, the committee, chaired by New Hampshire Senator Henry Blair, interviewed Adolph Strasser, president of the cigar-makers' union. Following a disquisition on the stimulating impact of shorter working hours on workers' consumption patterns, Strasser was asked if he did not contemplate a future beyond the contemporary exigencies of panic and overproduction, "some time [when] every man is to be an intelligent man and an enlightened man?" When Strasser did not reply, Sen-ator Blair interceded to elaborate the question. Still, Strasser rebuffed the queries, "Well, our organization does not consist of idealists . . . we do [not] control the production of the world. That is controlled by employers, and that is a matter for them." Senator Blair was taken aback.

> Blair. I was only asking you in regard to your ultimate ends.
> Witness. We have no ultimate ends. We are going on from day to day. We are fighting only for immediate objects—objects that can be realized in a few years. . . .
> Blair. I see that you are a little sensitive lest it should be thought that you are a mere theorizer. I do not look upon you in that light at all.
> Witness. Well, we say in our constitution that we are opposed to theo-rists, and I have to represent the organization here. We are all practical men.
> Blair. Have you not a theory upon which you have organized?
> Witness. Yes, sir: our theory is the experience of the past in the United States and in Great Britain. That is our theory, based upon actual facts. . . .
> Blair. In other words you have arrived at the theory which you are trying to apply?
> Witness. We have arrived at a practical result.
> Blair. But a practical result is the application of a theory is it not?[11]

On a cultural level, labor's critique of American society bore the same relation to Victorian respectability that its political radicalism bore to contem-porary liberalism. In both cases the middle-class and working-class radical variants derived from a set of common assumptions but drew from them quite different, even opposing, implications. No contemporary, for example, took more seriously than the Knights of Labor the cultural imperatives toward productive work, civic responsibility, education, a wholesome family life, temperance, and self-improvement. The intellectual and moral development of the individual, they would have agreed with almost every early nineteenth-century lyceum lecturer, was a precondition for the advancement of democratic civilization. In the day of Benjamim Franklin such values may well have knit together master craftsmen, journeymen, and apprentices. In the age of the factory system, however, the gulf between employer and employee had so widened that the lived meanings of the words were no longer the same.

No phrase was more frequently invoked in the litany of Knights' rhetoric and elaborate ritual than "nobility of toil." Like labor reformers in previous decades the Knights appropriated the classical economic labor theory of value to shower a sentimental glory on the toiler. No doubt the Knights' sanctification of work carried multiple meanings. In part labor drew on nostalgia for a preindustrial past, in part on a defense of devalued craft skills, but in part also on a transcendent vision of a cooperative industrial future. They dreamed of a day when even the enterprise of a Cornelius Vanderbilt or Jay Gould might be harnessed to "a different social system," which would replace the possession of "wealth" with "industrial and moral standard[s] of worth." For the Knights, in short, celebration of the work ethic came to serve as both a political and cultural badge of honor and even, as in the following news item, as a certificate of health:

A physician has lately written a work on the hay fever, in which he claims to have discovered for it a complete remedy. He has found a season of farm work a sure cure for the disease. He suggests that the susceptivity to that malady comes from eating too much in proportion to the physical labor one performs. It is a remarkable fact, that workingmen are not subject to the malady. It only appears to attack the idlers. The loafers will come eventually to understand that they *must* labor, if only to keep themselves in health. "Labor is the law of life."[12]

For the Knights the concept of the producing classes indicated an ultimate social division that they perceived in the world around them. Only those associated with idleness (bankers, speculators), corruption (lawyers, liquor dealers, gamblers), or social parasitism (all of the above) were categorically excluded from membership in the Order. Other social strata such as local merchants and manufacturers were judged by their individual acts, not by any inherent structural antagonism to the workers' movement. Those who showed respect for the dignity of labor (i.e., who sold union-made goods or employed union workers at union conditions) were welcomed into the Order. Those who denigrated the laborer or his product laid themselves open to the righteous wrath of the boycott or strike. Powderly characteristically chastised one ruthless West Virginia coal owner, "Don't die, even if you do smell bad. We'll need you in a few years as a sample to show how *mean* men used to be."[13]

This rather elastic notion of class boundaries on the part of the labor movement was reciprocated in the not inconsequential number of shopkeepers and small manufacturers who expressed sympathy and support for the labor movement. An exchange between John Keogh, a Fall River, Massachusetts, job printer and the Senate Committee on Labor and Capital is illustrative:

> Q. Conducting business for yourself?
> A. Yes, sir.
> Q. Are you a capitalist?
> A. No, sir. I was an operative for eleven years in the mills in Fall River.
> Q. But you have a little establishment of your own now?
> A. Yes.
> Q. You are a capitalist then, to that extent you control yourself and your own money, and do your own business as you please?
> A. Yes, but I do not consider myself a capitalist.[14]

In part, what "being considered a capitalist" implied was disregard for the workers' self-respect, the open defense of the laws of classical political economy, the working assumption of labor as a commodity.

If honest labor fulfilled moral and physical imperatives, too much of it not only damaged the individual physically but also interfered with the equally important imperatives of moral and intellectual development. The conditions of industrial life all too often made impossible the original bourgeois ideal of cultivated self-fulfillment. "That man who passes yonder with heavy footstep, hair unkempt, person dirty, dinner bucket in hand, and a general air of desolation," thus protested a Pittsburgh glass-blower, "is a 12 hour a day wage slave." The New York City tailors' union based its indictment of sweated labor on answers to the following circular sent to its members—"Are you compelled to work on Sunday to support your family? . . . Have you got time and means to visit Central Park or any other places of pleasure? Does your family or you go to hear public lectures?" A Saginaw Knight of Labor argued that lumbermen who toiled fourteen or fifteen hours a day were "not free men—[they] had no time for thought, no time for home." Petersburg, Virginia, streetcar workers justified their strike for shorter hours on grounds that they could not get to the theatre on time.[15]

Such public appeals were well calculated to appeal to middle-class sympathies, but workers' organizations took such concerns quite seriously too. Fall River spinners' leaders and workingmen's state representative Robert Howard approached the movement's instructional role with a missionary zeal: "We must get our people to read and think, and to look for something higher and more noble in life than working along in that wretched way from day to day and from week to week and from year to year." A Detroit Knight worried that long hours were rendering workers "incapable of doing anything requiring thought. . . . They will read trashy novels, or go to a variety theatre or a dance, but nothing beyond amusements." Through a network of reading rooms, traveling lecturers, dramatics societies, and the labor press, radical labor leadership hoped to awaken the masses of working people to a sense of their rights and responsibilities. Richard Powers, for instance, who had passed from cabin boy to ship's mate to president of the 7,000-member [Great] Lake Seamen's Union, measured his union's achievements by an educational standard. "Morally and intellectually the men we have out West have gained a good deal. For instance when they come off a vessel they have got a reading-room to go to, and they read now and study questions and know what is going on; they argue questions too." Boston typographers' leader Frank Foster boasted that "reading rooms and the various places provided for intellectual gratification were taken advantage of by printers more than any other trade." Perhaps nowhere was intellectual discourse within the Knights more highly valued than within the Socialist-led New York City District Assembly 49. "If you could hear our members quoting Spencer, Mill, Recardo, Walter, Mar, Laselles, Prouddon and other political economists," reported District Master Workman T. B. McGuire, "you would think you had struck a convention of teachers of the science which has enslaved us." Finally in Atlanta in 1885 approximately 800 people a week made use of the workers' Union Hall and Library Association, whose 350 to 400 daily and weekly newspapers made it one of best-supplied reading rooms in the South.[16]

Idealization of hearth and home, a mainstay of familial sentimentality in the Gilded Age, also enjoyed special status within the labor movement. For here, as clearly as anywhere in the radicals' world view, conventional assumptions had a critical, albeit ambivalent, edge in the context of changing social circumstances. Defense of an idealized family life as both moral and material mainstay of society served as one basis of criticism of capitalist industry. Machinist John Morrison argued before the Senate investigating committee that the insecurities of the unskilled labor market were so threatening family life as to make the house "more like a dull prison instead of a home." A self-educated Scottish-born leader of the type-founders, Edward King, associated trade union morality with the domestic "sentiments of sympathy and humanity" against the "business principles" of the age. Almost unanimously, the vision of the good life for labor radicals included the home. Grand Secretary of the Knights of Labor Robert Layton defined the relative success of skilled trade unionists like Pittsburgh rollers and puddlers by a domestic standard: "They often occupy an entire house themselves and have it neatly furnished; and if they have children that can play the piano, or if they have an ear for music, they will in many instances have a piano in the house, and generally they enjoy life pretty well." By the same rationale Knights' raffles would usually consist of small items to increase the comforts of domestic life. And when the Knights sought to reward grand old labor warrior Richard Trevellick for decades of service in abolitionist and labor circles, they found the ultimate gift in the provision of a cottage house, "to which he may retreat in the intervals of the conflict, and in the decline of life for that rest, that solace and refreshment which he has so nobly earned and so richly deserves."[17]

The importance of the domestic moral order to the late nineteenth-century radical vision also translated into an unparalleled opening of the labor movement to women. As Susan Levine has recently documented, the Knights of Labor beckoned both to wage-earning women and workingmen's wives to join in construction of a "cooperative commonwealth," which, without disavowing the Victorian ideal of a separate female sphere of morality and domestic virtue, sought to make that sphere the center of an active community life.[18]

Both their self-improving and domestic commitments converged in the working-class radicals' antipathy to excessive drinking. The Knights' oath of temperance, which became known as "the Powderly pledge," appealed in turn to intellectual development and protection of the family as well as to the collective interests of the labor movement. Like monopoly, the bottle lay waiting to fasten a new form of slavery upon the free worker. In another sense, as David Brundage has suggested, the growing capitalization of saloons together with expansion of saloon-linked variety theatre directly threatened a family-based producers' community. While most radicals stopped short of prohibition, exhortations in behalf of temperance were commonplace. In part it was a matter of practical necessity. Tension between the mores of traditional plebeian culture and the need for self-discipline by a movement striving for organization and power were apparent in Thomas Barry's appeal to Saginaw Valley general strikers. "My advice has always been in favor of sobriety. . . . If a man wants a glass of beer he should take it, but it is this going to extremes that is dangerous. The danger that would threaten us on the [picnic] grounds would be the system of treating. . . . If you are invited often drink pop. When you don't want to drink pop drop your pipe and smoke a cigar for a change. . . . I expect you all to act as deputy marshalls."[19]

In general, then, the labor movement of the late nineteenth century provided a distinct arena of articulation and practice for values that crossed class lines. Two aspects of this use of inherited values for radical ends merit reemphasis. First, to the extent that labor radicalism shared in the nineteenth century's cult of individualism, it established a social and moral framework for individual achievement. The culture of the labor movement stressed the development of individual capacity, but not competition with other individuals; while striving to elevate humanity, it ignored what S. G. Boritt has identified as the essence of the Lincoln-sanctified American Dream—the individual's "right to rise." The necessary reliance by the labor movement upon collective strength and community sanction militated against the possessive individualism that anchored the world of the workers' better-off neighbors. By its very nature, the labor movement set limits to the individual accumulation of wealth extracted from others' efforts and represented, in Edward King's words, "the graduated elimination of the personal selfishness of man."[20]

Second, in an age of evolutionary, sometimes even revolutionary, faith in progress and the future (a faith generally shared by labor radicals), the movement made striking use of the past. Without renouncing the potential of industrialism for both human liberty and material progress, radicals dipped selectively into a popular storehouse of memory and myth to capture alternative images of human possibility. The choice of the name "Knights of Labor" itself presented images of chivalry and nobility fighting the unfeeling capitalist marketplace. Appeals to the "nobility of toil" and to the worker's "independence" conjured up the proud village smithy—not the degradation of labor in the factory system. Finally, celebrations of historic moments of human liberation and political advancement challenged a political-economic orthodoxy beholden to notions of unchanging, universal laws of development. Indeed, so conspicuously sentimental were the celebrations of Independence Day and Memorial Day that Powderly had to defend the Order from taunts of "spread-eagleism" and "Yankee doodleism."[21]

This sketch of working-class radicalism in the Gilded Age raises one final question. Whose movement—and culture—was it? In a country as diverse as the United States, with a labor force and labor movement drawn from a heterogeneous mass of trades, races, and nationalities, any group portrait runs the risk of oversimplification. The varying contours of the late nineteenth-century working class do require specific inquiry, to which the next several chapters of this work contribute. Nevertheless, the Knights of Labor did provide a vast umbrella under which practically every variety of American worker sought protection. As such, the dynamic of the Order itself offers important clues to the general social context in which working-class radicalism as defined here flourished.

The ensuing case studies will support, I believe, the following argument. The articulate leadership of the Knights of Labor and the political movement that sprang from it included brainworkers (especially the editors of the labor press), skilled craft workers, and shopkeepers who looked to the labor movement as a source of order in a disorderly age. The self-conception of the radical labor leadership as a middle social stratum, balanced between the very rich and very poor, was evident in Powderly's 1885 characterization of his own ancestors—"they did not move in court circles; nor did they figure in police courts." Likewise the Union Labor party, heavily influenced by the Knights, was described by its national chairman, John W. Breidenthal, in 1887 as representing "the middle class of society . . . not the extremely rich or extremely poor. We stand on the middle ground. We have come here to organize and save this Government from the extremes of the one and the robbery of the other."[22]

This dominant stream within the labor movement included people who had enjoyed considerable control over their jobs, if not also economic autonomy, men who often retained claim to the tools as well as the knowledge of their trade. They had taken seriously the ideal of a republic of producers in which hard work would contribute not only to the individual's improved economic standing but also to the welfare of the community. So long as they could rely on their own strength as well as their neighbors' support, this skilled stratum organized in an array of craft unions showed economic and political resilience. But the spreading confrontations with national corporate power, beginning in the 1870s, indicated just how much erosion had occurred in the position of those who relied on custom, skill, and moral censure as ultimate weapons. Industrial dilution of craft skills and a direct economic and political attack on union practices provided decisive proof to these culturally conservative workingmen of both the illegitimacy and ruthlessness of the growing power of capital. It was they, according to every recent study of late nineteenth-century laboring communities, who formed the backbone of local labor movements. The Knights were, therefore, first of all a coalition of reactivating, or already organized, trade unions.[23]

In expressing the ideology of skilled workers, the Knights indicated that skilled workers in the early and mid-1880s were responding to their social predicament in an expansive and affirmative fashion. Instead of using their existing status as a badge of exclusion, the aristocrats of labor in communities all over the country offered their ideals as well as their power as a shield for all those below them. The teacherish invocations of the radical labor leaders toward the rank and file thus represented, in part, a measure of the real social distance among the members of the Order, despite a simultaneous (and sincere) egalitarianism of principle.[24]

For reasons of their own masses of workers who had not lost full and equal citizenship—for they had never possessed it—joined the skilled workers within the Knights. Wherever the Order achieved political successes, it did so by linking semiskilled and unskilled industrial workers to its base of skilled workers and leaders. The special strength of the Knights, noted the Boston *Labor Leader* astutely, lay "in the fact that the whole life of the community is drawn into it, that people of all kinds are together. . ., and that they all get directly the sense of each others' needs."

Lydia Drake of Battle Creek, Michigan, might therefore experience the Order as a schoolhouse of democratic virtues. "I have learned to love and honor it for the instructions it is ever ready to impart; the anxious care it sustains in behalf of justice and individual rights; the desire it expresses not only in words but in deeds to advance the cause of moral and intellectual culture; the hope it cherishes of harmonizing discordant factions; for the determined efforts it has already made to elevate the standard of labor, distribute more equally the profits thereof, and unite the interests of humanity in one common brotherhood."[25] How and why such heterogeneous groups of working people unified under the same organization are questions that point to the heart of the historical significance of the Knights of Labor. To answer them, however, we must turn to the specific experiences of the movement itself.

NOTES

1. Iorwerth Prothero, *Artisans and Politics in Early Nineteenth-Century London: John Gast and His Times* (Baton Rouge, La., 1979), 4; James B. Gilbert, *Work without Salvation: America's Intellectuals and Industrial Alienation, 1880–1910* (Baltimore, 1977), viii–ix, 3–13; Daniel T. Rodgers, *The Work Ethic in Industrial America, 1850–1920* (Chicago, 1978). See, e.g., Thomas Dublin, *Women at Work: The Transformation of Work and Community in Lowell, Massachusetts, 1826–1860* (New York, 1979); Alan Dawley, *Class and Community: The Industrial Revolution in Lynn* (Cambridge, Mass., 1979): Robert Sean Wilentz, "Class Conflict and the Rights of Man: Artisans and the Rise of Labor Radicalism in New York City" (Ph.D. diss., Yale University, 1980); Eric Foner, *Free Soil, Free Labor, Free Men: The Ideology of the Republican Party before the Civil War* (New York, 1970); David Montgomery, *Beyond Equality: Labor and the Radical Republicans, 1862–1872* (New York, 1967); John N. Ingham, *The Iron Barons: A Social Analysis of an American Urban Elite, 1874–1965* (Westport, Conn., 1978); and Ellen Carol Dubois, *Feminism and Suffrage: The Emergence of an Independent Women's Movement in America, 1848–1869* (Ithaca, N.Y., 1978).

2. Norman Birnbaum, *The Crisis of Industrial Society* (London, 1969), 107–8; Trygve R. Tholfson, *Working Class Radicalism in Mid-Victorian England* (New York, 1977), 25–28.

3. George McNeill, *The Labor Movement: The Problem of Today* (Boston, 1887), 491; *John Swinton's Paper* (hereafter *JSP*), Dec. 16, 1883, Nov. 15, 1885; *Report of the Committee of the Senate upon the Relations between Labor and Capital,* 3 vols. (Washington, D.C., 1885), I, 290; II, 438.

4. McNeill, *Labor Movement,* 459; Rochester (N.H.) *Anti-Monopolist,* Nov. 9, 1878; Saginaw *Courier,* Aug. 2, 1885; *Locomotive Fireman's Magazine,* Nov. 1889, 963–64; *JSP,* Aug. 19, 1885; Quincy (Mass.) *Monitor,* Dec. 1886; Richmond *Dispatch,* Oct. 12, 1886; Chicago *Knight of Labor,* Aug. 14, 1885.

5. *JSP,* Mar. 29, 1885.

6. *Journal of United Labor* (hereafter *JUL*), Aug. 9, 1888 *(translation mine);* Engels quoted in R. Laurence Moore, *European Socialists and the American Promised Land* (New York, 1970), 12–13.

7. Richmond *Whig,* Sept. 25, 1886; *Times* quote in Winfield (Kans.) *American Nonconformist,* Oct. 7, 1887.

8. Samuel Walker, " 'Abolish the Wage System': Terence V. Powderly and the Rhetoric of Labor Reform," 8–10, paper presented at the 1979 Knights of

Labor Symposium, Newberry Library, Chicago. For an older, eloquent, and still valuable assessment of these themes, see Chester McArthur Destler, *American Radicalism, 1865–1901* (Chicago, 1966), 1–31, esp. 25–27.

9. McNeill, *Labor Movement*, 486.

10. *JUL*, June 1882, Feb. 1884, Oct. 10, 1884; McNeill, *Labor Movement*, 485. For a recent upgrading of the role of Socialists in the Knights of Labor, see Richard Oestreicher, "Socialism and the Knights of Labor in Detroit, 1877–1886," *Labor History*, 22 (Winter 1981), 5–30, and Alan Dawley, "Anarchists, Knights of Labor, and Class Consciousness in the 1880s," paper presented at the 1979 Knights of Labor Symposium.

11. *Report . . . Labor and Capital*, I, 460.

12. *JUL*, Mar. 1883.

13. "Some people think it unreasonable to exclude a lawyer from the Knights of Labor, because he is somewhat of a carpenter. He can file a bill, split a hair, chop logic, dovetail an argument, make an entry, get up a case, frame an indictment, empannel a jury, put them in a box, nail a witness, hammer a judge, bore a court, chisel a client, and when the job is finished he will demand the highest wages and take the property." *JSP*, May 1, 1887; *JUL*, Mar. 1883.

14. *Report . . . Labor Capital*, III, 487.

15. *JSP*, Mar. 23, 1884; *Report . . . Labor and Capital*, I, 417–18; Saginaw *Courier*, May 5, 1885.

16. *Report . . . Labor and Capital*, I, 426, 648; *JUL*, Jan. 1884; John A. Garraty, *Labor and Capital in the Gilded Age* (Boston, 1968), 39; Atlanta *Journal*, Feb. 18, Mar. 16, 1885 (this information courtesy of Cliff Kuhn).

17. *Report . . . Labor and Capital*, I, 758–59, 688, 22; *JUL*, Nov. 1883.

18. Susan Levine, "Their Own Sphere: Women's Work, the Knights of Labor, and the Transformation of the Carpet Trade, 1870–1890" (Ph.D. diss., City University of New York, 1979), esp. 179–238. The "cooperative commonwealth" was one among many variants of the contemporary labor ideal; "commonwealth of toil," "commonwealth of labor," and the "association of producers" were also popular.

19. Terence V. Powderly, *Thirty Years of Labor, 1859–1889* (1890; reprint ed. New York, 1967), 311; David Brundage, "The Producing Classes and the Saloon: Denver in the 1880's," 25–26, paper presented at the 1979 Knights of Labor Symposium; Saginaw *Courier*, July 19, 1885.

20. The notion of movement culture is borrowed from Lawrence Goodwyn, *Democratic Promise: The Populist Moment in America* (New York, 1976), 88; S. Gabor Boritt, *Lincoln and the Economics of the American Dream* (Memphis, Tenn., 1978); Edward King, quoted in *Report . . . Labor and Capital*, II, 888.

21. The Knights preferred to think of themselves as part of a western tradition of innovators who included Galileo, Newton, Columbus, and Ben Franklin—"discontented" men who had made great contributions to "the progress of the world" (*JUL*, Apr. 10, 1886); David Montgomery, "Labor and the Republic in Industrial America: 1860–1920," *Movement Social*, 111 (Apr.-June 1980), 204; *JUL*, May 14, 1887.

22. Russell Hann, "Brainworkers and the Knights of Labor: E. E. Sheppard, Phillips Thompson, and the *Toronto News, 1883–1887,*" in Gregory S. Kealey and Peter Warrian, eds., *Essays in Canadian Working Class History* (Toronto, 1976), 35–57; *JUL,* Mar. 25, 1885; Steven J. Ross, "Strikes, Knights, and Political Fights: The May Day Strikes . . . and Rise of the United Labor Party in 19th Century Cincinnati," paper presented at the 1979 Knights of Labor Symposium.

23. See, e.g., Bryan D. Palmer, *A Culture in Conflict: Skilled Workers and Industrial Capitalism in Hamilton, Ontario, 1860–1914* (Montreal, 1979).

24. *Ibid.,* 239–43; R. Q. Gray, "Styles of Life, the 'Labor Aristocracy' and Class Relations in Later Nineteenth-Century Edinburgh," *International Review of Social History,* 18 (Pt. 3, 1973), 428–52.

25. Boston *Labor Leader,* Feb. 5, 1887; *JUL,* Mar. 1883.

2

The Uses of Political Power:
The Knights of Labor and the State

PERHAPS IN NO OTHER respect does the nineteenth-century American labor movement appear more self-deluded to our eyes than in its penchant for politics. Independent political efforts from the workingmen's parties of the Jacksonian era through Populism seem to have gone nowhere and resulted in few lasting accomplishments, while participation in the two-party system, if sometimes more fruitful, appears mainly to have sown the seeds of middle-class ideological assimilation and organizational fragmentation. Almost universally among labor historians, labor politics (at least until the CIO) is associated with illusion, weakness, and/or sellout within the working-class movement.[1] One might almost think that American workers would have been better off without the tempting apple of the suffrage, which they alone in the western world enjoyed throughout the century. But while historians have been quick to judge the effects of labor's political forays, they have largely ignored the reasons why and the manner in which the labor movement returned time and time again to the fray.

Modern understanding of the Knights of Labor has especially been affected by this political embarrassment. The critical gaze of Selig Perlman and Gerald Grob, for example, fixes the Knights' political activity in a social reform stream characterized by a "lack of mature class consciousness," meddling by politicians and professional reformers, and petit bourgeois dreams of reestablishing "the relationships of an earlier era." On the other hand, Norman Ware, in his admiring history of the Order as "a study in democracy," does his best to distance the Knights from ready identification as a political movement. Defining democracy as "a popular movement" (i.e., without necessary relation to "political" institutions), Ware associates (and embraces) the Knights as an example of a broad-gauged "reformism," equidistant from both "pure-and-simple trade unionism" and "politics," defined as "the outgrowth of reform or engrafted upon the movement by the farmers or the radical fringe of socialists and communists of one stripe or another." In this analysis the Knights fall into politics in 1886–87, then abdicate in 1890–94 as part and parcel of the paralysis of labor's national leadership and the natural inclinations of its now dominant agrarian or western sections.[2]

While these students touch some important bases, there are serious internal problems with both the Perlman-Grob and Ware approaches to the subject. Simply put, they largely miss a tide of electoral initiatives during the 1880s that represented the most important dimension of Knights' politics. The Knights' political activity may be encapsulated in three phases. The first was a national lobbying effort directed from the top and aimed at specific state and federal legislative action. This effort gathered strength from 1884 to 1886 and was crowned by the passage of a national contract labor law, state anticonvict labor legislation, and funding of the U.S. Bureau of Labor. The second—and most significant—phase was a grassroots entry into local politics by hundreds of district and local assemblies roughly between 1885 and 1888. Finally, the Knights moved into active association with a national third-party movement led by the farmers from 1890 to 1894.

Discussion of Gilded Age labor politics by both Grob and Ware center on the first and last of these phases which, while more convenient to analyze, inevitably create distortions. In both phases one and three political demands were explicitly spelled out, the protagonists neatly aligned, and the results rather easily measurable. It is from the Knights' national initiatives and later alliance with the farmers' movement that Grob draws his argument regarding the reform tradition from which the Knights derived. Similarly, the same record underscores to Ware the very hesitancy of the Knights regarding political action and, once in action, the weak-sister role that the Knights played to Populism. Even the conclusions drawn from such evidence are subject to some questions. On what grounds, for instance, can one separate the attitudes of the middle-class reform-minded leaders from those of the rank-and-file workers? In what sense can politics, as Ware maintains, flow directly from the basic energizing reform vision of the Order and yet at the same time (or alternatively) be seen as engrafted upon them from the outside?

More significantly, this national focus presents from the outset a circumscribed view of the relation of politics to the life of local assemblies, the heart of the Knights' organization. In the national lobbying phase, for the most part, one is dealing with the front office of what was in fact a sprawling, decentralized operation. And in the later alliance with Populism, the movement was already bereft of its dynamic core, namely the interaction of skilled trade unionists with previously unorganized urban industrial workers.

The second phase of the Knights' activities simply does not fit the present ways of understanding labor politics. First, the Knights in this period did not always enter politics with a specific reform program in mind. Second, the local assemblies showed a marked disinclination to coordinate their political activities with any larger political (as opposed to trade union) strategy or third-party movement beyond the local community. Third, the Knights' polit-

ical efforts of 1886–88 show little inheritance from agrarian political insurgency, as they generally preceded it. Finally, politics, even when it became a
major and sometimes successful endeavor, never during the prime of the
organization appeared to any Knights' faction as a solution to the movement's
needs, whether defined as immediate organizational stability or long-range
ends, such as the abolition of the wage system. Theirs was an attitude toward
politics not so much contravened as totally unexplained by both the Grob and
Ware presuppositions. There is, then, no adequate framework for understanding the political attitudes and behavior of the Knights of Labor. Unfortunately,
it is not simply that Ware, Grob, and others did not go far enough with their
researches. The problem lies in a wider lacuna in our understanding of the
relation of workers to the state in the nineteenth century. It may help to
reformulate the terms of discussion: within what general framework might
one best approach the relation of radical social movements toward politics
and the uses of the state?

American writings on the subject, notwithstanding their internal diversity,
have tended to assume the peculiarity of U.S. developments. Probably the
most helpful formulation on the record remains David Montgomery's *Beyond
Equality*. Unlike both Grob and Ware on the Knights, Montgomery recognizes
that the nineteenth-century movements did not "opt" for political strategies
instead of trade unionist ones; rather, along with workplace organization
workingmen's leaders turned "instinctively to political activity for reform."
Politics, in short, was part and parcel of the nineteenth-century labor movement, which often exerted "a significant influence on both the economic and
legislative fronts." Yet, as Montgomery argues in dissecting the thought of
labor reformer Ira Steward, the problem of labor politics is that while pressing
for political power and legislative changes, labor maintained a minimal role
for the state: "Steward, like all his contemporaries in the American labor
movement, had no conception of an active role for the machinery of state.
The sole function they attributed to government was that of enacting just and
general laws applying impartially to all citizens. Within the framework of
these laws, social development would take care of itself." From this perspective it is the political culture of American radicalism, in common with the
dominant liberal tradition, that apparently sets up the likely failures of the
continual political efforts. As if to underscore the ideological blind spot in the
American approach to government, Montgomery contrasts Steward (and by
implication American labor radicalism) with Karl Marx, for whom "the ultimate objective of the workers' movement was to seize state power and wield
it against the capitalists."[3]

While illuminating the travails of American labor politics, Montgomery
implicitly deflects the problem to the cultural realm of American exceptionalism, i.e., to the immaturity of American class consciousness and ideology,

even though he offers a different vision of maturity than Grob. Still, at the end of *Beyond Equality* one is left puzzled by the political commitment combined with self-limitation that defined the political philosophy of the labor movement. It is an uneasiness that is explained only if one is able to accept as definitive the peculiarity of American radical thought, separating the workers' movement from alternative, and apparently more clear-sighted, political agendas.

The exceptionalism of the American mentality remains the core assumption for David DeLeon's recent *The American as Anarchist*. An antistatist, antiauthoritarian libertarianism, innately suspicious and thoroughly cynical about government and the political process, DeLeon argues, runs through radical American attitudes from the Garrisonians to the Wobblies, from Tom Paine to Paul Goodman: "The black flag has been the most appropriate banner of the American insurgent." Statist radicalism—"traditional social democracy, communism, and other relatively authoritarian movements that rely upon coercive centers of state power (that is, on involuntary collectivism) rather than on cooperative associations," according to DeLeon—has not had a chance in a country living with libertarian dreams.[4] Despite its suggestiveness this argument fails to deal with the American radical's faith in republicanism (the word is not even listed in the index), which has brought American movements, again and again, to address the state as source of both grievance and rectification. It is a conceptual problem that rebounds to labor historians as well: how can American social movements be antipolitical and doomed by politics at the same time?

The paradox can be resolved if the intellectual context is shifted. In particular the Knights' ambivalence toward politics can better be understood as part of a halting reorientation of attitudes affecting Western radical political thought as a whole in the nineteenth and early twentieth centuries. Ironically, the worker's relation to politics, which has long served as an important explanation of why class consciousness failed to develop in the United States, might better be addressed by reassimilating American political culture into an international framework.

With a compelling analytical sweep, Swedish political theorist Daniel Tarschys has outlined four consecutive but overlapping visions of political utopia that engaged Marx and other nineteenth-century European radicals: the state, the democratic state, the association, and the commune. The last three of these visions also had considerable influence on American radicals and offer a useful starting point for reevaluating the ideology of the Knights of Labor. Veneration of the democratic state (following the Hegelian infatuation with the state *tout court*) accompanied the optimistic revolutionary rationalism of the late eighteenth and early nineteenth centuries. Nineteenth-century socialists, although increasingly critical and pessimistic, thus never "turned against democracy." For example, Marx and Friedrich Engels, who by the 1840s saw the democratic breakthrough as "no longer the end" but "the beginning" of the struggle, still (unlike their Leninist progeny) "anticipated the social transformation to begin immediately on the conquest of a democratic constitution."[5]

By the mid-nineteenth century a combination of setbacks (most notably, the 1848 revolutions) and disillusioning victories (most notably, the northern triumph in the American Civil War) for the radical political forces prompted an important strategic revision. Democratic hopes henceforth adhered less to either form of the state than to the association, the liberation of civil society through economic self-organization. This formation captures many of the goals of both the trade union and cooperative movements of the nineteenth century, with their emphasis not only on the self-organization of workers, but also, through this activity, on the more or less gradual creation of an ethically superior or "higher social order." The writings of Louis Auguste Blanqui, François Fourier, and Ferdinand Lassalle, as well as Marx, which themselves reflected the changing dimensions of the workers' movements, articulated a vision of the movement as community. Within this framework a humane social order would emerge less by direct intervention of the democratic state (although, to be sure, the priority placed on state support remained a key dispute among radicals, e.g., Marxists vs. Lassalleans) than by voluntary cooperation among workers themselves.[6]

The last great political vision of the century was represented by the Paris Commune, which can be envisaged as the reappropriation of the state by society. The Commune, at least in the eyes of Marxist interpreters and critics, represented the ultimate reunification of the workers' movement with the state and institutional centers of political-economic power. The "withering away" or "blowing up" of the state, the ultimate dream of so many nineteenth-century revolutionaries, meant (except to some very hard-core anarchists) not "blowing up society" but eliminating the "bureaucratic apparatus" that aided the social power of one class over another. Even the revolutionary initiatives of the Commune (and later, at least in their idealized form, of the soviets) thus aimed primarily at allowing rational self-government—the association redefined—to go forward. How extensive a role in coordination and on what scale the residual central governmental authority should occupy were questions that divided European theorists—especially Marx from the anarchists—but their answers did not contradict an essentially common vision of the desired and possible future: "If not interfered with by the authorities, the classical economic man would use all his faculties to promote his own welfare and thereby the public good. Marx's producer, released from the old social system, would just as certainly follow the precepts of his own reason and join together with his fellow men to organize a planned economy."[7]

Simultaneous commitment to politics as active citizenship and to subordination or minimalization of political or state-related society (as opposed to the civil society) defined important currents of late nineteenth-century radicalism. The first pillar of this faith can be broadly attributed to the democratic revolutionary spirit of the late eighteenth century and the second to the relative immaturity of monopolistic and bureaucratic concentration, for there does seem to be a rather sharp break in radical and socialist thought, roughly coincident with the rise of monopoly capitalism, around the turn of the century. Henceforth the state was now more often viewed as either the primary obstacle to or the major source of change. Responding quite differently, anarcho-syndicalists (as well as conservative trade unionists) tried, in principle, to avoid entrapment in the state apparatus, whereas social revolutionaries (as well as social democrats) made the seizure and use of state power the immediate focus of their activity.

It is against this European background of contending and changing strategies for the working-class movement that the assumptions and practices of the North American labor movement are to be studied. On reexamination, American labor radicals and the Knights of Labor in particular do not seem far removed from the major currents of thought affecting their European contemporaries. Rooted in revolutionary democratic enthusiasm (Paineite republicanism), American radicals by the era of the Knights were ambivalent about the role of the state and the proper political strategy for the labor movement. The reconsideration of basic strategy in European working-class thought is equally apparent in the Knights' own Declaration of Principles:

> This preamble well says, that "the alarming development and aggressiveness of great capitalists and corporations, unless checked, will inevitably lead to the pauperization and hopeless degradation of the toiling masses. . . ." The method of checking and remedying this evil is, first, the organization of all laborers into one great solidarity, and the direction of their united efforts toward the measures that shall, by peaceful processes, evolve the working classes out of their present condition in the wage-system into a co-operative system. This organization does not profess to be a political party, nor does it propose to organize a political party but, nevertheless, it proposes to exercise the right of suffrage in the direction of obtaining such legislation as shall assist the natural law of development. It is true that the demands are revolutionary, as it is the purpose of the Order to establish a new and true standard of individual and national greatness.[8]

In this statement, diagnosis of the threat, identification of the source of salvation, and ambivalence toward the exact means of redress all place the Knights within a larger Western radical tradition. It is worth noting that even the avowal of peaceful means, by which the Knights hoped to allay fears of a European-style insurrection, was not a point about which Marx himself necessarily disagreed.[9] For the Knights this intellectual juncture did indeed spawn rather conflicting attitudes toward the American political inheritance. Worshiping political nationhood, they displayed a mixture of fear and loathing for the prevailing uses of state power. As a result no contemporary organization celebrated the symbols of the Republic—the flag, the ballot box, the Fourth of July—with more enthusiasm than the Knights while steadfastly avoiding commitment to a state-oriented program or strategy.

To acknowledge transatlantic conceptual similarities, of course, is not to imply an explicit borrowing of ideas one way or the other. It is perhaps more likely that the specific and unique issues that radicals encountered within each national culture inevitably involved larger problems affecting working-class movements in all more or less liberal capitalist societies. Subjectively, it is clear that Gilded Age labor radicals attributed their political attitudes to a combination of pragmatic analysis and what they thought was good American common sense. The halting reorientation of the Knights' political stance in the 1880s is a case in point. High principles commingled constantly with immediate tactical decisions as new situations continually presented themselves. Initial aversion to electoral initiatives, for example, rested in part on the overwhelming failure of the Greenback-Labor party in the late 1870s. The difficulty and cost of such efforts, in which many of labor's high command had been involved (Terence Powderly, for instance, had served six years as mayor of Scranton), had left a sour taste about the possibilities of high politics in the United States. Exclusion of lawyers—the technicians of American politics—from membership in the Knights of Labor in part reflected a desired distance from the contaminated machinery of state. Again, from a practical point of view the very process of organizing a new political party risked further inflaming the partisan rivalries already undermining the unity of the producing classes. Beginning in 1880, therefore, the Knights had proscribed any official electoral activity by their assemblies, and Powderly quickly branded grassroots agitation for labor tickets in the mid-1880s as diversionary pipe dreams. Finally, the American embrace of an associationalist idealism tended to discourage political mobilization. The social and moral regeneration of the "commonwealth of toil" claimed highest priority with Powderly and many contemporaries. Their very dedication to the Order as a community and the exertions necessary to ennoble its internal life made irrelevant, if not pernicious, any protracted contact with the seamier sides of American politics. In support of this line a California district master workman reported to Powderly in 1883 that his assemblies were "growing slowly and recovering from an overdose of politics in the shape of Greenbackism, Prohibition and City Charter" and were "commencing to get back to first principles."[10]

Their resulting nonalignment policy placed the Knights in the anomalous position of advocating workers' political rights without offering a way to take advantage of those rights. Since 1879 the Knights' platform had included several planks directly addressed to legislative action. Internal education campaigns urged the worker to make use of "the high and sacred privilege of the ballot" but to beware of "machine hacks, scheming politicians, and money and land thieves." The conscientious Knight at one moment was advised to "let political parties and political clubs, of whatever name, severely alone"; the next moment he was told to "organize, co-operate, educate till the stars and stripes wave over a contented and happy people." It was very well for the official Knights' organ, the *Journal of United Labor,* to chastise Americans for voting away, like the French, "the freedom of a Republic" to "our Napoleon—the monopolists, corporations, and bosses." But how was the labor voter to make "a wise, independent, and individual ballot," when he could decide only between the representatives of two "cash-cursed" parties? A Newark machinist believed he had found the only consistent solution— "when I think there is no use of my voting as the monopoly ring will succeed anyhow; but my duty as a citizen demands my vote . . . I vote a clean blank ticket." One Thomas B. McGuire, a truck driver who had once owned an express company that had failed for lack of capital, voiced this same politically ambivalent strain of folk republicanism before the U.S. Senate Committee on Labor and Capital in 1883:

> McGuire. You [politicians] have got the power to see that every man gets what the Constitution guarantees to him—an opportunity to enjoy life, liberty, and the pursuit of happiness.
> Q. Do you understand it to be a fact that we have that power?
> A. Yes, the Constitution reads that way.
> Q. Is that all there is in the Constitution?
> A. This is about as far as I want to go.
> Q. That is in the Declaration of Independence, is it not?
> A. Well, have it the Declaration. When I was 13 years old I was in the Army of the United States, so I have had but little opportunity for education or study. . . .
> Q. Why do not the horny-handed sons of labor send men of their own choosing to make laws for them?
> A. Simply because the entire system from top to bottom is a system of bribery and corruption.[11]

The circumstances of the Great Upheaval of the labor conflict from 1884 to 1886 nevertheless led many Knights of Labor to reconsider the political option. Explosive growth in 1885–86 lent the labor movement greater potential for political action than ever before.[12] With large fractions of whole communities aligned with the Order, the numbers alone promised to carry substantial political weight if united in a common direction. Bruising defeats in strikes suffered in the unprecedented industrial conflicts of these years also resurrected the weapon of the ballot, if only as a last resort. Disorderly withdrawal from the Southwest Strike and the reverberations of the Haymarket Riot left Knights' assemblies across the country not only confused and demoralized but also open to serious retaliation by employers unless some new show of strength could be mustered. Indeed, widespread resort to the repressive judicial and military role of the state in putting down the Great Upheaval reinvigorated for many labor partisans an older radical Greenback message. As labor editor John Swinton wrote bitterly in mid-May 1886: "The country drifts from its ancient moorings. The constitutional method of reme-dying public grievances is disregarded. An anti-democratic Money Power is enthroned over the people."[13]

This juncture of resolve and circumstance fired what may still stand as the American worker's single greatest push for political power. Beginning with the early spring municipal elections and symbolically sanctioned by the spe-cial General Assembly in June 1886, the Knights flexed their political muscle virtually everywhere they were established. The secondary literature and the contemporary national labor press refer to labor tickets—called variously "Union Labor," "United Labor," "Knights of Labor," "Workingmen," and "Independents"—in 189 towns and cities in thirty-four (out of thirty-eight) states and four territories (Table 1). Close investigation by state or region, particularly if relevant two-party contests are included, would doubtlessly turn up scores of other cases where local elections were waged on the basis of allegiance or opposition to the aims of the labor movement. Areas affected ranged from Eureka, California, to Gardiner, Maine, from Red Wing, Min-nesota, to Fort Worth, Texas. The activity encompassed tiny rural hamlets as well as major metropolitan areas, frontier settlements as well as old New England towns, marketing centers as well as manufacturing and mining com-munities. The movement linked old immigrant farmers with new immigrant industrial workers, skilled white artisans with unskilled black laborers. Na-tionally, the biggest spotlight fell on Henry George's narrow and protested loss of the New York City mayoralty to Democrat Abram Hewitt (while trouncing Republican candidate Theodore Roosevelt) and on the Chicago United Labor party, which elected seven assemblymen and five judges while falling only sixty-eight votes shy of electing a Congressman. In less cele-brated contests a common wave of labor feeling brought a black miner to the mayor's office in Rendville, Ohio, replaced a prominent attorney with a bank janitor as mayor of Waterloo, Iowa, and secured several constables from the ranks of leather workers in Peabody, Massachusetts. Avoiding the continuing official ban on "direct" political activity by forming shadow "progressive" committees or political clubs, Knights' locals across the country marshalled their forces at the polls. A Leroy, New York, partisan celebrated in song the workers' turn to politics:

> The ballot box, the ballot box!
> There comrades, you will find the rocks
> To hurl against the tyrant's head;
> Nor iron, dynamite or lead
> Can match the ever-potent knocks
> Shot from our Yankee ballot box.

> The ballot box, the ballot box!
> No merely warlike weapon shocks
> With such effort the would-be boss;
> It closes his accounts with loss.
> Ho! rally to the polls in flocks
> Right's standard is the ballot box.[14]

For a brief period labor reform leaders held high hopes of building a national independent political movement. In addition to widespread inroads at the municipal level, in November 1886 the Knights claimed to have elected a dozen Congressmen (usually in fusion with one of the major parties). Envisioning "a Parnell party" in a partisanly split House of Representatives, the Order's Washington lobbyist, Ralph Beaumont, was jubilant: "God has answered our prayers and the Knights hold the balance of power in the organization of the 50th Congress." With the Knights and the burgeoning National Farmers' Alliance as a base, advocates of independent political action foresaw a powerful new party bringing together Greenbackers, socialists, single-taxers, and antimonopolists. Swinton threw his support behind just such a coalition of "new political forces" slated to convene in Cincinnati in late February 1887. Following a symbolic endorsement of the Knights' platform, the meeting chartered the National Union Labor party and set its sights on the 1888 federal elections. Readers following the crescendo of political successes recorded in *John Swinton's Paper* could well believe by the spring of 1887 that "there will soon be but two parties in the field, one composed of honest workingmen, lovers of justice and equality; the other . . . composed of kid-gloved, silk-stockinged, aristocratic capitalists and their contemptible toadies."[15]

But Swinton's senses as well as his sympathies had been carried away by the political fever. Efforts to create a national workingmen's party were hamstrung from the start by internecine strife. Powderly's order to "let political parties alone" together with general skepticism on the part of trade unions significantly reduced labor's involvement in the political project. Within the Farmers' Alliance as well, antipolitical tendencies still dominated outside of Kansas, Arkansas, and Texas. In New York squabbling between socialists and single-taxers destroyed George's Clarendon Hall coalition by the end of 1886; both, in turn, refused to work under the banner of the western-oriented Union Labor people. George's United Labor party even made certain to hold a separate convention in Cincinnati simultaneous with the Union Labor conclave. Transformed by the defections into primarily an agrarian and western instrument, the Union Labor party emerged as a weak forerunner to Populism. Within the Knights the battle to impose a coherent political strategy was won too late: the Order began to connect with the agrarian third-party movement in 1890 and completed the process with the deposition of Powderly in 1893; but by that time the Knights, having suffered at the hands of employers as

TABLE 1. Knights of Labor Political Tickets, by State or Territory, 1885–88

Alabama	*Georgia*	*Kansas*
Anniston	Macon	Argentine*
Mobile*		Kansas City*
Selma	*Idaho Territory*	Leavenworth
	Boise*	Ottawa*
Arkansas	*Illinois*	Parsons*
Hot Springs	Batavia	Weir City*
	Belvidere	Wellington
California	Cairo	Wichita*
Eureka	Chicago*	Winfield*
San Diego	East St. Louis*	
San Francisco	Elgin	*Kentucky*
Colorado	Galesburg	Covington*
Denver	Mattoon	Kenton County
Las Animas*	Minouk	Louisville
Leadville	Quincy	Newport
	Rockford	Prestonville*
Connecticut	Rock Island	
Beacon Falls	Salem	*Maine*
Bethel	Springfield*	Auburn
Branford	Streator	Biddeford
Danbury		Gardiner*
Derby	*Indiana*	Lewiston
Meriden	Evansville	Round Pond
Millburn	Fort Wayne	Salmon Falls
Naugatuck*	Indianapolis	South Berwick
New Britain	Loogootee*	Webster
New Haven	Marion*	
Norwalk	New Albany	*Maryland*
Norwich	Richmond	Baltimore
South Norwalk*	Terre Haute	
Rockville	Vincennes	*Massachusetts*
Seymour		Boston
	Iowa	Brockton
Dakota Territory	Boone*	Gloucester
Mandan	Burlington	Lynn*
	Cedar Falls*	New Bedford
Delaware	Cedar Rapids	Peabody
Wilmington*	Creston	Somerset*
	Des Moines	South Abington
Florida	Dubuque*	
Jacksonville	Muscatine	
Key West*		

Source: *JSP;* Edward T. James, "American Labor and Political Action, 1865–1896: The Knights of Labor and Its Predecessors" (Ph.D. diss., Harvard University, 1954); Philip S. Foner, *History of the Labor Movement in the United States,* vol. 2: *From the Founding of the*

TABLE 1. *(Continued)*

Michigan	*New Jersey*	*Pennsylvania*
Alpena	Bayonne	Bradford
Battle Creek	Jersey City	Harrisburg*
Bay City*	Newark	Philadelphia
Cadillac*	Paterson*	Pittsburgh
Detroit	Washington*	Scranton
Grand Ledge*		
Grand Rapids	*New York*	*Tennessee*
Iron Mountain*	Albany	Chattanooga
Ishpening*	Amsterdam*	
Jackson	Conajoharie	*Texas*
Jersey City*	Glens Falls*	Fort Worth
Lansing	Jamestown*	Houston
Manistee	New York City	San Antonio
Muskegon	Rochester	
Port Austin	Troy	*Vermont*
Saginaw	Yonkers	Fair Haven*
		Rutland*
Mississippi	*North Carolina*	West Rutland*
Water Valley	Burlington	
	Durham	*Virginia*
Minnesota	Fayetteville	Alexandria*
Minneapolis	Oxford*	Kanawha Falls
St. Paul	Raleigh*	Lynchburg*
	Statesville	Richmond*
Missouri		
Kansas City	*Ohio*	*Washington Territory*
Rolla*	Akron	Seattle*
Springfield	Alliance*	Tacoma
St. Louis	Ashtabula	
Willow Springs	Canton	*West Virginia*
	Cincinnati	Coal Valley
Montana Territory	Columbus	Fayette City
South Butte	Dayton	Kendalia*
	Eaton	Mountain Cove
Nebraska	Harrison	New Cumberland*
Norfolk*	New Philadelphia*	
St. Paul	Rendville*	*Wisconsin*
	Springfield	De Pere
New Hampshire		Eau Claire
Alton*	*Oregon*	Kenosha
Berlin Mills	Albina*	Marinette
Manchester	East Portland	Milwaukee*
Rochester*		Oshkosh
		Whitewater*

American Federation of Labor to the Emergence of American Imperialism (New York, 1955); plus local and labor newspapers.

*Reported electoral victory.

well as having experienced mass defections to the trade unions, had dwindled to relative insignificance among American workers.[16]

The content of labor's political vision in these years is best discerned in the multiple experiments at the local level in 1886 and in the year or two thereafter, when heady expectations were accompanied by real achievements. At least four uses of political power were articulated—sometimes separately, sometimes in tandem—in these locally diverse efforts. First, there was politics as a spillover effect. Organization of the local working-class population into Knights' assemblies tended in and of itself to undermine the legitimacy of the commercial-industrial elite as community leaders. Now that the community was voluntarily divided by differing conceptions of common need, the mere assertion of rights of citizenship led in some places almost inexorably in the direction of a labor ticket. In many cases, the Knights did not set out to do anything dramatically unconventional with political power. Rather, with new pride, solidarity, and power, workers determined to show not only that they could do what had previously been done for them but also that they could do it better. Thus, after the Knights took over a town meeting in Rochester, New Hampshire, in March 1886, one of their number boasted that whereas two days was "the usual time required to do the town business . . . on this occasion only three hours were consumed in adjusting affairs with everything done decently and in order." That the Knights in office were celebrating a social-political transformation accomplished primarily by mobilization and organization in civil society was apparent in an act of the 1887 Rutland town meeting. In a gesture more symbolic than substantive, the workingmen voted to place an American flag in every schoolroom.[17]

There were other ways as well in which the social reorganization of a community around the Knights produced an almost inevitable political spillover or partisan realignment. In Richmond, Virginia, for example, the Knights gave voice to an evolving coalition of interests between white skilled workers and black factory operatives and unskilled laborers. Since the two prevailing southern parties of the 1880s not only reflected but also sustained a world divided along race lines, the Knights had either to extend biracial cooperation into politics or, sooner or later, abandon it altogether.

The second use of politics—again essentially unrelated to the positive exercise of state power—derived from the need to curtail state repression of and interference with the life of the social movement. Most clearly in the wake of major strike defeats or massive counterthrusts to worker mobilization by the business classes, politics here emerged as at least one remaining way to "punish your enemies." Following the suppression of Milwaukee's eight-hour movement in the Bay View Massacre and the subsequent conspiracy trials, Wisconsin Knights' leader Robert Schilling in June 1886 announced his intention to "gain revenge—by the ballot." Response to antilabor use of the police and courts would similarly empower Chicago workingmen's efforts in the aftermath of Haymarket. In Kansas City, Kansas, too, control of the police power would emerge as a major political issue following the collapse of the Great Southwest Strike.[18]

Specific class-related legislation was the third use of local labor politics. Particularly where public bodies had assumed a direct administrative role in the economy, political conflict was assured. That the municipality was also an employer, for example, led to a variety of political demands. In addition to establishment of an eight-hour day for city workers and an end to municipal subcontracting, Richmond Knights, with many members in nearby quarries, insisted on the use of Virginia granite in the new city hall. Under similar labor pressures, in 1887 the town meeting at Quincy, Massachusetts, adopted a nine-hour statute and a minimum wage of two dollars and promised to employ only town residents.[19]

Expansion of the public sector emerged only slowly as a political issue in the era of the Knights of Labor. The nation's new intraurban transit systems, around which bitter strikes would swirl by the turn of the century, from the beginning evoked conflict between public and private interests. When Kansas City labor Mayor Tom Hannan insisted on a series of reforms in the street railway ordinance of 1887, for example, the local board of trade (appealing to the jurisdiction of the courts over the city council) enjoined the city's major public improvements bond issue. The urban transit controversy might in an abstract sense be compared to the contemporary fight of the farmers over railroad rates and, ultimately, railroad ownership. William Appleman Williams, most notably, has stressed the limited ideological reach of such political demands focusing on "commercial arteries" of the marketplace (railroads, telegraphs, telephones) while leaving the system of private enteprise otherwise untouched. An alternative and perhaps more convincing explanation for the centrality of transit and communication systems to the radical demands of the period lies in the fact that it was here that public authority appeared most baldly not only to have sanctioned but also to have colluded with private "monopoly."[20]

Within this third category of positive uses of state power, other tendencies of local Knights' regimes are worth noting. Depression in the 1890s did trigger demands for government to serve as employer of last resort. While the business classes encouraged private charity—provision of clothing and soap to needy youngsters, voluntary expansion of domestic service—Rutland labor representatives in 1894 pushed for short-term public projects like street-grading and landscaping to relieve widespread distress. Even so, demands for public welfare in the 1890s seem not to have advanced beyond the terms that Herbert Gutman has documented for the depression of the 1870s. Again, without necessarily breaking new ground, the Knights did act as a force for enlargement of public services and expenditures. In 1886 the first labor-dominated town meeting in Rochester, New Hampshire, for example, increased appropriations for street lights, poor relief, and education by 20 percent over the preceding year. In various ways the Knights also addressed the question of tax equity. Following the doctrine of Henry George, Rutland workingmen clamped a punitive tax on unoccupied land. Nevertheless, even allowing for the brevity of their tenure in office or the hopes they had while in office, the workingmen's substantive political experiences did not amount to an identifiable labor agenda. For them local politics was generally not an arena for imaginative effort or experimentation; rather, it was primarily a means of consolidation and preservation of gains created elsewhere.[21]

A fourth use of politics surfaced in only the most tentative form until the rise of the People's party in the 1890s. This was the path of the movement as politics, an effort to make political agitation and organization the focus of a national labor strategy. Particularly as the industrial campaigns of the Great Upheaval fell, one by one, into defeat, the attempt to revive the movement through politics gained credence in certain quarters. The United Labor party of Henry George, the 1887 agrarian-based coalition of "new political forces" in Cincinnati that led to the Union Labor party, and the Socialist Labor party all gave voice to this reaction. But by 1888 support for any third-party candidate beyond the local level was negligible, even where the Knights still exercised considerable influence.

Among the obstacles that third-party advocates faced and could not overcome was one of the Knights' own making. While becoming political, the Knights convinced themselves that they were doing the opposite, that they were really rescuing society from the depredations of politics. Thus at the local level they preferred to identify themselves as independent or nonpartisan; politics and parties in their minds were associated with social parasitism, "ring rule," and "baneful" central authority. To some degree, they came to this attitude by cultural inheritance. A disdain of partyism as an intrusion on individual will and conscience was deeply rooted in Anglo-American reform thought. Commitment to permanent party organization, moreover, implied a necessary relation to the state in their identity as a movement that the workingmen denied from the outset. Unless absolutely necessary, such a commitment was unlikely in an organization that could extol a candidate for the Vermont state legislature simply on grounds that he "has not been a politician because he was too honest to have anything to do with their dirty contemptible little tricks." The only way the Knights could cleanse the political process was to remain outside it, acting from political strength rooted in a moral order of their own making.[22]

Here it is worth considering an important difference between the paths of the Knights and the Farmers' Alliance. The Alliance, while rooted like the Knights in associated strength and sharing many of their ideological presuppositions, did, unlike the Knights, manage to shift effectively to a political strategy. Because the farmers found much of their oppression linked to institutions of circulation and credit (in which, through control of the money supply, the government was already involved), they could jump to a political demand—greenbackism and the subtreasury—to redefine their problems in a nationally coherent way. But the workers', and therefore the Knights', problems did not converge nearly so neatly on the public domain. Not the coordination of finance or transportation, after all, but the consolidation of corporate control over private production sent them into battle. To be sure, government and the political parties had everywhere made things more difficult for "the people to rescue the heritage which we received from our fathers from the grip of gold and greed." But, aside from sending men "untrammeled" and "closely identified with the struggling masses" into office to clean things up, no common or acceptable political solution could have saved the workers' movement. Indeed, precisely when politics became primary in the Order, the Knights could effectively count themselves dead.[23]

Some general propositions regarding the relation of the American labor movement to the international currents of political radicalism circulating in the mid- to late nineteenth century can now be presented. Essentially the events of the Great Upheaval led the Knights of Labor to a repoliticized associationalism, a vision they shared with others even if it was for them (as undoubtedly elsewhere) defined by particular national political circumstances. Thus, in the United States the contemporary industrial conflict threw a labor movement that would have preferred to go its own autonomous way back into contact and confrontation with state-organized power. To the extent that the state had become an appendage of the money power, the Knights believed that it had to be liberated before rational self-government, as organized by the people in civil society, might flourish. Reappropriation of the state by society, the political vision symbolized by the Paris Commune of 1871, in American translation became "recapturing government for the people." That the task here involved no insurrectionary mobilization does not necessarily imply that American workers were less radical but perhaps only that their circumstances were different. In a country that still waved its republican banner, a postmillenarian confidence dictated the use of the ballot rather than an apocalyptic appeal to rifle and cannon as the means of redress.[24]

Put another way, the Knights' attempts to control community politics could be compared with the evolving contemporary search for control at the workplace. Just as the late nineteenth-century "workers' control" impulse (Montgomery's phrase) tended to represent an extension of traditional craft autonomy into a changing and threatening work environment, so these local political efforts grew out of the adaptation, particularly on the part of skilled workers and small producers, to a demeaning of citizenship. While workers sought initially to defend themselves and their communities, the movement in politics, as on the shop floor, began to take unprecedented initiatives and even to envision a structurally altered environment.[25]

From a defense of their stake in civil society, the Knights took on the state to dispel its opposition and to identify its institutions with the interests of a well-organized body of producers. How events might have turned out had that body remained strong is a separate question that will not be discussed here. But such a perspective explains why the Knights could jump into politics enthusiastically without much of a political program. It also explains why, at the height of what appeared to middle-class Rutland as political insurrection, a regional labor leader could sincerely declare, "We stand as the conservators of society."[26] The Knights of Labor looked to self-organized society—not to the individual and not to the state—as the redeemer of their American dream. Neither ultimate antagonist nor source of salvation, the state represented a mediator in the conflict between the civil forces of democracy and its enemies. A source perhaps of both the Order's strategic strength and weakness, the Knights' perspective ought to be the initial point of departure for an evaluation of their actions.

Despite the passage of time and perspective, the Knights may nevertheless share more with their progeny than one would like to admit. The dilemma that they faced in trying to harness state power to democratic ends has continued to bedevil the American working-class movement (not to mention others). A comparatively modest scale of production, a feeble public administrative apparatus, and a rich nexus of local community ties all combined in the late nineteenth century to minimize radical demands on and expectations of the state. The problem for a powerful social movement seemed to be one of eliminating governmental roadblocks and perhaps of assimilating, by political control, certain limited state services to the needs of the movement. Essentially, however, the Knights made no imaginative leap with regard to the future relation of state and civil society. If anything, as labor radicals began to realize too late, it was their corporate antagonists who learned far earlier than they new uses of politics and state power.

Beginning in the 1890s the state took on more and more the role of coordinator of the socioeconomic order. The banking system and the money supply, the tariffs, the courts, and ultimately the enhanced regulatory role of government came to serve in crucial ways to stabilize a decreasingly democratic society. Faced with a practically irrevocable leviathan, radicals were forced into new but no less difficult choices. In telescoping many levels of activity over many years, it might be suggested that the craft unions abandoned a political strategy in favor of the immediate economic struggle. The Wobblies cloaked this same political retreat in more ambitious syndicalist terms. Socialists, labor progressives, and ultimately the communists, on the other hand, hoped to capture the state to overhaul society and in the meantime to squeeze from it at least a social welfare role. Neither approach proved very satisfactory. If to abandon politics meant to risk being hemmed in by leaving the state's powers in the hands of labor's enemies, to pursue the state-oriented strategy meant to risk assimilation and the taming of the movement that had launched it. The respective fates of the International Workers of the World and the CIO reflect the potential polarities. The pervasive, bureaucratic state, in short, has not only hampered efforts to implement radical change but also has stifled even the vision of democratic alternatives. No longer able by their own efforts to create oppositional forms of production or to convey an oppositional culture, labor unions and radicals alike have turned to the reformative power of government (e.g., the civil rights movement, labor-law reform, the war on poverty) as a partner in progress. But whether the political path can, indeed, be used at once to achieve practical ends and to invigorate a social movement still remains to be seen. That the Knights of Labor did not provide a definitive solution to the strategic dilemma of the relation of a democratic movement to the state should not, in retrospect, be surprising. Even in their failure, they were clearly grappling with one of the more important questions of modern times.

NOTES

1. For the most recent elaboration of these themes, see Alan Dawley, *Class and Community: The Industrial Revolution in Lynn* (Cambridge, Mass., 1979), 214–19, and Daniel J. Walkowitz, *Worker City, Company Town: Iron and Cotton-Worker Protest in Troy and Cohoes, New York, 1855–84* (Urbana, Ill., 1978), esp. 253–57. Also see David Montgomery, *Beyond Equality: Labor and the Radical Republicans, 1862–1872* (New York, 1967), 215.

2. Gerald N. Grob, *Workers and Utopia: A Study of Ideological Conflict in the American Labor Movement, 1865–1900* (Evanston, Ill., 1961), 34–59, 79–80, 58; Norman J. Ware, *The Labor Movement in the United States, 1860–1895: A Study in Democracy* (New York, 1929), xi–xiii, 350–70; Selig Perlman, *A Theory of the Labor Movement* (New York, 1970), 182–200.

3. Montgomery, *Beyond Equality*, 195–96, 249–60, esp. 259–60.

4. David DeLeon, *The American as Anarchist: Reflections on Indigenous Radicalism* (Baltimore, 1978), esp. 102–14, quotations from 102, 114.

5. Daniel Tarschys, *Beyond the State: The Future Polity in Classical and Soviet Marxism,* Swedish Studies in International Relations (Stockholm, 1971), 47–86, quotation from 65.

6. *Ibid.,* 77.

7. *Ibid.,* 86.

8. George McNeill, *The Labor Movement: The Problem of Today* (Boston, 1887), 485.

9. See William R. Schonfeld, "The Classical Conception of Liberal Democracy," *Review of Politics,* 33 (July 1971), 260–76.

10. On associationalism within American labor ideology see Brian Green-

berg, "Free Labor & Industrial Society: The Idea of a Cooperative Common-wealth in Mid-Nineteenth Century America," paper delivered at the Annual Meeting of the Organization of American Historians, New Orleans, Apr. 12, 1979; *Journal of United Labor* (hereafter *JUL*), Apr. 1883.

11. *JUL*, Dec. 1882, Jan. 15, Dec. 24, 1887; *John Swinton's Paper* (here-after *JSP*), Jan. 23, 1887; John A. Garraty, *Labor and Capital in the Gilded Age* (Boston, 1968), 152.

12. The Knights grew from 19,000 members in 1881 to 111,000 in 1885 to a reported 800,000 in 1886 before falling to 100,000 by 1888.

13. *JSP*, May 16, 1886.

14. *Ibid.*, Nov. 1, 1886.

15. *Ibid.*, Nov. 7, 1886, Apr. 17, 1887; Beaumont to Powderly, Nov. 5, 1886, Terence V. Powderly Papers, Catholic University, Washington, D.C.

16. Ware, *Labor Movement in U.S.*, 363.

17. *JSP*, Mar. 21, 1886; Rutland *Herald*, Aug. 27, 1886.

18. Milwaukee *Journal*, Oct. 4, 1886. The general point here is perfectly encapsulated in a resolution of the Workingmen's Convention, which gave rise to the Chicago United Labor party in 1886: "As the economic encroach-ments of aggregated wealth have caused the defensive organization of the producers into trade unions, Knights of Labor, and grangers, so much the political encroachments of the same aggregated wealth (which are still more dangerous to the liberty and existence of the people) inevitably force the people into defensive political organizations as distinct and antagonistic to capitalist political parties as the trade union is to the club, cabal, or clique of the monopolist" (*JSP*, Nov. 10, 1886).

19. Quincy (Mass.) *Patriot*, Mar. 5, Apr. 2, 1887.

20. William Appleman Williams, *The Contours of American History* (Cleveland, 1961), 334–38.

21. Herbert Gutman, "The Failure of the Movement by the Unemployed for Public Works in 1873," *Political Science Quarterly*, 80 (June 1965), 254–76; Rochester *Anti-Monopolist*, Dec. 12, 1885, Mar. 13, 1886, Mar. 11, 1887; Rochester *Courier*, Mar. 12, 1886, Mar. 11, 1887. The protective role of local working-class politics in another context has recently been noted by Joan Wallach Scott, "Social History and the History of Socialism: French Socialist Municipalities in the 1890s," *Le Mouvement Social*, 3 (1980), 145–55.

22. On antipartyism see Ronald P. Formisano, *The Birth of Mass Political Parties: Michigan, 1827–1861* (Princeton, 1971), 56–80, and Martin A. Schiesl, *The Politics of Efficiency: Municipal Administration and Reform in America, 1880–1920* (Berkeley, 1977), 6–24; Rutland *Herald*, Oct. 6, 1886.

23. See Lawrence Goodwyn, *Democratic Promise: The Populist Movement in America* (New York, 1976), for the argument offered here regarding farmer politicization; Kansas City, Kans., *Kansas Cyclone*, July 9, 1887; Rutland *Herald*, Oct. 6, 1886.

24. Frank M. Pixley, publisher of the nativist San Francisco *Argonaut*, returned from Paris in 1871 not only praising the "order and organization" of the Commune but also offering the following comment on the reception of

Americans by the Communards: "Americans had a universal pass in the city [along] with soldiers of the Commune. I treated a regiment of Vilette to half a cask of red wine. It was cheap, and I was paid in having them cheer the toast I gave them in very bad French—'The Republic of France and the Grand Republic of America. I shall live to see its realization' " (*American Non-Conformist*, Apr. 7, 1887, reprinted from *Argonaut*).

25. See David Montgomery, "Workers' Control of Machine Production in the 19th Century," *Labor History*, 17 (Fall 1976), 475–509.

26. Rutland *Herald*, July 25, 1887. From a diametrically opposite perspective the Chicago *Tribune*, even in its hostility, also understood that labor in politics primarily was aiming to buttress its role in civil society: "They [the United Labor party] want to control the police force so that they can throw bombs with impunity, the fire department so that they can ravage and burn without having their work of anarchy arrested, the machinery of taxation so that they can confiscate property by form of law and throw the revenues of honest enterprises into a common pool for plunder" (quoted in *JSP*, Mar. 27, 1887).

3

When Cleon Comes to Rule:
Popular Organization and Political Development.
Part I: Rochester, New Hampshire

UNTIL RECENTLY historians of New England tended to approach the nineteenth century as the beginning of the end of their particular version of the Old Glory. With national expansion, urbanization, the beginnings of industrialization, and immigration, the 1840s appeared to Charles Francis Adams, the consummate embodiment of the latter-day gentry in the Gilded Age, as a "somewhat dreary period in national history." Looking back on the history of his own Quincy, Massachusetts, for example, Adams concluded that the urban-industrial transformation signaled "a complete change in the character of the town," "a change for the worse." In a similar vein Barnes Frisbee, one of the distinguished elder citizens in Rutland, Vermont, during the 1880s, recalled that in the 1820s "social intercourse was more general, less formal, more hearty, more valued than at present." Frisbee recollected "very little of class or caste in the society of those years."[1]

For many who identified with what they preferred to remember of the times of their fathers, the shining star of the old order was local self-government. Steady disappearance of the town meeting served as the ultimate symbol of the insidious influence of new forces. All admitted that increasing population strained local institutions. But observers from the late nineteenth through the mid-twentieth centuries more than hinted that the final blow to town meeting issued from the outside. To Adams in the 1890s it seemed that a small, homogeneous community of freeholders had become a "heterogeneous mass of men with little knowledge of town traditions and less respect for them." A commentator fifty years later would likewise bemoan the "influx of strangers whose nationality and make up [were] immediately at odds with Town Meeting traditions."[2]

See epigraph, p. 1.

Scholars today have sketched a different picture of New England development from that of Adams and his ideological heirs. Colonial historians have made careful distinctions between village conformity and democratic decision-making, noting the narrow access to power maintained by gentrylike county elites. Stephan Thernstrom has emphasized the social heirarchy, religious closed-mindedness, and mercantile control exercised in the early nineteenth-century preindustrial town. Michael Frisch has demonstrated that the modern notion of "community"—implying areas of common public concern distinct from private interest—was realized less in the "good old days" than in the process of modernization, or "town-building." The debunking is carried even further by Page Smith who identifies the city, not the town, as the crucible of "modern democracy": "The town in its homogeneity, in its racial and cultural 'purity' was for the most part able to avoid those conflicts between rival groups and interests out of which modern democratic practice and theory have developed. As soon as alien groups moved in, town-meeting 'democracy' began to break down."[3]

The progressive as well as the nostalgic view of the transformation of New England community may, in fact, oversimplify the process of change. Industrialism was no neat package carrying new forms of work, socialization, and political relations under one wrapping. Rather, a changing social environment created pressures on old ways and set off a search for order in every corner of society. The new forms that would emerge depended on who was making the decisions at a given moment and perhaps just as important on what obstacles stood in the way of individual or group intentions.

An examination of political conflict in two New England towns—the textile and boot-making center of Rochester, New Hampshire, and the "marble city" of Rutland, Vermont—illuminates this largely neglected aspect of social change. Political organization from below, in this case the rise of the Knights of Labor, provided the chief stimulus to what some might call the modernization of community institutions. Specifically, the old town meeting gave way to representative city government, chosen by a socially inclusive two-party system. Neither the timing nor significance of this transition, however, derived from a general recognition that it was time for a change or from any conflict between traditionalists and modernizers. The institutional changes emerged as the by-products of a social struggle conducted both at the workplace and at the ballot box over the control and access to power in an age of industry.

In both Rochester and Rutland—as in Adams's Quincy and other New England towns[4]—workingmen's political slates, organized by the Knights of Labor, scored stunning electoral victories in 1886. The mass mobilization involved in such an accomplishment had complex roots. In part, labor organizations of the Gilded Age were able to draw on established traditions of political dissent, such as radical Greenbackism. But there was also something quite new about this moment of the mid-1880s. Through the Knights of Labor native American workers joined forces with an immigrant, and especially an Irish-American, industrial labor force that was preparing for the first time to claim its full rights of citizenship. This combined producing class played a key role in the transformation of politics in both cities, even though it did not shape the outcome in its own image. Dislodging an older system of party, power, and privilege, these New England movements hastened the arrival of a new social compromise, which ultimately invited the workers to take part in the machinery of state after divesting them of the capacity to run that machinery for themselves.

Rochester climbed to full-fledged industrial status in the half-dozen years following the Civil War. Until then it had served primarily as handmaiden to its agrarian hinterland. Set off from its Strafford County neighbor of Dover in 1722, the tiny English colony lying less than five miles from the Maine border along the Cocheco River raised corn and potatoes while periodically fending off Indian attacks. Twenty-one villagers fought and died in the Revolutionary War. Until the turn of the nineteenth century a few saw and grist mills and a tannery constituted the town's only manufactures. Then, in 1811, a store-keeper and plowhandle-maker secured a carding machine and established the Gonic Woolen Mills. The town's wealthy men—three trader-merchants—traveled twice a year to Boston to buy their goods; before 1834 they banked at Strafford, thirteen miles away, or stored their accounts inside a padlocked safe. John McDuffee, of Scotch-Irish ancestry, who married into the family of one of the old merchants, took the initiative in chartering the Rochester Bank and for the next sixty years served as patron of local economic development. He also nursed a small forerunner to the Norway Plains woolens firm through the lean late 1830s. When the first railroad opened in 1849, the village of 3,000 specialized in the manufacture of woolen blankets and possessed a rudimentary leather and shoe-making trade. The industrial hamlets of Gonic and East Rochester were separated by farmland—still the town's greatest resource—from the main village of Rochester.[5]

With the coming of the Civil War one ambitious Rochester family found itself particularly well positioned. Ebenezer G. and Edwin Wallace, the twin sons of a Maine Universalist minister-farmer, first had apprenticed as tanner-curriers; they then applied their trade while working their way through Phillips Exeter Academy. Hard-pressed financially, the brothers did not attend college but settled in Rochester in 1847 to take up leather-making. Setting out on the gold rush of 1849 with a Protestant caravan determined to "live together, work in common and divide equally" but destined to splinter as soon as they hit the fields, Ebenezer returned three years later with a modest sum. By 1858 the Wallace brothers had built a small but healthy leather-making business, employing six to eight hands. Cut off from the normal finishing market by the outbreak of war, the brothers extended production to encompass boot-making. Exigency became prosperity. Their labor force swelled through wartime demand to more than 100 workers, and Ebenezer and Edwin Wallace became the town's richest and most influential citizens. Meanwhile, even though Ebenezer used a combat substitute, his service to the Union cause did not go unrecognized. He held center stage at the town's eulogy to the nation's martyred president in 1865. As if to seal their newfound gentility, the Wallace brothers would see that their sons went to Dartmouth.[6]

By 1873 the town of Rochester had more than 5,000 residents. Local witnesses enthusiastically reported a building boom, connections with three railways, and the charter for a fourth. In addition, McDuffee had purchased a large interest in the Dover Cocheco Woolen Company and quickly added three mills in Rochester. New churches and schools sprang up, and the town's first newspaper, the weekly Rochester *Courier,* appeared in 1864. In 1874 the town boasted forty-five merchants, eleven manufacturers, eight doctors and dentists, and five lawyers.[7]

The Wallace family itself stood at the center of much of the town's postwar development. When the Strafford County Improved Peat Company was organized by John McDuffee's son in 1864, Ebenezer Wallace helped subscribe the initial capital. When the Rochester Savings Bank was chartered in 1872, Ebenezer Wallace was one of twenty-four incorporators. The Rochester Loan and Banking Company, established in the same period, boasted Edwin Wallace, president, and Ebenezer's son, Albert, fresh from Dartmouth College, vice-president. By 1870 both brothers had served in the state legislature. The family firm had grown in tandem with the town. In the 1880s the Wallace company occupied five acres of ground, including two multistoried factories. By 1885 the company employed 500 men and 150 women, making it one of the largest leather works in the country.[8]

The census of 1880 captured the overall social impact of the town's quickening industrialization. Nearly half of the nearly 2,000 citizens, defined as adult males eligible to vote and approximated in Table 2, in the town of 6,000 people were directly involved in the production of woolen or leather goods. Two woolens manufacturers, the Cocheco and Norway Plains companies, had already joined the Wallace firm as employers of 200 or more workers. While a bare quarter of this once overwhelmingly agricultural center were still engaged on the land, the expansion of services, schools, shops, and banks concomitant to industrialization was reflected in the numbers of independent professionals, merchants, clerks, teachers, and skilled craftsmen. By 1890, in fact, Rochester had become a respectable partner to neighboring Dover with a population of 7,000 people.[9]

The dominance of the factory system had perhaps its most dramatic effect on the young women in the town, or at least upon those who came from laboring families. While family responsibilities claimed married women of all classes (only 5 percent of employed women were married), the mills and

TABLE 2. Male Occupational Structure in Rochester, 1880

Occupations	Percent of Total Population
Non–Wage Earners	30
Capitalists (manufacturers, bankers, insurance agents)	1
Professionals-merchants	8
Salaried positions (clerks, teachers)	4
Farmers	17
Working Class	70
Skilled tradesmen	11
Industrial workers	42
Boot and shoe	28
Woolens	14
Unskilled laborers (rural and urban)	17
Total (*N* = 1,764)	100

Source. U.S. Tenth Census, 1880, population manuscript.
Note. Data are based on males, aged twenty and older.

factories took the great majority (70 percent) who entered the labor market. Indeed, domestic work, which nationally still commanded by far the largest number of female wage earners, represented a mere 14 percent of women employed in this industrially dominated town (Table 3).[10] It was the young daughters of industrial operatives, not surprisingly, who most often went to work in the mills; 85 percent of women in both the shoe and woolens industries were less than thirty years old, and in woolens, which claimed a majority of all working women, precisely half were under twenty (Table 4). Again, two-thirds of the fathers (identifiable by occupation) of the female woolen workers were themselves operatives in the town's two major industries.

Nor was it that industrialization had simply augmented and rearranged the tasks of the urban population of New England, male and female. The factories also became the special preserve of a growing immigrant population arriving mainly from Ireland, England, Scotland, and French-Canada. While together in 1880 they represented about a quarter of the total Rochester labor force, first- and second-generation immigrant families were, compared to the native population, overwhelmingly concentrated in the manual working class and, more particularly, the woolen trades. Indeed, in the woolen mills the immigrants and their children comprised 60 percent of the work force (Tables 4 and 5). Among these immigrant groups the French-Canadians occupied the lowest socioeconomic positions; more than 40 percent of males were engaged in unskilled rural or town labor. Whole families including young children commonly entered the woolen mills, and French-Canadian boys accompanied their fathers into the most unsavory branch of the leather trade, the tanneries.

TABLE 3. Female Occupational Structure in Rochester, 1880

Occupations	Percent of Total Population
Non–Wage Earners	6.5
Capitalists	—
Professionals-merchants	1.5
Salaried positions (clerks, teachers)	5
Farmers	—
Working Class	93.5
Skilled trades	—
Industrial workers	70.5
Boot and shoe	17.5
Woolens	53
Garment trades (tailor shop, seamstress, dressmaker)	9
Domestic	14
Total ($N = 461$)	100

Source. U.S. Tenth Census, 1880, population manuscript.
Note. All women employed are included. Dash = no woman in that position.

TABLE 4. Women's Employment in Rochester, 1880: Age and Ethnic Distribution within Occuptional Groups

	Age		National Origin	
Occupations	Under 20	Under 30	Native[a]	Immigrant[b]
Non–Wage Earners ($N = 30$)	7	63	80	20
Professionals–merchants ($N = 7$)	14	14	95	5
Salaried positions (clerks, teachers) ($N = 23$)	4	78	50	50
Working Class ($N = 431$)	38	78	59	41
Industrial workers ($N = 326$)	44	85	52	48
Boot and shoe ($N = 81$)	26	85	85	15
Woolens ($N = 245$)	50	85	42	58
Garment ($N = 40$)	18	60	87	13
Domestic ($N = 65$)	19	52	77	23
Total ($N = 461$)	36	75	61	39

Source. U.S. Tenth Census, 1880, population manuscript.
Note. All data are given as percentages of N.
[a]Includes native-born women with native parents only.
[b]Includes foreign-born women and those with one or both foreign-born parents.

Manufacturers in menial trades like brick-making also availed themselves of the pool of young Quebec men by boarding them at the yards.[11] English and

TABLE 5. Rochester Social Structure, 1880: National Origins and Occupational Groups

Occupations	Percent Native-Born[a]	Percent Immigrants[b]
Capitalists (N = 22)	94.5	5.5
Professionals and merchants (N = 139)	86	14
Salaried positions (N = 68)	90	10
Farmers (N = 300)	97	3
Skilled tradesmen (N = 200)	88	12
Industrial workers (N = 730)	68	32
Boot and shoe (N = 481)	(81)	(19)
Woolens (N = 249)	(42)	(58)
Unskilled laborers (N = 305)	65	35
Total (N = 1,764)	77	23

Source. U.S Tenth Census, 1880, population manuscript.
Note. The basis for this comparison is all males, age twenty and older.
[a]Includes native-born of native parents.
[b]Includes foreign-born and those with one or both foreign-born parents.

Scottish immigrants fared considerably better, entering the factories as well as skilled trades, while the Irish as a group were located roughly halfway between the French-Canadians and the British on an occupational scale (Table 6).

In contrast to larger cities, industrialization had not altogether altered Rutland's social geography. The economically varied residency patterns of a preindustrial community remained. Manufacturers' residences lay interspersed with the houses of employees. A small shoe manufacturer still took in a few of his workers as boarders. An editor lived next door to a teamster. However, by 1880 a small clustering of Irish families suggests an established ethnic enclave within the larger settlement. But the Irish were not set entirely apart from the rest of the population. Only the French-Canadians seem to have suffered social isolation as well as general poverty. Unlike the English-speaking immigrants, they were crowded into a section of town noted for its tenements instead of separate dwellings.

Public affairs in Rochester had largely ignored the social and economic transformation of the town. As a local chronicler noted in 1880, "Rochester has been conservative in action and not easily moved to adopt changes. The disposition of her voters seems to have been to 'let well enough alone.' " From the late 1870s through 1885, for example, contending forces at local elections included, in the order of their usual finish, Republicans, Democrats,

TABLE 6. Occupational Structure in Rochester, by Ethnic Groups, 1880

Occupations	Yankee[a]	French-Canadian[b]	Irish	British[c]
Non–Wage Earners	37	2	10	11
Professional	2	—	—	1
Merchants	9	—	5	8
Salaried positions	5	1	1	1
Farmers	21	1	4	1
Working Class	63	98	90	89
Skilled tradesmen	13	3	6	9
Industrial workers	36	51	61	72
Boot and shoe	28	22	29	18
Woolens	8	29	31	54
Unskilled laborers (rural and urban)	14	43	24	8
Total	100	100	100	100
N	1,361	150	140	90

Source. U.S. Tenth Census, 1880, population manuscript.
Note. Immigrant groups include those who are foreign-born and those with one or both parents foreign-born. All data are given as percentages and are based on males, age twenty and older.
[a]Includes native-born population with native-born parents.
[b]The French-Canadians were distinguished by their names. British-Canadians, i.e., those with parents born in England or Scotland, were listed under British. Similarly, Irish-Canadians were listed under Irish.
[c]Includes English, Scottish, and Welsh.

Prohibitionists, and Greenback-Laborites. But no great partisan issues or heated rivalries were invoked in these contests.[12]

Until the mid-1880s, in fact, the political and social leadership overlapped conspicuously with the town's economic elite. Town leaders tended to be native-American men of independent means, Republican in politics, Masonic in associational life, and prominent in the administration of one of the community's Protestant churches. Republicans and Democrats, while offering distinct tiers of leadership, seem to have drawn their representatives from substantially the same social pool. Identifiable Republican candidates from 1878 to 1885 included: ten merchants, nine farmers, a doctor, and a shoemaker. In these same years Democrats put forward seven merchants, two farmers, a shoe manufacturer, a spinner, a trimmer, and a granite worker. The only hint of social reform tendencies within either major party lay in the local and statewide connection between some Democrats and the New Hampshire Grange. Elsewhere, Democrats might represent ethnic, especially Catholic, constituencies. If there was any tendency in this direction in Rochester in the early 1880s, Democratic names like Philander Varney, Silas Hussey, George Springfield, Russell Wentworth, and J. L. Duntley kept the fact well hidden.[13]

Not surprisingly, political leaders were well connected to other centers of the town's associational life. At least five Republican officeholders during the early 1880s also held executive positions in the two local Masonic lodges. The banker McDuffees, for example, had long been active in Masonic affairs, with the first lodge dating to 1810. McDuffee Hall served as the Universalists' meetinghouse. The Wallaces were also Universalists, and the family was represented on the parish committee. Anna Evans, wife of the substantial young farmer and Republican selectman Edward E. Evans, served as one of two female approved ministers of the Friends' Society. S. O. Hayes, closely associated politically with the Wallace family, belonged to the Episcopal church, where his wife was the Sunday organist. A. S. Parshley, insurance agent and frequent Republican candidate during the decade, was clerk and superintendent of the Free Baptist Sunday School.[14]

The local citizenry, it appears, normally approached the annual March town meeting with more a dutiful than passionate commitment to the exercise of self-government. To be sure, the weekly Rochester *Courier*, edited for eighteen years by Republican teetotaler, Charles W. Folsom, had once led an excited charge against the "rum-sellers" who congregated around the Grand Army of the Republic's annual drills and musters. Like the bloody shirt, the temperance issue remained a stock in trade of Republican campaigns, but by 1880 it was no longer a matter of partisan dispute. The town would vote overwhelmingly for a state prohibition amendment in 1889.[15]

Rules governing the relation of government to business enterprise were equally taken for granted. Although the larger manufacturers seldom ran for local office, their needs were not neglected by town government. Starting in 1872, the town exempted from taxation "any new establishment for cotton, wool, wood, iron, boots and shoes, and any other material with a capital investment of $1000." Over the years other legislation had granted additional exemptions to particular enterprises.[16]

Generally devoid of debate over the larger nature or uses of the public prerogative, town democracy echoed with a jockeying for individual position and argument over moral character and conduct. For the major political parties, contests at the local level offered minor steppingstones of influence toward the primary seat of partisan interest, the state legislature. For the office seekers themselves, however, more was at stake. Town politics represented not only a test of social prestige but also tangible control over the nuts and bolts of town-building. How much to spend on schools, whether to build a bridge or extend a road, where to lay a macadam crossing, how much to invest in street lights, whether to float a bond issue—these were the bones of contention for a town of Rochester's size and stage of municipal development. Even the more spirited local campaigns thus rested less on differences of principle than on whether or not the "ins" had betrayed an intangible public trust. In 1882, for example, strong party men, both Republicans and Democrats, combined as "ringbreakers" to unseat an old board of selectmen accused of cowtowing to seventy-year-old Ebenezer Wallace and the "Factory Ring." Two years later, however, the old board group was back in office as Regular Republicans. If factions developed within parties, the boundaries of both factions and parties proved elastic. So fluid were Rochester's political lines that Democrats and Republicans took precautions in 1884 to hold their party caucuses at exactly the same time "to prevent either caucus from being captured by the other."[17]

Within the general consensual framework of local affairs, two minority groups, the Prohibition and Greenback-Labor parties, stood out as exceptions for the fundamentally ideological inspiration of their political engagement. The Prohibitionists formed a tight, native-American circle whose demand for moral self-discipline set them closer to labor reformers of the period than might be expected. The Rochester party ran continuously from 1870 through 1888, displaying a hardy commitment as they repeatedly placed the same names before an unwilling electorate. In a given election they could count on some forty to one hundred loyalists out of a total of 800–1,400 participating citizens. In their associational ties as well as in their occupational status, the Prohibitionists also differed from the major parties. Eleven Prohibition candidates identified through mid-decade included four farmers, four workers (two mechanics, a laster, and a loomfixer), two grocers, and a trader. The farmer Albert M. Horne seems to have given leadership to the movement. One Prohibitionist was a local Grange officer, another was active in the Odd Fellows, a fraternal lodge whose membership included considerably more of the Rochester laboring population than did the Masons. Not surprisingly, wives of the Prohibition men led the Women's Christian Temperance Union, itself a reform organization with broader women's rights as well as labor reform interests. Local evidence does not reveal direct ties between Prohibitionist and labor organizations, but the Prohibition party and the WCTU maintained cordial relations with the Knights of Labor in many areas of the country, including neighboring Maine.[18]

The Greenback-Labor party attracted even less support locally during the 1880s than did the Prohibitionists. In the party's best showing of the decade, George G. Berry, native Rochesterian and editor-printer of the weekly *Anti-Monopolist,* mustered twenty-three votes for selectman. The ten stalwarts of the Greenback Weavers and Chambers Club fit comfortably inside the newspaper's office for their regular meetings. Despite their negligible electoral strength, however, the Greenbackers represented something more in local affairs than a group of isolated eccentrics. A dozen party activists in the 1880s included one merchant (a tin and stove dealer) and two farmers, one of whom doubled as a milkman. The rest consisted of a railway station agent, Berry the printer-publisher, three shoemakers, three textile workers (a boss weaver, a boss finisher, and a trimmer), and one man of unspecified occupation who shared lodging with a sawyer. These men, in short, formed the kernel of

Rochester labor politics, at once a vestige of the larger growth of the late 1870s and the seed for what would come some half dozen years later.

Chartered nationally in 1878, the Greenback-Labor party was the third-party heir to Radical Republicanism. Depression, entrepreneurial failure, and industrial unrest combined for a brief moment to see this native-reform force lay claim to substantial sections of the original Republican constituency of manufacturers and small producers. In New Hampshire, in fact, signs of such economic dissatisfaction had cropped up as early as 1870 with the strong showing of an independent Labor Reform candidate for governor. In that same year Rochester elected two reform selectmen, one as a Democrat and Labor man, the other with a Temperance and Labor label. Simultaneous to the establishment of the national party in 1878, the farmer Henry M. Kelley, running as a Greenbacker and Democrat, defeated the Republican candidate for moderator at town meeting. While Kelley and most of his supporters soon merged back into the dominant Republican party, they had nevertheless established a foothold for independent reform politics, and the stubborn few gathered around the *Anti-Monopolist* lived off that promise for the next dozen years.[19]

The Greenback faith derived from a deep-seated ideological antagonism to the apparent rise of an all-powerful financial monopoly expropriating both the liberty and prosperity of American citizens. Public subsidies, land grants, and privileged low interest bonds issued to railroads and other corporate developers through the banking system were part of a chain of economic and political chicanery that had been cemented by "the crime of '73" in which silver was demonetized. Greenback radicals during the depression of the late 1870s avowed that democratic abundance would return only after the money and credit supply were removed from control of financial elites, monopolies (particularly railroads and banks) were deprived of legal protection, and all other class legislation was abolished. Like the Radical Republicans and radical Jeffersonians before them, their emphasis was upon "equal rights to all citizens"; and in a community like Rochester where crowds still flocked to see *Uncle Tom's Cabin,* comparisons between the old servitude and the new forms of subjugation found more than a few attentive listeners.[20]

Through the pages of the *Anti-Monopolist,* Berry and his son, Frank P., kept the cutting edge of inherited republican beliefs very much alive. The paper painted the nation's new industrial-financial rulers as an "upper ten . . . who sit in their spacious and luxuriant offices and devise schemes to draw into their possession the total net results of all the toil of the laborers." Having captured the machinery of government, this parasitical elite "always had the law on their side." Those who courageously attacked the system of plunder were, of course, immediately assailed as "unpatriotic" by the Blaines and Garfields, hortatory puppets of the new aristocracy. The "people" had few defenses. "Even the slaveowners, whom these 'upper ten' now decry as cruel," had fed and clothed "those by whose toil they were enriched." Not so, the "relentless lords of labor." As American "patriots" the Greenback critics promised to overturn the present "system of oppression." Their forces, the *Anti-Monopolist* assured its readers, would one day be remembered "side by side with . . . the immortal heroes of the revolution and emancipation."[21]

A rationalist and free-thinker, Berry represented a kind of last gasp of "Enlightenment radicalism" (to use Anthony Wallace's phrase) in an age dominated by evangelical pieties. In 1880, for example, the Methodist minister, John Chessman, interrupted his remarks before the regular Sunday afternoon temperance society meeting to condemn Berry's criticism of the local clergy and even to urge the *Anti-Monopolist's* suppression. Responding to the assault, Berry did not sound intimidated: "For the information of all we plead guilty and confess that we don't care a whit more for the clergy than we do for ordinary terrestrial beings and we shall attack them or their doctrines (for sufficient cause) . . . as soon as we should the money Shylocks or Republicanism." Berry stated his philosophy succinctly and pugnaciously: "We don't believe in monopolies of *any* kind. We don't believe the manufacturer ought to have a corner on labor and thus make slaves of thousands of human beings. And we don't think the clergy ought to have a corner on soul-saving and damn every one that don't believe in the Christian religion." In support of the beleaguered editor, one reader, a man of both Greenback-Labor and temperance persuasion, denounced Chessman as the clerical tool of industrialist Edwin Wallace.[22]

The Greenback-Labor partisans were undoubtedly most effective on the attack, storming the battlements of entrenched privilege. In 1879, for example, the desire of several Rochester women to vote in school board meetings aroused considerable opposition. The *Anti-Monopolist* was adamant. "Ladies, it is your right and privilege to attend. . . . Rebuke the insults you have suffered." Within a year of the initial protest, Mrs. George G. Berry and Mrs. Frank McDuffee, a weaver's wife, were active regulars at the board meetings.[23]

Greenback militants also carried with them the weaknesses of the home-grown radical tradition. So vigorous in asserting general principles, they offered few tangible reforms, particularly at the state or local level. What was worse, the defense of republican values against the intrusions of capital sometimes degenerated into suspicion of alien labor as well. A series of letters in the *Anti-Monopolist* helped to prevent a public appropriation for Rochester's night schools. Most of those who would benefit, the correspondent "America" feared, would be French-Canadians, "imported across the line for the express purpose of cheapening and undermining the resources of honest Americans." To "America," it seemed that night schools were no more than the "upper ten" shifting their responsibilities to working-class taxpayers. "Let it be done through private charity," he urged, "by special aid of those for whose benefit they were imported." Nativist logic justified and only barely masked a simple racism. The French were "no good" for the community. Many had "a faculty for cheap living" and returned "whence they came with a well-lined purse with which to buy up 'zee leetle farm.' " "Without the least compunction," they applied for public relief and were altogether "a disgrace in this great, highly civilized and christianized republic."[24]

These glimpses of Rochester's political life in the early and mid-1880s suggest the existence of diverse associational and ideological networks within a small community. Even within the Protestant native-American population during a relatively stable period, political heterodoxy flourished. Such embers of dissent no doubt contributed to the coming brushfire.

A new social configuration emerged in Rochester in 1886 with the formation of seven Knights of Labor local assemblies. To be sure, pockets of labor organization had existed earlier in the decade, notably among shoemakers. Although industrial regimentation had undermined much of their once-proud craft status (a fifty-nine-hour week, for example, was the norm in the local shoe factories), New England shoemakers still displayed a robust line of descent from the "rebel mechanics" of an earlier day. Their presence has already been noted among the core of Rochester's Greenback radicals.[25]

The Lasters' Protective Union, the first known local labor organization, comprised the trade's most skilled men. In the late 1870s it had picked up the freshly fallen mantle of the first great commonwealth of shoeworkers, the Knights of St. Crispins. In the spring of 1884 the lasters alone managed to resist a general wage cut instituted by the Wallace company. In November 1885, when the company resumed full operations following a lengthy slump in trade, the union sent a regional official to request a 10 percent increase above the daily $1.56 wage. When refused by an "indignant" Mr. Wallace, they walked out "leaving everything in excellent order." After a two-week strike the lasters' demands were accepted.[26]

Shoeworkers were the first to join the Knights of Labor. The lasters' victory along with the Order's national growth stimulated the entire shoe-working community. A lone Knights' local, formed in 1882, claimed but ninety members in 1885. That year shoecutters and shoe operatives joined the Knights' movement and formed separate Rochester trades assemblies; East Rochester shoeworkers also combined. The lasters maintained their own union but also joined the Knights, a common pattern within the labor movement of the day. By March 1886 an unfriendly Rochester correspondent could write: "The Knights of Labor constitute a large element here, as might be expected where there is a large shoe interest. For some reason or other shoe help seems to be in the direct line of fermentation, whatever be its source." In 1885 a short-sighted Lynn shoe manufacturer had relocated in Rochester to avoid the union and its wage demands. But already in January 1886, Walter Jones, the Lynn heelers' master workman, was busy signing up Rochester shoeworkers at the rate of "a 100 a night." Workplace organizing expressed only one side of the shoeworkers' wide-ranging collective endeavors. The various divisions of the Wallace factory, for example, teamed up in organized baseball games, and the lasters' union staged an evening of old-time drama at the local opera house.[27]

Rochester shoeworkers appeared to have combined the status of semiskilled factory workers with the behavior of self-confident skilled artisans. By economic criteria only, they were industrial workers. Four-fifths were under forty years old, fully half under thirty. For all but a few, therefore, work had begun in an industry already dominated by the factory system. The possibility was not nearly as open to them as it had been to the Wallaces to move from craftsman to entrepreneur. What explains the continuity, then, between the older organizations of shoeworkers (led by ex-artisans) and the activism of these younger factory workers? Direct transmission of values from one generation to the next provides one explanation. In Rochester such a process was aided by familial ties as well as workplace relationships. A census sample indicates that nineteen out of every twenty shoeworkers lived in familial settings. Boardinghouse arrangements were scarce. Half the fathers of young (dependent) shoeworkers in the factories by 1880 were themselves shoeworkers (Table 7). Another quarter of the fathers were either artisans or textile workers. Only a tenth of the young shoeworkers came to the factories from the farm. Rochester's shoeworkers appear, therefore, to have encountered the rigors of industrialization with significant cultural resources. They were thoroughly familiar with the artisan's control of production and social fellowship. If they had largely lost control over the tools of their trade by the 1880s, they retained the tools of experience and an inherited belief in their rights within the workshop and the world outside.[28]

TABLE 7. Occupations of Shoeworkers' Fathers in Rochester, 1880

Occupations	Percent of Total
Merchants	2
Farmer-farm laborers	10
Skilled tradesmen	15
Shoeworkers	50
Textile workers	13
Unskilled laborers	10
Total (*N* = 106)	100

Source. U.S. Tenth Census, 1880, population manuscript.
Note. The table includes only those households of dependent male shoeworkers in which the occupation of the head of household (either father or father-in-law) is listed. The households headed by widowed mothers or retired fathers (with no occupation listed), which came to roughly 10 percent of the original sample, were not included in the table.

Once the shoeworkers stirred, other Rochester workers also expressed interest in the Knights of Labor. Weavers and spinners together formed a woolens' assembly in 1886. House-builders, including carpenters, masons, painters, and lathers, also joined the Order as a unit. Two mixed-trade assemblies completed the picture of Rochester organization. A new newspaper, the Rochester *Leader,* also appeared in December 1885 as "an advocate of the Labor Interest." Altogether the town proved one of the most dynamic locales in a statewide Knights' drive that saw forty locals and more than 5,000 New Hampshire members by the end of April 1886.[29]

There is reason to suspect that Irish-Americans in particular played a disproportionately large role in the revived labor movement. Already by 1880 there were signs of the outspokenness of local Irish-American workingmen. The temperance meeting that featured the clash between evangelical conservatism and the radical *Anti-Monopolist* witnessed another confrontation as well. When Wallace rose to blame drunkenness on immigrant carriers of Old World "degradation," an Irish shoecutter jumped up to remind the industrialist that the "true cause" of Ireland's plight was "the landlords who own nearly the whole of the land." By October 1886 the influential Manchester *Union* estimated that "a large majority" of the state's Irish population were members of the Knights of Labor.[30]

The Knights' activity coincided with a growing self-assurance within New England's Irish-Catholic communities. In the 1860s St. Mary's parish had grown from ten to several hundred families as the Irish streamed into the town's factories. When newer French-Canadian Catholics split off to form their own parish in 1883, the Irish parishioners, not to be outdone, constructed a second and more elaborate St. Mary's. In November 1886, at the height of local labor influence, the second St. Mary's Church unveiled a new pipe organ and huge bell, secured by massive outpourings of small contributions. The same period also witnessed large Irish nationalist rallies, no doubt including contingents of Rochester supporters, in nearby Dover. Taken together, these events suggest a serious coming of age of the the overwhelmingly working-class Irish community, asserting itself and its interests on every front.[31]

By the beginning of 1886 organization through the Knights of Labor had cut deeply into the life of the community. Differences of social identity that had always divided the people of Rochester now coalesced more dramatically around a single issue. "Public opinion here has changed wonderfully within a few months past, or since the recent labor troubles," commented one anonymous local labor partisan in March 1886. "Unionism has enlarged its borders and is bound to assert its power in the advancement of liberty and justice to all men."[32]

The day following the March 1886 annual town meeting, the Rochester *Courier* spoke of a "new factor" that had dealt "party politics in Rochester

. . . a stunning blow." Men with "no previous experience" had been elected selectmen, town clerk, treasurer, and tax collector. The pattern was extended the next week when the new selectmen completed the roster of local government by appointment. The United Labor ticket, formed at a secret joint meeting of the Knights of Labor and the lasters' union, had made its strength abundantly clear in the days before the town meeting. The Democrats had met and endorsed the labor ticket. Republicans, after initially slating two labor men under their own banner, had reconsidered the idea and withdrawn from the field. In a peculiar case of consensus politics, the labor representatives secured a nearly unanimous verdict from the four-hundred-odd citizens in attendance. The lower-than-average turnout suggests that the opposition preferred not to be embarrassed by a direct confrontation.[33]

The Knights' triumph in March 1886 was not a one-time affair. For three-and-a-half years, United Labor, Union Labor, or just plain Labor candidates went undefeated in local elections. Against Republican opposition the Knights elected a five-member delegation to the state legislature in the fall of 1886. They swamped a Citizens ticket attempting to appeal to loyalists of both major parties at the 1887 annual town meeting. A year later, they supported a grocer named George L. Hayes, who polled 1,200 votes in a town that contained only 2,200 voting-age males. A Concord paper commented that Rochester's old parties "have become mere side shows in that town." By the fall of 1888 the Republican town of Rochester was reduced to a solitary Republican legislator.[34]

The labor movement left its mark in other parts of the state as well. The 1886 gubernatorial race pitted Republican woolen manufacturer Charles H. Sawyer against wealthy Democratic farmer-lawyer Colonel Charles Cogswell. The Democrats made direct appeals to the Knights of Labor, emphasizing Sawyer's opposition to a state ten-hour bill. In addition, the Reverend Luther F. McKinney, the pastor of a Universalist congregation in Manchester, ran for Congress in the First District (which included Rochester) as a Knight of Labor with Democratic backing. To a traditional Greenback-Labor platform advocating inflationary measures, McKinney added demands for nationalization of the railroads and telegraph system. The Republican Concord *Evening Monitor* alarmingly compared the labor-oriented thrust of the Democratic state campaign to the anarchism of "Spies, Most, Kearney, and [the] *Arbeiter Zeitung*." Nevertheless, McKinney narrowly won. Cogswell battled Sawyer to a standoff that was resolved in the Republican's favor only by a decision of a partisan state legislature. In solidly Republican Rochester, where labor-backed candidates including McKinney had now secured over 55 percent of the vote, the Republican oracle found the results "hard to believe" and the Knights of Labor entirely "to blame."[35]

The available evidence suggests that the Knights' political movement in Rochester represented less a party than a mass protest against the self-selected guardians of the public trust. The political parties, in this sense, only masked the real issue, which was the nature of popular access to power. So long as the people—through the Knights of Labor—could be elected to office, the movement seemed willing to work through the existing parties. Labor forces, for example, slated three Republicans and two Democrats for the fall 1886 legislative ticket. On one level, organization of the local work force had simply added muscle to the old Greenback excoriation of social parasitism. An attack on Old Board politicos prior to the 1886 town meeting as, among other things, a "rum ring . . . winked at by the clergy" testified to the translation of a particular social critique into mass political action. So, too, did the verse (to be sung to the tune of "Rally Round the Flag") of a Keene, New Hampshire, Knight of Labor.[36]

> We build gilded carriages, fine mansions and halls,
> But not for the brave sons of labor,
> And we go to work when the bell or whistle calls,
> But where are the fruits of our labor?
>
> Chorus: Labor forever, hurrah! boys, hurrah!
>   'Tis the life of the nation and prop of the law,
>   And we'll rise it to that station, where no man can draw,
>   Millions from our labor, hurrah! boys, hurrah!
>
> While the law has the banker and broker for pets,
> Who fatten on the fruits of labor,
> The brawny wealth producer, a thought never gets,
> Though working day and night at labor.
>
> Chorus:
>
> But now we're determined and bound to get what's right,
> For all men and women who labor,
> And when we're united we'll beat them in the fight,
> With the ballot our shield and sabre.
>
> Chorus:

Transferral of public responsibilities out of the normal orbit of influence of the town fathers had an utterly exhilarating effect on local labor partisans. "[Previously] the common herd would form into line at the crack of the party whip, and, with lockstep, march to the polls and to victory in the interest of capitalist monopoly," explained a Rochester correspondent to *John Swinton's Paper* in New York City. "How great and radical the change!" Less sympathetic observers also noted the difference. The Concord *Evening Monitor* attacked the appearance of the mongrel legislative ticket in the fall of 1866 as an inappropriately "partisan" act, violating as it did the more dignified nominating process ordinarily carried out among the town's "best men."[37]

The most tangible impact of the labor reform movement on the town's political life was the de facto shift in the social origins of officeholders. With the possible exception of the Greenback-Labor group, workers were represented on the Knights' tickets out of all proportion to their place in the old parties. Over the three-year period 1886–88, of thirty-seven candidates identified under the labor banner, 80 percent were from working-class occupations, including eight shoeworkers, seven carpenters, and four woolen workers. The political movement thus directly represented the most important blocs within the Knights of Labor. At a typical 1886 labor political caucus, shoemaker Clarence Chamberlain presided, and Horatio Cate, printer-editor of the *Leader,* acted as secretary.[38]

The character of labor's political leadership offers other important clues to the meaning of the movement. First, it is apparent that the laboring community was governed by an internal hierarchy of skill and ethnicity as well as by a well-developed sense of social status. The Knights of Labor and their supporters tended to designate their most respectable and socially successful members as official representatives and emissaries before the public. Particularly for the elected positions of selectman and state legislator, they reached no further down on the social ladder than lasters, cutters, or carpenters. It was symbolic that labor's biggest vote-getter had worked his way up from clerk to independent grocer. The appointment of the edge-setter, John H. Pingree, as police chief and his subsequent election as county sheriff appeared at first a striking exception to the rule. However, Pingree was already a deacon in the Masonic order when he took office. He was not alone in moving from a position of authority in the lodges into labor politics. At least six titled Odd Fellows and one other Masonic officer became labor spokesmen, candidates, or officeholders. Camaraderie as well as leadership experience gained in these explicitly nonpolitical associations may well have convinced certain less wealthy citizens that they were just as capable of running the town as anybody else. The absence of Irish-American and French-Canadian shoeworkers from the ranks of labor candidates suggests again that in seeking an electoral majority, the labor reformers were conforming to local notions of respectability. In this respect the labor effort represented a carefully qualified revolt from below.[39]

Second, the Knights of Labor and its independent brand of politics obviously appealed to significant sections of the town's middle class. A real estate auctioneer, a mill overseer, a hardware store owner, a grocer-bookkeeper, a livery stable owner, a hat and cap merchant, a tailor with his own store, a cashier, and the town postmaster—all served under labor's banner. For some small proprietors, reliance on working-class consumers may have facilitated identity with labor's cause. In any case, lines between occupations were not as rigid as they later became. Fred Crocker, for example, appointed as a policeman by the labor forces in 1886, worked as both a mason and a hairdresser. But how do we account for an overseer within the workingmen's ranks? An index to political consciousness in this case might not have been the man's own social position but that of neighbors and kin. Supervisory personnel were not necessarily far removed from the status of wage earner. The grown sons of one woolen mill overseer, for example, were shoemakers. In another case, French-Canadian brickyard workers boarded with their overseer. Personal contact in a managerially unsophisticated industrial system might yet bridge a widening class divide.[40]

Third, the political evidence hints at a significant rural/urban split among the local population. Farmers did not generally enlist in Rochester Knights' campaigns; indeed, the local head of the Grange campaigned against a labor man in 1887. The rural section of the Knights that existed in New Hampshire—a prosperous farmer served as master workman in the nearby town of Strafford—made little headway in separating area farmers from their traditional political loyalties. Generally resisting encroachments from town authority, the farmers may well have associated labor with a coming host of urban problems. They may also have had in mind their own potential labor problem.[41]

Finally, and perhaps most curiously, none of the recognized group of Greenback regulars gained office during labor's political ascendancy. To be sure, the Greenbackers did not oppose the labor tickets, and the *Anti-Monopolist* appeared sympathetic. Why, then, were these steady tillers in the field unrewarded when a harvest finally arrived? One may only speculate. In his national survey of late nineteenth-century labor politics, Edward T. James found that the Greenback party was "largely ignored if not rebuffed" by the labor tickets of 1886–87. Specifically, in Manchester Labor and Greenback conventions in 1886 could not agree on a common endorsement of candidates. The new political movement received its greatest stimulus from the idea that citizens, not politicians, were taking power. In this sense, Greenback reformers may have been just as unacceptable as other party men. Indeed, ideological affinity may have only increased fears that the Greenbackers would dominate the political neophytes. Then, too, the purely native-American coloration of the older movement may have set it apart from the Knights and their Irish-American support. With a trace of paternalism and a touch of surprise, the *Anti-Monopolist* congratulated the laboring men for joining in town affairs with "no drunkenness" and "no arrests." The *Anti-Monopolist* remained an independent community newspaper, while the *Leader,* edited by twenty-eight-year-old printer Horatio Cate and twenty-seven-year-old shoeworker and Adventist I. M. Horne, evidently spoke directly for the Knights. Printed in the same office, the two papers as well as the movements they represented may have been separated by a subtle generation gap as much as by anything else. Of eight labor partisans identified by age, six were less than forty years old in 1886. They served an industrial constituency whose youth has already been noted.[42]

Ideologically, the Rochester Knights combined emergent class feelings with certain residual preindustrial values. As workers they resisted the claims of factory owners to absolute authority at the workplace and to a disproportionate influence in public. They criticized the principle of tax exemptions for factories on grounds of the labor theory of value, arguing that "the whole thing would be worthless but for the laboring class." At the same time Rochester's labor partisans desired social harmony and wished to preserve the sense of individual moral accountability possible in a small town. In this ambivalence they were probably quite close to the timid radical at the head of the Order, Terence Powderly. Identifying the "isms" with disorder and permanent social polarization, the Rochester Knights joined Powderly in condemning socialism and anarchism following the May 1886 Haymarket explosion.[43]

George P. Hayes, Rochester shoemaker and Union Labor supporter, has left revealing testimony of the intellectual spirit behind the political labor movement. An avid reader of *John Swinton's Paper,* Hayes paid homage to Henry George and Robert Ingersoll, both of whose views the paper had recently featured. George's writings had convinced Hayes that a scourge had settled upon the nation's essentially decent institutions and made servants and slaves of citizens and workers. "O that such vital truths might be instilled deep into the sluggish minds and hearts of a long-suffering, deceived and oppressed people," Hayes wrote from Rochester, "that they might be nerved and impressed with a full sense of duty and the God-given right and power to purge this Government of a corrupt political system, and make it one of purity, justice, and equality."[44]

"What a rattling of dry bones would result among the uppertendom," Hayes mused, "if only a giant intellect like Ingersoll would lead the movement." The famous free-thought and Republican orator who had once sworn off any imputation of conflict between labor and capital changed his mind in the mid-1880s. He had begun preaching that in place of the "dream of 1776 . . . we have kings and princes, lords and peasants" in the form of "Monopolists, corporations, capitalists, and workers for wages." For a brief period Ingersoll even suggested that "the foundations have been laid for a new party. The people who have done the work of the world begin to see that they have the power to control." The supreme spokesman for bloody-shirt Republicanism went so far as to support George for mayor of New York in 1886. These were writings that could stir a Rochester shoeworker.[45]

It was in keeping with the whole tenor of their movement that the Knights, once in office, exercised power with great restraint. Their record indicates greater interest in airing and cleaning out local government than in any major rearrangement of government function or program. "Believing that traps have been set into which they have walked with open eyes," the Knights allegedly sent their people to the polls to "find out who pays the tax and what becomes of the money." But even after taking a look around, the labor majorities acted with utmost circumspection. Local labor rule, for example, did not end tax exemptions for business. Indeed, the only labor action to arouse significant controversy was the vote to construct a concrete pedestrian crossing from the Knights of Labor hall on one side of the street to the clothing store of German-Jewish Simon Wolf, a labor partisan and town treasurer, on the other. Labor's first town meeting increased appropriations for street lights, poor relief, and education by 20 percent over the preceding year. Again in 1887–88, a labor board appropriated extra money for highways, schools, a new town hall, a reading room, and a Memorial Day celebration. Small in themselves, these actions may have signaled a subtle shift toward an attitude to government described by Michael Frisch as an instrument of "more general, public ends" rather than "simply the place where overlapping and conflicting private claims for public favor could be adjusted." Being a broadly based institution, the Knights may thus have qualitatively stimulated the process of town-building.[46]

A limited caretaker role—to show that they could do what had been done for them—generally defined the scope of labor's ambition in local government. At best, political participation offered proof of equal citizenship, a denial that increasing wealth and authority at the top of society were justified by mass ignorance and passivity at the bottom. Labor politics, however, was clearly only the end product of the organization and mobilization of a working-class community. Even the occasional bravado of Knights' representatives did not mask the limited area of their political operation.[47]

The labor tickets in Rochester grew up as an extension of the strength of the Knights of Labor. So, too, the decline of independent labor politics was undoubtedly a corollary to the collapse of its constituent organization. The causes, of course, were complex and national in scope. Only the manner in which the once-robust movement was locally laid to rest is treated here.

The shoeworkers—the crux of Rochester labor organization—were never as strong industrially as their numbers suggested. From 1886 they seem to have experienced a long and painful downhill slide. At least five work stoppages affected the local shoe industry between 1886 and 1893. Not a single one ended happily for the workers. The first, by Wallace company lasters in July 1886, failed after one month to stave off the introduction of nonunion men. In November of the same year, F. W. Breed employees in East Rochester accepted a new price list offered by the company after a three-week protest. The following January, lasters at the Fogg and Vinal company in East Rochester brought 250 men and women out in a futile demand for a higher wage scale. In May 1887 a 10 percent wage reduction was imposed on 120 stitchers in one of the Rochester factories. The resulting walkout lasted for more than six months, until the 250 workers in the plant returned, having managed only to limit the reduction. Thus, with utter intransigence the factory owners met labor's demands during the latter's headiest days of local political influence. The rout of the shoeworkers continued into the 1890s. Wallace successfully imposed a wage reduction on 700 workers in 1890 by means of a lockout. He hired sixty hands from "other places" after the struggle. In 1893 even a five-month strike by 175 skilled cutters could not avert a 10 percent wage cut.[48]

A coordinated offensive by eastern shoe factory owners probably contributed to the plight of Rochester's workers. The Boston *Labor Leader* reported a January 1887 conference of shoe manufacturers determined to break the Knights' grip on their factories. Following this conference, strikes erupted in a number of Massachusetts shoe towns over the posting of notices for "yellow-dog employees only." A few months later, Philadelphia shoe manufacturers engineered a mass lockout at the end of which women who had been earning $12 per week found their wages cut to $7 per week.[49]

The Knights' organization, rooted as it was in local resentment of arbitrary political and industrial authority, proved incapable of dealing with powers that did not respect the sovereignty of local sentiment. Local 2200's Master Workman and shoeworker S. W. Brock worried as early as January 1886 that "these country shoe manufacturers are afraid they will have to pay what others pay for their work and wood like to bust this Assembly or get men in to it who will run it in thair intrese [*sic*]." One New England manufacturer had already let it be known that he would not complete the installation of a factory in Rochester so long as Knights' organizers from the stronghold of Lynn, Massachusetts, were around the town. In Brock's opinion scare tactics passed along in this instance from a shoe owner to a bookkeeper who was also a popular Knight had a debilitating effect on the Order's rank and file.[50]

The tactics of antiunion employers put the shoeworkers on the defensive, but the shoeworkers were also weakened by an internal collapse. Feuding broke out in 1887 between the lasters' union and the Knights of Labor, opening wounds in places like Alton, just up the river from Rochester. Formation of a national trades assembly of shoe and leather workers within the Knights failed to solve the growing jurisdictional and craft conflict in the industry. Rochester sent representatives in the spring of 1888 to an area-wide organizing meeting of the United Boot and Shoe Workers National Trade Assembly, a federation that, after frustrated dealings with Powderly, entirely cut its ties to the Knights. Not until formation of the Boot and Shoe Union in 1895, however, did the organized factions within the trade begin significantly to recompose. According to Norman Ware, "Shoeworkers have never since been so thoroughly organized as they were under the Knights of Labor."

Fracture of the mainstay of Knights' support in Rochester provides the most convincing explanation of their precipitous fall from political power by the end of 1888.[51] In the fall of 1888 the independent formula had clearly lost its promise. A. J. Streeter, the Union Labor candidate for president, received only two votes in the town. By the spring of 1889 the few individuals running as self-styled labor men seemed to have had little connection to the earlier movement. One clue as to the possible redirection of popular ferment after the defeat of this labor movement was provided by an unsuccessful statewide prohibition referendum in March 1889. Almost alone among urban centers (Nashua was the other exception), Rochester voters overwhelmingly endorsed the amendment, 1,224 to 683. The townspeople, it appeared, had switched from one source of moral and civic renewal to another.[52]

Demise of the Knights of Labor and their political tickets, however, did not end workingmen's influence in local and state affairs. Republican boards in Rochester in 1889 and 1890 included among their elected members the grocer George Hayes as selectman, the hat merchant Fred Chesley as town clerk, and the shoeworker Frank Decateur as tax collector. All three had entered government under labor's banner. At the state level Republicans had also moved toward the new constituency, enacting a ten-hour law, weekly payments' legislation, and a prohibition on child labor in mills and factories.[53]

Even more assiduously and effectively than the Republicans, the Democrats cultivated labor's old support. The secretary at labor's congressional nominating convention of 1886, shoemaker Benjamin M. Flanders, became a Democratic legislative candidate in 1888. He was joined by Sheriff Pingree, who had also switched to the Democratic label. In the same election Democrats opposed the young Republican industrialist Sumner Wallace with a rallying cry of "labor versus capital." While Democratic candidates from the president on down (including Congressman McKinney) were handily defeated in New Hampshire in 1888, they still carried the old Republican town of Rochester. Significantly, in addition to accommodating the workingmen's leaders, Democrats had placed the local head of the Hibernian society on their ticket in 1887.[54]

The political elites of Rochester had effectively defused the threat of an independent labor movement by a combination of the carrot and the stick. Through the agency of the Knights, smoldering social grievances at first turned local politics on its head. Control of the mechanisms of state power, even at the lowest level, however, was soon undermined by the overwhelming influence of the business classes over civil society. Nevertheless, reaction to organization and demands from below did affect both the content and form of local politics. Rochester became a city in 1892 and returned to predominantly Republican voting habits for the next fifteen years. The polite, clublike atmosphere of the good old days, however, had been banished into history.[55]

NOTES

1. Charles Francis Adams, *Three Episodes of Massachusetts History,* 2 vols. (Cambridge, Mass., 1894), II, 949, 968; H. P. Smith and W. S. Rann, eds., *History of Rutland County* (Syracuse, N.Y., 1886), 70–73. A sense of

faded dreams and a consequent reemphasis on the bright days of yore seem to have affected even the preservation of documents. The state of Vermont, for example, which has carefully catalogued an extraordinary variety of records for the 1790s, has not bothered much with the next century. Not until the turn of the twentieth century were official papers of the governors collected; similarly, correspondence (meticulously recorded in great letter books) of the state's leading political family from the late 1870s through the 1930s (the Proctors) rested at least until 1976 uncatalogued and practically untouched in the basement vault of the small local library where they were first deposited.

2. Fascination with the forms and origins of local and especially town government was evident in the first studies issuing from America's new professional historians in the late nineteenth century. *Johns Hopkins University Studies,* vol. 1 (1883), edited by Herbert B. Adams, for example, included essays on "Germanic Origins of New England Towns" and the "Genesis of a New England State." Adams, *Mass. History,* 966, 986; John Gould, *New England Town Meeting: Safeguard of Democracy* (Brattleboro, Vt., 1940), 59–60. See also John F. Sly, *Town Government in Massachusetts, 1620–1930* (Cambridge, Mass., 1930), 107–9, and Adna F. Weber, *The Growth of Cities in the Nineteenth Century* (Ithaca, N.Y., 1899), 429.

3. Thernstrom, *Poverty and Progress: Social Mobility in a Nineteenth-Century City* (New York, 1970), 33–56; Michael H. Frisch, *Town into City: Springfield, Massachusetts, and the Meaning of Community, 1840–1880* (Cambridge, Mass., 1972), 32–47, 219–50; Page Smith, *As a City upon a Hill: The Town in American History* (New York, 1966), 110–11. For an excellent overview of the colonial town see John M. Murrin, "Review Essay," *History and Theory,* 11 (1972), 226–76.

4. Only one New England state has really been surveyed in this period for labor politics. Labor candidates or a labor political effort of some sort appeared in almost every industrial community of Maine. See Charles R. Scontras, "Organized Labor and Labor Politics in Maine, 1880–1890," *University of Maine Studies,* Ser. 2, no. 83 (1966), esp. 17–47.

5. Franklin McDuffee, *History of the Town of Rochester from 1722 to 1890,* 2 vols. (Manchester, N.H., 1892), II, 367–78. The city's first historian was the son of the banker, John McDuffee. Federal Writers' Project, *New Hampshire, a Guide to the Granite State* (Cambridge, Mass., 1938), 246–47; Alonzo J. Fogg, *The Statistics and Gazetteer of New Hampshire* (Concord, 1874), 316–19.

6. D. H. Hurd, *History of Rockingham and Strafford Counties* (Philadelphia, 1882), 750–53; McDuffee, *Rochester,* 207, 287, 459, 474–75, 483.

7. Fogg, *Gazetteer of N.H.,* 316–39, 418–19.

8. McDuffee, *Rochester,* 474–75, 480, 483; U.S. Commissioner of Labor, *Third Annual Report* (Washington, D.C., 1888), 316–23.

9. U.S. Eleventh Census, 1890, *Compendium of the 11th Census, 1890, Population,* Pt. 1 (Washington, D.C., 1892), 274–75; Concord *Evening Monitor,* Mar. 8, 1886.

10. Compare Rochester's low proportion of domestics to the statistics cited

in David M. Katzman, *Seven Days a Week: Women and Domestic Service in Industrializing America* (New York, 1978). Katzman (Table A-3, 284) found nearly twice as many women nationally employed in household service as in manufacturing in 1880. Similarly, in twenty selected large cities the proportion of domestics to total women employed (Table A-6, 287) ranged from Rochester, New York, with 28.8 percent to Buffalo with 84.3 percent, all substantially higher than in the smaller town of Rochester, N.H. Whether Rochester as an early seat of semiskilled factory production had simply anticipated the servant problem that Katzman makes clear all cities came to share or whether its small-town ways created less of a demand for a genteel lifestyle facilitated by servants is unclear. In any case the relation of servants to the self-image of people in different settings seems a subject worthy of further investigation. It is worth noting in this regard that the wealthy manufacturer Edwin Wallace retained but a single live-in servant and that the extreme of conspicuous luxury in the town was set by banker John McDuffee, who kept two household servants. A complaint did, however, accompany the opening of a local shirt factory in the early 1880s regarding the scarcity of young women for domestic work.

11. U.S. manuscript census, 1880.

12. McDuffee, *Rochester,* 543; Rochester, *Anti-Monopolist and Local Record,* Nov. 9, 1878, Oct. 16, 1880, Mar. 18, 1882, Mar. 15, 1884; Rochester *Courier,* Mar. 13, 1885.

13. Candidates' names were drawn from the newspapers 1878–85 and matched with the city directory of 1885–86. The Yankee names of Democratic candidates do not preclude the possibility that the party was attracting Irish votes. If that were the case, the anomaly between candidates and constituency would still make the Irish very much second-class citizens; the New Hampshire State Grange, in any case, was often quite orthodox in its socioeconomic views. Solon J. Buck, *The Granger Movement* (Cambridge, Mass., 1913), 114.

14. Rochester city directories, 1885–86, 1887–88, Rochester Public Library.

15. McDuffee, *Rochester,* 190–92; Concord *People and New Hampshire Patriot,* Mar. 14, 1889.

16. McDuffee, *Rochester,* 544.

17. Frisch, *Town into City,* 41–42; Rochester *Anti-Monopolist,* Mar. 18, 1882, Mar. 15, 1884.

18. The New Hampshire Prohibitionists' convention of 1870 protested the "overabundance" of legislation for "private and corporate interests." *The American Annual Cyclopaedia,* X (New York, 1871), 538. See Scontras, "Organized Labor and Labor Politics," 319, on Prohibition–Knights of Labor ties in Maine. Francis Willard, head of the WCTU, was a good friend of Knights' leader, Terence Powderly. The Odd Fellows in Rochester dated only to 1875, suggesting with other evidence that its local roots were a bit more plebeian than the Masons. A study of workingmen's associations in England in the nineteenth century finds the Oddfellows [*sic*] primarily peopled by skilled artisans. See P.H.J.H. Gosden, *The Friendly Societies in England* (Manchester, 1961), 74–75.

19. Rochester *Courier*, Mar. 11, 1870; McDuffee, *Rochester*, 190–92. For the political evolution of the Greenbackers, see David Montgomery, *Beyond Equality: Labor and the Radical Republicans, 1862–1872* (New York, 1967), esp. 340–56.

20. The Rochester *Anti-Monopolist* regularly endorsed the Greenback platform; see, e.g., Feb. 27, 1886. See, generally, Allen Weinstein, *Prelude to Populism: Origins of the Silver Issue, 1867–1878* (New Haven, 1970).

21. Rochester *Anti-Monopolist*, Nov. 9, 1878.

22. *Ibid.*, Feb. 28, 1880, May 22, 1886. See also Anthony F. C. Wallace, *Rockdale* (New York, 1978), 243–400.

23. Rochester *Anti-Monopolist*, Mar. 8, 1878, Mar. 29, 1879.

24. *Ibid.*, Mar. 8, 1879.

25. For an excellent overview of attitudes and organization among New England shoeworkers, see Alan Dawley, *Class and Community: The Industrial Revolution in Lynn* (Cambridge, Mass., 1979).

26. U.S. Commissioner of Labor, *Third Annual Report;* on the behavior of shoeworkers, see Paul Faler, "Cultural Aspects of the Industrial Revolution: Lynn, Massachusetts, Shoemakers and Industrial Morality, 1826–1860," *Labor History*, 15 (Summer 1974), 367–95, and Gregory S. Kealey, *Toronto Workers Respond to Industrial Capitalism, 1867–1892* (Toronto, 1980), 37–52.

27. Jonathan Garlock and N. C. Builder, "Knights of Labor Data Bank: Users Manual and Index to Local Assemblies" (1973), manuscript at the University of Rochester, N.Y.; Norman J. Ware, *The Labor Movement in the United States, 1860–1895: A Study in Democracy* (New York, 1929), 204–5; *John Swinton's Paper* (hereafter *JSP*), Jan. 10, 1886; Concord *Evening Monitor*, Mar. 8, 1886, Mar. 9, 1887; Rochester *Anti-Monopolist*, Mar. 3, May 1, 8, 1886. Scontras notes that about half the members of the Lasters Protective Union in Maine belonged to the Knights and that the Knights formed assemblies in every town where the lasters had previously established themselves. He also quotes George McNeill to the effect that in 1886, at the peak of Knights' strength in New England, almost half the members of the order were shoeworkers. "Organized Labor and Labor Politics," 10–11.

28. The figures on age are based on a sample of 250, or a little more than one-half the total number of shoeworkers listed in the 1880 census. Figures on household structure are based on a slightly smaller sample, or a little more than one-third of the total. Dawley, *Class and Community*, 143–48, 176–77.

29. Rochester *Anti-Monopolist*, Apr. 24, 1886; Garlock and Builder, "Knights of Labor Data Bank." Dover, N.H., for example, with almost twice the population of Rochester produced only two assemblies and 2,000 members.

30. Rochester *Anti-Monopolist*, Feb. 29, 1880; Manchester *Union*, Oct. 27, 1886.

31. McDuffee, *Rochester*, 291–92; Rochester *Anti-Monopolist*, May 8, 1886.

32. *JSP*, Mar. 21, 1886. It was not a happy time for those left off the bandwagon. Silas Hussey, a granite worker and Democratic politician, complained bitterly about being excluded from the Knights. He was, he said, no

"banker, lawyer, professional gambler, or liquor seller [all proscribed from membership in the order]," and he denied being a professional "office-seeker." "Many of my most beloved friends are there and several by my advice." The victim of a grudge or of legitimate scruples, Hussey likened "hoarders of power" within the organization "who flippantly use the black ball to gratify a personal spite" to the "arrogant capitalist" outside the Order. Rochester *Anti-Monopolist,* Jan. 23, 1886.

33. Rochester *Courier,* Mar. 12, 1886; *JSP,* Mar. 21, 1886.

34. Rochester *Anti-Monopolist,* Nov. 6, 1886; Rochester *Courier,* Mar. 11, 1887, Mar. 16, 1888; Concord *People and New Hampshire Patriot,* Mar. 22, 1888; Concord *Evening Monitor,* Nov. 9, 1888.

35. Concord *Evening Monitor,* Sept. 21, Nov. 3, 24, 1886.

36. *JSP,* Mar. 21, 1886; Thomas F. Leahy to Terence Powderly, May 19, 1886, Powderly Papers, Catholic University, Washington, D.C.

37. *JSP,* Mar. 21, 1886; Concord *Evening Monitor,* Oct. 23, Nov. 3, 1886.

38. Of the workingmen active in labor politics the five not listed in the text included (one each): a railroad baggage master, a mason and hairdresser, a machinist, a laborer, and an employee in an axe-handle factory. Names listed in the newspapers were paired with the city directories; Rochester *Courier,* Oct. 29, 1886.

39. Rochester city directories, 1885–88. The outward similarity between Knights of Labor and lodge structures was no doubt more than coincidental. The morality of social conformity that the lodges encouraged through elaborate ritual may have rebounded to the advantage of labor organization, particularly in a small town, where popular lodges and unions must of necessity have laid claims to the same people. Scattered reports from other labor centers in the period corroborate this hypothesis. Unionized workers in Framingham, Massachusetts, reported to the labor press on the excellence of their new Odd Fellows hall. Participants similarly compared Knights' successes in Wilmington, Delaware, to "Knights of Pythias fever several years ago" (Haverhill [Mass.] *Laborer,* Mar. 13, 1886). Charles Ferguson wrote suggestively in 1937 that "class-consciousness, American style . . . expressed itself through the characteristic medium of social clubs and secret orders. The native technique of reform is, first of all, to demand three raps and a high sign." *Fifty Million Brothers: A Panorama of American Lodges and Clubs* (New York, 1937), 173. Work on popular associations is much better developed for England than for the United States. In a study of British working-class life in the third quarter of the nineteenth century, Neville Kirk found the Oddfellows' publications openly friendly to trade unionism. "Class and Fragmentation: Some Aspects of Working-Class Life in South-East Lancashire and North-East Cheshire, 1850–1870" (Ph.D. diss., University of Pittsburgh, 1974), esp. 151–52, 174–75, 225.

40. Compiled from local newspapers, city directories, and notes from the 1880 manuscript census. See, too, Daniel Nelson, *Managers and Workers: Origins of the New Factory System in the United States, 1880–1920* (Madison, Wis., 1975).

41. When C. F. Montgomery, Strafford master workman, ran for county

commissioner in 1886, opponents spread rumors that he had worked his farm laborers eighteen hours a day and fed them skim milk. Rochester *Anti-Monopolist,* Oct. 30, 1886.

42. Edward T. James, "American Labor and Political Action, 1865–1896: The Knights of Labor and its Predecessors" (Ph.D. diss., Harvard University, 1954), 311; *Granite State Free Press,* Sept. 24, 1886; Rochester *Anti-Monopolist,* Mar. 13, 1886. Unfortunately, no issues of the *Leader* have survived. McDuffee, *Rochester,* 190–92; U.S. manuscript census of 1880.

43. Rochester *Anti-Monopolist,* Dec. 12, 1885, May 8, 1886. See, generally, Raymond Williams, "Base and Superstructure," *New Left Review,* 82 (Nov.-Dec. 1973), 3–16.

44. *JSP,* Oct. 3, 31, 1886.

45. *Ibid.,* Nov. 28, 1886, Mar. 13, 20, 1887.

46. Rochester *Courier,* Mar. 12, 1886, Mar. 11, 1887; Rochester *Anti-Monopolist,* Mar. 13, 1886, Mar. 11, 1887; Manchester *Union,* Mar. 19, 1888; Concord *People and New Hampshire Patriot,* Mar. 22, 1888; Frisch, *Town into City,* 43.

47. *JSP,* Mar. 21, 1886.

48. U.S. Commissioner of Labor, *Third Annual Report,* and *Tenth Annual Report* (Washington, D.C., 1896), 562–73, 1318–21; Concord *Evening Monitor,* Nov. 16, 20, 1886; Concord *People and New Hampshire Patriot,* Jan. 13, June 2, 1887; Ware, *Labor Movement in U.S.,* 205–6.

49. Boston *Labor Leader,* Jan. 29, 1887.

50. Brock to Powderly, Jan. 4, 1886, Powderly Papers.

51. Ware, *Labor Movement in U.S.,* 205–9; Haverhill *Laborer,* Nov. 27, 1886; John Laslett, *Labor and the Left* (New York, 1970), 55–56.

52. Rochester *Anti-Monopolist,* Mar. 16, 1889; *Strafford County Record* (beginning in 1890 the paper removed *Anti-Monopolist* from its title), Mar. 14, 1890. The farmer James F. Foss, for example, secured both the Democratic and Labor endorsements for selectman in 1888. Two years previously he had opposed the Labor ticket in the Citizens party; Concord *Evening Monitor,* Mar. 14, 1889.

53. Manchester *Union,* Mar. 14, 1890, Mar. 13, 1891; Concord *Evening Monitor,* Sept. 17, 1886; *Journal of United Labor,* Sept. 17, 1887.

54. Manchester *Union,* Sept. 22, 1886; Rochester *Anti-Monopolist,* Nov. 10, 1888; Concord *Evening Monitor,* Nov. 12, 1888. The Irish-Democrat Patrick H. Hartigan ran for treasurer against Simon Wolf (Rochester *Courier,* Mar. 11, 1887). Compare Rochester to Stamford, Connecticut, where the Irish entered local political life in the early 1890s, and older, amateur paternalists simultaneously gave way to professional politicians. Estelle F. Feinstein, *Stamford in the Gilded Age: The Political Life of a Connecticut Town, 1868–1893* (Stamford, 1973), 230–32.

55. John Scales, *History of Strafford County, New Hampshire, and Representative Citizens* (Chicago, 1914), 478.

4

When Cleon Comes to Rule:
Popular Organization and
Political Development.
Part II: Rutland, Vermont

IN 1911 A LOCAL HISTORIAN of Rutland, Vermont, recounted that the surrounding territory had lived through five jurisdictions—Indians, French, English, the independent republic of Vermont, and statehood. Had he been writing twenty years earlier, the author might have been tempted to add as a sixth jurisdiction the regime of the Knights of Labor. For here, in the largest settlement of the most rural and most Republican state in the Union, a tenacious workingmen's movement seized political power in 1886 and did not fully relinquish it for ten years. The duration of labor's influence in Rutland provides the opportunity for an uncommonly close look at the relationship between politics and social change in the Gilded Age. Questions regarding the nature of labor's challenge to established authority and the reactions to labor rule—subjects barely introduced in the case of Rochester—here receive fuller exploration.[1]

A visitor in 1850 might easily have miscalculated Rutland's future course of development. Nestled among the western Green Mountain slopes of south-central Vermont, the town appeared, like much of the rest of New England, to have passed through a natural cycle from youthful exuberance into quiet old age. From its initial settlement in 1770, Rutland grew by 1830 into a small manufacturing center for woolens, agricultural implements, stoves, and iron ware, whiskey, and cider brandy. Locked in its mountainous terrain without navigable waterways, the village missed the early stages of the "transportation revolution" and entered a general decline by mid-century. Half the size of Burlington to the north, the Rutland population increased by only 1,500 between 1800 and 1850. The slow growth of one of the state's principal urban centers only hints at the vast out-migration that Vermont had suffered. A late nineteenth-century guide could boast that Vermont had more native sons per capita in *Who's Who* than any other state; the same statistics, however, indicated that almost all the distinguished citizens had left Vermont to apply their talents.[2]

A combination of rail and rock reversed Rutland's slide into historical obscurity. During the 1850s, when practically every community in America was competing for a piece of the tie, six railroad lines connected Rutland to Troy and Albany, New York, jealous rivals seeking both Vermont markets and a passage to Canada. The town, as champion of the state's older southern counties, experienced new growth. By the end of the decade, those far-seeing men who had acquired Rutland real estate realized fifty times the lands' original value. (Even Jay Gould spent three years in Rutland as railway superintendent and managed to land his partner in a Vermont jail.) Local capitalist Charles Clement took charge of the Rutland Road in the 1860s and built it into a formidable contender with the Vermont Central line to the north. The railroad men soon discovered that they had outdone themselves. Dividends from the Vermont roads were none too good, and the Rutland Railroad Company, in poor straits by 1870, was leased to its upstate rival for twenty years.[3]

The town of Rutland gained whether the railroads themselves were profiting or not. In the early 1850s the town freemen voted funds to cover sewage ditches and to extend plank sidewalks throughout the residential neighborhoods. During the 1860s and 1870s considerable public investment was made in a gas light company and in the local water system. A daily newspaper established in 1861 both symbolized and in itself furthered local development. At the local centennial celebration in 1870, Judge Walter C. Dunton compared Rutland "more than any other town in all New England" to "the thriving and prosperous towns of the West." As if to strengthen the analogy, the western fringe of the town was nicknamed "Nebraska." After doubling in size between 1850 and 1870, Rutland reached 12,000 inhabitants by 1880, surpassing Burlington as the state's largest metropolis. To those looking back at the end of the century, it seemed as if a group of native and adopted sons of Rutland had suddenly "awakened from lethargy," outfitted themselves as captains of industry, and assured the town's economic preeminence. As late as 1937 the Federal Writers' Project would comment that of the state's three industrial centers (Barre, Burlington, and Rutland), "Rutland alone maintains the vigor which her railroad gave. Rutland, more typically than either of her rivals, is the small American city."[4]

Rutland's late nineteenth-century ascent was linked inseparably to marble-quarrying excavations in the surrounding countryside. Rutland in 1880 was composed of four distinct villages separated by hills and farmland: the original village of Rutland (population 7,500) and the three smaller marble-milling centers of West Rutland (2,000), Sutherland Falls (1,000), and Center Rutland. The American marble industry began slowly. Despite its rich natural deposits, New England had shown little taste for elaborate stone construction until expanding wealth and conspicuous consumption generated new building styles in the early nineteenth century. Quarrying in Rutland County, carried on sporadically since 1795, became a continuous operation in the 1840s through the enterprise of Charles Sheldon (1839) and W. Y. Ripley (1844). Once the railroad network fully opened the mineral-rich lands to exploitation, banker investors like E. P. Gilson and Clement also bought into the trade. Not until the intervention of Redfield Proctor in the 1870s, however, did the industry reach maturity.[5]

The Proctor family dominated the Vermont marble business with an acumen characteristic of the Gilded Age. Born in 1831 in a Vermont village named for his Revolutionary forebearers, Redfield Proctor by age twenty-five had graduated from Dartmouth College and had become director of a Vermont local bank. After Civil War service Colonel Proctor entered a law partnership and was soon appointed receiver of the ailing Sutherland Falls Marble Company. For ten years Proctor paid out no dividends, plowing all profits back into production. The firm adopted the newest labor-saving machinery and brought George J. Wardwell, one of the industry's key inventors, into the front office. Proctor also expanded the business vertically to include monument finishing (1876) and exterior finishing (1880) and began to organize his own market outlets. In the process the Proctor interest surpassed all of its rivals. Proctor bought out his biggest competitor, the New York–owned Rutland Marble Company with operations in West Rutland in 1880, giving him control of 55 percent of the trade. He formed the Producers' Marble Company in 1883, a price-fixing partnership to which all Rutland-produced marble was sold, then resold at a uniform standard. Unfortunately, by discouraging managerial efficiency and innovation among the older firms, this system proved vulnerable to outside competition. Proctor therefore terminated the arrangement after four years and returned to a monopolistic strategy. By 1891 his company had purchased most of his former partners, swallowing Ripley and Sons and Gilson and Woodfin to become the largest marble company in the world, employing 1,800 workers in 1894. The village of Sutherland Falls, practically owned and operated by the Vermont Marble Company, was appropriately renamed Proctor in the early 1880s.[6]

Proctor's achievements were not limited to the business world. During the consolidation of the marble industry, Proctor became a pillar of the state Republican party. His political career included tenure as governor of Vermont between 1878 and 1882, President Benjamin Harrison's secretary of war between 1888 and 1892, and U.S. Senator from 1891 until his death in 1908. Proctor's service in the Senate was highlighted by his help in triggering U.S. entry into the Spanish-American War. Proctor bequeathed the presidency of the marble company to his twenty-nine-year-old son, Fletcher, in 1889; Fletcher followed his father to the gubernatorial mansion in 1906,[7] and the Proctor dynasty (including two more Governor Proctors) continued to dominate state politics through the 1940s.

A career of effort, power, and success molded the mind of this Gilded Age titan. Redfield Proctor believed his roots to be the very sinews of American civilization—"those men of Anglo-Saxon stock" who "within two hundred years" have done "more than all others combined to subdue and develop the wild regions and peoples of the earth." Having grown up in symbiosis with the productive explosion around him, Proctor tended to see business and sometimes life itself as one huge dynamo operating under inexorable laws of motion and force. As governor, he had urged rigid economy and opposed taxation that "drives away capital and clogs the wheels of business." No man, in Proctor's view, was too good to do honest labor; in his early days as company president he sometimes handled a truck, loaded cars, or selected specimens of stone. Labor organization and protest, on the other hand, disturbed Proctor's natural order. When copper miners in Ely, Vermont, rioted in 1883 after learning that the company had defaulted on months of back pay owed to them, the National Guard was rushed in to quell the disturbance. Among Rutland's thirty-eight volunteers stood ex-Governor Proctor.[8]

In a class by himself as a businessman and expressing little interest in economic enterprises outside his marble empire, Redfield Proctor nevertheless fit comfortably into a group of thirty to fifty families who could properly be considered Rutland's economic and social elite. The group sprang from a homogeneous Yankee background. E. P. Gilson, banker and marble man, for example, traced his family to Massachusetts settlers of 1635. W. R. Page, a director of the Howe Scale works, Rutland's largest manufacturer with 230 employees in 1880, also came from an old Rutland family. His grandfather was the original Bank of Rutland cashier, and his father nursed railroad and banking interests before luring the scale works away from the neighboring hamlet of Brandon. John A. Mead, who would buy out Howe Scale in 1888, was the great-grandson of the first known white settler in the territory that still bore the landmark of Mead's Falls. The Tuttle family, owners of the daily Rutland *Herald* as well as a share of a local bank, had likewise lived in the town since 1798. John W. Cramton was also a member of this elite but differed from the others in his early poverty (as well as his Roman Catholic upbringing). Raised on a nearby Vermont farm, he had made a living as a peddler before opening a Center Rutland tinshop, buying Rutland's major hotel, and eventually holding directorships in the *Herald* and several banking and industrial establishments.[9]

Besides a common heritage, Rutland's business elite shared numerous active social and cultural ties. They congregated at the older, less enthusiastic Protestant churches (the Episcopal and Congregationalist denominations in particular) and fraternized at the Masonic lodge or Elks Club. Most of the leading business figures had been to private academies, if not to college as had Proctor. Their artistic refinement was, nevertheless, probably not much more than mid-brow for the period. Shunning participation in the more plebeian cornet band, the town's upper class made sure to replace the old Ripley Music Hall with a new opera house, where comedies with names like *Harvard Versus Yale* were performed. Another standard of educated taste appeared in the poetry of Julia Caroline Ripley Dorr, "poetess-laureate" of Vermont and daughter of marble merchant E. W. Ripley. Dorr's work followed the canons of gentility, avoiding all expression which could not with propriety be read to children.[10]

During the secession crisis Rutland's prominent families acted with a true sense of mission. The old banker Hugh Henry Baxter rode at the head of the first column of Vermont troops in 1861. Two sons of marble merchant E. W. Ripley and his wife Zilma Delacy Thomas (whose French family had fled the slave insurrection at St. Domingue in 1791) were decorated as generals by the end of the Civil War. John A. Sheldon, son of the town's first marble owner, joined the Vermont Volunteers just as his great-great-grandfather had fought with the Massachusetts Revolutionary army. The war itself projected some new figures into the local elite. Hardware merchant Levi G. Kingsley served as lieutenant under Generals Baxter and Ripley. After the war, Kingsley married Baxter's sister-in-law; soon General Kingsley (promoted for having reorganized the state's National Guard in 1874) became a director of the Baxter National Bank.[11]

Social philanthropy complemented battlefield decorations as signs of local stewardship. Redfield Proctor built the Proctor Free Library, endowed the state's first tubercular hospital, and financed construction of several churches. E. P. Gilson served as trustee for the state mental hospital. Corporate counsel Joel Baker was active in the YMCA. Many activities of a charitable or benevolent nature fell within the special province of the town's upper-class women. The list of women library commissioners, for example (including a Baxter, a Clement, and the poet Dorr), provides as good an index as any to the best families in town.[12]

For the local elite politics served at least two interrelated functions. On the one hand, governmental connections at both the state and local levels might further a business career. J. Gregory Smith, for example, president of the Vermont Central, had held the governor's chair at a decisive juncture in his successful rivalry with Rutland's Clement family. Redfield Proctor's entrepreneurial temerity, particularly his manipulation of New York investors in 1880, was also backed by the seal of the statehouse. In general, the state's role in industrial development (affecting railroad rights, land grants, tax exemptions, bank charters, and similar matters) made notable economic assets out of both legal training and political activism. Local men like Proctor, Baker, and John Prout (who moved from local railroad counsel to a seat on the state supreme

court) found that their private legal practices led directly to business investment and political influence.[13]

On the other hand, for the substantial men of the community, tenure of
public office was itself a mark of social prestige, a symbol of community
respect, a social validation of wealth and power. During the 1870s and early
1880s, members of marble families including the Ripleys, Sheldons, Reding-
tons, and Gilsons had all served multiple terms in the public trust. Baker, for
his part, had been elected school superintendent, grand juror, probate regis-
trar, and deputy city clerk. Dr. J. D. Hanrahan, a director of the Howe Scale
works, had served six terms as town trustee.[14]

Ordinarily the two hands worked together, attached to the businessmen's
central nervous system, the Republican party. In a state without one Democratic governor between the Civil War and 1962, the local business elites were
overwhelmingly Republican. A rare exception like Democratic attorney L. W.
Redington might still be classified by contemporaries as being Republican in
his social life. Notwithstanding state and national political loyalties, Rutland's local office seekers often proceeded in a relatively nonpartisan fashion.
Deference to an older corporate ideal tended to discourage organized political
divisions in favor of a search for consensus among the town elders. In 1884,
for instance, an identical slate of officers was presented to and approved by
pre-election caucuses of Republicans and Democrats in Rutland and West
Rutland. The list, moreover, contained only a single change from the roster
of incumbent town officers. With such informal agreements worked out in
advance, the town meeting itself would witness only isolated contests waged
on the basis of group interest or personal popularity.[15]

Public office, to be sure, was not the sole preserve of the local business
elite. Out of a citizenry including all adult males with a nominal financial
stake in government (i.e., as signified by the state's poll tax) there emerged a
governing class extending roughly through the top third of the town's occupational ladder. In addition to the wealthy businessmen, farmers, shopkeepers, clerks, supervisors, and even a few skilled craft workers held office in
Rutland in the years prior to 1886. As in Rochester, New Hampshire, the
occupational profile of officeholders corresponded neatly to another index of
social status—that class of citizens that could hire servants or otherwise
minimize household labor. Taken together these two indices may well have
defined an unspoken line of social respectability, which separated the Rutland
elite and that upper third of the citizenry who might aspire to their material
and cultural standard from the mass of the town's working people. In these
circumstances the openness of the institution of local government, just like
the freedom of the marketplace, probably reinforced the legitimacy of the
town's wealthy few. By providing a regular rendezvous for all citizen-taxpayers,
the town meeting, in particular, reassured many Gilded Age New Englanders

of an unbroken link to the Revolutionary republican past. During Rutland County's 1881 centennial commemoration, the *Herald* (apparently unimpressed by the claims of the German forest or the American frontier) could thus point complacently to "the principles of freedom which are found dominant in the dwellers among mountains."[16]

The two-thirds of the social structure absent from the councils of government formed Rutland's lower classes. They ranged from artisanal craftsmen and skilled industrial workers (including ironworkers and scaleworkers) to unskilled laborers. If one judges by their ability to hire domestic servants, it appears that the most prosperous workers (railway engineers and conductors, tinsmiths, blacksmiths, and some carpenters) more closely resembled small shopkeepers and clerks in their standard of living than any other social group. The mass of workers fell well below this standard. Except for a relatively few skilled cutters and carvers, the marble workers (quarrymen, millworkers, and polishers) formed a semiskilled labor pool earning $.80 to $1.15 a day. Together with the unskilled laborers, they represented three-fourths of the local working class. Their lives involved a continual struggle against abject poverty and dependency. An accident at the quarries or a winter without alternative casual employment might push a family over the brink. The marble workers, in particular, filled the annual rolls of both local relief and criminal convictions. For these people the local poll tax of one to two dollars was more than a token payment. There are no firm contemporary figures, but a more recent analysis suggests that the Vermont poll tax indirectly disfranchised many citizens.[17]

More than economic position, however, separated the wage earners from the governing or respectable citizens. Social class and ethnicity substantially overlapped in Rutland. The capitalists, professionals, merchants, white-collar employees, and farmers were between 80 and 90 percent old-line Yankees, and their dominance of the town's most influential positions only masked the fact that by 1880 immigrants and their sons composed a majority of Rutland's adult male population, made up almost two-thirds of the working class, and had a virtual monopoloy on the lower rungs of manual labor (Table 8). Of greater significance, nine of ten marble workers were of foreign extraction. Six of ten were of Irish birth or parentage; two of ten were French-Canadians. The rest divided among English-Canadian, Swedes, and native-Americans. Among the latter, foremen and supervisors made up the single largest job categories. An aggregation of diverse ethnic substructures therefore composed Rutland's overall occupational structure (Table 9).

In many respects, ethnicity served to underline the class cleavage in Rutland. The resident guests at the town's best hotel on the day the 1880 census was taken were all native-Americans of native parentage, while twenty of twenty-one hotel staff workers were of Irish and French-Canadian descent. In

TABLE 8. Native and Immigrant Components of the Occupational Structure in Rutland, 1880

Occupations	Total Number	Native-Born of Native Parents (%)	Foreign-Born or Foreign-Parents (%)
Non–Wage Earners	788	83	17
Capitalists and professionals	159	89	11
Merchants and shopkeepers	234	80	20
White-collar employees	173	79	21
Farmers	222	85	15
Working Class	2,291	32	68
Skilled tradesmen	767	57	43
Scale workers	114	53	47
Marble workers	672	12	88
Unskilled laborers	616	65	35
Farm laborers	122	71	29
Total	3,079	50	50

Source. U.S. Tenth Census, 1880, population manuscript.
Note. Data are based on all males, aged twenty and older.

the same period twenty-four of thirty-three citizens admitted to Rutland's poor farm were immigrants. The distinctive character of the Irish-American working-class community was symbolized in the nickname, "Stonepeggers," affixed to West Rutlanders. Twentieth-century folkloric explanation of the name has pointed variously to 1859, when marble bosses had thrown stones at workers loafing at their labors; to 1863, when irate Irish citizens resisted the attempts of deputies to draft them; or to 1879, when local partisans had pummeled a visiting baseball team. At times such spirit had taken the form of labor protest. In the 1860s a series of marble strikes reportedly ended with the importation of French-Canadians, the eviction of Irish families, and continuing difficulties between the two groups. Another work stoppage by West Rutland quarrymen in 1880 represented the longest marble strike of the ensuing decade.[18] The de facto correspondence of the poorer, less educated, and sometimes unruly element of the population with a particular national and immigrant background lent a special character to the contemporary ideology of New England's elite citizenry. To Charles Francis Adams, for example, New England's civilization seemed peculiarly adapted to "Yankee" temperament and peculiarly unfit for "alien" consumption: "Quick of impulse, sympathetic, ignorant and credulous, the Irish race have as few elements in common with the native New Englanders as one race of men well can have with another."[19]

TABLE 9. Occupational Structure in Rutland, by Ethnic Groups, 1880

Occupations	Percent within Total Population	Yankee[a]	Irish[b]	French- Canadian[b]	English- Canadian[b]
Non–Wage Earners	25	42	8	2	9
Capitalists and professionals	5	9	1	—	1
Merchants and shopkeepers	8	12	2	1	1
White-collar employees	5	9	2	—	6
Farmers	7	12	3	1	1
Working Class	75	58	92	98	91
Skilled tradesmen	25	28	11	20	34
Scale workers	4	4	4	1	6
Marble workers	22	5	44	54	21
Unskilled laborers	20	14	31	20	29
Farm laborers	4	6	2	3	1
Total	100	100	100	100	100
(*N*)	(3,079)	(1,534)	(899)	(254)	(239)

Source. U.S. Tenth Census, 1880, population manuscript.
Note. Data are based on males, aged twenty and over, and are given as percentages. Dash = number too negligible to calculate percentage.
[a]Native-born, native-parents.
[b]Foreign-born and those with one or both foreign-parents.

In another sense, however, ethnicity also modified the class divisions within the population. National origins—not economic rank—defined neighborhood boundaries. Within the immigrant marble-working communities of West Rutland and Proctor, native-Americans clustered together on the same streets within a few-block area. Even within more economically diversified Rutland village, the population divided into ethnic neighborhoods. An Irish-American lawyer or merchant, for example, was more likely to live next to Irish laborers than among the native-American middle class. Among the immigrants themselves, Irish and French-Canadians were grouped separately, except for those at the very bottom of the social scale who apparently had no control over living arrangements. Even the boardinghouses respected ethnic as well as class lines. One house catered to skilled young Canadians, another to Irish general laborers, and so on. At work, national solidarity within an immigrant population may have helped to bridge class differences. Edward Copps, a machine foreman for the Vermont Marble Company, was active in local Catholic social and temperance societies and had conducted the old West Rutland band. He was married to Bridget Maloney, sister to Democratic lawyer Thomas W. Maloney and Father Maloney of Middleton. When Copps was killed in a quarry accident in 1886, six marble workers served as pallbearers.[20]

Cross-class social ties undoubtedly influenced the political consciousness of the immigrant community. Thus, while the great proportion of Rutland's Irish-Americans were classified as unskilled and semiskilled labor, those who escaped from a subsistence standard of living may still have played an important role in shaping the aspirations of the proletarian majority. As Stephan Thernstrom found in Newburyport, a limited, but significant, dimension of mobility was available to immigrant workers and their children in Rutland or at least so it must have seemed in 1880. The percentage of those in poor working-class jobs (marble quarrying, mill work, and general labor) dipped from 68 percent among the immigrant generation of Irish to 56 percent for the second generation. The improvement produced no measurable expansion of the Irish middle class (this sector remained equally small among both first- and second-generation Irish-Americans); rather the significant shift occurred into the skilled working class. In Rutland village, for example, little more than 10 percent of the immigrant population held artisanal, skilled manufacturing, or skilled marble-working assignments, while 30 percent of the second generation were so employed.[21] Historiographical arguments about the political meaning of late nineteenth-century social mobility must begin with these skilled workers. They may well have set the definitions of respectability and right conduct in the Irish-American world—with a level of income, job security, and skill beyond that of the masses of poor immigrant laborers, but one to which the latter might justifiably aspire.

During the decade beginning in 1886, Rutland's lower orders dramatically narrowed the political distance separating them from the business elite. The Knights of Labor was the agency of transformation, harnessing both class and ethnic grievances to a cadre of politically minded skilled workers and small businessmen. Reacting to the dismal performance of incumbent public officials, a United Labor convention, based on the organizational unity of the Knights, met in August 1886 to draft candidates for the upcoming village elections. On September 7 the largest town meeting ever held in Rutland elected a full slate of independent labor candidates, including the town's first Irish-American and French-Canadian officeholders. Word quickly went out from local labor circles to the New York mayoral campaign of Henry George, "Try to do as well as we did in Rutland." The Rutland *Herald*, on the other hand, dolefully pronounced the election results under the headline, "RUTLAND'S QUAKE."[22]

The public unveiling of the Rutland Knights of Labor occurred in late January 1886 when a *Herald* reporter was conducted, blindfolded, to a meeting and returned "amazed at what has been going on in our very midst." A week earlier a Boston Knights' organizer had initiated Rutland's first local assembly following months of preparation. Local Assembly (L.A.) 5160 contained people whom the *Herald*'s man recognized "from almost every department of work in town." A spokesman reassured the journalist that "there will probably be no call for violent measures." "We want Rutland capitalists, however, to recognize the organization and we also want to help forward the cause all over the country by sympathy with its principles and contributing funds when necessary to advance its interests." From this brief exposure to the new phenomenon, the reporter shrewdly noted the combination within the Knights of the "mysticism of the masonic lodge, . . . the beneficiary elements of a mutual aid society, and the defensive and protective phases of a trade union after the old English pattern." Nor did it escape his attention that "those who believe in the ballot . . . find ample opportunity to make known their views in the debates on 'Labor in all its interests' which, by the constitution, must be discussed for at least 10 minutes every meeting."[23]

According to a local labor leader, the Knights' progress in 1886 was marked by a period of "gradual growth" followed by a period in which "a wild desire to join the Order seemed to take hold of our people." During the first period, skilled craft workers and local labor reformers made the Order their home. V. C. Meyerhoffer, hotel owner and Canadian-born son of Hungarian parents, symbolized the link between the Order and previous attempts at labor organization. A charter member of the typographers' union in 1852, delegate to the Industrial Congress in 1874, and an active Co-operator and Sovereign of Industry in the mid-1870s, Meyerhoffer must have been nearly sixty years old when he brought the printers into the Knights in January 1886. Newspaper reports indicated that local cigar-makers also acted as one of the entering wedges of spreading Knights' activity. The continuing infusion of skilled workers into the Order was evident in the October 1886 report that 60 percent of Rutland Knights of Labor owned property and that 70 percent held deposits in savings banks.[24]

Hegemony by the skilled workers was also suggested by the early and continuing leadership role exercised by a small group of self-educated labor reformers. James J. Fay, a self-employed bookbinder and the first master workman of L.A. 5160, was an ardent disciple of Henry George. Following a visit by George to Rutland in 1881, Fay and his friend the carriage painter, A. A. Orcutt, took it upon themselves to distribute twenty-five copies of *Progress and Poverty*. Orcutt wrote George in 1883: "I have studied Political Economy a considerable since you were here. I have learned to believe that in it is embraced the fundamental principles of religion. I have come to believe—aside from Nature's productions—that he who obtains of the productions of mankind without in some way—either mentally or physically—having done his part is a liar and thief and the truth is not in him. Am I not right?" It may well have been through the ministrations of Fay and Orcutt that a young Irish-American marble polisher named Thomas H. Brown first took up the radical faith. Brown, who would become Rutland's first district master workman (1887) and a key figure in local politics, along with Fay, Orcutt, and a few other local Georgeites, organized a chapter of Father Edward McGlynn's Anti-Poverty Society in 1887.[25]

The second explosive period of Knights' growth coincided roughly with the entry of the lesser-skilled marble workers into the Order. Not surprisingly, West Rutland, with its history of stubborn, sometimes rough-and-tumble, self-assertion provided the first base of organization among the marble workers. As early as March 1886 the West Rutland assembly had recruited over 100 members. One important factor in labor's expansion within the poor, marble-working bastion of West Rutland was the sympathy of the religious leaders of St. Bridget's Irish-Catholic parish. Such sympathy had apparently become a tradition by the 1880s. Father Picard was fondly remembered as a defender of Rutland's first strikers in 1859. During the "Golden Age of St. Bridget's" (between 1869 and 1897), the Irish-born Reverend Charles O'Reilly commanded universal respect. This stern, temperate priest, who was known to use a cane at drinking and dancing parties, lived in a parish house surrounded by the homes of poor laborers. In October 1886 Father O'Reilly attended and won a prize at the first annual Knights' fair. The priest provided one important symbol of the social coloration of the local Knights; a picture of Parnell that hung among the row of prizes at the fair provided another. Together these symbols offered some explanation for the fact that of Rutland's entire marble work force of 1,500 to 2,000 men, the "large majority" had entered the Order by the end of 1886. Two of the four Rutland assemblies established during the year were based in West Rutland. Assemblies had also sprouted in three other hamlets of Rutland County.[26]

The exact pace of the Order's growth in 1886 is difficult to determine, but several signs testified to the Knights' increasing size, self-confidence, and community impact. Local merchants provided one signal. By March a Rutland bootery was advertising "the Knights of Labor shoe." In April, while local Knights were busy subscribing funds to aid the Gould strikers, newspapers carried the message of a "Great Strike in Rutland! Over 5000 Working People have already struck against the credit system." So said a local merchandiser who dealt only in cash. These appeals to labor-minded consumers coincided with the lifting of secrecy around Knights' activities. At the end of April shorthand announcements of Grand Army Hall meetings began appearing in red chalk all over the town's white marble slab sidewalks. By the summer Knights' baseball teams were competing openly. Even the dismissal of several members by hostile employers did not dissuade the Order from a more public posture.[27]

Notwithstanding their numerical strength, Knights' leaders hesitated to do battle with Rutland's large employers. They pointedly did not rush into industrial confrontation. Indeed, the only tangible economic gains reportedly secured by organized Rutland workers came in the wake of the September 1886 electoral successes. Howe Scale foundrymen, although not formally recognized by their employer, restored a 6 percent pay cut exacted from them the previous year. Then, in December, 300 young women at Rutland's new shirt factory walked off their jobs until the employer granted them overtime rates. Depression in the marble trade, no doubt, contributed to the Knights' unaggressive shopfloor performance. The year 1886 witnessed the collapse of several small firms, victims of a price competition that alarmed even Redfield Proctor. Corresponding with General Ripley in July, Proctor sadly noted a steady decline in marble prices—"it is the tendency of all business, and though it has been long postponed it is coming now rapidly." By the end of the year, the Marble King was explaining to stockholders, "Our profits are not and cannot be what they have been." No protest was registered by the organized marble workers until February 1887, when West Rutland Knights demanded an increase of $.10 to $.35 cents a day and uniform scales for piece work among skilled cutters and polishers. Yet, when the company balked—citing its patient indulgence of older, less productive workers and promising to reexamine pay scales during the spring's better weather while warning that the well-stocked firm could more easily withstand a shutdown than the men themselves—the Knights withdrew their demands.[28]

Compared to the industrial front, the political sphere must have looked positively inviting to Knights' strategists. By the mid-1880s, Rutland was the country's largest urban settlement retaining town government institutions. Local businessmen had tried to incorporate as a city in 1880, hoping to substitute a single authority for the maze of competing village, town, and county jurisdictional lines. But opposition from outlying agricultural areas, the Proctor interest, and the rural sympathies of the state legislature doomed the attempt. Meanwhile, direct democracy of the traditional lax and honorific sort proved increasingly inadequate to meet the needs of municipal development. Now retired Judge Walter C. Dunton, for example, blasted local government in January 1886 for its total lack of public planning. He cited the waste involved each winter when gravel was hauled onto the dirt roads only to be hauled off a few months later as mud; Rutland's officials, according to Dunton, "talked as if macademized roads were only an experiment," allowing the town to be embarrassed by rivals like Burlington. In the same period, a woman who called herself "Justitia" scoffed at the lack of support from town fathers for a public library when "even little villages around here have [them]." "Why should women care," she asked, "if the men do not? Are the women owners of marble quarries, presidents or directors of the banks or the railroads?"[29]

While local officials neglected long-term community needs, the business they did conduct brought them little honor. Private interests, for example, had no trouble attracting government attention. Proctor presented the trustees with his plans for a new public road to be built through Vermont Marble Company property. Electric and gas interests sought political allies while competing for a municipal light contract. The new electric light company tried to shame authorities for remaining "almost alone" in keeping the old gas system. The gas company, for its part, predicted financial disaster from electricity bills, not to mention the costs of litigation from the suit it would file to inhibit any change of contract. When the gas company ultimately agreed to slash operating rates in half, it became apparent to many citizens just how much the town had previously been bilked by the utility.[30]

Municipal stumbling produced a genuine fiscal crisis by the beginning of February 1886. The trustees reached the end of the year's budget almost two months before the village meeting and voted to shut off the lights and dismiss the police rather than assume legal responsibility for the debt. The trustees had spent money, which the previous village meeting had earmarked for other services, on sewers; now, according to angry critics, they were showing a willingness to make Rutland both a "laughing stock" and a "hoodlum's nest." An emergency village meeting resolved the impasse, but not without mutual recrimination among the traditional officeholders. John D. Spellman, an ambitious Democratic lawyer-politician, lambasted his home town in April as the "worst managed village in Vermont."[31]

Meager efforts at self-reform followed the revelations of government mismanagement. General Levi Kingsley, State Supreme Court Judge Wheelock G. Veazey, attorney Spellman, and the *Herald* all called for a new day of civic responsibility. A special public meeting heard reference to the growing impatience with local government felt by the "working people." While candidates at the April village meeting all claimed to represent cleansing influences, the *Herald* fingered Dr. Hanrahan, running against Kingsley for village president, as a tool of the electric light company. Even after Kingsley was elected, the *Herald* feared that the reform impulse had gathered little momentum. Some of the most influential local families, meanwhile, remained preoccupied with other political interests. The Sheldons, for example, were locked in a statewide contest as "bolters" from the Republican candidacy of Senator George F. Edmunds. Proctor was busy trying to protect the autonomy of his bailiwick at Proctor, Vermont. With a business that did not depend on local trade, he saw in the recurrent attempts at municipal incorporation only the prospect of expanded public authority and concomitant higher taxation. As a remedy to the municipal nemesis, Proctor had settled on a project of permanent town division by state statute.[32]

In this atmosphere of rudderless local government, the young Knights of Labor seized the political initiative. "The time has come when we propose to have a share in the legislation by which we are governed," declared quarryman and West Rutland Master Workman James Gillespie on August 26, 1886, at the first workingmen's convention ever held in Rutland.[33] "You have candidates of your own," Gillespie thundered, "and will leave the old political issues aside." United Labor speakers—for even the name that local Knights had chosen for their political vehicle copied that of the New York movement—echoed Henry George's theory that "monopoly" ownership inevitably spread from land and manufacturing to control of the state and the established political parties. Edgar B. Moore, a middle-class student of George's who lived with his father, a stove manufacturer, compared United Labor delegates to the "horny-handed sons of toil" who had marched behind Andrew Jackson's assault on "ring rule."[34]

The workingmen settled on a political platform shaped by local and state conditions. It included six demands: abolition of the trustee process; weekly cash payments of wages; election rather than appointment by the boards of civil authority of the overseers of the poor; an employer's liability act; free evening schools for six months of the year in all major towns; and a ten-hour law. Because of the complicated trustee system, employees of failing businesses had suffered long delays in payment of wages—and sometimes permanent loss. The second reform related to the coupon system by which Proctor and other large marble owners had forced workers to do business at company stores. The boards of civil authority, target of the third demand, were bastions of corporate influence and advocates of a parsimonious welfare policy. The accident-prone quarries, in particular, stimulated demand for liability legislation. Without it, the owners tended to contest each case of injury. The educational plan reflected the artisanal commitment to self-improvement. It emphasized practical instruction, e.g., mechanical drawing courses for men, cooking and housework instruction for women. The ten-hour demand, coming as it did at the end of the package, suggested that the Knights held small hope of pushing such a major reform through a rural Republican-dominated state legislature.[35]

The ticket selected by the United Labor convention represented a sharp break with political tradition. For the sixteen positions (one state representative and fifteen justices of the peace) to be filled on September 7, the Knights selected men who would most likely never have appeared on any other list of nominees. Fourteen candidates for justices of the peace identified by trade included four marble workers (a cutter, a polisher, a quarryman, a plain "marble worker"), three carpenters, two laborers, one shoemaker, one clerk, one owner of a meat market, one country store owner, and one small farmer. The French-Canadian marble worker, Megloire Ducharme, was among their number. At the top of their ticket the workingmen chose James F. Hogan, a Catholic clothing store owner and son of an Irish quarryman, as their candidate for the state legislature. Hogan had grown up in Rutland and worked in the quarries until he was sent to Holy Cross College in Worcester, Massachusetts, on the earnings of his brothers and sisters. He was a much-respected but shy man who faltered at the podium, unable to express his feelings before hundreds of applauding workers who had just endorsed his nomination. Thomas H. Brown rescued the candidate by smoothly eulogizing Hogan as "a God-fearing man, who will work for justice and right and not in the interest of monopoly . . . who has not been a politician because he was too honest to have anything to do with their dirty contemptible little tricks, and who will serve the people better because he is untrammeled and closely identified with the struggling masses."[36]

The initial reaction of the older parties suggests that neither Republicans nor Democrats viewed the workingmen's actions as much more than a temporary protest. The dominant Republicans treated the reformers with polite condescension. The *Herald,* for instance, complimented the United Labor meeting as "probably as good looking, well dressed, and well behaved a body of workingmen as any town in the world can show . . . instead of being a mob as sometimes happens . . . in large cities." With paternal hauteur, Proctor acknowledged Hogan's presence on the ballot as the first local Irish-Catholic to run for high office. The Republican party, he noted, had opened the political system to the "colored" races in the first place; now, a "colored" man nominated at a recent labor caucus" provided a further "living instance" of the Republican principle of equality. Proctor expressed surprise and even a little hurt that the workingmen had taken such extreme measures to support their moderate reform demands. Proctor, for one, admitted the need for changes in the trustee laws. Nor need the laboring men have worried so about the company stores. "I suppose that was intended to hit me," the Marble King reflected. "I will only say in reply that if I am concerned in any company store that does not benefit the workingman, I will either set it right or remove it." Aside from such gestures of conciliation, however, the Republicans held fast to their faith in the town's traditional guardians. For state representative they nominated Hiram Smith, a marble quarry superintendent, leading Congregationalist, and Masonic officer. In form they remained a closed ethnic caste. Their response, it appeared, was to win back community confidence in the governing elite but not to tamper with the composition of that elite.[37]

The Democrats were prepared to go further in response to the new party. They evidently regarded the workingmen's movement less as a rebuke than as an opportunity. If nursed properly, this new, already-organized constituency might propel them from a long-suffering minority status to the premiere political force in the county and, ultimately, maybe even the state. At the labor nominating convention, Democratic attorney Spellman had sought in vain to dissuade the Knights from an independent course. The Democrats even offered James Hogan their party's nomination. When he refused, they slated inventor-manufacturer, George J. Wardwell, instead and shaped him in labor's image: "Though he may not have worked in the quarries [like Hogan] in his younger days . . . [he] worked in the marble yards of those quarries.

He represents the true, healthy type of American working man, self-made, self-educated, upright and true: he has hewn success out of life by his untiring industry and productive brain." Composed of smaller manufacturers, lawyers, merchants, farmers, and a few skilled workers (including a foreman, a carpenter, and a mechanic), Democratic caucus delegates adopted a platform nearly identical with that of the labor party's. They distinguished themselves in only two particulars. They discountenanced "class distinctions of every name and nature," asserting that "no political party ought to be organized on any such basis." The Democrats also made opposition to the Proctor-backed plan for "dismemberment" of the community of Rutland a major issue, behind which they hoped to attract cross-class support.[38]

Neither Republican nor Democratic strategy, however, dampened the labor fever running through Rutland. The night before the balloting 1,000 Knights rallied at the Rutland skating rink to hear their leaders implore them to "stand behind Hogan" and shun beckoning taverns on election day. With a turnout nearly one and one-half the size of the previous local elections, Hogan swept into office with 1,645 votes, 400 ahead of his Republican challenger. The labor candidacy reduced the Democrats to an almost impotent irrelevancy, with Wardwell gathering only 245 votes. All fifteen labor justices of the peace took office. On election night crowds paraded through the streets. Stopping in front of Hogan's house, one group burst out in song. Mrs. Hogan, an accomplished pianist, returned the favor with a serenade of her own.[39]

Rutland's Knights of Labor did not have long to celebrate their victory. The prospect of labor rule in Rutland summoned up less a loyal opposition than a counterrevolution. Within days of the town election, Proctor dusted off plans he had been nursing for some time to rid his business of potential legislative interference and unnecessary taxation by the central government in Rutland town. Through influential contacts at Montpelier, he began a vigorous lobbying effort to divide Proctor from Rutland's political jurisdiction, and he encouraged West Rutland to do likewise. As he put it in private correspondence, in a large town "interests are so mixed and varied that a large part of the voters had little interest in them and never understand them but are led by demagogues and go with the mob." Small-town citizens were less likely to make such mistakes because "the questions are brought right to their doors." In the one-industry village in which only thirty-five homes were independently owned, overwhelming endorsement of a prodivision petition circulated door to door by Redfield's son, Fletcher D., tended to prove his point.[40]

The Proctor family could count on powerful political support for their initiative. Business connections alone would bring the other marble owners to the Proctors' side. But Proctor also figured that labor's electoral victory would soften natural commerical opposition within Rutland village to town division. "Fear of foreign rule," Proctor advised his counsel, "had produced a wondrous change in public feeling." The influential *Herald,* for example, did not attack the division plan. This, then, was the opportune moment to appeal to the rural bias of the Vermont legislature (beginning with its Legislative Redistricting Committee) against the ineffectual, and now possibly dangerous, government of the state's largest urban center.[41]

But Proctor also had his opponents in the form of a coalition between some of Rutland's older citizens, independent businessmen, Democrats, and Knights of Labor. A blue-ribbon committee to save the town mixed retired Judge Dunton, the elderly bankers Charles Clement and John Baxter, the merchants E. D. Keyes and Harley C. Tuttle, Democratic attorney John Spellman, and federal Judge David Nicholson with Master Workman James J. Fay. Since several of these men had previously pushed for a municipal charter on grounds that town government was too unwieldy, they could not easily defend the status quo of local government from the attacks of the division lobby. Instead, the antidivision forces concentrated on the deleterious economic and political effects of the legislative proposals. Their most passionate argument concerned the private motives behind the call for the rupture of old community boundaries. L. H. Granger, an insurance agent, attacked the protagonist of the division forces as if he were the modern-day representative of England's Old Corruption: "Governor Proctor is a man of iron. It is questioned whether he is not strong enough to dismember this largest town in Vermont; whether he is not powerful enough to carve out for him a pocket borough." To Granger, twin dangers confronted the American republic in the Gilded Age. One involved "the anarchists who seek to destroy; the other, greater because insidious—the encroachments of great corporations, which seek to control and pervert our political institutions, until we shall live only in their shadow."[42]

The Knights of Labor were as interested as other citizens in the division question, but, unfortunately, they found themselves lined up on both sides of the issue. Representative Hogan probably upheld the dominant opinion in labor circles by speaking forcefully against division from the floor of the legislature. In addition, workers filled a mass meeting in Rutland village to protest what they called "the scheme" for division. In West Rutland, however, sentiments were quite different. Two men who would soon become identified as Knights' leaders spoke for the division of West Rutland at legislative committee hearings. They claimed that nine of ten West Rutlanders favored division. While theirs were not the economic motives of West Rutland merchants who wished to be able to regulate the excursion trains carrying shoppers away to Rutland center, the West Rutland workers shared the general complaint of government inattention to the roads, sidewalks, and other needs of their community. One other factor likely influenced popular prodivision feeling in West Rutland. An Irish political majority would almost surely accompany political separation of the Stonepeggers. P. J. Donnergan, an Irish-American marble worker who had "always lived" in West Rutland, thus spoke approvingly of attaining "home rule." Given the differences of opinion within their own ranks on the division question, the Knights of Labor remained officially neutral and unconcerned. An official of L.A. 5160 boasted that the Order would carry all three towns separately if necessary. "If any one is favoring a division with the hope of averting the baneful effect of the political action of the Knights, he is laboring under a delusion."[43]

State legislators apparently thought differently and overwhelmingly approved the creation of the new towns of Proctor and West Rutland in late November 1886. To those who had followed the lawmakers' deliberations, no mystery surrounded the final outcome. The most telling prodivision argument in Montpelier, said the *Herald*, "was that Rutland was at the mercy of irresponsible men." From the beginning of their investigations, rural Republican members of the Redistricting Committee had apparently expressed shock at the local political climate. "From the fact that the laboring men elected a representative by such an overwhelming vote," an antidivision man sadly reflected, "they seemed to infer that we were in a state of anarchy down here." Prior to the decisive vote, rumors circulated in the legislative chamber that the new Rutland governors might apply "excessive taxation to support a strike or to carry out Henry George's theory of the distribution of property." One representative had openly counseled an antidivision delegation of Rutland businessmen, "Division is your only salvation. You are in bad shape politically and something must be done for relief."[44]

By the end of their deliberations, the legislators' basic decision surprised no one. But in the final hours of the last legislative session the lawmakers tacked on some additional unadvertised items to the division bills. By amendment to the original Rutland charter, the state withdrew the town's right to elect a municipal judge, making it an appointed position. Another statute hurriedly enacted required local trustees to furnish bonds ranging from $1,000 to $5,000 before taking office. Finally, the legislature voided the tenure of the fifteen Rutland justices of the peace elected in September on grounds that they did not properly represent the new districts that had just been carved out. The governor was authorized to appoint interim justices. While the division vote rested on a variety of motivations and explanations, the object of these collateral actions was unmistakable.[45]

In the end the legislature went farther than anyone in Rutland had, at least publicly, advised. Together the actions amounted to placing the town in a virtual state receivership. The *Herald* tried to head off a vituperative reaction, belatedly blaming the new statutes on "outsiders" and proclaiming that the "best people" in town really had "had no fear of labor organization, but on the contrary respected the methods thus far employed by the workingmen." Loss of more than a third of Rutland town's population as well as its largest revenue-producing properties, the conservative newspaper reported, might be offset "by the belief that we will have a better and safer government" with "property more secure and therefore more valuable." Other citizens, however, were unwilling to adopt the *Herald*'s spirit of reconciliation. Spellman proclaimed that practicing before the labor justices would not have embarrassed him. The legislative package, according to Spellman, was the creation of "capitalists (sometimes appropriately called monopolists)" organizing "for their special protection." Presiding (elected) Rutland municipal Judge Albert Landon was the most indignant of all. "The industrial classes have become sufficiently intelligent to undertake to right their wrongs at the ballot box. And this is a mad attempt to wrest that dreaded weapon from their grasp." If the logic of the legislature were extended, Landon agrued, "the pride of New England—the boasted divinity of its town system of government—could be wiped out by the stroke of a pen."[46]

Rutland's political evolution had thus been staked to the outline of social conflict. First, in one great surge, the organization of Rutland workers had dramatically reshaped the substance of local politics; then the reaction to their initiative had upset even the physical boundaries of the political community. Forced to choose between political pacification and civic growth, the division forces betrayed fears that underlay the surface exuberance of an Age of Progress. For their part, Rutland Knights of Labor had been treated to an elementary lesson in the costs of inexperience among political professionals. Political dismemberment, in itself, however, did not ensure the success of the opposition strategy. Whether town division would, in fact, disrupt labor's political momentum depended on the specific social configurations within the new jurisdictions of Rutland, West Rutland, and Proctor.

A magisterial rule—at once benevolent and arbitrary—quickly settled over the new town of Proctor. In the spring of 1887 the first Proctor town meeting began by electing Redfield Proctor moderator and proceeded to endorse a company-backed slate by acclamation. For decades to come, the Proctor family, itself a bulwark of the state Republican party, would be able to count on solid, conservative Republican majorities in their town. An apparent absence of working-class organization and activity from 1887 on seemed to signal the dispersal of what had always been a relatively weak Knights' presence in Proctor's mills. Effective control of the town's social and political life, henceforth, emanated from a single center of power.[47]

Proctor family rule combined power with discretion. As early as 1886 the Vermont Marble Company chartered a company cooperative store and an employees' savings bank. While disclaiming direct liability for quarry accidents, it hired the country's first industrial nurse in 1895. Soon, a fully equipped hospital was providing free medical care to all Proctor employees. The company also built and funded programs for the local YMCA. Redfield Proctor commited himself to his town and company and tried to ensure that the employees would do likewise. In December 1886, for example, "in these times of labor troubles," he bought back shares of stock from large shareholders in order to resell them at reduced rates to foremen and salesmen "to bind them all the more closely together." Proctor also worked hard, almost scientifically, at securing a docile labor force. He requested the Cunard Line in 1887 to send 200 to 300 Swedes to the quarrying center: "We want good rugged men and much prefer men from the country rather than such as go from the city." During the same period he took pains to recruit a particular Chicago building contractor known for employing "men who have not got the 8 hour craze and are not controlled by unions." Proctor pointedly did favors for the local clergy and as pointedly expected loyalty in return. The ambivalent nature of acquiescence in the town of Proctor—rendered in part out of desperation and in part of gratefulness—explains why the local marble workers paraded in welcome whenever the governor or his son entertained visiting dignitaries or why 3,000 men waited for hours through a severe March snowstorm in 1908 for the Marble King's casket to pass in final review.[48]

Nearly twice the size of Proctor, the new town of West Rutland possessed more of both the substance and spirit of democratic self-government. A relatively autonomous labor and ethnic communal organization created the basis for political pluralism, but it was a most moderate pluralism that quickly prevailed there. Postdivision West Rutland was, in short, at once dominated by the unabashed assertiveness of its Irish working-class constituency and by the limitations of that same community. At the inaugural town meeting on March 1, 1887, West Rutland independent labor forces did sweep the field as predicted. By the next year, however, a nonpartisan group calling itself the Citizens caucus had gained control of local government, and at least through the mid-1890s local affairs were untroubled by independent labor political agitation.

Several factors seem to have influenced the new town's general political quiescence.[49] The need to establish fiscal solvency was perhaps most important. Division left West Rutland with considerable debts owed to the old town authority, and the new government had to issue bonds immediately just to maintain local projects already under way. The new town stood on an uncertain economic base in any case; as in Proctor, practically everyone depended on the health of the marble industry. From the beginning of their tenure, therefore, West Rutland labor selectmen cooperated with local businessmen and even deferred to the advice of a marble company lawyer. One of their first acts budgeted public funds for roads requested by local marble companies. M. W. Cannon, a farmer (and former quarryman), Knights of Labor master workman, and a leader of West Rutland labor political forces, boasted that "there is no element of our population that will make greater efforts for the maintenance of law and order, for the security of person and property and for the economical administration of town affairs than the workingmen. No action of the workingmen will ever mar the progress of the new town."[50]

If labor's West Rutland representatives displayed a willingness to work with other local interests, businessmen also accepted the necessity for collaboration. Before the first West Rutland town meeting, several Knights' leaders were offered places on the businessmen's Citizens ticket. When the Knights refused, other marble workers were nominated to take their place. Indeed, the initial 1887 election amounted almost to a competition in representation from below. In reaction to the call of the Citizens caucus for a government of all the talents, the labor caucus pressed for election of "all nationalities," adding two French-Canadians (a carriage manufacturer and a marble worker) to a ticket weighted with Irish marble workers. Looking over the town's governors in 1887, a visitor noted that West Rutland possessed "the most common representatives I have run across." By the year's end, however, the workingmen's politicians appear to have accepted the political hospitality of town elders. In 1890, for example, Cannon was elected selectman alongside two other nonpartisan candidates: one, a marble worker and former United Labor man, the other, a superintendent of the Sheldon Marble Company. From the beginning local Democratic politicians showed skill in accommodating to and making use of intraclass political formations in West Rutland. As early as 1886 Democratic businessmen like cigar manufacturer A. H. Abraham and insurance executive L. W. Redington diplomatically contributed gifts to a Knights' raffle. That West Rutland was the only site in the county to carry for Grover Cleveland in 1888 suggested the particular turn that labor's political strength had taken there.[51]

In taking stock of the relations between the labor movement and the community power structure that gave rise to such a political juncture, it is important to note that class conciliation in West Rutland took place not in the flush of labor mobilization but during the ebb tide of organized labor strength. As early as mid-1887 employer hostility and intransigence before labor's wage demands were reportedly taking a heavy toll in demoralization and loss of membership among area marble workers. While four Knights' assemblies, including two based in West Rutland, survived until 1892, they did so with a much attenuated community presence.[52] The collapse of labor leadership and mass discipline (following the national fate of the Knights of Labor) left the movement without confidence in its own future. In less polarized relation to local government the labor constituency henceforth served only as a residual opposition, setting limits rather than a clear direction in the public sphere. The case of West Rutland also highlights the economic limits on labor's political autonomy in a small one-industry town, even a class-conscious and organized one. That such a fledgling community should reach a consensual public *modus operandi* is not surprising. Localism and a climate of civic unity under adversity in the end predominated over internal divisions. That a self-consciously working-class party should run such a town, even for a year, is surely the more incongruous idea and remarkable achievement.

While the two new towns, for one reason or another, settled into a relatively quiet resolution of their internal affairs, the situation in what remained of old Rutland town (which contained roughly two-thirds of the original population) took on an entirely different complexion. If the state legislators had meant to wipe out Rutland labor politics by town division, they failed. Except for the loss of population and taxable property, the only new political factor in Rutland town after 1886 was the added stigma of betrayal attached to many of the town's business leaders. As a result labor politics there was not foreshortened but prolonged. As in West Rutland, the Rutland United Labor party swept the February 1887 town meeting, then fell off the following year. But the circumstances were quite different. Unlike the situation in the new town to the west, the underlying social tension separating workers from the Yankee elite did not evaporate in old Rutland. Its greater size—Rutland was finally incorporated as a city under mayoral-aldermanic government in 1892—and its more complex economy militated against political manipulation by a few employers. Drawing on this comparatively urban environment, no shortage of confident young Knights of Labor were willing to challenge the older town guardians for control of the community's future. Rutland workingmen unlike those in West Rutland thus found it possible to regroup after their first electoral setbacks, and they recaptured important positions under United Workingmen's banners in 1890, remaining a legitimate independent threat through 1892. Even as the numbers behind the Knights dwindled, the constituency that the Order had created endured. When labor finally transferred its strength to the Democratic party, it infused that party with new prospects and with a new character derived from the workingmen's movement.[53]

Rutland town's 1887 workingmen's government offers a revealing glimpse of the Gilded Age labor movement at full strength. A remarkably high 75 percent of all eligible voters participated in labor's postdivision triumph. In many individual contests workingmen's candidates achieved majorities of 60 percent or more. The personnel of the town's labor government indicates that the movement effectively straddled the middling and lower tiers of the social structure. Labor's officeholders varied markedly in background. Thus, while a horseshoer and a farm laborer assumed the post of fence-viewers (regulator of rural property boundaries), a clerk, an insurance agent, and a dairy dealer willingly put their accounting skills to work as United Labor town auditors. For school superintendent the new labor school board endorsed James Merrill, a twenty-four-year-old law student two years out of Yale College. Anchored by the disciplined loyalty of their rank and file, Knights' leaders like machinist John Huffmire and Henry Georgeites James J. Fay and Edgar Moore all assumed key positions in the town's administration. In April a local opponent complained that "the Knights of Labor are controlling almost entirely this village and town." A hostile upstate press smirked at the political avalanche in "the wicked city." Everyone, more or less, acknowledged the new turn of affairs. A May announcement in the Rutland *Herald* attracted readers with the banner "K. OF L." Beneath the boldly printed initials, one found an endorsement of Carter's Little Liver Pills, "rightly called the King of Linaments." To stay abreast of the regnant local feeling, a merchant renamed his store the Anti-Monopoly Clothiers. By July the town even hosted a new daily local labor newspaper called the *People's Journal*.[54]

A generational as well as a social cleavage had suddenly opened up in Rutland local politics. The *Herald*'s editors were not altogether biased in charging that Rutland's 1887 town officers "read like a strange directory," derived "largely from one class of inhabitants" who were "unfamiliar with public affairs." At least half of labor's selectmen and school board members in 1887 were thirty years older or younger. With the exception of Meyerhoffer, the Knights' senior local strategists were Fay, aged forty; Huffmire, aged thirty-seven; and T. H. Brown, aged twenty-nine. It was no wonder, then, that the *Herald* would rally antilabor troops in 1888 by appealing particularly to "every old citizen of this town" to remember his "life-long friends, substantial men who have never misled [him]."[55]

The youth of the insurgent leaders suggests that Rutland's previous sociopolitical consensus may have broken down, in part, because of an anachronistic world view of the local elite. For, despite the fact that Rutland town had gone through dramatic changes since the Civil War, the people who had presided over those changes preferred to think that the social fabric was still cut from the original cloth. They recalled the days when Redfield Proctor personally took a hand at the quarrying operations. They toasted the image of Jonas Putnam, whose fifty-two years of work for a local organ manufacturer indicated the "permanency of relations between old-fashioned New England employers and their workmen." The exemplary worker who "took as much interest in the establishment as his employer" could, the *Herald* believed, expect an eventual advance in his social position. The town burghers clung to the idea that wage labor functioned as a temporary incubator—conditioning the hard-working young man to the qualities necessary to rise to independent status. "How a Laborer Became a Capitalist" ran a local headline. "Pluck, Economy, Perseverance, and Minding His Own Business Did It."[56]

The world confronting Rutland's younger workers, however, lent little credibility to the picture of economic harmony and upward mobility painted by the town elders. Given the concentration of industry and the cost of new technology, the relations of production no longer encouraged the workingman to think that by emulating his employer he could climb to the top himself. A marble worker who came of working age in the 1870s and 1880s (55 percent of Rutland marble workers in 1880 were under thirty) could—if he remained in town—expect to spend his entire adult life in the quarries or mills.[57] Similarly, a skilled iron molder or scaleworker, far from heading toward independence, faced a steady fall from aristocrat to commoner even within the working-class world. In the case of the Irish and French-Canadian citizenry consideration of both their economic and political positions might well have convinced them that they had never really been invited into the organic community of the *Herald*'s dreams in the first place. In such circumstances, the constant invocation of the theme of opportunity within complacent middle-class rhetoric may only have bred frustration and resentment among a new generation of working people every bit as ambitious as their predecessors. A tone of impatient group arrival thus echoed in Brown's remarks to an election-eve crowd: "When the workingmen strike they are told by a thousand newspapers that it is all wrong, that they must right their wrongs at the ballot box, and tonight we are assembled here, knowing no Frenchmen, no Irishmen, no Swedes, no Yankees; we came here knowing our right and knowing, dare maintain."[58]

Even those workers who had successfully acquired a trade and in some cases moved on to self-employment did not necessarily fit the mold of contemporary middle-class expectations. For it was precisely this upper stratum within the working-class world who provided the leadership for the Knights of Labor. It may well be, for example, that Rutland's second-generation Irish-Americans, weighted toward the skilled trades and industrial positions, contributed a critical mass of confidence and maturity required for independent political activity (Table 10).

The workingmen's respectable self-image was certainly apparent in the platform upon which they ran for office in 1887. On the whole, the United Labor architects took a prudent but expansionist approach to the role of local government. Citing individual cases of corruption and mounting public debt, the platform demanded "strict account of all public transactions . . . rendered so as to be perfectly understood" and "just and equitable taxation." An emphasis on balanced budgets was a matter of direct self-interest to working-

TABLE 10. First- and Second-Generation Components within the Irish-American Working Class in Rutland, 1880

Occupations	Total Number	Percent Irish-Born	Percent Native-Born of Irish-Parentage
Skilled tradesmen	152	49	51
Scale workers	33	51	49
Marble workers	484	49	51
Unskilled laborers	275	72	28
Farm laborers	17	65	35

Source. U.S. Tenth Census, 1880, population manuscript.
Note. Data are based on males, aged twenty and over.

men who owned their own houses and small plots of farmland. For families struggling to make ends meet, debt service paid from property assessment appeared not only unproductive but also an exploitative form of taxation in its own right. In addressing the contents of the town budget, the workingmen made clear that they were modernists favoring an expansion of the public sphere of influence. In no way antigovernment traditionalists, labor in its program called for the permanent surfacing of roads, a higher school tax, and a substantial public appropriation for the new town library. In sum, their attitude reflected an optimistic faith in themselves and in the community's future development.[59]

These attitudes were quickly translated into practice. Rutland's first labor-dominated town meeting in 1887 adopted a tax rate of $15 per $1,000 of listed property, which even the *Herald* admitted was "generous if not extraordinarily high." An exceptional 10 percent of the augmented local budget was earmarked for the stalled construction of the town's memorial to the Civil War dead. In addition, the workingmen set aside the first public allotment (2 percent of taxes) toward a free library. The *Herald* candidly acknowledged that "the same men would not have voted so much if they did not feel responsibility for town government."[60]

Indeed, on many issues the Knights' approach to government corresponded to that of the most development-oriented members of the business community. In educational matters, for example, the labor voters joined forces with local bankers and the *Herald* to replace the old district system with a town school board and consolidated administration. For years residents of outlying areas of the county—including both farmers and industrialists like Redfield Proctor—had jealously guarded the tiny district schools from the higher taxes and centralization of power associated with urban authority. Brown, on the other hand, wholeheartedly defended the plan for upgrading the educational system: "We never growl at school taxes and you will not hear us protest at paying out money for school purposes." The degree of working-class interest in education was evident in the attendance of 500 citizens, "a large majority of whom were Knights of Labor," at Rutland's first school board meeting. Joseph Austin, a blacksmith and labor school board candidate, expressed commitment to "liberal education and the expenditures of all the money necessary to establish creditable schools." Other workingmen's spokesmen advocated "radical improvements" in the system including a new school building and the hiring of several additional teachers. Such reform-mindedness prompted one reorganization opponent to compare the workingmen's political moves to the "Anti-Masonic excitement" and "Liberal anti-slavery crusades" of earlier generations. To this senior observer it seemed that the Knights had "grown up like Jonah's gourd." "It has taken control of town meetings and of schools. [There is] no guarantee that ignorant Italians, anarchists, and infidels cannot and will not control the town meeting and as a result all the schools in the town."[61]

Maneuvering room for the workingmen's representatives, to be sure, was far from a position of total control. From their first day in office, the new men reckoned with a negative business climate left over from the bitter election campaigns and town division; as such they frequently emphasized their interest in a strong and stable commercial climate. A manufacturer who had expressed fears in March 1886 about locating his plant in Rutland thus drew an immediate and official response from the Knights of Labor: "The workingmen of Rutland are ready to help, morally and financially, any business enterprise that may locate here." The Knights pointed with pride to "honorable, upright" town officials, reduced drunkenness, and "scarcely any business for our police courts" since labor's coming to power. The Order's spokesmen, furthermore, denied interest in "labor strife" and promised that workers would "never interfere with the prosperity of Rutland." Indeed, in an allusion to their interest in cooperatives, the Knights pointed out that they contemplated the establishment of "enterprises of our own." Labor's willingness to cooperate with business leaders was evident in village president James Fay's acceptance of a five-year municipal contract for the electric light company. Democratic attorney Colonel V. A. Gaskill, who had joined remonstrants wanting to restrict the utility to a one-year contract, angrily dared the local labor legislators to "tell Powderly what they had done."[62]

The workingmen's approach to governmental efficiency was, if anything, too zealous for some local businessmen. Labor's representatives campaigned for an accelerated schedule of improvements as well as for streamlined governmental structures. Demanding an end to "the days of mud and mire in the streets of Rutland," Fay advocated acquisition of an expensive "stone-crusher" to macademize the roads of the town's commercial center. Both Fay and E. B. Moore attempted to convince the Businessmen's Association of the merits of a city charter to replace the competing jurisdictions and duplicated functions in what Moore called the "hydra-headed monster" of divided town and village government, boards of water commissioners, overseers of the poor, and civil authority. Moore lectured the local merchants and capitalists that "good, economical, practical government is impossible with such complicated machinery and such varying interests." "Let us clean up your mess" seemed to be labor's message to the town elders. Moore, in particular, went so far as to hold up Pullman, Illinois, as a model of efficient administration, citing its "magnificent streets, splendid sewerage and many other improvements." While agreeing with the main thrust of labor's proposals, the *Herald* considered them a bit "radical" and "too sweeping" in their embrace of centralization.[63]

Confrontations with Rutland's old establishment during labor's first year in office centered on symbolic issues of influence and power rather than on specific differences in direction. Using its remaining pockets of governmental authority, the old guard attempted to fulfill their predictions of labor mismanagement. Recalcitrant village trustees, for example, aided by a ruling from the Republican village attorney, blocked the town's decision to purchase a stone-crusher. In addition, the trustees checked Fay's effort to appoint Knights of Labor policemen, touching off a protracted dispute over the prerogatives of the village president. Despite these obstacles, most of the routine business of local government passed smoothly. A typical meeting of the divided board of trustees moved without dispute to purchase two new police billyclubs, install a fire alarm box, investigate the possible acquisition of a hook-and-ladder truck, and fund a new sewer project. Unanimously, conservative trustees could agree with labor representative V. C. Meyerhoffer to ignore a complaint against ball-playing in the public streets.[64]

A few details of local administration reflected a unilateral labor influence. Rutland village advanced the wages of stonecutters on construction projects. Brown struck down a proposal for wire fences along the highways because "the present board fences result indirectly in giving employment to many laboring men in winter." The board of selectmen reprimanded a policeman for harassing Salvation Army marches and musical parades. These agents of the social gospel had first appeared in Rutland in January 1886 and reportedly attracted "a new class not used to church going." Their enthusiastic operations apparently bothered other Christians who compared them to the "orgies of a fanatical group of superstitious negroes at a southern revival," but the workingmen's government, which included Salvation Army member and selectman John Huffmire, ignored the protests. A more positive assertion of cultural and religious identity was registered in West Rutland, where the 1887 Knights' administration declared a general suspension of work on St. Patrick's Day, and where a tear-filled audience that evening watched a cast of marble workers perform *Pike O'Callahan*, the drama of a young Irish patriot forced to flee his homeland. Finally, it appears that a thoroughly traditional form of political influence was registered in 1887 Rutland town archives, which list Meyerhoffer and Huffmire as the recipients of $200 for road-building work.[65]

Labor's performance in office bespoke an exuberant civic pride and self-conscious patriotism. They had taken the forms of democratic citizenship seriously and, in so doing, had come to see themselves as the true and proper guardians of the public welfare. Even the *Herald* acknowledged the comparative zest with which workingmen attacked municipal responsibilities. "[High] Society," it mused, "demands cynicism . . . so the idealism of the labor movement [is] working on suppressed enthusiasm like a spark on tinder." The Knights of Labor held the only Independence Day ceremony in town in 1887. Several months later Moore introduced a motion at town meeting to fly the American flag over public buildings. Taken together these actions describe a movement self-consciously bent on renewal rather than a redrafting of republican principles. In words with which his audience agreed wholeheartedly, A. A. Carlton, regional lecturer for the Knights of Labor, addressed a public forum sponsored by Rutland's Georgeite Anti-Poverty Society in July 1887. "We stand today," he said of the Order, "as the conservators of society. We have watched the growth of a privileged class and of a vast army of tramps. If these extremes come together there will be a crash. We are building between them a platform upon which all men may stand on an equality."[66]

The premium attached to self-improvement and refinement within the movement's culture buttressed labor's claims to political legitimacy. Within their own circles, the organized workers particularly appreciated those who by their own efforts had smoothed over the rough edges of working-class existence. A taste for what might be called "popular gentility" was manifest in personal qualities as well as the public activities of those associated with the labor movement. The Knights delighted in an orator like Brown who could respond in verse to the *Herald*'s attacks on Henry George. Mrs. James Hogan was an accomplished pianist. Labor trustee and marble cutter J. S. Carder had taken singing lessons. A Rutland "Knights of Labor concert" directed by the visiting vocalist, "Professor Cassavent," in 1894 would feature a potpourri of selections ranging from popular romantic songs and polkas to bits of comic opera and overtures from romantic classical symphonies. The air of gentility carried over to the Knights' emphasis on education and temperance. The same values would motivate Fay to demand a crackdown on "gambling dens . . . where men and young boys are lured from the paths of virtue" in his first official declaration. The Knights sanctioned gambling only at their own lotteries, where both men and women might win small domestic adornments—a silver butter dish, an easy chair, lace curtains, a bed quilt, or a set of crockery. In self-defense against the spector of increasing degradation at the workplace, the Knights may thus have given a special meaning to the general contemporary enshrinement of family autonomy and domestic purity. With the family as the basic unit of participation in its organized community life, the movement kept issues of social and self-reform inseparable.[67]

The Knights struggled simultaneously for strength and intelligence. "Every faculty within us," counseled Carlton, "should be developed for the benefit of humanity. We do not wish to displace this system until we have something to put in its place." Thus it was that the movement combined a demand for power with the most cautious exercise of that power. Politically, the Knights advocated fairly modest reforms. They tried hard to win the respect and support of middle-class elements. On many matters, in fact, they did not disagree with their traditional governors over the way things ought to be run— only, as self-appointed conservators of society, they intended to be its managers as well.[68]

Unfortunately for the workingmen, their moderate policies and demeanor did not make them any more acceptable to an opposition stung by the organized disloyalty of the town's employees. The very foreignness of the new governors together with their potential for mischief set the business community into an attitude of implacable hostility and made it impossible for the labor administration to substantiate its claims to managerial competence. As a result in Rutland, as elsewhere, labor strength quickly began to fall off as a consequence of external attack and internal discouragement.

The workingmen's declaration of candidacy in 1887 touched off a fury among those who had hoped that somehow, amidst political division, the labor interest would just go away. Now the previous public air of polite condescension dissipated before the recognition that the reformers intended not to stage a protest but to build a stable political base. Violating the system of "good, honest, impartial local government," the Knights' political organization appeared to the *Herald* "unrepublican, undemocratic, and un-American," "a threat to the personal and political liberty of the individual." To the old town stewards who idealized the forms of town meetings, it seemed that the labor party was now introducing social class as a qualification for local office. The traditional way, insisted the *Herald,* involved selection of "the best men for the several positions, regardless of what honorable calling they pursue for getting a living." Now suddenly "a man is of no account if he is only a plain citizen. He must be a workingman or something or other."[69]

Republican oracles predicted the most dire consequences from labor rule. In the aftermath of town division, "preservation of property [values] and credit" constituted the priorities of local government, according to the *Herald.* Any "labor disturbance" in these circumstances might "set the town back ten years." A week prior to town meeting Rutland's daily newspaper described the streetcar workers' protest in Cambridge, Massachusetts, with an extended comment: "It is almost always a calamity to a city to fall under democratic control. If a riot is to be suppressed or violators of the liquor law are to be punished, or vice to be driven out . . . officials who are but the creatures of the disorderly element—the very vomit of the saloons—are the last men in the world upon whom the friends of law and order can depend for the protection of peace, life and property." Given control of government, the Republican organ suggested, Rutland Knights might conceivably undertake such "unpatriotic designs" as the provision of public relief to the unemployed. Appealing to all "intelligent workingmen," the *Herald* pleaded, "Let us have no class movements, no grab for offices, no raid upon the treasury." A group of Rutland business leaders publicly expressed outrage at the thought of "being put under control . . . of the leaders of a secret order whose history and doings elsewhere are bordering upon anarchy and communism."[70]

Halfway through the first term of the labor officials, the discrediting process acquired some teeth. The announcement in October 1887 that the Rutland Shirt Company planned to transfer its operations touched off a mild panic that business and jobs were about to abandon the town. "The labor movement has frightened outside capital for the time being," declared the *Herald*. "That makes it all the more incumbent on local capital to re-establish confidence." Within months, two new businessmen's organizations—one a private club, the other a merchants' association—were seeking simultaneously to refurbish Rutland's image abroad and to activate its "men of education and standing" at home. While the old guard regrouped, the *Herald* provided a steady diet of invective against "class government." In particular, it aimed at political leaders like Huffmire, Moore, Fay, and Brown. The *Herald* caricatured these "friends of the workingmen" as "glib-tongued fellows who have ceased to earn their living by the sweat of their brows, finding it easier to pose as reformers and let the workingmen support them." Through a mysterious cabal, the *Herald* charged, these men had taken over public affairs, holding over their constituency "the most odious form of tyranny—the discipline of an Order and the feeling of fraternity." Under the "monstrous pretense" of protecting the public interest, the political invaders were threatening the already-beleaguered town with new debts, increased taxes, and the potential loss of investment.[71]

The key political problem facing the antilabor forces, of course, was how to refashion an electoral majority. To this end the town's business leadership, in a sharp break with tradition, abandoned not only the personalism and informality of older times but also retreated from the framework of partisan loyalty to unite behind the widespread contemporary phenomenon of a nonpartisan Citizens party of order. Though the effort initially amounted to little more than dressing up the old ruling Republican faction in new outfits, it soon became a most effective counterweight to independent labor politics. Proclaiming "Rutland Redeemed," the Citizens ticket captured the 1888 town meeting and generally dominated local government until it liquidated itself in 1894. Though not exactly the association of "Republicans, Democrats, and workingmen joining hands . . . to secure the public good" that it claimed, the Citizens party was more than an instrument of middle-class fear and repression. As early as 1888 Rutland Democrats like attorneys J. D. Spellman and T. W. Maloney, who had joined in the antidivision fight and generally enjoyed good relations with organized labor, were taking an active role in the Citizens' activities. Antidivision activists like Judge W. C. Dunton similarly rejoined those they had denounced as "designing men" the year before. In addition, young professionals and businessmen like school superintendent J. A. Merrill, selectman James Creed, and town auditor Richard Ryan initially elected on the labor ticket, were endorsed for reelection by the challengers. The Citizens crowned its 1888 ticket with the nomination for town meeting moderator of acting State Supreme Court Judge Walter G. Veazey, who had also forthrightly opposed town division in 1886. Unlike the old party caucuses a mass public meeting ratified the Citizens slate in 1888; in future elections the candidates themselves were nominated at open meetings.[72]

This outside assault coincided with a deflation of interest within labor's own ranks. As early as June 1887, District Master Workman T. H. Brown confided to Terence Powderly that local quarrymen were expressing disappointment that they had not gained "an immediate benefit in the shape of increase in wages" through "the power of the order." Unable to move forward on the industrial front, the Knights at best were just "about holding our own." A few months after Brown's assessment, the Vermont Supreme Court set labor's hopes back further by convicting striking Knights' granite workers who had intimidated scabs in the upstate town of South Ryegate for conspiring in restraint of trade. By the end of the year, several assemblies in the state's marble centers had collapsed.[73]

Organized labor had lost its local numerical superiority. By 100- to 200-vote margins, the Citizens ousted the slate now calling itself the United Workingmen at the 1888 town meeting. General Levi Kingsley, a political moderate and senior local citizen who since the town division business had attached himself to labor's cause and received their nomination for selectman, alone escaped the electoral reverse. The returns suggest that an erosion of labor's organized strength rather than any massive shift in popular sympathies contributed to the electoral turnaround. The Citizens advanced 150 votes over the previous year's showing and that increase with the reduced turnout (more than 100 fewer votes) accounted for the difference.[74]

The more successful the Citizens became, however (i.e., the more it resembled a truly democratic consensus), the less well it served its originators' purposes. Bipartisan inclusiveness had proved the key to its winning ways beginning in 1888 but also risked loss of control over the direction of the movement. As early as the 1888 village election, Citizens' leaders were expressing fears that the Knights had infiltrated preliminary meetings and secured nomination of some of their men in Citizens' costumes. Two years later Republican and Democratic businessmen opened what they called a nonpartisan caucus with a pledge of willingness to select men from all competing parties. The organizers withdrew quickly, however, when workingmen in alliance with a dissident Democratic faction proposed a genuine unity slate. The *Herald* described it most coolly "as a whole not the men who naturally would be selected to conduct the business of any corporation equal in importance and with equal interest at stake to the town of Rutland." Again in 1891 workingmen upset the official slate with a caucus victory for an iron molder for street commissioner. Even if steered through the uncertainties of the caucus, business-endorsed candidates still might face a stiff labor challenge on election day. Both in 1890 and 1891, after achieving partial success within the nonpartisan slate, workingmen won other positions—and even secured a

Georgeite tax on unoccupied land—on the strength of their own independent tickets.[75]

The Citizens or nonpartisan approach thus proved an unhappy compromise with the tidy control that the business elite acting through the Republican party had once exercised over local affairs. As early as 1888, J. D. Spellman had ruffled the feathers of the socially homogeneous Republican inner sanctum with whom he was formally cooperating by publicly protesting the exclusion of a Jewish-Republican merchant tailor from the Citizens ticket. By substituting personal popularity and skillful campaigning for party loyalty and social standing, the new system allowed maverick Republicans and ambitious Democrats such unwelcome openings. Republican leaders of the antilabor coalition watched helplessly as their Democratic partners wooed the opposition forces, steadily enlisting them under the banner of the minority party. The growing ties between the Democrats and what was left of the labor movement were apparent in the representation of Vermont's District Assembly 200 at the 1890 Denver Knights' convention by the editor of Rutland's new Democratic *Evening Telegram*. In the same year the *Herald* depracatingly labeled the emerging pattern of electioneering "Spellmanism."[76]

It was not long, therefore, before the same people who had condemned labor's party politics in 1886–87 for having no place in local affairs summoned it to active duty. By 1894, two years after incorporation, the *Herald* had decided that "non-partisan" city government was proving no better than the "old town meeting mobs." "Narrow ward interests," in the *Herald*'s view, were leading irresponsible Citizens representatives toward unnecessary street and sewer construction, pushing up both taxes and municipal debt. "A Republican town," the paper advised, "should have Republican government." Indeed, once oft-repeated elegies to New England town democracy had given way to a growing pessimism about local self-government. The *Herald* argued in 1895 for the appointment of a professional city engineer and the transfer of "elected committee duties" to "executive [appointed] officers." One could not expect government to improve, this line of logic ran, until the "substantial men of the city—the men with real interests at stake" took charge. To protect the city from the vicissitudes of local politics, the Republican party made its own structural changes. The party's city committee tightened local organization in 1895 with the formation of a stable executive leadership and permanent ward committees. In addition, the Republicans prepared to operate closed primaries and asserted the right to remove local delegates who flaunted the city committee's authority.[77]

With the dissolution of the Citizens ticket, a competitive two-party system generally reasserted itself over the young city's government. The Republicans, to be sure, remained the majority party, but they frequently faced a stiff challenge from the revitalized Democrats. Certain areas of the city simply transferred their bloc-voting support from independent labor to Democratic candidates. The same district, for example, which in 1887 elected a United Labor marble worker, J. S. Carder, to the board of selectmen by a vote of 136 to 1 was the single defector in 1904 from Theodore Roosevelt's sweep of the city. An even more direct link was provided in the personage of Thomas H. Brown, the Knights' district master workman; throughout the 1890s he secured nearly automatic claim to the seventh ward's Democratic aldermanic seat.[78]

Labor's political presence after 1888 rested on continuing workplace and community-centered organization. The Rutland Knights remained a town presence well into the 1890s; as late as 1892 four local assemblies—one mixed, one of marble cutters, one of marble polishers, and one Martha Washington women's local—were still active. In 1893 a new Central Trades and Labor Council replaced the Knights as the coordinating unit for the local labor movement. Within the labor council typographers, machinists, iron molders, carpenters, and journeymen barber craft units joined old marble workers Knights' assemblies. While organization in the city's largest industry was obviously not what it had once been, associations of skilled marble cutters were listed sporadically in Rutland directories through 1904.[79]

The Irish-Catholic community remained at the center of working-class social and political life. Two Hibernian societies and the Young Mens' Catholic Union (YMCU) were chartered during the 1890s. The officers of one Hibernian club included a cigar-maker, a mechanic, and a marble polisher. The Central Trades and Labor Council held their regular meetings at the YMCU. In contrast to the local YMCA, which had invited the *Herald*'s owner to refute Henry George's theories in 1888, the YMCU sponsored a debate in 1892 concerning nationalization of the railroads and telegraphs. The union's president in the early 1890s was Democrat Richard Ryan, who as a young clerk had served as secretary of a West Rutland Knights' local and had run on the labor ticket in 1887. From the late 1880s through the 1890s the heavily Irish and French Canadian working-class wards seven and eight proved bastions of both independent labor and Democratic electoral strength. In 1904 the *Herald* referred to the "reputation of Ward 8," which had sent a procession of Irish names to the aldermanic bench, as the city's "most obstreperous ward." In the national elections of that year wards seven and eight provided the largest number of Socialists as well as Democratic votes within the city.[80]

The continuing cleavage in Rutland's political life revealed itself most clearly during the bitter depression winters of 1894 and 1895. With hundreds of marble workers out of work by January 1894, Thomas Brown found many in the seventh ward with "barely the necessaries of life and certainly none of the comforts." The overseer of the poor, James Battle, himself a Knight of Labor, worried that many self-respecting unemployed citizens would refuse to ask for help. These circumstances, the workingmen's representatives insisted, required some modification of the iron laws of the marketplace. Marble worker and Democratic alderman John McGuirk insisted that unemployed millworkers and quarrymen should not have to "raise money on [i.e., mortgage] their little homes." Instead, he proposed city works programs of street grading and landscaping. At a labor council mass meeting Democratic leaders like Spellman and Brown sharply attacked the laissez-faire "Board of Trade attitudes to the unemployed." Huffmire likewise declared it the city's "duty . . . to provide work," and the meeting as a whole resolved that the city "open up to as great an extent as possible public works to . . . worthy laboring men, many of whom have contributed in the years that have gone in building our city up to its present proportions." Labor had gone further than ever before in advocating the positive use of government authority.[81]

The Republican majority on the city council, however, took a different view of the situation. Their attitude was summed up in the *Herald*'s designation of emergency relief measures as "Tammany charity," and of the "friends of the workingmen" who proposed such schemes as "the most pestiferous nuisance in the community." The city administration refused to do more in 1894 than continue the services of seventy-five men who had been on work relief since the summer digging the foundation for a new power station and setting electric light poles. For its part the business elite emphasized private and voluntary means for treating the widespread distress. Hoping to put "every penny where it will do the most good," the *Herald* launched a subscription drive to distribute clothing and soap to needy children. In addition, a special newspaper column appeared calling attention to the number of laborers for hire (e.g., "Pierre Du Bas chips wood"). Meanwhile, the wives of the city's leading businessmen tried to relieve "the present misery and poverty" with a program of their own. The Women's Exchange, a kind of bazaar of female crafts, aimed "not only to lend a helping hand to artists but to any intelligent [women] who are not and never can be artists, but who, when changed circumstances and common sense demand that they shall help themselves, have the wisdom to do what they can do well." Like the soap for the hungry poor, the effort bore the mark of condescension as well as impracticality.[82]

With bitterness on both sides, Rutland workingmen foisted Democratic Mayor Thomas Brown—"that spared monument of the old rounders," as the *Herald* called him—onto an otherwise Republican-controlled government in 1896. Ten years of grappling for political influence had obviously changed the mood among working-class voters. The optimism reflected rhetorically and programatically in 1886–87 had given way to a surly and defensive attitude. Now, it seemed, the working-class constituency mobilized most powerfully around negative issues. It was no coincidence that two referenda—one concerning a $40,000 bond issue for a new high school and the other a five-year tax exemption to a new shirt factory—failed on the same ballot that brought Brown to office. Indeed, bellwether ward eight voted down both resolutions overwhelmingly, 189 to 18 and 175 to 27, respectively. When the workingmen had first came to power in 1886, they had willingly taxed themselves to promote community growth across class lines. American flags had flown over Rutland buildings, proclaiming their faith in a prosperous yet moral order of democratically regulated capitalistic growth. By 1896 such a vision must have appeared a youthful fantasy. The Rutland workers did not have to look to Pullman or Homestead for lessons. The most minor tools of decision-making had been wrenched from their control as if it were not a revised grand list, public works, or even union organization they had been dealing with but dynamite. Now it was a reeducated local elite that had assumed the responsibility for public planning. In response, the workingmen seem to have edged into a mood of general resistance to governmental initiatives for which they could not see an immediate return.[83]

In their own way Republican city fathers matched the workingmen's stubbornness, reacting to a Democrat in power just as they had to out-and-out labor officials. Mayor Brown, who had promised to clean out corruption from the street departments and other city agencies, found himself frustrated at every turn. His appointments were blocked, and government was at a near standstill. Halfway through Brown's term, the banker Percival W. Clement, head of the city's Board of Trade, warned that the Howe Scale Company might leave town unless business confidence were quickly restored. In the same breath he declared his willingness to succeed the mayor. Brown responded immediately by stepping down from office, explaining simply that the opposition could not manage "a Republican town." No opposition confronted mayoral candidate Clement in the 1897 special election.[84]

In the end labor's political breakthrough in Rutland facilitated a degree of mobility for some individuals but resulted in ambivalent consequences for local workers as a whole. Unquestionably, the workingmen's movement had successfully opened the political process to those of nonelite background; henceforth, the legitimacy of an Irish, French-Canadian, or marble worker seeking office would never again provoke the questions it had in 1886–87. Indeed, identification with the laboring classes might well prove a valuable political asset. At the same time the consequences of such openings, as noted by David Montgomery, must be considered: "The capacity of America's political structure to absorb talent from the working classes was perhaps the most effective deterrent to the maturing of a revolutionary class-consciousness among the nation's workers during the turbulent social conflicts of the late nineteenth century. The ability of working-class leaders to attain at least personal political success through the medium of the two major parties certainly militated against the successful development of a definite Labor party and kept the labor parties that frequently did appear distinctly local in scope."[85]

A select few within labor's high command in Rutland did achieve a degree of social success and assimilation, despite the collapse of the movement in which they first gained prominence. What is more, their very success coincided with an apparent moderation in their political views or at least a modification of their relation to the rank-and-file worker. James J. Fay, for example, master workman, United Labor village president in 1887, and United Workingmen village auditor in 1891, was reelected city auditor in 1895 with bipartisan support. E. B. Moore even more explicitly made his peace with the city's orthodox businessmen. By 1895, having advanced from his father's stove company into a real estate business of his own, he was elected to a year's tenure as president of the city's Board of Trade, succeeding Clement. When workers castigated "Board of Trade attitudes" about unemployment during the depression, they may well have remembered the moderator of the first labor town meeting with a touch of bitterness.[86]

In his case, Moore need not necessarily have abandoned his old beliefs. He may simply have followed a strict construction of Georgeite principles toward a more business-minded progressivism. In 1888, for example, Moore had opposed a bill that would have made mortgagers (banks and insurance companies) share in the taxes on mortgaged property with mortgagees. Moore saw his stand as consistent with the single-tax idea and feared that the proposed legislation would drive investment money out of the state. Taking the opposite position, the *Herald* strangely enough wound up defending "justice in taxation first" and accusing Moore of insensitivity to the plight of the state's farmers and small property owners. Moore placed complete faith in industrial expansion and multiplying productivity. For him, the single-tax theory served primarily to point the way to free-market prosperity. It was therefore not surprising that when workingmen voted down resolutions for industrial tax exemptions and a new high school in 1896, Moore found himself lined up on the other side.[87]

Brown offers an even more dramatic example of how the labor movement might function as an agent of sociopolitical mobility. The young labor politician always showed a zest for the intricacies of government. By 1892 he had combined his natural eloquence with a commanding experience of local affairs. In a single town meeting, for example, he directed the passage of five resolutions ranging from building a footbridge over a set of railroad tracks to a $100 appropriation for a Memorial Day demonstration to an increased wage and nine-hour day for municipal workers. While remaining an effective and popular legislator in the 1890s, Brown had moved some distance from his roots. As assistant to General Kingsley in the auditor's office in 1887, Brown learned new skills and perhaps new ambitions. The marble polisher of 1887 became a clerk in a provision store in 1891. Following his unnaturally shortened mayoral term, the "last of the old rounders" again improved himself. After studying law with the Catholic attorney P. M. Meldon, Brown joined both the bar and the Elks Club in 1899. Appointed Chinese inspector in the

Treasury Department under both Presidents Cleveland and William McKinley, he might have communed once more with Powderly, who was commissioner-general of immigration from 1897 to 1902. Brown undertook another prestigious assignment as Democrat national committeeman in 1908.[88]

The Encyclopedia of Vermont Biography (1912) says nothing of Brown's early labor and political experience. Did the omission reflect the subject's own preferences? A tone of moderation had already crept into Brown's once-impassioned oratory by the early 1890s. Supporting demands for public work at an 1894 meeting, Brown counseled the firebrands in the audience that it was "not fair" to blame city government for the problem. "It was easy to say that the city government ought to furnish employment for all the men, but it was another matter to do it."[89]

Finally, there was even the possibility that the road to respectability was paved with an extra "e." From the early 1880s through the mid-1890s, an extensive written record consistently lists the man's name as Thomas H. *Brown*. Suddenly, just before the mayoral campaign of 1896, his name became *Browne* without explanation. Indeed, the city directory of 1901–2 lists the address of the attorney T. H. *Browne* alongside that of his mother, Mrs. Henry *Brown*. Perhaps no one bothered with exact spelling of this working-man's name until he became a well-established figure. But perhaps he did not bother about it either until rising social status encouraged him to emphasize the neglected spelling of his proper name or maybe even to make his name more "proper."[90]

From the experiences of Brown and Moore one might well conclude that politics had indeed better served the "friends of the workingmen" in Rutland than it had the workers themselves. But a "politics corrupts" generalization does not altogether fit the Rutland events either. Like the stable functioning of the two-party system itself, the breaking away of the labor leadership from its original constituency occurred only in the aftermath of the weakness and disintegration of the labor movement. To be sure, it might be argued that the workers squandered a precious resource by fixing the attention of men like Brown and Fay on the electoral process in the first place to the possible neglect of workplace agitation. The facts, however, warrant equally as well another conclusion. This is that political power provided the Rutland labor movement with an added life, including influence, unity, and community sustenance, that might otherwise have been snuffed out entirely amidst a trade depression and employer hostility. From this latter perspective the moves toward public power and planning by Rutland workingmen appear as much the apex as the anticlimax of the Gilded Age labor movement.

Political structures in Rutland had changed dramatically over the course of a decade. Labor's 1886 assault had begun by destroying the cozy, nonpartisan self-selection process among the town's best men and replacing it with two opposing political formations, each of which saw itself outside of or above the bounds of partisanship. Ironically, the period of social polarization had ended in the institutionalization of the two-party system in local affairs. The change also roughly coincided with the dissolution of town-meeting democracy into the representative structures of city government. If one looked only at the before (say 1885) and after (say 1895), Rutland might indeed seem to fit conventional expectations of political modernization and progressive municipal development. Such a view, however, by attending only to external benchmarks and neglecting the impact of popular organization and working-class mobilization would miss the substance of what had happened in Rutland and why. In this sense Rutland's modernization was a by-product of the larger contest shaking the town and much of the rest of the nation over the exercise of private power and public authority. Two-party competition, in particular, became the norm of local politics only after and as a result of the storm that had preceded it.

Even the establishment of active two-party pluralism did not entirely foreclose the option of independent workingmen's politics. In 1904, when Republicans withdrew from yet another Citizens coalition formed during renewed unrest by marble workers, J. S. Carder won the mayoralty on an independent labor slate. The city's first official labor mayor was a marble cutter and union leader who had first served as selectman during the Knights' heyday seventeen years before.[91]

NOTES

1. F. E. Davison, *Historical Rutland: An Illustrated History of Rutland, Vermont, from the Granting of the Charter in 1761 to 1911* (Rutland, 1911), 4.

2. H. P. Smith and W. S. Rann, eds., *History of Rutland County, Vermont* (Syracuse, N.Y., 1886), 170; WPA Federal Writers' Project, *Vermont, a Guide to the Green Mountain State* (Cambridge, Mass., 1937), 127–29; Dorman B. E. Kent, *One Thousand Men* (Montpelier, 1915), 12–13; Vermontville, Michigan, a colony of Rutland County emigres, provided a testament to the general exodus from the state's inland agricultural districts. Page Smith, *As a City upon a Hill: The Town in American History* (New York, 1966), 113.

3. Smith and Rann, eds., *Rutland County*, 158–59, 161–62; Edward Chase Kirkland, *Men, Cities, and Transportation: A Study in New England History, 1820–1900*, 2 vols. (Cambridge, Mass., 1948), I, 166–67, 229–30, 339, 346; Jim Shaughnessy, *The Rutland Road* (Berkeley, 1964), 358, 471. The panic of 1893 forced even the Vermont Central line into receivership, and it was not until the twentieth century that the Clement family plucked the railroad from the neglect of the New York financiers and restored it to prosperity.

4. Davison, *Historical Rutland*, 20–26, 41–42; Edward Love Temple, "Old Rutland—Sidelights on Her Honorable and Notable Story, 1761–1922" (no

date), 34–53, Local Archives, New York Public Library; *Vermont Historical Gazetteer*, III, pt. 2 (Claremont, N.H., 1877), 1036; U.S. Tenth Census, 1880, *Statistics of the Population*, 1 (Washington, D.C., 1883), 355; Federal Writers Project, *Vermont*, 127, 129; Smith and Rann, eds., *Rutland County*, 161–62.

5. *Rutland County Gazetteer and Business Directory, 1881–1882* (Syracuse, N.Y., 1881); U.S. Tenth Census, 1880, *Report on the Building Stones of the U.S. and Statistics of the Quarry Industry*, X (Washington, D.C., 1885), 109–11. The population of Center Rutland was negligible at the time of the census.

6. *Ibid.*, 35–36; Smith and Rann, eds., *Rutland County*, 190; Frank C. Partridge, "The Vermont Marble Company, Its Past and Future," address at a general conference in Proctor, Vt., Dec. 28–31, 1920; Walter H. Crockett, *Vermont, the Green Mountain State*, 5 vols. (New York, 1921), IV, 98–99; Paul A. Gopaul, "A History of the Vermont Marble Company," 42, 47, manuscript at St. Michael's College, Winooski, Vt., 1954. The Wardwell channeler, running on a portable track, replaced the more tedious method of cutting into the stone with chisel and wedge.

7. Crockett, *Vermont*, 96–97, 262–68, 388; Duane Lockard, *New England State Politics* (Chicago, 1959), 12–18.

8. Jacob G. Ullery, *Men of Vermont: An Illustrated Biographical History of Vermonters and Sons of Vermont* (Brattleboro, 1894), xi; Crockett, *Vermont*, 100, 131–34; Proctor's private correspondence revealed a man obsessed with power and business achievement. Depressed by the stagnation of the Producers Company in 1885, he confessed to a woman stockholder: "If I was not in the marble business I should not go into it now nor invest in it, but I am in it all over and know nothing else and can do nothing else. . . . It is an old proverb that money is power. [We] . . . reversed this and thought power would be money and it proved so. We developed and gave our neighbors such forcible competition that we made ourselves and our business felt in the marble business. We worked for that more than we did for mere profit. . . . The Rutland Marble Co. put their business in our hands because they felt our power and that gave us greater success and profit than we could have got by the conservative course others might have taken." Proctor to Mary H. Myers, Dec. 21, 1885, Proctor Family Papers, Proctor Free Library, Proctor, Vt.

9. Hiram Carleton, *Genealogical and Family History of the State of Vermont* (New York, 1903), 406–7; Smith and Rann, eds., *Rutland County*, 321–23, 894–95, 916–18, 220–21; *Book of Biographies, Biographical Sketches of Leading Citizens of Rutland County, Vermont* (Buffalo, N.Y., 1899), 113–15; Temple, "Old Rutland"; Rutland *Herald*, Nov. 30, 1900.

10. The religious and associational ties of the elite were drawn from previously cited local histories and city directories, 1884–85, 1889–90, at the New York Public Library; Rutland *Herald*, Mar. 3, 1884, Feb. 26, Aug. 20, 1886; Davison, *Historical Rutland*, 55; Carleton, *Genealogical and Family History*, 46–47, 406–7; *Dictionary of American Biography*, V: 381–83, XV: 245–46.

11. Temple, "Old Rutland"; Davison, *Historical Rutland,* 45–47; *Book of Biographies,* 51–53; Smith and Rann, eds., *Rutland County,* 907, 912–13, 925–26; Rutland city directories.

12. Rutland *Herald,* Jan. 29, Feb. 5, 22, 1886; Davison, *Historical Rutland,* 68. Through the spreading mandate of domestic morality and child welfare, women in this period were gradually enlarging their arena of public activities from benefit fairs and suppers, as well as their own "Fort-nightly's" and Chautauqua circles, to involvement in the temperance question, public instruction, and poor relief. This process was not without its tensions. In Rutland, for example, a controversy arose around the propriety of women who had gotten the library project started by serving as official library commissioners. The marble merchant J. C. Barrett urged caution in the matter of female responsibility. A man might want to contribute $5,000 or $10,000 to the library but not want "to leave it with a lot of silly women." On the significance of a library in local development, see Michael H. Frisch, *Town into City: Springfield, Massachusetts, and the Meaning of Community, 1840–1880* (Cambridge, Mass., 1972), 93.

13. Carleton, *Genealogical and Family History,* 685; Smith and Rann, eds., *Rutland County,* 389–92; Crockett, *Vermont,* 166–67.

14. Rutland *Herald,* Mar. 4, 1880, Mar. 6, 1884, Feb. 24, 1886; Carleton, *Genealogical and Family History,* 684–85.

15. Andrew E. and Edith W. Nuquist, *Vermont State Government and Administration* (Burlington, 1966), 13, 55–56; Smith and Rann, eds., *Rutland County,* 907–8. Regarding the dominance of the Republican party, see John D. Buenker, "The Politics of Resistance: The Rural-Based Yankee Republican Machines of Connecticut and Rhode Island," *New England Quarterly,* 47 (1974), 212–37.

16. Rutland *Herald,* Mar. 4, 1880, Mar. 5, 1881, Mar. 6, 1884, Feb. 24, 1886. A list compiled in 1886 of thirty-two citizens who had served one or two terms as village trustee included seven capitalists, three professionals, two building contractors, five clerks, one farmer, two supervisors, and six skilled workers. The last category included two masons, two blacksmiths–carriage makers, one carpenter, and one cooper. In addition, William B. Thrall, a former president of the Brotherhood of Locomotive Engineers, had been elected four times to the position. The distribution of servant-hiring households, derived from the 1880 manuscript census, paralleled that of Rochester's, with one exception. Where one servant represented a conspicuous sign of wealth in the smaller New Hampshire town, Rutland displayed more of a hierarchy in this area. The banker, Baxter, for example, set the pace with seven servants, plus a hostler and gardener. He was followed by John B. Page with four servants. Redfield Proctor kept three servants (one Irish, one French-Canadian, one native-American); so did other marble men like William Ripley, Charles Woodfin, and Charles Clement. Two domestics still suggested a handsome staff; in this category fell Charles Sheldon, foundry owner Joel Harris, and Judge Dunton, as well as real estate agents, contractors, lawyers, merchants, and even a well-regarded clergyman. Professional men, prospering merchants, some clerks, and the cream of the skilled work-

ing class seemed capable of procuring the services of at least one fellow townsperson, most often a girl of Irish or French-Canadian extraction. The distribution pattern of home labor-saving devices, which had made some impression on Rutland by the late 1880s, followed that of personal service. An 1890 advertisement for Hamer's "Perfect Washer" listed forty-two Rutland homes making use of the new consumer product. The breadwinners of these families included seven capitalists, seven professionals, fourteen shopkeepers, eight farmers, and three workers (a railroad conductor, a machinist, and a scale maker). The argument is that the correspondence in class base of the citizens who could relieve their wives of menial household labor with the town governors suggests a conscious feeling among these people of their relative "respectability" and "worthiness."

17. Rutland *Herald,* Mar. 3, 1880; Thomas H. Brown to Terence Powderly, June 20, 1887, Terence V. Powderly Papers, Catholic University, Washington, D.C.; Town of West Rutland, Annual Report, 1888, West Rutland Town Hall. The poll tax was equivalent to the sum of local rates. Appleton's *Annual Cyclopaedia, 1881* ([New York, 1882], 863) refers to a prevailing state poll tax of two dollars; Andrew E. Nuquist, *Town Government in Vermont* (Burlington, 1964), 54. See Alan Dawley, *Class and Community: The Industrial Revolution in Lynn* (Cambridge, Mass., 1976), 167–72, for a description of living standards of workers.

18. Patrick T. Hannon, *Biography of St. Bridget's Parish, West Rutland, Vermont* (West Rutland Free Library, n.d.), 38, 41–42; Rutland *Herald,* Mar. 3, 1880.

19. Charles Francis Adams, *Three Episodes of Massachusetts History,* 2 vols. (Cambridge, Mass., 1892), II, 957–58.

20. Rutland *Herald,* Feb. 11, 22, 1886, Nov. 5, 1888.

21. *Poverty and Progress: Social Mobility in a Nineteenth Century City* (New York, 1970), 80–114. The occupational comparisons of first- and second-generation Americans are based on calculations from the manuscript census of 1880.

22. *John Swinton's Paper* (hereafter *JSP*), Sept. 26, 1886; Rutland *Herald,* Sept. 8, 1886.

23. Rutland *Herald,* Jan. 29, 1886.

24. Brown to Powderly, June 20, 1887, Powderly Papers; Rutland *Herald,* Jan. 29, Oct. 22, 1886, May 26, 1887. Four mixed assemblies of the Knights took shape in Rutland in 1886, and six others were chartered in other parts of the county during 1886–87. Jonathan Garlock and N. C. Builder, "Knights of Labor Data Bank: Users Manual and Index to Local Assemblies" (1973), manuscript at the University of Rochester, Rochester, N.Y.

25. Henry George to "Bigelow," June 10, 1881, Fay to George, Jan. 31, 1883, Orcutt to George, Feb. 11, 1883, Henry George Papers, New York Public Library; Rutland *Herald,* Mar. 21, 1887.

26. Hannon, *Biography of St. Bridget's,* 70–80, 140–41; Rutland *Herald,* Oct. 22, 1886; Brown to Powderly, June 20, 1887, Powderly Papers; Garlock and Builder, "Knights of Labor Data Bank." Robert H. Wiebe thoughtfully noted that the Irish Knights of Labor "behaved as if their organizations were

a personal plea for recognition." *The Search for Order, 1877–1920* (New York, 1967), 68.

27. Rutland *Herald,* Apr. 23, 30, May 1, Aug. 25, 1886. As the Knights moved into the open, their meetings were announced by simple, coded etchings on pavements all over town. The symbol 4 | 30
| 8X
| 5160 indicated a meeting
of L.A. 5160 on Apr. 30 at 8 P.M.

28. *Ibid.,* Sept. 8, 15, Nov. 23, Dec. 1, 1886; Proctor to Ripley, July 13, 1886, to Emil Oelbermann, Jan. 1, 1887, Proctor Family Papers. Proctor may have been poor-mouthing the company *in extremis* to justify to stockholders a decrease in dividends. Still, he had reasons to be worried. Whether there were many businessmen besides Proctor who had accepted the Marxist notion of the falling rate of profit is an interesting question in itself. Rutland *Herald,* Feb. 25, 1887; Hannon, *Biography of St. Bridget's,* 70–80.

29. Rutland *Herald,* Jan. 2, 29, 1886.

30. *Ibid.,* Jan. 5, 27, 1886.

31. *Ibid.,* Feb. 3, Apr. 17, 1886.

32. *Ibid.,* Apr. 17, 29, June 9, 10, 1886.

33. Unlike the situation in Rochester, New Hampshire, Rutland appears to have been relatively uninfluenced by Greenback-Laborism as an organized movement. Although the National (Greenback) party elected eight representatives to the 1878 Vermont state legislature and fielded Greenback candidates through 1882, there is no sign that Rutlanders ever took a prominent part in its proceedings. Indeed, the 1882 Greenback gubernatorial candidate received only one vote from Rutland. This is not to say that Greenbackism as an ideology had no local influence. The Greenback-Labor party of 1880 was the first in Vermont to raise the issue of equal taxes and the just administration of the grand list of property valuations, which became rallying points for Rutland United Labor and United Workingmen campaigns in later years. "Vermont," *Appleton's Annual Cyclopaedia, 1878, 1880, 1882, 1884;* Rutland *Herald,* Sept. 6, 1882.

34. Rutland *Herald,* Aug. 27, 1886.

35. *Ibid.*

36. *Ibid.,* Aug. 27, Sept. 6, Oct. 6, 1886.

37. *Ibid.,* Aug. 27, Sept. 2, 1886. Within certain contemporary circles, "white" and "colored" seem to have taken on meanings that did not imply strict racial referrents so much as "us" and "them." Proctor, for example, wrote to a stockholder in Washington, D.C., as follows: "You were a good, faithful man, and a pretty good fellow anyway, a good Republican and a white man and have shown your good will in many ways." To Henry W. Taylor, Mar. 26, 1886, Proctor Family Papers.

38. Rutland *Herald,* Sept. 3, 1886.

39. *Ibid.*

40. Proctor to William P. Dillingham, Sept. 14, 1886, Proctor Family Papers; Rutland *Herald,* Nov. 1, 3, 1886; "Division of Rutland, Argument of

Remonstrators before Committee in Representatives Hall, November 9, 1886," Proctoriana Collection, Vermont State Library, Montpelier.

41. Proctor to Dillingham, Sept. 14, 1886, Proctor Family Papers; Rutland *Herald,* Nov. 4, 1886; Burlington *Free Press,* Oct. 22, 1886. "Don't fail me this last time," the ex-governor wrote to E. H. Ripley, in summoning him to testify for the division forces. Nov. 15, 1886, Proctor Family Papers.

42. Rutland *Herald,* Oct. 23, 29, 30, 1886.

43. *Ibid.,* Oct. 15, 23, Nov. 2, 1886; Burlington *Free Press,* Nov. 17, 1886.

44. Rutland *Herald,* Nov. 20, 1886; Burlington *Free Press,* Nov. 20, 1886. The workingmen's representative must have struck the state legislators as only marginally more responsible than his constituents. Taking the floor for the first time in the assembly, Hogan tried to turn a discussion of a technical amendment to the division bill to the question of a referendum of all Rutland citizens on the subject. He was quickly reprimanded for being out of order. *Herald,* Nov. 17, 1886.

45. *JSP,* Dec. 5, 1886.

46. "Division of Rutland"; *JSP,* Dec. 5, 1886; Rutland *Herald,* Nov. 20, Dec. 3, 7, 10 (letter from Dr. John Crowley), 1886.

47. Rutland *Herald,* Mar. 2, 1887.

48. David C. Gale, *Proctor, the Story of a Marble Town* (Brattleboro, 1922), 213; Proctor to Elizabeth H. Arnot, Dec. 24, 1888, to Emil Oelbermann, Jan. 1, 1887, to Francis B. Riggs, Jan. 5, 1887, to The Cunard Line, Nov. 15, 1887, to F. R. Brainerd, July 8, 1887, to Rev. J. C. McLaughlin, Mar. 12, 1886, Proctor Family Papers; Crockett, *Vermont,* IV, 394–95.

49. Rutland *Herald,* Oct. 23, 1886, Mar. 2, Nov. 18, 1887, Mar. 29, 1888.

50. Minutes of the Selectmen, Oct. 22, Nov. 1, 1887, West Rutland town archives; Rutland *Herald,* Feb. 28, 1887.

51. Rutland *Herald,* Feb. 28, 1887; Annual Reports of the Board of Officers, Feb. 19, 1890, West Rutland town archives; Rutland *Herald,* Oct. 22, 1886, Nov. 7, 1888.

52. Brown to Powderly, June 20, 1887, Powderly Papers.

53. Postdivision Rutland retained sections of the Vermont Marble Company, a few smaller marble concerns, the Howe Scale Company, several foundries and machine shops, wood-working establishments, two shirt factories, railroad shops, print shops, and binderies. By 1890 Rutland town's population stood at 11,760 compared to West Rutland (3,680), Proctor, (1,758), and the village of Rutland Center (786).

54. Rutland *Herald,* Mar. 1, 2, 19, July 29, 1887.

55. *Ibid.,* Mar. 2, 1887. The men's ages were figured from the manuscript census of 1880.

56. Rutland *Herald,* Mar. 30, May 5, 1887.

57. Based on calculations from the manuscript census of 1880.

58. Rutland *Herald,* Mar. 1, 1887.

59. *Ibid.* A candidate for selectman explained labor's economic logic: "[It] has sometimes been argued by capitalists that a public debt is a public bless-

ing. This may be true so far as the money lender is concerned, but is not true as to the poor man, or to one whose property is in real estate" (*ibid.*, Feb. 26, 1887).

60. *Ibid.*, Mar. 2, 1887. The standard grand list rate was 1 percent of assessed valuation or $10 tax on $1,000 valuation. Labor's interest in education was also manifest at the Fair Haven town meeting, where workingmen initiated a $1 library tax.

61. *Ibid.*, Mar. 2, 10, 1887, Feb. 24, Oct. 26, 1888. "RCT," who lashed out at labor's plans for the schools, may well have been a rural citizen to whom all the foreign-born were "Italians"; the workingmen's emphasis on centralized schooling, it might be noted, contrasts with the image of popular opposition to reform pictured in Michael B. Katz, *The Irony of Early School Reform* (Boston, 1968), esp. 19–115. Opposition to high schools, upon which Katz concentrates, may have been a special case, an exception (see later in this chapter) to the embrace by organized labor of educational rationalization.

62. Rutland *Herald*, Mar. 21, Apr. 4, 1887.

63. *Ibid.*, Mar. 31, 1887. The issue of street paving divided labor's supporters. Some protested that pedestrian sidewalks be given priority over the commercial thoroughfares. *Ibid.*, Feb. 6, 7, 1888.

64. *Ibid.*, Apr. 5, 6, 8, May 17, 19, 1887.

65. *Ibid.*, Jan. 6, Feb. 2, Apr. 13, 1886, Mar. 7, 1888. On the Salvation Army in New England, see Edmund M. Gagey, "General Booth with His Big Bass Drum Enters into Haverhill, Massachusetts," *New England Quarterly*, 45 (1972), 508–25; Rutland *Herald*, Nov. 10, Dec. 16, 1887; Town of West Rutland, *Annual Report*, 1888.

66. Rutland *Herald*, Apr. 21, July 5, 1887, Mar. 7, 1888.

67. *Ibid.*, Oct. 22, 1886, Apr. 5, Sept. 20, Nov. 23, 1887, Jan. 18, 1894. Cf. David J. Pivar, *Purity Crusade: Sexual Morality and Social Control, 1868–1900* (Westport, Conn., 1973).

68. Rutland *Herald*, July 25, 1887.

69. *Ibid.*, Feb. 26, Mar. 1, 1887.

70. *Ibid.*, Feb. 26, 1887.

71. *Ibid.*, Feb. 6, Mar. 2, 6, 9, 1888.

72. *Ibid.*, Mar. 3, 7, 8, 1888.

73. Brown to Powderly, June 20, 1887, Powderly Papers; Rutland *Herald*, Apr. 26, 1887. That Brown's pessimistic report came one month after machine helpers and other workers had walked out on strike at two small quarries suggests that the strikes quickly collapsed in failure (there were no follow-up reports) and discouraged other marble workers. *Ibid.*, May 6, 1887. Rutland attorney Joel Baker counted the "Ryegate Conspiracy Case" as one of his most notable performances before the bar. Carleton, *Genealogical and Family History*, 685. See also *Granite Cutters Journal*, May-July 1886.

74. Rutland *Herald*, Mar. 29, 30, 1888. On Citizens' tickets see, e.g., Zane L. Miller, *Boss Cox's Cincinnati: Urban Politics in the Progressive Era* (New York, 1968), 88–89; Michael J. Cassity, "Modernization and Social Crisis: The Knights of Labor and a Midwest Community, 1885–1886," *Journal of American History*, 66 (June 1979), 57; Cliff Kuhn, " 'Democratic

Confusion': Working-Class Politics in 1880s Atlanta" (1980), manuscript at the University of North Carolina at Chapel Hill.

75. Rutland *Herald,* Mar. 27, 1888, Mar. 3, 4, 1890, Mar. 13, 1891.

76. *Ibid.,* Mar. 27, 1888, Mar. 3, 1890; Knights of Labor, "Proceedings of the General Assembly, 1890," Powderly Papers.

77. Rutland, *Herald,* Jan. 23, 1894, Jan. 29, 30, 1895.

78. *Ibid.,* Jan. 21, 1888, Mar. 14, 1892, Mar. 2, Nov. 9, 1904.

79. City directories, 1891–1904; Garlock and Builder, "Knights of Labor Data Bank"; R. S. Ryan to John W. Hayes, June 17, 1892, Patrick Gallagher to Hayes, Nov. 28, 1892, John W. Hayes Papers, Catholic University, Washington, D.C. Gallagher pleaded for a Swedish-English organizer to relieve a "very poor condition" of organization in West Rutland.

80. City directories, 1891–1904; Rutland *Herald,* Jan. 21, 1888, Mar. 14, 1892, Mar. 2, Nov. 9, 1904. The Proctor YMCA, dedicated in 1909, was built by the Vermont Marble Company. At the opening ceremonies Senator Proctor expressed the hope that this organization that included employers, foremen, office men, and laborers and "all races, classes, and creeds . . . will help to solve the labor problem . . . will insure a better quality of work . . . and will be a perpetual reminder of the concern of this Company for the moral and physical well-being of its employees" (Gale, *Proctor,* 219). A clue to the social character of contiguous wards seven and eight, separated from the rest of the city by the railroad yards and depot, was suggested by the location there of St. Peter's Catholic Church, parish, and convent house, and both the Irish-Catholic and French-Catholic cemeteries. Map of Rutland, Tuttle Company, 1889–90, New York Public Library.

81. Rutland *Herald,* Jan. 5, 17, 1894.

82. *Ibid.,* Jan. 3, 17, 18, 1894, Feb. 7, 1895.

83. *Ibid.,* Mar. 4, 1896.

84. *Ibid.,* Feb. 19, 1896, Feb. 10, 15, Mar. 3, 1897.

85. David Montgomery, *Beyond Equality: Labor and the Radical Republicans, 1862–1872* (New York, 1967), 215.

86. City directories, 1884–96; Rutland *Herald,* Mar. 3, 1891, Mar. 6, 1895.

87. Rutland, *Herald,* Oct. 22, 1888, Mar. 2, 1896.

88. *Ibid.,* Mar. 2, 1892.

89. *Ibid.,* Jan. 17, 1894.

90. City directories, 1884–1904; Knights of Labor, "Proceedings of the General Assembly, 1887," Powderly Papers; Rutland *Herald,* 1886–96.

91. Rutland *Herald,* Feb.-Apr. 1904.

5

City-Building and Social Reform:
Urban Workers within the Two-Party System, Kansas City, Kansas

TWELVE HUNDRED MILES from the disturbances overtaking New England town government, labor's Great Upheaval possessed an equal fury. The railroad strikes of the mid-1880s, highlighted by the Great Southwest Strike of 1886 against Jay Gould's Union Pacific empire, shook the entire social order of the trans-Mississippi West. While adding impetus to a growing agrarian rebellion against monopoly control of the marketplace, the railway conflicts had an even more immediate political effect on the urban terminals through which the trains passed. In addition to places like Ft. Worth and St. Louis, Kansas City, Kansas, was one city so affected. Here, as elsewhere, the powerful combination of workers represented by the Knights of Labor led to more than simply economic contests. In Kansas City, the path of municipal progress became obstructed by a fierce debate over the very definition of progress and the question of whose interests it would serve.

Exploring the conflict that occurred at Kansas City requires reference to the larger statewide political tapestry, to which the local events both contributed and responded. Since the bloody 1850s, the state of Kansas had served as one of the nation's most sensitive barometers of social and political conflict. The active presence within the state in the 1880s of Greenbackers, Grangers, prohibitionists, women's rights activists, Alliancemen, and Knights of Labor testified to a continuing social turbulence. Indeed, by 1890 Kansas activists would be leading the country's radical political forces toward a third-party Populist crusade. In this sense the Great Southwest Strike, along with its immediate local ramifications, may properly be seen as part of a larger, evolving political storm.

It is equally important, however, to note that urban labor politics even in Kansas City operated at some remove from the general contemporary evolution of western political radicalism. Unlike the venerable traditions of town meeting, politics in the Middle Border cities were, by the early 1880s, a rough-and-tumble mixture of interests fueled by feverish commercial speculation. In Kansas City not only did the two major parties compete vigorously for working-class votes at election time, but also professional politicians had already erected the semblance of urban political machines. It is not surprising, therefore, that labor reform politics in Kansas City took root within the two-party system, specifically through the aegis of the Republican administration of Mayor Thomas Hannan (1886–89). This penetration of local political power in the 1880s, moreover, seems to have been among the factors that detracted from rather than enhanced the appeal of the People's party to urban workers in the 1890s. The resistance of urban wage earners to the great third-party movement rising around them offers a unique perspective on the complicated mosaic of American politics near the end of the century.

For years businessmen on the Kansas side of the Missouri and Kansas rivers had struggled to emerge from the shadow of their counterparts in Missouri. In early spring 1886 the Kansas state legislature rewarded them by consolidating three neighboring Wyandotte County settlements—Wyandotte (population 12,086), Kansas City (3,806), and Armourdale (1,582)—into a new city called Kansas City. A catastrophe for the post office, and a disappointment to many who preferred the old Indian name, the new creation survived initial abuse and by 1890 surpassed Topeka and Leavenworth to become the state's largest city.[1]

Although its history stretched back scarcely forty years, the consolidated city of the mid-1880s retained only a trace of the influence of a remarkable group of original colonizers. Led by Silas Armstrong, several hundred Wyandot Indians, descendants of the Iroquois nation and the last tribe driven from Ohio, settled in Kansas in 1843 in an area traversed by John C. Fremont and Kit Carson only a year before. While retaining their own language and group cohesiveness, the Wyandots had substantially assimilated through intermarriage and cultural adaptation to Euro-American society. Through real estate acquisitions and control of the ferry to Westport Landing, Missouri, Wyandot merchants like Joel Walker and Mathias Splitlog became quite wealthy. Assuming the leadership of the Northwestern Confederacy of Indian tribes, the Wyandots also played a key role in the economic and political development of the Kansas territory. In collaboration with Pacific railroad interests, William Walker, a "mostly white" Wyandot and outspoken antislavery advocate, was elected "provisional" territorial governor by a rump convention of Indians in 1853. Indeed, apprehension at Indian initiatives by southern proslavery forces in Leavenworth and across the border in Kansas City, Missouri, helped to spur passage of the Kansas-Nebraska Act of 1854. Under a revised 1855 treaty most of the Wyandots sold their land and relocated to the Indian Territory. By 1859 when the county of Wyandotte was organized, the old Indian village had grown to a population of over 1,000. Armstrong and Splitlog avenues would continue to evoke the town's pioneer days. Another prominent reminder of the town's Indian roots was Russell D. Armstrong, wealthy publisher of the conservative Republican Wyandotte *Gazette* and a descendant of Silas. When it suited them, the *Gazette*'s political opponents recalled the publisher's heritage, smearing him, for example, with the "rape of innocent women" by "his brethren, the Cheyennes and Arapahoes."[2]

Kansas City's critical years of growth owed less to its own initiatives than to spillover effects from the spreading regional metropolis across the state line. Through a combination of corporate intrigue and political maneuvering, Kansas City, Missouri, in 1867 beat more populous rivals like Leavenworth and Atchison in laying the first bridge across the Missouri River and thereby assured itself of a key position on the Union Pacific's Central Line. From a wartime low of 3,500 people, the tide of settlement rode expectations of economic boom as Kansas City emerged as a major reshipment point for southwestern Texas cattle. When Chicago's Armour meatpacking company decided in that year to extend operations southward, a major new local industry was inaugurated. Within a decade it doubled the capital investment of any other local industry. Not until the depression and the Rocky Mountain locusts arrived together in 1873 did growth slacken in Kansas City, Missouri. The lull was only temporary, and by the 1880s the area witnessed renewed urban expansion and booming land sales. Population of the "young, western giant" climbed to 130,000 by 1890.[3]

The same events that proved the undoing of larger Kansas towns along the Missouri River provided a new spark of life to the old settlement of pioneer Indians and western traders at the mouth of the Kansas River. The orientation of Kansas City, Missouri, to its western hinterland and railroad connections, together with Kansas's cheap real estate and low taxation, gradually induced city industry to cross the state line. A tiny triangle wedged among the Kansas River, the Missouri state line, and Kansas City stock yards, the old town of Kansas City, Kansas, was given over to warehouses, workers' tenements, and low-life entertainment. Peering down on old Kansas City from the bluffs on the other side of the Kaw (as the Kansas River was known) stood the town of Wyandotte, a residential center with small, diversified industry that served as the primary escape route from Missouri's appreciating land values. Local interests boasted in 1879 that "Wyandotte promises to be to Kansas City what Brooklyn is to New York." With total confidence Wyandotte contracted for the nation's first intraurban street railroad in 1883, with construction to begin in 1886. By the early 1880s, Wyandotte had also annexed the bordering southern hamlet of Armstrong, which housed the Union Pacific shops. South of Armstrong lay the complex of stock yards, packinghouses, and railroad connections known as Armourdale, where Armour and Company alone employed 1,900 workers. Finally, a few miles upstream on the Kaw, the town of Argentine had sprouted around the shops of the Atchison, Topeka, and Sante Fe. A smelting and refining works there produced nearly a fifth of the country's silver and lead. By 1885 these industrial concentrations made Wyandotte County by far the densest county in the state with less than 20 percent of its population still employed in agriculture.[4]

It was not only the economic character of Kansas City, Kansas, which distinguished it from the state's largely rural, native-American communities. There were probably few more socially heterogeneous places in America than this industrial city on the edge of the prairie. The demand for skilled craftsmen, semiskilled operatives, and menial day laborers for the varied enterprises of the young city brought a steady stream of German, Irish, and later Afro-American recruits. By 1880 less than half of the adult male working population in the three towns that would form Kansas City, Kansas, derived from white, native-American families, while fully a third were immigrants or the sons of immigrants and nearly one quarter were Afro-Americans. The first- and second-generation foreign-born population divided roughly evenly between the Irish and the Germans, with a mixture of English, Scottish, and Swedish arrivals making up the remaining third of the immigrant stream.

These ethnic groups differed markedly in economic standing. The Yankee population dominated the capitalist and professional strata and held a disproportionate share of white-collar, agricultural, and upper-skilled working-class positions (Table 11). The German and British immigrant communities composed a smaller but still significant proportion of the city's non-wage-earning population. But overwhelmingly these latter two groups were rooted in the skilled crafts, such as railroad shop workers, slaughterhouse butchers, and

TABLE 11. Ethnic Distribution within Occupational Groups in Kansas City, 1880

Occupations	Native White	Immigrant[a]	Black
Non–Wage Earners (N = 565)	59	35	6
Capitalists and professionals (N = 131)	93	28	8
Merchants (N = 210)	53	45	2
Salaried positions (N = 166)	61	37	2
Farmers (N = 58)	50	24	26
Working Class (N = 2,664)	39	35	26
Skilled workers (includes butchers, railway shopmen) (N = 1,288)	50	45	5
Unskilled workers (includes packinghouse laborers) (N = 1,376)	29	25	46
Total (N = 3,229)	42	35	23

Source. U.S. Tenth Census, 1880, population manuscript.
Note. Data are based on males, aged fifteen and over, and are given as percentages.
[a]Includes foreign-born and those with one or both foreign-born parents.

artisans. Irish-Americans occupied a distinctly inferior place in the city's economic life, best revealed by the comparative size of their unskilled working class. While unskilled laborers represented approximately one quarter of the Yankee, British, and German settlers, they made up nearly half of the Irish-American community (Table 12).

Below even the Irish in socio-economic position stood the Afro-Americans. Nearly seven out of eight employed black males were unskilled laborers, nearly twice the percentage of the Irish. (By counting only those fifteen and older, this figure underestimates the proportion of black menial labor. The labor force at a Wyandotte brickyard, for example, included several black males aged ten to thirteen.) Drivers of express wagons, laborers on rock piles, railway depot porters, personal servants, and "chore-runners"—so uniform was the complexion of these workers that the tasks themselves were commonly considered "nigger work."

The origin, as well as still uncertain status, of one segment of the black community was evident in the 1880 census description (in place of occupation) of thirty lodgers in one boardinghouse simply as "Exodusters." Indeed, of some 6,000 lower South blacks who traveled in groups up the Missouri River to Kansas in 1879, nearly a third had landed at Wyandotte. The old abolitionist governor, John P. St. John, had encouraged the generally impov-

TABLE 12. Occupational Structure in Kansas City, by Ethnic Groups, 1880

Occupations	Percent within Total Population	Native Whites	Blacks	Irish[a]	Germans[a]	British[a]
Non–Wage Earners	18	24	5	15	24	17
Capitalists and professionals	4	7	1	3	3	3
Shopkeepers	7	8	1	6	14	8
White-collar employees	5	8	1	6	6	6
Farmers	2	2	2	1	2	—
Working Class	82	76	95	85	76	83
Skilled workers	40	47	9	43	59	60
Unskilled workers	42	29	86	42	17	23
Total percentage	100	100	100	100	100	100
Total number	3,229	1,369	740	361	340	214

Source. U.S. Tenth Census, 1880, population manuscript.
Note. Data are based on males, aged fifteen and over, and are percentages. Dash = number too negligible to calculate percentage.
[a]Includes foreign-born and those with one or both foreign-parents.

erished refugees, proclaiming the state the "asylum of the oppressed," but the newcomers generally met a less than hospitable welcome. While local black political leader Corvine Patterson helped to set up temporary barracks for the Exodusters, Judge R. E. Cable probably expressed the prevailing concern of local residents by insisting that the black migrants be transported out of Wyandotte, "peacably if we can, forcibly if we must." Within one month of their arrival, Wyandotte had clamped a freeze on river embarkments, and most of the refugees had reportedly moved on to Topeka, Parsons, and other interior settlements. Those who remained fared poorly during the area's general boom. A sample of Kansas City Exoduster households conducted by the state Bureau of Labor in 1886 found black adult male laborers earning an average of $262.75 annually; the average annual income for white laborers was $333.09.[5]

The considerable imbalances of wealth in the Kansas City area were reflected in three patterns of residential clustering. Skilled workers tended to live alongside the upper classes within Wyandotte's developed older section; the unskilled were concentrated among streets unnumbered in the census, presumably at the edge of town. Second, a few local boardinghouses catered especially to young male skilled workers such as carpenters, machinists, and shoeworkers. A railroad engineer, for instance, kept a maid to look after him and a houseful of railroad conductors. Third, blacks lived physically apart from the rest of the citizenry. The Exodusters had first erected shanties on the levee; many remained there, although by 1885 roughly a third of Wyandotte's black population had established themselves in a small suburb at the rear of town. As late as 1886, Wyandotte's densely black third ward still lacked a permanent schoolhouse in which to hold even segregated classes. The few whites scattered among the black residential sections were almost all unskilled workers. A white Virginia-born dishwasher lived and worked with a black cook, and a Scottish boatman had as neighbors a black sawyer and a black carpenter.[6]

Consolidation of Kansas City, Kansas, in 1886 let loose a tide of civic boosterism. If the "energetic capitalists" spread round the state of Kansas would just "concentrate their energy at this point" went the local argument, Kansas City might one day not merely dwarf its namesake across the state line but also rival St. Louis or Chicago. With such heady ambitions political and business leaders readied plans for municipal improvement complete with a local version of manifest destiny.[7]

Just as the nation had required a transportation network to bind together its shores, so Kansas City determined to construct one grand, paved street from the northern limits of Wyandotte to the southern tip of Armourdale. Not only roads, but also railroads, intraurban street railways, schools, and sewers were contemplated to make the city attractive to outside capital. Gas lamps, an elevated railroad, and new bridge to Missouri figured immediately in booster plans. The city fathers appeared unintimidated by the responsibilities of urban planning. Indeed, when several members of the local Board of Trade journeyed to Havana, Cuba, they found it a "model city" in most respects but insisted that it "could be improved a little by widening the streets and permitting theatres to sell season tickets."[8]

Amidst the stream of civic success stories pouring out of the new city, the one note of caution concerned the quality of local government. Sympathetic property tax evaluation, bonding power, and assurance of public order, of course, were all important to the securing of private investment capital, and all were in public hands. Early in 1886 the *Gazette* reported wealth pouring in "despite a lack of internal initiative." Repeated calls to the community for a "good business mayor" and "a majority of good business men in the council" suggested that all was not well. Business apprehension, in fact, centered on the April 1886 election of the consolidated city's first mayor, Thomas Hannan, and the unpredictable set of forces that surrounded him.[9]

Until 1885 local politics had turned on a combination of personal following, ward organization, ethnic factionalism, and residual national partisan loyalties. The greatest testament to the dominant moral feeling in an overwhelmingly native-born Protestant, rural Republican state was the passage of the nation's second prohibition law in 1880. Democrats made much of popular urban opposition to the statute, but by lax enforcement local Republicans also accommodated themselves to the antiprohibition constituency and through the early 1880s usually carried both Wyandotte and old Kansas City. Circumstances in Kansas City provoked the complaint in 1884 that the town "swarms with the worst element of gamblers, those who run what is called the *skin* games where those who play cannot possibly gain anything. There are more than thirty dealers in Misery and Death on our main thoroughfare . . . in spite of our prohibitory Con'Amendment!" Among the city's ethnic groups, only the Irish were securely lodged in the Democratic camp, while Afro-Americans normally could be counted on by the Republicans. Fanatically antiprohibition, the Germans were nevertheless inclined toward the Republicans. As in Rutland no one in Kansas City embraced the symbols of political citizenship more zealously than the hyphenated Americans. Despite the lack of any official celebration, Independence Day in 1885 was heralded by both "German" and "Colored" picnics in Wyandotte.[10]

While seldom attracting the direct involvement of big railroad and packinghouse owners (most of whom resided elsewhere), local political life combined the economic interests of bankers, real estate investors, and their attorneys with popular mobilization. The scramble for office and influence sometimes embarrassed business leaders looking to polish the long-term reputation of the city. In 1885, for example, conflict had broken out between high-minded *Gazette*–Board of Trade interests and incumbent Wyandotte Republican Mayor

T. C. Foster. According to the *Gazette,* the local regime was shamefully riddled with conflicts of interest, and open collusion existed between police and saloon owners. When Foster won renomination with well-organized black Republican backing, reform-minded Young Republicans together with the Board of Trade took the extraordinary step of endorsing his Democratic opponent. Pointing to the "menace" of the "colored vote" massed "as one man," Democratic physician J. C. Martin was voted into office in April 1885. While the election returned the Republican party to business control, the episode did indicate the rough-and-tumble, plebeian nature of city political appeals. A purified Republican slate managed only a partial victory in the 1885 fall elections, when blacks, annoyed at being taken for granted, split their ballots among Republicans, Democrats, and a "Young Turk" Colored ticket. The *Gazette* expressed dismay that the Democrats not only had gathered in their usual "saloon men" but also had attracted new recruits, among them "Knights of Labor thronging to the polls."[11]

The Knights became entangled in local politics almost from the time they had appeared, sprouting three mixed assemblies and three trade assemblies of coopers and carpenters, harness and saddle-makers, and (most likely black) barbers, hod carriers, and laborers in 1882–83. As early as 1883, Kansas City Knights' organizer John Cougher had moved into alliance with the skillful Republican County machine of state Senator William J. Buchan. The successful campaign of wealthy businessman R. W. Hilliker, Buchan's candidate for mayor of old Kansas City in 1883, received Cougher's active support. The Cougher-Buchan alliance flourished for two more years. After Senator Buchan introduced legislation that established the Kansas Bureau of Labor and Industrial Statistics in 1885, Wyandotte Knight and old Greenbacker F. H. Betton became the state's first labor commissioner, and Cougher was appointed his assistant. Republican Governor Martin named another Knight state mine inspector. The early cooperation between the Order's leaders and a section of the Republican party hierarchy was also evident in second district Congressman E. H. "Farmer" Funston's sympathetic attitude on the House Labor Committee.[12]

Labor's ties to the county Republican organization burst asunder in the Knights' 1885–86 confrontation with Jay Gould, which reshaped the entire state political climate. First, shopmen on Gould's Wabash line and the Missouri, Kansas, and Texas road successfully resisted wage reductions in March 1885. Second, in September sympathetic action all along the Gould system broke a lockout against Knights' shopmen on the Wabash line. The settlement, arbitrated by Governor Martin, was "the most important . . . the Knights ever made." The Gould strikes opened the Order to the mass recruitment of both railroad and packinghouse workers who formed five trade assemblies between them in Wyandotte County. New members filed in at the rate of 200 a week.

By the end of the year only the coal counties in the state's southeast corner approached the concentration of 4,000 Knights grouped in the Kansas City area's twenty-one assemblies.[13]

The Knights' growing industrial strength was quickly reflected in an independent political stance as well. As early as 1884 some local assemblies were chafing under John Cougher's political rule of the Kansas City assemblies. Carpenters' leader Richard Edwards wrote General Master Workman Terence Powderly that Mayor Hilliker had made "glorious promises which were not kept" to the workingmen, while Cougher ran the assemblies for the Republican organization, expelling members who exercised alternative political judgments. The coopers' master workman, William Fletcher, added to the protest in December 1885 by claiming that Cougher "trains right in with the monopolist-political serpent and against the rest of us all the time." It was essential, wrote Fletcher to Powderly, that "this apple of discord be cooked." By the time of Fletcher's letter, however, Cougher's influence was already on the wane (within the year he would be suspended from the Order). In the spring municipal elections of 1885, the Kansas City Knights helped to oust Hilliker from office and to replace him with the "independent" Republican James Phillips, a master carpenter and boss machinist at the Fowler packinghouse. The fall 1885 elections offered further evidence of labor's potential political power. A candidate for district judge who had taken a tough, antistrike position was one of only two Republicans defeated. On the other hand, Sheriff James Ferguson, a boss railroad carpenter by trade, had outpolled the field. The previous March, "when asked to take a posse and clean out the Wyandotte strikers," Sheriff Ferguson "went down and talked kindly to the men, gave good advice and returned to his office." Within the year reports suggested that the sheriff had actually joined the Order.[14]

Local affairs were further disrupted by the Great Southwest Strike, the third and final confrontation between Gould and the Knights of Labor. Dismissing a Knights foreman in Marshall, Texas, on February 18, 1886, railroad management openly called the Order's bluff in precipitating a work stoppage across the Missouri and Texas Pacific lines. This time, Gould's general manager, R. M. Hoxie, wanted no part of negotiations or arbitration sought by the Order's overextended and unprepared officials. The striking workers, for their part, jumped at this test of strength to confront long-standing grievances. Unskilled laborers such as yardmen, section hands, and coal heavers, for example, took advantage of the situation to demand a minimum daily wage of $1.50. Kansas City railroad machinists forced a "tyrannical" master mechanic to retire. In the face of armed guards sent to protect railroad property, the strikers simultaneously exercised restraint over their own numbers while intimidating potential strikebreakers. Kansas City strikers, for example, caught a few running crews and "rocked them in the yards at night [calling] them rats, sons of bitches, scabs." Similar tactics were employed to gain the cooperation of the reluctant railway brotherhoods. At Atchison, the following anonymous handbill appeared, addressed to skilled engineers and firemen:

> BOYS: We warn you not to run trains out of Atchison. It is with regret we tell you, as we call you Brothers. If you do your life will pay the forfeit. Boys, we want to throw off the Yoke of Serfdom and be FREE MEN like yourselves. Don't deny us what at one time you prayed for.

At Kansas City the strike brought local commerce to a near standstill by the end of March; even the packinghouses were forced to suspend operations.[15]

The dramatic confrontation with the Wizard of Wall Street offered numerous signs of the depth of support that the Knights had built up over the previous year in Kansas. The extent of labor influence among respectable upper-working-class and lower-middle-class elements was perhaps most evident in Governor Martin's private dismay that several lodges within his beloved Independent Order of Odd Fellows had become infested with Knights' loyalties. Equally disturbing to state authorities was the extraordinary solidarity with the strikers exhibited by the poorest urban workers. John L. Waller, a black political crony of the governor's, complained in April of the "great influence being brought to bear upon colored men" to join the Knights. Already by November 1885, for example, one black assembly had been chartered in Kansas City, and two more were reportedly being formed. According to Waller, the feeling had spread that "should colored men take hold of the order, there will be chances for the young men of the race to become skilled laborers, and the avenues of business and trades now closed to them will be instantly thrown open." Hailing the general "refusal of working people to take the place of the strikers, notwithstanding gaudy inducements," the *Boycotter* (a Knights' paper started in protest against the anti-union policies of the mass-circulation Kansas City, Missouri, *Journal*) underlined the larger, symbolic meaning of the struggle. "Organization," noted the *Boycotter*, "had had its influence even among the unorganized."[16]

Anxious from the beginning to resolve an unwanted conflict, the harried national leadership of the Knights proved no match for the skills of railroad management. Having forfeited all strategic advantage by allowing Gould to renege on a March compromise agreement, the Knights' general executive board practically washed their hands of an increasingly hopeless situation and left St. Louis strike commander Martin Irons with few resources. By the beginning of April, state militia had placed Ft. Worth, Texas, and Parsons, Kansas, under martial law. On April 9, deputies fired into an East St. Louis crowd of strikers and killed nine people. Around Kansas City several trains with scab crews were derailed before a mysterious April 26 train-wrecking near Wyandotte killed two firemen. Labor's final defeat in the Southwest Strike, accepted ignominiously on the same day as Chicago's Haymarket affair, left hundreds of union men without jobs and dozens scattered in jails along the railroad route. It also let loose a torrent of abuse against both the Knights and the urban "mobs" who appeared not only to have tolerated but also to have abetted the work stoppages.[17]

The strike had proved both a terrifying and unifying experience for the business classes of Kansas. Many had come to view the Knights and leaders like Irons as seditious elements to be curbed by whatever means necessary. Particularly as the strikers' own efforts flagged, the opposition grew more vociferous. Early in April, for example, 150 of Atchison's "best citizens" had sent Gould a message of support. Governor Martin's ultimate intervention must, in part, have been precipitated by communications like the one he received from Wyandotte businessman Henry J. Armstrong, which warned that in the present "condition of anarchy," "firmness at the outset is the most efficacious remedy." The antistrike reaction did not merely await the actions of lawful authorities. Beginning in Sedalia, Missouri, and spreading throughout the strike belt, a secret, extralegal society appeared in the form of the Law and Order League. Mimicking the Knights with its secret passwords, grips, and recognition signs, the league promised to protect railroad property and "replacement employees." Some 350 "responsible men" formed a branch of the organization in Kansas City, Kansas, shortly after the April train-wrecking. After the strike the Kansas league took on the task of maintaining social control in the state's urban areas, focusing at once on the eradication of lower-class drinking and gambling dens and on the elimination of alleged "socialists and red flags" from labor organizations.[18]

Law-and-order vigilantism ultimately gave way to a more permanent institutional response to lower-class social and political upheaval. In December 1886 a wave of nativist and antilabor fervor pushed a metropolitan police bill through the state legislature. The bill substituted a governor-appointed board of police commissioners for local urban jurisdiction over prohibition violations and other transgressions. That Senator William Buchan took charge of the legislation indicated the hardened poststrike line of state Republican leaders as well as the degree of political realignment in Kansas City.[19]

The poststrike reaction, to be sure, did not go unanswered. "The companies called 'Law and Order Leagues' and the State Militia of Kansas," wrote one labor partisan, "are occupying the same position to enslave whites as the 'Border Ruffians' did to enslave blacks." Petitions, including 300 signators from Wyandotte, poured into Governor Martin, protesting his use of the militia to put down the strike. As for the Law and Order League, the Kansas City *Boycotter* laughed at the claims of pot-bellied, middle-class hypocrites to civic virtue: "It is true that many of you carry at your front some resemblance to 'ornamental' bay windows. These you have built carefully by many a good dinner as well as by many an inner bath, taken in violation of the prohibition law; but fear not; remember that the walls of Jericho fell down at the blast of a ram's horn. You are a whole army of Gideon's, and if blowing will maintain order you can beat a Dakota cyclone." Topeka Knights of Labor formed a special committee of safety to bring before the courts "test cases" involving "arbitrary police power against the poor." The committee soon claimed credit for the arrest of one officer "for a needless and cruel assault upon a twelve-year-old colored boy."[20]

The first municipal election in newly consolidated Kansas City, Kansas— coming as it did in the first week of April 1886—thus could not escape the passions touched off on both sides by the Southwest Strike. Local Republican leaders had hoped to nominate ex-mayor R. W. Hilliker, a reliable business- man who had cultivated numerous labor connections. But their plans went awry. As the *Gazette* later put it, "All classes of men . . . without regard to party lines" had swarmed into the Republican convention and captured the mayoral nomination for the maverick Irish-Catholic stonemason, Thomas F. Hannan. Conservative Republicans tried to recover by forming an *ad hoc* Citizens ticket to which they hoped to attract Democratic participation. V. J. Lane, Democratic postmaster and influential publisher of the Wyandotte *Her- ald,* quickly buried the idea: "Democrats will not be catspaws for them and mere tools to put the city in their power and help them wreak vengeance on the Knights." The Democrats proceeded to nominate banker Nicholas Mc- Alpine; his 672 votes were more than enough to throw the three-way election to Hannan. The new city council, meanwhile, divided unpredictably between warring Republican and Democratic factions.[21]

Above all, Hannan owed his election to the Knights of Labor and the Order's political unification of previously antagonistic ethnic communities. A regular Republican by upbringing—his father, a contractor-mason, served on the party's city central committee—Hannan had opposed the renomination of "corrupt" Wyandotte Mayor T. C. Foster in 1885, but, unlike the *Gazette–* Board of Trade group, had remained on the biracial ticket to win a school board seat. In the 1886 election, Hannan enjoyed victory margins of nearly 85 percent in old Wyandotte's black-dominated wards two and three. Appar- ently mindless of the Order's own biracial composition, the *Gazette* fairly blamed Hannan's triumph on "the Knights . . . assisted by the colored men." From beneath labor's umbrella, Hannan had also effectively reached out to many erstwhile Democrats. His own roots endowed him with a natural appeal among the city's Irish-Americans, and he built bridges to "saloon shyster" Jack Sheehan and other Irish political bosses. As mayor, Hannan was always publicly identified with the Knights, and it is possible that he was already a member when elected. His first mayoral address set forth the Knights' goal of an eight-hour day and increased pay for municipal workers, including a $1.50 wage for common laborers. The first documented proof of his affilia- tion, a December 1887 letter praising Powderly for his strong protemperance position, also suggests Hannan's political acumen. By supporting the Knights' voluntaristic approach to temperance (rather than prohibition), the mayor neatly sidestepped the community's major ethnocultural schism.[22]

With Hannan's election, the atmosphere of limitless boosterism surrounding the infant metropolis gave way to an extended conflict over the specific pathways of city-building. The new administration staked its reputation to a public taming of the corporations. Wherever it could, Hannan's city government made tangible and explicit its inherent right to regulate, even administer, the multiplicity of contracts between private companies and municipal authority. Its initiatives derived from an informal prolabor coalition between the mayor and members of the faction-ridden city council. Hannan's closest allies on the council were Republican Charles Bohl, a carpenter by trade, and Democratic Council President William Clow, a preacher and mechanic known both for his prudent watch over the public treasury and his antisaloon radicalism. As a sign of things to come, Clow inaugurated the business of the new council by directing an increase in license fees for packinghouses and streetcar companies while totally exempting "the milk peddler with his own cow."[23]

The central reform thrust of the Hannan regime involved the use of bond issuance and contract-approval authority to exact public tribute from the chief industrial beneficiaries of such decisions. In July 1886, for example, the mayor delayed a $30,000 bond issue to the Northwestern Railroad, owned by ex-Governor George T. Anthony, insisting on a formal pledge that the road would locate its shops (thereby expanding local employment) as well as its tracks within city boundaries. Soon afterward, the Hannan forces surprised the Corrigan Cable Car Company, owned by one of the most powerful citizens in Kansas City, Missouri, with a proviso that a city contract be contingent on extension of track three blocks beyond company intentions. If stretched to the outermost limits of the city as the mayor proposed, the road would enhance municipal development. Hannan publicly dismissed the company's cost estimates with figures based on his own experience in laying railroads and foundations "since I was eight years old." When the council passed the street railroad bill along company lines, the mayor promptly vetoed it, adding to earlier objections demands for an employer liability clause and for the cession from the courts to the city government of the right to enforce or abrogate the contract. Over the railroad's protest that "courts are safe, councils are not infallible," the veto was sustained, and the company soon capitulated with slight compromise to the mayor's terms. Before he signed the bill, Hannan required a final modification in the track design and shaved off a year on the completion date.[24]

A second cable-car ordinance, submitted in January 1887, met an equally rigorous reception from city hall. Initially passing the council's scrutiny, the bill was nevertheless returned unsigned by the mayor who insisted on a clause guaranteeing a single fare from all points in Kansas City, Kansas, to Union

Depot in Kansas City, Missouri. When the ordinance, so amended, returned to his desk, Hannan balked again, this time commanding the company to improve the grading of streets on which it proposed to lay track.[25]

Not surprisingly, such actions did not appeal to the city's business establishment. Quickly, the business press exchanged its drumroll of commercial boosterism for apocalyptic warnings about the course of municipal affairs. Then in August with its alienation from the local administration reaching exteme pitch, the Board of Trade took the unprecedented step of blocking by injunction a $50,000 public improvements bond issue overwhelmingly approved in council and already signed by the mayor. Agreeing that it was now more important for the city to stop "the Hannan gang" than to go forward under adverse conditions, the *Gazette* emphasized both that the "best men" of the community had not been consulted in drawing up the improvements charter and that Hannan had continually "bled" the corporations for political payoffs. While the latter charge remained unsubstantiated by example, the mayor may indeed have played favorites among his corporate antagonists. His appointment to city assessor of a man with financial connnections to the large Fowler packinghouse at least suggested no political puritan at the local helm of state.[26]

The mayor's actions might have raised less of a storm had they taken place outside a revival of passions stemming from the Southwest Strike. In July 1886 the Missouri Pacific Railroad declared that an ingenious bit of detective work had not only broken the April Wyandotte train-wrecking case but also implicated several local Knights of Labor in the crime. Thomas Furlong, chief detective of the Gould line, reportedly had inserted himself under an alias into the Order in St. Louis. He had then traveled to Kansas City–Wyandotte, where he posed as a semiofficial troubleshooter for the general executive board in the affair. In Kansas City he met with the original suspect then under arrest and arranged bail. The undercover agent had been welcomed by Mayor Hannan who had promised all possible assistance to the defense team. In the course of his exertions the detective claimed to have discovered the involvement of Wyandotte Master Workman George Hamilton and several others in the planning of the train-wrecking. When Furlong came forward with his evidence in late July, Hamilton along with five other Knights were arrested and ordered to stand trial in six months. Well before the formal proceedings, however, the *Gazette* expressed the opinion that the mayor "should share prison with them." The pledge of loyalty to the labor organization by the mayor, city marshal, and the entire police force constituted a "danger to the peace and prosperity of the city." In the circumstances "the better citizens of town" warned that they might have "to rely on an alternate armed force, the Law and Order League."[27]

Despite the abuse rained down upon him, Mayor Hannan showed little inclination to treat with his detractors. If anything, the administration's irreverence toward respectable Republican opinion grew more pointed. In September Hannan revoked the *Gazette*'s contract as official city newspaper (i.e., printer of all city business and contracts) and handed it over the the Kansas *Pioneer,* a German-language publication that circulated among only a few hundred readers and lacked even its own press. A two-page English supplement was added for the occasion.[28]

The Knights of Labor had thus become the center of attention in Wyandotte County politics, with their adherents and detractors defining the contending factions within the two major parties. In the fall 1886 primaries, when Buchan's organization rejected a slate of labor candidates for county office, "Knights of Labor influence" swung in the direction of the Democrats. At the state level as well, the minority party had formally recognized the new political force, nominating a Knight of Labor for lieutenant governor. Master Workman William Fletcher explained to Powderly that the Order had "learned to ignore party affiliation and unite harmoniously . . . on men who will do most for the masses." The Southwest Strike had convinced Fletcher that "in strikes capital is the stronger" and that labor's refuge lay in the political realm. He emphasized that the new tactic implied no radical adventurism: "we are not socialists, nor anarchists, nor evil wishers of our country." The "principles represented by the star-spangled banner," said Fletcher, were creed enough for the Kansas City Knights. While Republicans generally swept the state in November's elections, labor-supported Democrats notched victories in Atchison and Leavenworth and in a most "unnatural" break with tradition took the majority of offices in Wyandotte County.[29]

A further test of the local political climate was provided by the January 1887 trial of George Hamilton for his participation in the train-wrecking. Both prosecution and defense willingly placed the Order as a whole in the docket along with the defendant, and both spoke to an audience larger than the jury. In a controversial move the state borrowed counsel—eight attorneys in all—from the Missouri Pacific company. The smaller defense panel was distinguished by the presence of Charles P. Johnson, former Democratic lieutenant-governor of Missouri, and ex-Missouri Republican Congressman Major William Warner. Among the jurors drawn from one of the county's agricultural districts sat one Knight of Labor, singled out for special admonishment by the prosecution. The defense based its case on evidence of poor track conditions and argued that no crime may, in fact, have occurred—despite the fact that William Vossen, one of the suspects, had already confessed and turned state's witness. Hamilton's lawyers, however, also counterattacked against the prosecution, a tactic clearly dependent upon the political currents at large in the community. Hamilton, Johnson charged, was being prosecuted "not because he is a murderer . . . but because he was the leader of the Knights of Labor in Wyandotte." As to the handiwork of Chief Furlong,

Johnson dismissed it with political sarcasm: "I don't like some snakes, but I like all snakes better than I do a detective." In his final remarks the defense counsel practically turned the verdict into a referendum: "Pausing for a moment the speaker walked up to the railing of the jury box. Striking a dramatic attitude he declared that it was the same old fight that had been going on since the world began. It was the struggle of the poor and oppressed toiling masses against wealth, against despotic power, against monopoly. He was proud to say that the fight was on. He was thankful for an opportunity to engage in it."[30]

The first Hamilton case ended in a hung jury, with the defendant returned to his cell pending a retrial. Five jurors including the Knight of Labor had voted for acquittal. The state moved quickly to transfer the Vossen case out of Wyandotte County, apparently because Nathan Cree, who had been elected Democratic county attorney in November 1886, had vowed to prosecute the state's witness despite his cooperative attitude. A less direct consequence of the verdict was Senator Buchan's introduction at Topeka of a jury qualification bill, which would empanel only property holders, and a jury commission bill, which would transfer from county to state-appointed officials the administration of jury lists.[31]

The April 1887 municipal election promised a clear-cut popular verdict on the proper degree of the Knights' political influence. Well before the scheduled party conventions, the Kansas City Board of Trade, acting through its Committee of One Hundred, threw its weight behind a "non-partisan" Citizens slate as their alternative to the "Hannan gang." Heads of the city's coal, construction, and real estate firms initiated the new formation—a much-better organized affair than the patchwork job of 1886—with a controlled statement expressing "anxiety" that "little, if any, good has come from the consolidation." Prominent Democrats like banker Nicholas McAlpine and former Wyandotte mayor Dr. J. C. Martin joined conservative Republicans on the Citizens' side. So did the perennial black politician, Constable Corvine Patterson. The *Gazette* spearheaded a campaign that assailed the stonemason-mayor not only for his alleged incompetence—"Would he be employed to transact business by capitalists or even by men in the lower walks of life?"—but for shielding criminals.[32]

At the top of their ticket the Citizens once again nominated R. W. Hilliker for mayor. Selection of this veteran politician over the *Gazette*'s choice of a more statesmanlike businessman suggested that Senator Buchan's machine was really running the nonpartisan show. For all the fuss over Hannan's political deals and the unchecked presence of policy shops and liquor dealers under a labor administration, Hilliker was a most unlikely candidate to eradicate urban vices. Hilliker's appeal was not to reform of any kind but to the collaboration of business and workingmen in the governmental pork barrel. In 1887 he called for a vast new system of public boulevards, attacking the mayor's "penurious spirit" even while aligning with those who had suppressed all municipal improvements during the mayor's tenure.[33]

The opposition's very resort to the Citizens' strategem confirmed Mayor Hannan's consolidation of the local Republican party machinery. The Republican convention (packed, said the *Gazette,* with "Knights-of-Labor-Democrats") resolved unanimously to renominate "the wise, patriotic, conservative" incumbent. Speakers saluted Hannan for reducing the city debt and encouraged him to continue to protect the "people's interest" with his veto power. Senator Buchan, the *Gazette,* and the metropolitan police act were all roundly denounced as "un-Republican" and "subversive of the rights of the people." That half of the city's Republican committeemen were drawn from the ranks of workingmen (including four carpenters, two Union Pacific shop foremen, two blacksmiths, one telegraph operator, one postal courier, one express driver, and one laborer) indicated the core of Hannan's strength. In characterizing the mayor's appointments as the "bummer element of a *class* of . . . honest, industrious mechanics and laboring men," the *Gazette* indirectly testified to the transformation in the social base of local political power.[34]

There were further clues to the constituent elements of the Hannan Gang. The *Gazette* specifically identified four men—"Fletcher, Weil, 'Alley' Taylor, and Foster"—as the leading Republican "shysters" behind the administration. William Fletcher, one of the city's oldest Knights of Labor, master workman, and an executive member of District Assembly 69 at Cherryvale, Kansas, symbolized the administration's direct ties with the labor order.[35]

T. C. Foster's presence within Hannan's inner circle suggested the continuing effectiveness that the mayor had made of party factions unmotivated by any reform impulse. The contractor-politician Foster, identified along with Hannan in 1885 with manipulation of the "nigger element" of the party, had lost out to the Hilliker-Buchan forces but retained a degree of influence, particularly among saloon operators along old Kansas City's waterfront. Foster's attachment to the "labor Republicans" reflected both his own ambitions and Hannan's manipulation of the levers of political power.

Most dramatically, the adherence of C. H. J. "Alley" Taylor to the labor Republicans suggested one pole of an extraordinary new popular alliance. By 1887 Taylor had already proved himself one of the country's shrewdest black politicians. He had distinguished himself as one of only three black lawyers to practice before the U.S. Supreme Court. Before coming to Kansas he had served as deputy attorney general in Indiana. In the largely Democratic town of old Kansas City, Taylor had accommodated himself to the political hierarchy and gotten himself appointed city attorney. Claiming that the Republicans had always taken the black vote for granted, Taylor urged a completely free-floating flexibility upon black voters; in 1889, after a year's appointment by President Grover Cleveland as U.S. minister to Liberia, he would transfer the Negro *American Citizen* from Topeka to Kansas City and turn it from "a hidebound, partisan [Republican] sheet" into an instrument of his own designs. Upon Hannan's accession to the mayoralty, Taylor, condemned by Buchan Republicans as an "unscrupulous trickster," had not only dealt with the labor mayor but allegedly also extracted certain patronage powers in exchange for his loyalty.[36]

By 1887 the Hannan–Knights-of-Labor–Taylor alliance had created deep fissures within the black political community. Regular Colored Republican clubs as well as black Knights' locals backed the mayor's reelection bid, while the Young Men's Colored Republican Club bolted to the Citizens ticket. Although Hannan had made few explicit moves to the black community, his generally worker-oriented policies had had some positive side effects. Councilman Charles Bohl, for example, delayed a railroad ordinance until he received a guarantee that "squatters on the levee" in the path of the proposed route would be removed only when they had been provided with homes at company expense. For blacks, the most controversial side of the Hannan administration involved its aggressive use of patronage power. The anti-Hannan Young Republicans, citing the turnover in offices that extended to the dozen black schoolteachers, attacked the mayor for appointing "only Knights of Labor from among the colored people, when the Knights of Labor organization of colored people numbers but a small fraction of the colored Republican vote of this city." Citizens city council candidate, Professor J. H. Jackson, who had lost his position as black elementary school principal after joining the nonpartisan slate in 1886, convened a preelection meeting on the politicization of the schools. But when he insisted on "no d——d Hannan men in the hall," most of the assembled black citizenry reportedly got up and walked out.[37]

For their part, pro-Hannan blacks staged a vigorous attack on Robert Hilliker's record as mayor of old Kansas City in the early 1880s. A local correspondent calling himself "Afro-American" claimed that Hilliker had refused to suppress a gang known as the Dirty Dozen, "who made a specialty of insulting unprotected colored women on their way home from work." On another occasion, Hilliker was alleged to have condoned a vigilante hanging of a black man with the words, "It was good enough for every black son of a b——." As the new police board's secretary, Hilliker promised jobs to blacks, but the Hannan partisan cautioned the black voter "that what may be to his individual interest may be directly against the interests of a majority of our race."[38]

Louis Weil, the fourth of Hannan's "shyster"-boosters and editor of the German-language *Pioneer,* symbolized the link between the labor administration and the skilled white ethnic working-class community. Devoting a full page to news from the mother country, Weil's newspaper was also intensely involved in local reform politics. Like Hannan, the *Pioneer* encouraged regulation of railroad and coal monopolies and opposed prohibition. The secularist German-American editor based his allegiance to the Republican party on its antislavery nationalism and on "the principles upon which the . . . party was organized . . . rather than the party itself."[39]

In addition to the *Pioneer,* Hannan received the endorsement of the newly chartered *Kansas Cyclone,* a breezy, independent, and mildly reformist organ. Edited by Louis Rosenthal and Mark Cromwell, the *Cyclone* addressed a biracial audience and received the patronage of the few Jews in the city, including "Meidle the Tailor" and "Hayter the Jeweller." Advertising union meetings and excerpting stories from Knights' papers around the state, the *Cyclone* declared its allegiance to the "labor party of Wyandotte County" and "Tom Hannan, the workingman's friend."[40]

During one controversial year in office, the Hannan administration had molded a constituency that included Irish Catholics, Germans, and Afro-Americans. Through the influence of the Knights, the Kansas City party system had reorganized primarily around the great "labor question." In recognition of his unusual base of support, the mayor had even added an "Independent People's" line to his regular Republican line on the spring 1887 municipal ballot. The Law and Order League, underground counterpart to the Citizens' respectable front, defined the class nature of the upcoming electoral contest most sharply. A private league circular leaked by the *Cyclone* asked for assistance in preventing "the scum of the Tin-bucket Brigade from taking possession of our beautiful city" and driving the "cultured portion out." Rule by Hannan and the Knights, "that unlawful body of reprobates," augured "no more boulevards or parks, no more beautiful homes . . . but in their stead the meagre homes of the poverty scums such as is found in 'Mississippi town' in this city, the abode of the bosom friends and colored cronies of this fellow Hannan and his gang."[41]

The out-and-out race and class hatred to which the Law and Order League appealed was, in fact, complicated by three political factors. First was the loyalty of certain veteran Republican politicians to the local reform regime. Citizens' movement organizers, for example, had fully expected Republican Councilman James Phillips, machine shop superintendent at Fowler's packinghouse, to repudiate the Hannan faction. When he refused, the Board of Trade president visited George Fowler and urged him in vain to dismiss Phillips. Since Phillips had himself trounced Hilliker for mayor of old Kansas City in 1885, his association with the labor party in 1887 was particularly nettlesome to the nonpartisan slate. Second, continued maneuvering for governmental favor by individual businessmen discouraged antilabor Citizens' solidarity. A week before the election, for instance, the banker McAlpine, trying to steer a railroad ordinance through the council, publicly complimented the members on their "good acts."

Finally, an important segment of the Democratic party had likewise simply refused to affiliate with Hannan's opposition. V. J. Lane and the *Herald,* for example, again endorsed a slate of their own that undermined the Citizens' bipartisan approach. The *Gazette* accused the "young democracy" in particular of secret connivance with the Hannan forces. Besides enjoying a natural following among traditionally Democratic Irish-Americans, Hannan had gone to considerable trouble in cultivating the minority party, offering Democrats the bulk of high appointed posts in his administration. Symbolically, on election eve Henry George arrived in Kansas City to be introduced by the Democratic grocer, Michael J. Manning, Hannan's hand-picked police judge.[42]

The "Hannan Gang" looked secure as it overcame Hilliker and the Citizens ticket with a 53 percent majority in an election in which the turnout of the previous year nearly doubled. Hannan's party captured two-thirds of the council and school board and elected two constables and half the justices of the peace as well as the police judge. "The hard-fisted Dirty Bucket Brigade," boasted the *Cyclone,* "have completely routed the shylocks, usurists, and ringsters." The *Pioneer* claimed that German voters had been "einstimmig" [unanimous] for Hannan and deserved not only "the greatest thanks" but a more "influential" role in city affairs for their efforts. As for the black vote, wards two and three again gave the incumbent his largest margins of victory.[43]

The fortunes of Kansas City's labor party were at high tide. In addition to winning a popular mandate, Mayor Hannan had finally received judicial clearance for the sale of the stalled municipal bonds. Within a week investors had purchased the entire issue. The administration also unveiled plans for a new city park, a municipal library, and a centralized sewer system. Then, within five months of Hannan's reelection, the retrial of George Hamilton presented a final local rebuff to the forces of law and order. After a fourteen-month incarceration Hamilton confidently entered the docket looking less an outlaw than "the best-dressed man in the courtroom." When the jury, which included three black workers and a white carpenter, acquitted the defendant, the prosecutors dropped charges in the remaining train-wrecking cases, citing overriding local prejudice against the railroad company. Spreading alarm among Topeka lawmakers over "the terrible farce our jury system has become," the Hamilton case speeded passage of the Buchan jury commission act.[44]

Kansas City's reform organs echoed in 1887 with a renewed sense of pride and patriotism. The *Pioneer,* for example, called for an "old-fashioned" Fourth of July celebration to "boom our grandest national holiday with as much fervor as we boom real estate, manufacturing and business." The appropriate organizers of such a celebration, in the newspaper's opinion, were the Knights, for "no other civic organization could carry it out as successfully." As the plan took shape, a labor spokesman called on citizens to come out with "music and families and banners and baskets" to renew the meaning of Independence Day: "This government belongs to the people, and in spite of any defects in it it is the best and most beneficient the human mind ever conceived of. At this time it is especially fitting that we do this, that we may both revive our faith and notify rings of monopolists that their day of misrule is ended; that we, the people, intend to rescue the heritage which we received from our fathers from the grip of gold and greed and transmit it purer and better to our children."[45]

From 1886 to 1889 the Hannan administration roughly fit historian Melvin G. Holli's characterization of the "social reform" regime. Like Detroit's Hazen S. Pingree, who in Holli's words established the "first significant social reform administration in any large city of the time" in 1889, Hannan drew on organized labor to reshape the constituency of the urban Republican party. Like Pingree, too, Hannan opposed "goo-goo" (good government) or structural reform issues as exemplified in his opposition to police reorganization and in his indifference to moral uplift legislation such as prohibition.[46]

Hannan's second term, in fact, focused as much on the reorganized police force as it did on policing the corporations. While friction with the newly appointed metropolitan police commissioners (and especially with their first secretary, bitter rival R. W. Hilliker) was predictable, the issue, like all controversies involving the mayor, became a larger symbolic battleground as well. After a series of petty humiliations suffered at the hands of these new authorities, Hannan arbitrarily dispatched a sergeant-at-arms of his own to act as an alternate police emissary to city hall. The metropolitan commissioners openly expressed outrage when the city council, backing the mayor, refused to approve their budget.[47]

The mayor's hostility to such structural reform as the police act ideologically placed him closer to the anticentralist tendencies of the Democrats than to the modernizationist thrust of his own party. It was the Democratic county attorney and constitutional lawyer, Nathan Cree, for example, who most neatly articulated the antipolice consolidation sentiment: "We are in favor of Home Rule for Kansas as well as in Ireland." Cree effectively lent to Hannan's obstructionist tactics both legal and intellectual justification, placing the police act in a framework of reaction to the "growing discontent in the laboring classes" and a "steady growth of sentiment among the wealthy classes . . . in favor of a strong government that will depend on force alone for the maintenance of public order." Consolidated police authority, by this interpretation, signified "class rule of the rich over the laboring people, distinctly *so intended*." Citing precedents in English law rejecting "all measures assuming the incapacity of the people for self-government," Cree set himself against the spreading system of "centralization" and demanded a reduction of "delegated power" and greater local governmental authority. His opinions made little headway in the state at large but convinced enough Wyandotte County voters to tip the 1887 fall balloting again in the Democrats' direction. Hilliker wrote the governor in disgust that "our worthy 'Republican Mayor' is fighting the whole Republican ticket."[48]

Hannan's was a rough-hewn generalship, displacing the business-dominated party machine with a combination of organization, dash, and substance. His greatest resource was his own ethnic working-class background. Taking a direct interest in the details of city-building, he made public power more than a rubber stamp for the plans of railroad and utilities. He also presided over the elevation of wages to municipal workers. Doubtlessly, the mayor did not lose votes in Kansas City for his ungrammatical constructions and colorful tirades. Hannan's was a personal and, by the end, even a cantankerous regime. When, on his own initiative, he tried to pardon an impoverished black held in jail on a misdemeanor, he was overruled by an indignant city council. Similarly, after he had dragged out the police payment question until mid-February 1888, resisting any attempt at conciliation, a weary council finally overrode his veto unanimously. Hannan's detractors understood that his appeal rested on "always trying to create the impression that he is fierce in his fight against corporations." They may also have been correct in suspecting that the mayor carefully curbed his wrath at those who cooperated with the city administration. For, above all, the Hannan regime depended on a fiercely loyal working-class public, who suffered the mayor's manipulation of diverse voting blocs.[49]

Nothing emphasized labor's contribution to social reform politics more than the dissolution of Hannan's organized following. The Knights declined drastically in the years following Hannan's reelection. Rout in the Southwest Strike followed by Powderly's pusillanimous retreat from confrontation with Chicago packers in October 1886 served as national symbols of the Order's strategic weakness. In Kansas City defeat in these key local industries carried particularly disastrous consequences. Internal jurisdictional problems also weakened the Order. Kansas City Knights' locals had initially affiliated to four different district assemblies, and the coordination problems inherent in such an arrangement apparently only worsened with time. Journalistic mention of the Order as a key factor in local politics ends in 1888; contemporary records report only a handful of functioning assemblies by the following year. While the entire edifice had probably not collapsed quite so precipitously as this evidence suggests, the local labor movement was indeed unraveling. It did not revive until some 2,000 trade unionists—half the number organized by the Knights at the end of 1885—affiliated with the Central Trades and Labor Council in the American Federation of Labor in 1891.[50]

In these same years social reform politics utterly lost its electoral foothold. By the time of the 1889 spring elections, for example, the mayoral race had again become more a contest of personalities and party loyalty than of major social divisions. Since returning to the city council in the aldermanic election of 1888, Hilliker had successfully recouped much of his lost political authority. Mayor Hannan had not improved his public standing, when, in a characteristic move, he assigned his old nemesis to only one of sixteen council committees while his friends served on five or six. A new majority on the council quickly solidified their positions by redrafting the city's ward structure. At the same time the Buchan faction skillfully reasserted its control of the party. The county organization had always managed to deny labor Republicans any but city offices. In 1888, however, the machine opened the path to county sheriff for the Knights of Labor mayor of Argentine. Party leaders also stepped up their appeals to blacks, nominating a black realtor for register of deeds in 1888 and arranging for Corvine Patterson's elevation to the board of police commissioners. As his opposition mobilized, Mayor Hannan was unable to keep his own fences mended. When the *Kansas Cyclone* failed to get the official city imprimatur, it mercilessly swung its guns against the "Hannan ring" before bowing out of existence in mid-1888. With a cry of "anything to beat Hannan," Buchan, Patterson, and *Gazette* Republicans coalesced to drive the mayor from the field at the 1889 party convention and replace him with merchant William A. Coy. Upon Coy's election, the *Gazette* was awarded the city printing contract, and within weeks the *Kansas Pioneer,* the last journalistic support of the labor faction in the Republican party, had folded.[51]

The demise of labor's political power entailed less a wholesale change of faces than the resubmersion of labor politicians into a less fractious political order. Once deprived of an independent base of operations, for example, even a Hannan might become useful to party professionals. Thus, in 1891 when the uninspiring reign of Mayor Coy appeared to have given Democrat J. C. Stout, a former master painter at the Union Pacific shops, a perfect shot at the city's top office, the party hierarchs allowed the once-accursed Hannan to bear their standard again, this time with tacit approval from both Hilliker and Buchan. Old "Honest Tom" worked his magic again in 1891, edging out his Democratic opponent by 186 votes. C. H. J. Taylor, who had joined young black leaders in sponsoring an independent black protest slate, which garnered only 100 votes, afterward blamed the election on the fanatic loyalty of Hannan's Irish-American supporters.[52]

The third Hannan administration, 1891–93, bore slight resemblance to the first two. Frustrated by a conservative council in attempts to appoint old friends including Knights of Labor to city offices, the mayor acquiesced in effective rule by Board of Trade city developers. His term, in fact, ended in a scandal of skyrocketing debt produced by contracts for a water works and electric light franchise. Practically all that remained of the spirit of Hannan's earlier command was his cultivation of ethnic loyalties. Thus, the mayor made sure to express a public welcome to Bishop Louis M. Fink and the new Catholic archdiocese that relocated in Kansas City in 1891. In another symbolic gesture Hannan asked all businesses to close on St. Patrick's Day.[53]

Nor were the Irish the only group to yield to the blandishments of ethnic brokerage. Failing to punish Hannan, Taylor brushed aside the idealism of young blacks after the election and returned to clubhouse bargaining with the powers that be: "We made him do right when first elected Mayor. . . . We know his methods and understand his nationality." Taylor counseled a *quid pro quo* deal with "Hannan and the Irish"—"whatever they do for one of our number is compulsory." Shortly after these peace signals were sent out by the *American Citizen* to the city administration, a black grocer and part-owner of the Negro newspaper was named city street commissioner. "Sometimes by silence you get what you want," Taylor concluded.[54]

Even though the Kansas City Knights of Labor had lost their once-commanding influence by 1891, their support was still sought on behalf of one politician or another. Correspondence to John Hayes, the Order's general secretary-treasurer, from the neighboring railroad and smelting town of Argentine expresses repeated complaint about the destructive impact of political machinations. Already reduced to fifty-five members, Argentine smelters Local 1521, for example, was reportedly divided, night shift against day shift, on the basis of murky political factionalism. "Politics broke up our old assembly," a local officer wrote bitterly in 1891, "and a J.P. elected by the Knights is now trying to break up 1521." Figuring in the "political ring" which had helped to stir up "bad blood" among the Argentine Knights was "one T. F. Hannan of Kansas City."[55]

The fate of Kansas City reform politics offers important clues to the related historical problem of why the Populist movement generally failed in the cities and failed particularly to excite the urban working classes. Tom Hannan's 1887 reelection as a labor mayor on the Republican ticket coincided with the beginnings of the independent political formation (initially, the Union Labor party) that would in a few years emerge as the powerful Populist movement. Kansas activists appeared as the spearhead of this most successful political challenge to the emerging national corporate-industrial political order. At the first national congress of the People's party in 1890, for example, Kansas held 400 of 1,400 delegate positions. Within the state the third-party men experienced their own power as early as 1891 when, after sweeping the legislative elections, they turned the venerable Republican Senator John J. Ingalls out of office. With some help from the Democrats, Kansas Populists gained the statehouse in 1892 and remained a powerful force for several years, carrying the rock-ribbed Republican state overwhelmingly for William Jennings Bryan in 1896.[56]

For all their statewide success the Populists met with remarkably little response from the industrial centers in Kansas. Union Labor electoral strength in 1888, for example, despite the efforts of party chairman and state Knights of Labor Master Workman John W. Breidenthal, was concentrated in the agricultural counties in the middle third of the state; the People's party did not so much depart from as improve upon the performance of the Union Labor party, turning strong minority showings in given counties into lopsided majorities. A few examples suggest Kansas City's (and to a lesser extent Wyandotte County's) generally countervailing electoral winds. The 1890 Populist gubernatorial candidate made a strong second-place statewide showing with 37 percent of the vote (compared to the Republicans' 39 percent). In Wyandotte County the results were reversed—Democrats, 53 percent, Republicans, 40 percent, and People's Alliance, 7 percent. Within the city itself the third-party candidate received a mere ninety-five votes. The Populists gained but still received only one of every four local votes cast in their fall 1891 triumph. They ran a full municipal slate in 1892 and elected no one. In most three-way races waged in the county during the early 1890s, the Populist could almost always expect to run third, cornering perhaps 20 percent of the city vote while doing a bit better in the townships. Only when they fused with the Democrats as in November 1892, when "Potato King" Edwin Taylor finally unseated Senator William Buchan, did the Populist presence make a difference. Even in coalition, Kansas City Democrats treated the Populists as a weak sister. Democrats snubbed their allies entirely in the local 1893 slatings; in response a Populist newspaper protested only to the extent of demanding representation in a single ward.[57]

In conjunction with the swelling base of the southern-affiliated National Farmer's Alliance, Kansas Knights played a critical role in initial third-party developments. Three-fourths of the delegates to the state's first Union Labor convention in August 1887 were Knights of Labor. And Breidenthal continued to head third-party organization in Kansas from its Union Labor beginnings through the 1890s. Given the Order's own mid-1880s urban political impact, why was it that third-party reformers received such a frosty reception in these same cities?[58]

The answer, according to the evidence from Kansas City, hinges on a combination of Populism's basically agrarian-oriented political program and cultural inspiration with the urban political vacuum left by the collapse of the Knights. While the leadership of the labor movement showed sympathy to the third party, the laboring-class voter generally did not. Within the Kansas countryside, the mortgage-cursed family farm constituted the third party's class basis. Mercantile and railroad influence, together with the hard-money loyalty of the Republican party hierarchy, carried a clearly defined social conflict into the political arena. But in Kansas City the lines between the Populists and their opponents became more of a blur. In probable deference to the local labor-Republican coalition, the Union Labor party never ran a separate slate in Wyandotte County. The *American NonConformist*, a leading Union Labor organ edited by Henry Vincent and family in Winfield, Kansas, had saluted Hannan as a comrade-in-arms as late as January 1888. Third-party organizers and organized labor nevertheless continued on friendly terms.

When the Populists held their first local meeting in June 1891, several Knights of Labor including Hannan's old friends M. J. Manning and William Fletcher were among the delegates, while Knights and Alliancemen jointly celebrated Independence Day a month later. C. C. Bishop, local leader of the typographers and an officer in the Kansas Federation of Labor, also lent his support to the Populists. A packinghouse foreman active in the Southwest Strike and three railroad workers, among them a member of Eugene V. Debs's newly formed American Railway Union, all ran on the fall 1894 People's party ticket. In short, what was left of reform labor leadership was pro-Populist.[59]

But labor was only one part, and not necessarily the dominant part, of the urban-Populist coalition. The Citizens' Alliance, formed in 1890 to organize third-party support in the cities, managed to attract at least a significant segment of middle-class elements who had had nothing to do with labor's political upheaval a few years previously. Their recruitment seems to have hinged on the Populists' promise to restore prosperity and a degree of institutional autonomy to the region's economy, even while on local matters they remained quite conventionally conservative. One of the county's prominent Alliancemen, for example, was implements merchant W. S. Twist, future president of the Kaw Valley Telephone and Electric Light Company. W. S. Beard, representing the Single Tax Club at the 1891 meeting to form a third party, was president of the Security Savings Bank. Porter Sherman, vice-president of the Wyandotte National Bank and a leading Alliance spokesman, opened his office to Citizens' Alliance meetings. A Yale graduate and former professor of political economy, Sherman had once argued that universal compulsory education offered young men "well up in dime novels, the *Police Gazette,* and obscene literature" a virtuous path away from " 'mobs,' 'riots,' 'communists,' 'cranks,' 'revolutionaries,' and 'white-kid glove reformers.' " The pro-Populist *Labor Review* may well have been correct in insisting that the People's party contained some of the "most conservative men in the county."[60]

It was not simply that some urban Populists did not fit the image of Hannan's old Dirty Bucket Brigade, but rather that the reform content of Citizens' Alliance activity in the city also had a distinctly middle-class thrust. After asserting the central Populist demand for "cooperative" institutions "so that labor may be emancipated from the thraldom of the money power," Alliance reformers in 1891—now arrayed against Mayor Hannan—focused their attention on exorbitant governmental salaries, municipal indebtedness, and political corruption. By August 1891 the costs of suburban road-building and the "electric light swindle" under Hannan rule had triggered the formation of a Taxpayers' League, which at one meeting of 800 supporters rhetorically threatened to lynch the city council. The league had the support of Democrats like Nathan Cree who had always feared excessive governmental power. Also expressing outrage at heavy-handed attempts to quash an anticonsolidation movement, the *Weekly Sun,* a Citizens' Alliance paper, joined in the attack on Hannan's "ward heelers" and "wire pullers." In an ironic political turnabout, the Republican *Gazette* defended the Hannan administration's ambitious municipal development plans and counterattacked the "Alliance-reform" forces as destructive "tax-jumpers" and "repudiators." In some respects, then, the local reform movement had assumed a good-government-against-the-machine cast, or, to use Holli's schema, it appeared to be concentrating on "structural" rather than "social" reform.[61]

Markedly unsuccessful in dislodging local Republican machine rule despite the outside Populist buildup, the opposition forces tried an old ploy in 1895. The banker-political economist Porter Sherman headed a Citizens ticket of "all the parties." With depression-related unemployment an acute local problem, the wealthy realtor and Republican "ring candidate" George J. Twiss borrowed a page from the previous decade by openly promising workers new jobs through extensive street construction and a special relief fund. Sherman labeled the Twiss plan "communism pure and simple." He addressed workers as taxpayers and homeowners, arguing that high taxes lowered property values. A few days before the balloting, a Citizens' meeting was broken up by a crowd described as "city politicians, Republicans, and Negroes." A group bearing a similar description had reportedly disrupted Taxpayers' League meetings in 1893. Had part of Hannan's old following now become the strong arm of the Republican machine? In any case, Twiss scored a smashing victory in the mayoral election. Even the voice of the Kansas Federation of Labor noted approvingly that many Democrats and Populists had defected from Sherman's candidacy.[62]

One other problem of the Populists in the city bears mention. The significant role of prohibitionists and women's suffrage advocates within Populist ranks highlighted an ethnocultural conflict between native-American radicalism and the attitudes of urban working-class communities. The state's People's party had been formed in 1890 in a coalition of Union Labor and Prohibition party camps. The prohibitionist, moral reform strand within Populism was well represented in Wyandotte County. The old Prohibitionist and Greenback-Labor radical, attorney Hiram Perkins Vrooman, was one of the first organizers of the Wyandotte Citizens' Alliance in 1888 and a candidate for district judge on the People's ticket in 1891. S. S. King, an Alliance journalist who had moved to Wyandotte County from Chariton, Iowa, undoubtedly drew popular approval for his colorful tirades against the "demands of Wall Street" and his pleas for a party "on the side of labor against capital . . . on the side of the proletariat against the plutocrat." But his peculiar place in local politics was suggested when the Law and Order League recommended King in 1892 for the position of special prosecutor in liquor cases.[63]

The strength of the women's rights movement within Kansas Populism also suggested a source of likely friction between the third party and the urban working classes. By the early 1890s leaders like Mary E. Lease, Annie Diggs, and Fanny Randolph Vickery had turned Kansas into what historian Mari Jo Buhle has called the "organizational epicenter for Populist women." The key to this development was the growing politicization of the Women's Christian Temperance Union (WCTU), which, from an initial commitment to prohibition, had branched out to a variety of reform activism. When women in first- and second-class Kansas cities were enfranchised in 1887, the WCTU's role naturally took on added importance. Although they enjoyed good relations with Knights' leaders in the state, WCTU organizers met resistance from German ("who love der liberty and der beer") and Irish (whose women were reluctant to vote) immigrants. From the beginning, therefore, Kansas City's women's rights–prohibitionist forces and the "Hannan Gang" found themselves aligned on opposite political sides. Amidst the highly charged mayoral campaign of 1887, for example, the WCTU's voter registration drive received aid from the Law and Order League and leading local businessmen, and the pro-Hannan *Pioneer* accused the WCTU of marshalling only upper-class supporters to the polls. Echoing the same social cleavage politically, an astute anti-Populist Democrat in 1892 vowed never to entrust the responsibilities of the district attorney's office to "any church committee, Law and Order committee, or any old women's committee." Given the growing isolation of agrarian radicals from the cities in the 1890s, it is perhaps not surprising that women's rights advocates should finally overcome opposition to a strong suffrage plank in the 1894 People's party platform while simultaneously predicting that newly enfranchised women would offset "the ignorant foreign vote." Populist leader P. P. Elder worried aloud about the colliding paths of the native reform movement and the working-class vote. At the St. Louis industrial conference in 1892 he had lectured fellow Populists that "prohibition and woman suffrage would have meant certain defeat in Kansas for the new party. They would not have brought us a single vote and would have lost us 10,000 German votes and a large Irish Catholic vote."[64]

There was, in short, and not surprisingly so, an intrinsically Protestant, moral reform character to the agrarian movement that undoubtedly restricted its appeal among urban wage earners. It was not simply that the movement was sprinkled with Protestant clergymen like the Reverend Charles Anderson, one of the first Alliance spokesman in the House of Representatives. Nor was it that the Populists were openly intolerant; the powerful pillar of Kansas Populism, the *American NonConformist,* for example, continually warned its readers against anti-Catholic bigotry. Perhaps it was simply that the spirit of the revival informed the substance of radical organizing in Kansas. On a swing through western Kansas in 1887, Knights' lecturer Colonel Jesse Harper, for example, wisely chose as his topic, "The Dignity of Labor from a Bible Standpoint." At the country town of Burrton all businesses closed "to hear the economic gospel expounded" at labor's "love-feast": "the colonel was in

excellent spirits and carried the emotions of his audience on a balance between explosive laughing and tears for nearly three hours."[65]

The most radical edge of this native American Protestant tradition, a tradition in which many Knights of Labor as well as Alliancemen were obviously
at home, was perhaps best represented in Wyandotte County by the careers of
Hiram Perkins Vrooman and that of two of his sons, Harry and Walter. Hiram
Vrooman, chairman of the People's party Central Committee and Populist
candidate for district judge in 1891, had entered politics in the 1850s as a
Missouri Democrat opposing centralized government. In the early 1870s he
was swept up in the liberal Republican following of Carl Schurz and elected
judge. Judge Vrooman's continuing antipathy toward concentrated power soon
led him to radical Greenbackism; in 1880 he ran for governor of Kansas on
the Greenback ticket and by 1884 was lending support simultaneously to Ben
Butler's Anti-Monopoly party and the National Prohibition party. In 1886
Judge Vrooman and his sons together with a minister named John Melvin
organized a Knights' newspaper in the tiny town of Quenomo, Kansas; young
Walter's efforts soon earned him the reputation as "the boy orator" of the
labor movement. By 1888 Hiram Vrooman had apparently moved his legal
practice to Wyandotte County, for he was listed as one of the early organizers
of both the local Union Labor party and the Citizens' Alliance.[66]

The radicalism of the Vrooman family neatly knit the moral regeneration
of the individual into a larger theme of social justice. Hiram was an active
prohibitionist as well as antimonopolist. Following the theological concerns
of their older brother Frank, who would become a powerful exponent of the
Social Gospel, Harry and Walter Vrooman early mixed lay preaching in Con-
gregational churches with their entry into Kansas politics in the 1880s. Politically, Harry was attracted while a student at Topeka's Washburn College to
the anarcho-syndicalism of Burnette G. Haskell's Red International. To Harry
in 1885 the red flag of socialism symbolized "the gospel Paul preached on
Mars Hill, that God 'hath made one blood of all nations,' " and he boasted,
while helping to arrange a visit from Albert Parsons, that the string of Socialist clubs in thirteen Kansas counties included ministers, lawyers, doctors,
school teachers, and college professors, "as well as some of the ablest members of the WCTU." Soon a more gradualist approach would place Harry
Vrooman in the forefront of the Christian socialist movement with the Reverend W. D. P. Bliss as well as within the ranks of Edward Bellamy's Nationalist clubs, commitments he would ultimately pursue from the pulpit.[67]

Walter Vrooman's political odyssey was perhaps the most complex of all.
His early political work in Kansas was itself antedated by brief fame as a
phrenologist and apostle of diet cures (especially whole wheat and apples),
which remained an abiding interest. While preaching from a Kansas City
pulpit in 1888, he was already a member of the Socialist Labor party. In later
years Walter Vrooman would join Charles Beard at Ruskin Hall and other

workers' cooperative education experiments. The moral and aesthetic emphasis to his radicalism unfortunately also led Walter by the end of the century to
champion a white Anglo-Americanism in the face of "Slavic and Asiatic
despotism." Altogether, of course, the Vroomans touched many different
bases within the radical political culture of their day. It does seem clear,
however, that except for their brief intersection with the Knights of Labor
what energized individuals like the Vroomans was simply not part of the
contemporary diet of urban working people.[68]

While the cultural baggage of Populism would, in any case have made for
an awkward reception in the cities, there is no doubt that the fall of the
Knights of Labor seriously exacerbated the problem. The argument could be
made that the Knights' leadership, itself thoroughly at home with the thinking
of the WCTU's Frances Willard, the Vincents, Vroomans, and others served
as a mediator, indeed transmitter, of a native-American radical political philosophy to Gilded Age industrial workers. The Knights, of course, carried
strong moral reform principles themselves and continuously strove to discipline their members in a direction which native-American radicals, including
the Populists, generally applauded. A movement that could simultaneously
embrace Walter Vrooman and Tom Hannan appealed across a wide spectrum
indeed. Had it existed as a more powerful force within Populism, the labor
movement might also have helped to steer the agrarian-based party more
clearly toward the concerns of urban workers. But without an organization to
subordinate issues of individual morality to the needs of general, social, and
specifically working-class advancement, cultural issues flared (as they had
done previously in American politics) into great symbolic political dividers.

As it was, by the time the Populists came along, Kansas City politics
offered little room for ideas that were not couched in terms of immediate
interest, power, and position. The relation of local blacks to the party system
offers an exemplary case of the reigning ethnic brokerism. Black politics had
assumed a no-holds-barred quality. In the 1891 elections, for instance, J. W.
Vorhees, a black shoe manufacturer, put out word that "any colored man who
would not vote for Corvine Patterson," the black Republican ward boss and
candidate for register of deeds, "ought to have his throat cut." When a black
employee rebuked Vorhees, declaring that no man owned his vote, he was
summarily fired. Vorhees himself reportedly had once "catered to" the Populist but left them on finding no "boodle" there. The local Populist press, to
be sure, did carry an idealistic message to black citizens. "The free slave is
the poor man of this country," argued one woman writer. "You are tired of
being the foot ball kicked from one side to the other by two parties . . . come
over to the Lord's side and live." But the influential maverick, C. H. J.
Taylor, based his political moves on entirely different considerations, namely
how many jobs (particularly political offices) for blacks could the Populists
guarantee? In 1891 he had caustically accused the Alliance gubernatorial

candidate of insulting the black race by helping to defeat a black aspirant for minor office. Then, as Democrats generally moved into fusion with the third party in 1892, Taylor switched his position and stood unsuccessfully on the People's party ticket for state legislator. Alignment with the Populists had, in any case, implied no general assimilation of radical principles. In 1891 Taylor's *American Citizen*, reacting to the racist exclusionism of the railroad craft unions and convinced that blacks could not afford to oppose the railroads, defended black strikebreakers and called Jay Gould "as great a benefactor and philanthropist as the world has ever seen." The political realities that prompted such a statement spelled doom for the Populists in the cities.[69]

NOTES

1. Kansas State Board of Agriculture, *Fifth Biennial Report including Decennial Census for 1885* (Topeka, 1887), 34–40; Wyandotte *Gazette,* Apr. 6, 9, 1886.

2. *Wyandotte County and Kansas City, Kansas, Historical and Biographical* (Chicago, 1890), 148. When the Wyandots first reached supposedly vacant lands ceded to them by government treaty, they found them already occupied, but the friendly Delawares and Shawnees quickly negotiated space for the new arrivals. In their Ohio farming community, most Wyandots had converted to Methodism. In Kansas the new settlers quickly erected a Methodist church and a log jail as well as a saw mill and grist mill; they also established a temperance society. Besides Armstrong, a few other prominent citizens had Indian connections. Hiram M. Northrup, a white trader from Missouri, settled in Wyandotte as early as 1855, married an Indian woman, and soon established the town's first bank. The daughter of Joel Walker married Nicholas McAlpine, whose real estate and banking interests would make him one of the county's richest capitalists by the 1880s. Charles P. Deatherage, *Early History of Greater Kansas City, Missouri and Kansas, 1492–1870* (Kansas City, Mo., 1927), 75, 695, 699. Two hundred Wyandot Indians survived in the Kansas county in 1890; Wyandotte *Herald,* May 2, 1889; A. Theodore Brown, *Frontier Community, Kansas City to 1870* (Columbia, Mo., 1963), 50, 53, 65; Kansas City (Mo.) *Pioneer,* Oct. 30, 1878.

3. Charles N. Glaab, *Kansas City and the Railroads* (Madison, Wis., 1962), 122, 168–69; Deatherage, *Early History,* 490–93; Wyandotte *Gazette,* Apr. 28, May 28, Nov. 12, 1886; U.S. Tenth Census, 1880, *Report on Social Statistics of Cities* (Washington, D.C., 1887), Pt. 2, 554–60; U.S. Eleventh Census, 1890, *Population* (Washington, D.C., 1895), Pt. 1, 384.

4. "Kansas City in 1879," pamphlet, New York Public Library; Perl W. Morgan, *History of Wyandotte County and Its People,* 2 vols. (Chicago, 1911), I, 335; Wyandotte *Gazette,* Aug. 27, Oct. 31, Dec. 17, 1886; *Wyandotte County,* 345; *Kansas Decennial Census, 1885,* 592–98.

5. *Kansas Decennial Census, 1885,* 35. Distribution of the urban immi-

grant population differed in important respects from the statewide count. By 1890 one in ten Kansans was foreign-born. Germans, who had homesteaded there as early as the 1850s, were by far the largest group, two-and-a-half times the size of the English immigrants. Swedish and Irish groups followed in size of settlement. Walter T. K. Nugent, *The Tolerant Populists: Kansas Populism and Nativism* (Chicago, 1963), 35–37; Glen Schwendemann, "Wyandotte and the First 'Exodusters' of 1879," *Kansas Historical Quarterly,* 26 (Autumn 1960), 240–43; Kansas Bureau of Labor and Industrial Statistics, *First Annual Report* (Topeka, 1885), 249–52; Nell Irvin Painter, *Exodusters: Black Migration to Kansas after Reconstruction* (New York, 1977), 257; on the general Exoduster experience see both Painter and Robert G. Athearn, *In Search of Canaan: Black Migration to Kansas, 1879–1880* (Lawrence, Kans., 1978).

6. Wyandotte *Gazette,* May 7, 1886; U.S. manuscript census of 1880.

7. Wyandotte *Gazette,* Dec. 17, 1886.

8. *Ibid.,* Apr. 23, May 14, 1886; Wyandotte *Herald,* Mar. 27, 1890.

9. Wyandotte *Gazette,* Apr. 30, Nov. 5, 1886.

10. Richard Edwards to Terence V. Powderly, June 15, 1884, Terence V. Powderly Papers, Catholic University, Washington, D.C. By 1891 one observer counted 300 saloons operating in the consolidated cities (Kansas City *American Citizen,* Sept. 4, 1891). The state's Prohibition party justified itself by proclaiming the farce made in practice of the amendment. Owen Nugent, who had served time for saloon-running in Kansas City, produced a popular comedy entitled *Prohibition in Kansas;* Wyandotte *Gazette,* Apr. 8, 1881, Apr. 6, 1883, June 5, 1885; Wyandotte *Herald,* July 9, 1885.

11. Wyandotte *Gazette,* Mar. 27, Apr. 3, Oct. 30, Nov. 6, 1885; Wyandotte *Herald,* Apr. 2, Nov. 5, 1885; Wyandotte *Kansas Pioneer,* Nov. 17, 1887.

12. Jonathan Garlock and N. C. Builder, "Knights of Labor Data Bank: Users Manual and Index to Local Assemblies" (1973), manuscript at the University of Rochester, Rochester, N.Y.; C. A. Henrie to Powderly, Dec. 23, 1887, William Mattfeldt to Powderly, Dec. 9, 1885, Powderly Papers.

13. Norman J. Ware, *The Labor Movement in the United States, 1860–1895: A Study in Democracy* (New York, 1929), 134–50, quotation, 144; Garlock and Builder, "Knights of Labor Data Bank"; *John Swinton's Paper* (hereafter *JSP*), Feb. 15, May 3, 17, June 14, 28, 1885.

14. Edwards to Powderly, June 15, 1884, Fletcher to Powderly, Dec. 7, 1885, C. A. Henrie to Powderly, Dec. 23, 1887, Powderly Papers; Wyandotte *Herald,* Nov. 5, 1885; Wyandotte *Gazette,* Mar. 20, Nov. 6, 1885, July 23, 1886.

15. For an extended narrative of the strike see Ruth A. Allen, *The Great Southwest Strike* (Austin, Tex., 1942); U.S. Congress, House of Representatives, *Investigation of Labor Troubles in Missouri, Arkansas, Kansas, Texas, and Illinois,* 49th Cong. 2d sess., H. R. 4174, Pt. 1 (Washington, D.C., 1887), 185, 200, 206, 215, 217, 223; unidentified clipping, Mar. 22, 1886, Powderly Scrapbooks, Powderly Papers.

16. J. H. Codding to Martin, Apr. 16, 1886, Waller to Martin, Apr. 12,

1886, Governor John A. Martin Papers, Kansas State Historical Society (hereafter KSHS), Topeka; *JSP,* Nov. 8, 1885; Kansas City (Mo.) *Boycotter,* Mar. 20, 1886.

17. Jeremy Brecher, *Strike!* (San Francisco, 1972), 35; Scandia, Kansas, taxpayers (antimilitia) petition to Martin, Mar. 27, 1886, Governor Martin Papers; Wyandotte *Gazette,* Apr. 30, May 7, 1886; Kansas City (Mo.) *Star,* Jan. 8, 1887.

18. S. H. Kelsey to Martin, Apr. 9, 1886, Armstrong to Martin, Mar. 26, 1886, Governor Martin Papers; Clarence E. Bonnett, *History of Employers' Associations in the United States* (New York, 1956), 248; Wyandotte *Gazette,* Apr. 30, 1886, Feb. 11, 1887.

19. Wyandotte *Gazette,* Nov. 12, 1886, Mar. 4, 11, 18, 1887. The police act took effect in March 1887; the transfer of the police from local to metropolitan or state control in Kansas was part of a national pattern. Kansas City, Missouri, had undergone the change earlier in the decade; in New York City the state government had taken over the force in 1857. Although circumstances differed, the general motives were the same. See Wilbur R. Miller, "Police Authority in London and New York City, 1830–1870," *Journal of Social History,* 8 (Winter 1975), 86, 94–95.

20. Antimilitia petitions to Martin from Republic County, Mar. 27, 1886, from Labette County, Apr. 2, 1886, from Wyandotte County, Apr. 12, 1886, Governor Martin Papers; *Boycotter* quoted in Wyandotte *Gazette,* May 14, 1886. Parsons, Kansas, Knights of Labor dealt the Law and Order League a more theatrical counterpunch. At an Independence Day celebration over the downfall of the labor organization, the city's "better classes"—"from the national banker down to the pawn broker"—organized a jubilee at the fairgrounds under the password, "No Knight of Labor Need Apply." But a secretly organized people's committee had made plans of its own. As the Fourth of July dawned, farmers' wagons rumbled into town, and iron molders gathered behind them in a procession of flags, banners, and drums. A wagon carrying little girls in white dresses with "Liberty caps" followed. Hose and hook-and-ladder companies and hundreds of other citizens on foot brought up the parade. Together, the Parsons Knights of Labor marched past the "grand marshals of the 'sham' Law and Order League," to celebrate, said one participant, "the 110th anniversary of our independence in a becoming manner." *JSP,* June 27, July 11, 25, Aug. 8, 29, 1886.

21. Wyandotte *Gazette,* Apr. 9, Sept. 24, 1886; Wyandotte *Herald,* Apr. 5, 1886, Hannan's total over Hilliker was 1,338 to 1,301 votes.

22. Wyandotte *Gazette,* Mar. 27, 1885, Apr. 2, 9, 16, 1886; Wyandotte *Herald,* Mar. 26, Apr. 9, 1885; William Fletcher and T. F. Hannon to Powderly, Dec. 18, 1887, Powderly Papers.

23. Wyandotte *Gazette,* Apr. 16, May 21, Aug. 20, Oct. 1, 1886.

24. *Ibid.,* May 7, July 23, Oct. 1, 8, 22, 1886.

25. *Ibid.,* July 23, 1886, Jan. 21, Feb. 4, 11, 1887.

26. *Ibid.,* Feb. 11, Apr. 1, 1887.

27. *Ibid.,* July 23, Sept. 10, 1886.

28. *Ibid.*, Sept. 17, 1887.

29. *Ibid.*, Nov. 5, 11, 1886; Fletcher to Powderly plus clippings, Nov. 15, 1886, Powderly Papers.

30. Wyandotte *Gazette*, Jan. 7, 1887; Kansas City *Star*, Jan. 8, 13, 1887. For Knights' efforts to raise money for the defendants and their families, see Fletcher to Powderly, Sept. 21, 1886, Jan. 2, 1887, and J. L. Delay to Powderly, Apr. 3, 29, 1887, Powderly Papers.

31. Kansas City *Kansas Cyclone*, Apr. 2, 1887.

32. Wyandotte *Gazette*, Feb. 4, Mar. 18, 25, Apr. 1, 1887; Kansas City, Kans., directory, 1891.

33. Kansas City *Kansas Cyclone*, Apr. 2, 1887; Wyandotte *Herald*, Apr. 5, 1886; Wyandotte *Gazette*, Mar. 18, 25, 1887.

34. Wyandotte *Gazette*, Mar. 18, 1887; Wyandotte *Herald*, Mar. 24, 1887.

35. Wyandotte *Gazette*, Apr. 1, 1887; Fletcher to Powderly, Sept. 21, Nov. 21, 1886, Powderly Papers; Argentine *Labor Review*, Oct. 24, 1891.

36. Kansas City *American Citizen*, Sept. 4, 1891; Wyandotte *Gazette*, Apr. 1, Aug. 13, 1886.

37. Wyandotte *Gazette*, Mar. 18, 1887; Wyandotte *Kansas Pioneer*, Mar. 17, 1887.

38. Kansas City *Kansas Cyclone*, Apr. 2, 1887.

39. Wyandotte *Kansas Pioneer*, Jan. 6, May 26, June 2, 1887.

40. Kansas City *Kansas Cyclone*, Apr. 2, May 21, 1887.

41. Wyandotte *Gazette*, Apr. 8, 1887; Kansas City *Kansas Cyclone*, Apr. 3, 1887.

42. Kansas City *Kansas Cyclone*, Mar. 26, 1887; Wyandotte *Gazette*, Mar. 4, 11, Apr. 1, 22, 1887; Wyandotte *Herald*, Mar. 24, 1887.

43. *JSP*, May, 1, 1887; Wyandotte *Kansas Pioneer*, Apr. 7, 14, 1887; Kansas City *Star*, Apr. 5, 1887.

44. Wyandotte *Kansas Pioneer*, Apr. 28, June 10, 1887; Wyandotte *Gazette*, Aug. 26, Sept. 16, 1887; *Wyandotte County*, 275; Wyandotte *Herald*, Aug. 30, 1888.

45. Winfield *American NonConformist and Kansas Industrial Liberator*, Mar. 8, 1888; Wyandotte *Kansas Pioneer*, June 2, 9, 1887; Kansas City *Kansas Cyclone*, July 9, 1887.

46. *Reform in Detroit* (New York, 1969), esp. xiii, 169, 226*n*. The comparison with Pingree and other "social reform" mayors (e.g., Toledo's "Golden Rule" Jones) is meant only to suggest the similarity in the broad outline of their appeals. Pingree, too, drew on Knights' bloc support and added to it the votes of Poles and other ethnic minorities. In other ways the two men were quite different. Pingree was a reformed businessman welding a working-class constituency, Hannan a workingman riding the crest of a politicized labor movement. See also Richard J. Oestreicher, "Solidarity and Fragmentation: Working People and Class Consciousness in Detroit, 1877–1895" (Ph.D. diss., Michigan State University, 1979), esp. 480–83.

47. Wyandotte *Gazette*, May 6, June 10, 1887.

48. Wyandotte *Herald*, Nov. 20, 1887. Cree's views are summarized here

from documents published in the *Herald,* Aug. 23, 30, 1888, but the Democratic position had been articulated earlier, e.g., Wyandotte *Gazette,* June 10, Aug. 5, 1887; *Herald,* Nov. 20, 27, 1887. Resistance to the metropolitans took an even more extreme form in the railroad and silver-smelting town of Argentine, where organized labor was also strong and politically powerful. Local Argentine officers stopped an investigation by the metropolitans in 1891 by arresting them. *Ibid.,* May 14, 1891.

49. Wyandotte *Gazette,* Nov. 18, 1887, Feb. 10, 17, 1888; Kansas City *Kansas Cyclone,* Apr. 3, June 11, 1887.

50. Ware, *Labor Movement in the U.S.,* 152–54, The Knights' national leadership did not lack for ideas from the rank and file on how to cope with the nation's most concentrated industries. James Lillis, master workman of Kansas City's packinghouse assembly no. 7321, who had worked "in most every packing house in this country" and knew "just about how they work" scoffed at directives from general headquarters to "reason with the packers" for an eight-hour day. Explained Lillis, "There ain't any influence that can be brought to bear on them that would have any effect at all." Instead the master workman proposed a military strategy of industrial packinghouse assemblies (many packers were in mixed assemblies ill-equipped to deal with an industry-wide strike) combined with exemplary distributive cooperatives that could deal directly with farmers to "supply fresh meat to the public" in case of a strike. Expecting trouble in the spring of 1887, Lillis warned Powderly that if any action was anticipated, "I would like it to be well done—fix up all the packing points and make it universal." This was just the sort of action the general master workman never countenanced. Lillis to Powderly, Feb. 6, 1887, Alfred Taylor to Powderly, Feb. 24, 1886, E. G. Wright to Powderly, July 14, 1886, Powderly Papers. District 69 centered at Cherryvale, Kans., District 39 at Denver, and District 107 at Kansas City, Mo., all had Kansas City, Kans., affiliates. Creation of a statewide assembly by the end of 1886 probably came too late to make much difference; Garlock and Builder, "Knights of Labor Data Bank"; Kansas City *Labor Review,* Oct. 24, 1891.

51. Kansas City (formerly Wyandotte) *Gazette,* Apr. 6, May 25, 1888; Kansas City *Kansas Cyclone,* May 19, 26, 1888; Wyandotte *Kansas Pioneer,* Oct. 27, Nov. 17, 1887, Mar. 31, 1888, Mar. 23, Apr. 6, 13, 27, May 4, 1889; Wyandotte *Herald,* Nov. 10, 1887, Apr. 4, 1889.

52. Kansas City *Sun,* Mar. 20, Apr. 3, 1891; Kansas City *Gazette,* Apr. 9, 1891; Kansas City *American Citizen,* Apr. 10, 1891.

53. Wyandotte *Herald,* May 14, 21, July 16, Aug. 20, 27, 1891, Apr. 6, 1893.

54. Kansas City *American Citizen,* Apr. 17, May 22, 1891.

55. William W. Woodruff, John Doyle, et. al. to Hayes, Jan. 28, 1891, Woodruff to Hayes, Mar. 10, 1891, B. M. White to Hayes, Apr. ?, 1891, John W. Hayes Papers, Catholic University, Washington, D.C.

56. Nugent, *Tolerant Populists,* 45, 51–54, 137; Lawrence Goodwyn, *Democratic Promise: The Populist Moment in America* (New York, 1976),

esp. chs. 7, 8. "If Texans led the farmers into the Alliance, Kansans led the Alliance to the People's Party" (195); Wyandotte *Herald,* Nov. 2, 1896.

57. See Raymond C. Miller, "The Background of Populism in Kansas," *Mississippi Valley Historical Review,* 40 (Mar. 1925), 469–89, esp. 483–85; see also O. Gene Clanton, *Kansas Populism: Ideas and Men* (Lawrence, Kans., 1969), and Clarence J. Hein and Charles A. Sullivant, *Kansas Votes: Gubernatorial Elections, 1859–1956* (Lawrence, Kans., 1958). Even before the Union Labor party, political radicalism in Kansas had established itself outside the urban centers. In 1878–80, for example, the Greenback-Labor party showed best in the wheat-growing areas of the eastern third of the state, notably bypassing every county (excluding the coal-mining region in the southeastern tip of the state) with an urban or industrial concentration. Kansas City's electoral pattern of the late 1880s also fit that of other industrial centers in the state which had experienced strong labor organization. In Labette County, for example, the Union Labor party made one of its best runs in the fall 1888 gubernatorial election, grabbing 31 percent of the vote. Parsons, the county's largest town, however, contributed a bare 20 percent of its votes to the third party (Kansas City *Star,* Nov. 7, 1888). The vote for the Union Labor party was likewise negligible in Atchison and Leavenworth, and the Populist vote there a couple years later also fell well below the statewide average; Wyandotte *Herald,* Nov. 12, 1891, Mar. 31, Nov. 10, 1892; Kansas City *Gazette,* Nov. 3, 1891; Kansas City *Sun,* Nov. 11, 1892, Apr. 7, 1893.

58. Winfield *American NonConformist,* Aug. 11, 1887.

59. *Ibid.,* Jan. 26, 1888; Argentine *Labor Review,* June 20, 1891; Wyandotte *Herald,* June 18, 1891; Kansas City *Labor Record,* Nov. 2, 1894. The political potential of a labor-Populist alliance in areas where a radical labor movement survived in the 1890s is suggested by two examples. Shelton Stromquist has recently demonstrated the direct connection between the Knights of Labor and the formation of the American Railway Union in 1893; the union, in turn, offered significant support to the Populist party. "The Knights of Labor and Organized Railroad Men," paper presented at the 1979 Knights of Labor Symposium, Newberry Library, Chicago; see also the comprehensive analysis of labor-Populist relations in Illinois by Chester McArthur Destler in *American Radicalism, 1865–1901* (Chicago, 1966), 162–254.

60. Perl W. Morgan, *History of Wyandotte County, Kansas and Its People,* 2 vols. (Chicago, 1911), 2: 852–53; Wyandotte *Herald,* June 18, 1891; Kansas Bureau of Labor and Industrial Statistics, *Third Annual Report* (Topeka, 1887), 309–17; Kansas City *Labor Review,* June 20, 1891. While a thorough study of the Citizens' Alliance remains to be written, Goodwyn (*Democratic Promise,* 649n24) has noted that both the "moderate" Citizens' Alliance and a more "radical" National Citizens' Industrial Alliance (each with roots in Kansas) were seated as urban extensions of the third-party movement at the founding convention of the People's party in 1892 at St. Louis. Newspapers in Kansas City simply referred to the "Citizens' Alliance." In private discussion with the author, Goodwyn has also noted the key role that Briedenthal played in corraling several western bankers to the ranks of the third party.

Peter H. Argersinger has also drawn attention to the "political deals and compromises" of the Kansas Citizens' Alliance in his *Populism and Politics: William Alfred Peffer and the People's Party* (Lexington, Ky,. 1974), 122–23.

61. Kansas City *Labor Review*, June 12, 13, 1891; Kansas City *Sun*, Feb. 27, Oct. 23, 1891; *Wyandotte Herald*, Aug. 13, 1891.

62. Wyandotte *Herald*, Mar. 28, Apr. 4, 8, 1895; Kansas City *Labor Record*, Mar. 29, 1895.

63. Wyandotte *Herald*, Oct. 18, 1888, June 18, 1891; Kansas City *Labor Review*, July 18, 1891. See also the comprehensive study by Ross E. Paulson, *Radicalism and Reform: The Vrooman Family and American Social Thought, 1837–1937* (Lexington, Ky., 1968), although Paulson is apparently wrong in citing Hiram Vrooman's 1884 candidacy on the Anti-Monopoly ticket as his last campaign; see Kansas City *Sun*, May 1, 8, 1891.

64. Mari Jo. Buhle, *Women and American Socialism, 1870–1920* (Urbana, Ill., 1981), esp. ch. 2; Wyandotte *Gazette*, Mar. 18, June 17, July 6, Aug. 20, 1887; Kansas City *Kansas Pioneer*, Feb. 24, 1887. By 1891 the women's vote had risen to one-fifth of the total local electorate; the returns of that year (the first to be recorded by sex) gave a slight female edge to Hannan's opponent in the mayoral election. Black women represented nearly one-third of those registered (Kansas City *Sun*, Apr. 4, 1891). On the WCTU's reform role in Kansas, see also Robert R. Dykstra, *The Cattle Towns* (New York, 1968), 287; *Woman's Journal* quoted in Rutland (Vt.) *Herald*, Apr. 18, 1887. On the relation of suffragists, Populists, and immigration, see Jack S. Blocker, Jr., "The Politics of Reform: Populists, Prohibition, and Woman Suffrage, 1891–92," *The Historian*, 34 (Aug. 1972), 614–32; Alan P. Grimes, *The Puritan Ethic and Woman Suffrage* (New York, 1967), 95, 140–41; Aileen S. Kraditor, *The Ideas of the Woman Suffrage Movement, 1890–1920* (New York, 1971), 106–7.

65. *JSP*, Oct. 17, 1886; Winfield *American NonConformist*, Jan. 20, 1887.

66. Paulson, *Radicalism and Reform*, esp. 23–25, 37, 50–52; Wyandotte *Herald*, Oct. 10, 1888.

67. Paulson, *Radicalism and Reform*, 46; Kansas Bureau of Labor and Industrial Statistics, *First Annual Report*, 98–100.

68. Paulson, *Radicalism and Reform*, 49–50, 54–55, 58, 60n80, 150. Walter Vrooman published a book in 1897 entitled *Sacred Biography for Boys and Girls: An Illustrated Story Book for Young and Old, Written to Encourage Modern Heroes as Well as to Praise Ancient Ones*. On page 125, he compared biblical figures to contemporary radicals as follows: Moses—Bryan, David—Lee Meriwether, Nehemiah—John Peter Altgeld, Elijah—"Sockless" Jerry Simpson, Isaiah—George D. Herron, Jeremiah—Henry D. Lloyd, Amos—Keir Hardie, Daniel—W. D. P. Bliss, and Ezekiel—Edward Bellamy.

69. Kansas City *American Citizen*, Apr. 24, Oct. 21, 1891; Kansas City *Labor Review*, Aug. 15, 1891; Kansas City *Gazette*, Nov. 10, 1892; William H. Chafe, "The Negro in Kansas Populism" (M.A. thesis, Columbia University, 1966), 39.

6

Together but Unequal:
Southern Knights and
the Dilemmas of Race and Politics,
Richmond, Virginia

SOCIAL DIVISIONS AMONG American workers have nowhere asserted themselves more strongly than in the biracial South. The case of the Knights of Labor in Richmond, Virginia, offers an illustration of the profound implications and of the profound difficulties posed by the race question for a radical political realignment in the 1880s. Richmond was one of at least twenty-one cities in nine southern states to witness a workingmen's political movement.[1] Following impressive economic advances by the Knights of Labor, a labor reform slate swept control of municipal elections in May 1886 and went on confidently to challenge the conservative incumbent Congressman the next fall. Success rested on the cooperation of disaffected white Democrats with black Republicans. Many observers felt that they were witnessing the beginning of a major political and social upheaval. Yet, on November's election day, no labor candidate appeared on the ballot, and within a year no more labor politics, to speak of, existed in Richmond. The explanation for this sudden turn of events leads at once to the actions of a particular cast of characters at a given moment and to a longer drama of interracial cooperation and disillusionment.

Richmond's postwar recovery, delayed by the panic of 1873, hit its stride in the 1880s. As the nation's tobacco capital and a longstanding commercial and transportation center of the Southeast, the city's population steadily grew from 63,600 to 81,388 over the decade. A manufacturing boom accompanied the growth in population. Richmond's iron industry, including the famous Tredegar Works of Joseph T. Anderson, tripled in value and helped boost Virginia from sixteenth to seventh largest producer in the nation. Older industries including marble and stone quarries, flour mills, and boot and shoe factories also showed signs of renewal. Most of all, however, Richmond prospered by the continuing good fortune of King Tobacco. By 1885 some fifty tobacco processing factories meant triple the product from any other trade in sales and value. The 1870s had inaugurated a new branch of the tobacco industry: cigarettes. Of the latter Richmond produced 3 million in 1875 and 65 million six years later. By 1886 in the largest factory of its kind in the world, employing 1,000 women and children, more than a million cigarettes a day were turned out. Peaking at 7,300 employees around mid-decade, the tobacco work force represented a quarter to a third of all those involved in local manufacturing.[2]

Socially, Richmond was two cities—one white, one black. Almost every area of social life indicated that white Richmond wished to distinguish itself from the more than 40 percent of the population who were black. Following the briefest of Reconstruction periods, white officials had sought to confine black residency, social organization, and political power to the huge Jackson Ward, created in 1871 around the old free-Negro settlement area. By the late 1880s official segregation in Richmond had reached the point that white and black children were walking to and from school on separate sides of the street. Howard Rabinowitz has demonstrated that even segregated access to municipal institutions was often an improvement over policies of total exclusion. It took years, for example, before the city provided a park, adequate asylum, or almshouse for Jackson Ward.[3]

Nowhere were Richmond's caste lines drawn more clearly than in the world of work. On the basis of the manuscript census of 1880, Herbert Gutman has discovered that in 1880 95 percent of Richmond's black male population in 1880 were wage earners, the remaining 5 percent representing mainly hucksters and small food dealers. Indeed, while blacks comprised 44 percent of the city's total population, they represented six out of every ten workers. Within the wage-earning labor force the racial distribution was even more striking. Eighty percent of the skilled workers, according to Gutman's figures, were white; 80 percent of the unskilled workers were black. Published statistics from the 1890 census (when blacks made up 40 percent of the total population) reaffirm the racial segmentation of the Richmond labor market. Blacks comprised 9 percent of all nonwage earners, 25 percent of the skilled trades, 39 percent of all industrial workers, and 77 percent of all unskilled laborers (Table 13). If anything, these aggregate figures mask the concentration of blacks in particular trades and underestimate the segregation of employment by race, including the total exclusion of blacks from whole categories of work, as well as the barriers to black occupational mobility.[4]

The white norm of social separatism was most strictly enforced among women workers. White women represented less than one-third of the female labor force in 1890. Even this minority, however, did not enter a general female labor market. Every one of the city's 223 female paper box-makers, for example, was white, while domestic and personal service, which encom-

TABLE 13. Male Occupational Structure in Richmond, 1890

Occupations	Number	Percent White	Percent Black
Non–Wage Earners	6,852	91	9
Capitalists and professionals	1,261	95	5
Merchants	2,551	86	14
Salaried positions	3,040	95	5
Working Class	14,642	50	50
Skilled trades	4,732	75	25
Industrial laborers	4,128	61	39
Unskilled laborers	5,782	23	77
Total	23,466	63	37

Source. U.S. Eleventh Census, 1890, *Population*, Pt. II (Washington, D.C., 1895), 718–19.
Note. The total population includes 1,972 individuals of unspecified occupation. Data are based on white and black males, aged ten and older.

TABLE 14. Female Occupational Structure in Richmond, 1890

Occupations	Number	Percent White	Percent Black
Non–Wage Earners	1,043	81	19
Merchants	296	81	19
Salaried positions (teachers, saleswomen)	747	81	19
Working Class	10,301	23	77
Skilled trades (tailoresses, printers)	169	82	18
Industrial laborers (garment, tobacco)	2,572	67	33
Unskilled laborers	122	15	85
Domestic and personal service workers	7,438	6	94
Total	11,761	30	70

Source. U.S. Eleventh Census, 1890, *Population*, Pt. II (Washington, D.C., 1895), 718–19.
Note. Total population includes 218 individuals of unspecified occupation. Data are based on white and black females, aged ten and older.

passed two of three employed women, was 94 percent black (Table 14). The tobacco factories, which employed large numbers of women of both races, took special precautions. A visitor in 1879 did "not see any mixture of black and white women; that does not seem to be allowed."[5]

Black workers in the 1880s sought to preserve positions of employment and skill that they had occupied at Emancipation. Concentrated both in unspecified general labor and in the semiskilled, mass-production industries, they continued as a near labor monopoly in the tobacco trade. The only exceptions were the white skilled cigar-makers. The iron industry depended on blacks less exclusively. Since Anderson's successful experiments at the Tredegar works, blacks had provided the menial labor at the foundries, while whites generally took the more skilled, better-paid assignments as rollers and puddlers.[6]

Except for trades where free Negroes had established footholds before 1860, blacks were virtually excluded from the artisan crafts through 1890. The pattern of nearly total exclusion held for stonecutters, printers, machinists, cabinetmakers, and men's custom tailors. These crafts generally had organized early on the basis of tight control of entry. For example, not a single free Negro machinist was found in 1860 (out of 161); only thirteen (out of 462) black machinists were reported in 1890. In other skilled work, including the building trades, blacksmithing, harness and saddle-making, and coopering, blacks held on in varying degrees of strength to positions carved out years before through the urban employment of free Negroes and, to a lesser extent, of slaves. Black plasterers, for instance, dominated the trade in 1890 just as had free blacks in 1860. For skilled black craftsmen in general, however, the trend was indicated in the estimate of apprentices in 1890–212 whites, 24 blacks.[7]

Politically, white supremacy in Richmond had been vouchsafed by astute city business leaders who themselves had directed the statewide Conservative party of Redemption since 1870. Combining old Bourbon Democrats and ex-Whigs in a marriage with northern banking and industrial interests, the Conservatives had never really been tested in their home base. They had a powerful organ of persuasion in the daily Richmond *Dispatch,* owned and edited by Henry K. Ellyson, who had succeeded to the mayoralty in the racially charged campaign of 1870. Beginning in 1880 the Conservatives were represented in Congress by former state's attorney George D. Wise, nephew to the popular antebellum governor, Henry A. Wise who had among other accomplishments presided over the execution of John Brown. Even the powerful Readjuster rebellion led by General William Mahone, which gained control of state government from 1879 to 1883, failed to dent Conservative control of Richmond. Until 1886 Richmond's Conservative power-brokers, popularly known as "The Ring," handpicked candidates for the common council primary and then dominated all but the black Jackson Ward on election day. Indeed, the 1880s in Richmond as in Virginia as a whole appear in retrospect to have prepared the ground for an era of unchallenged one-party rule. The symbol of the new-model Bourbon conquest of state authority was, appropriately enough, General Fitzhugh Lee, nephew to the heroic Confederate commander, elected governor in 1885.[8]

This is not to say, however, that the city's Democrats could afford to take their opposition lightly. In addition to its own shrewd political leaders, the local Republican party could count on the overwhelming loyalty of the city's sizable black citizenry. "The typical black," complained the *Dispatch,* "recognized the white Democrats as his friends during 364 days of the year. On the remaining day he is a Republican." Despite obstacles ranging from bribery to vote-stealing to physical intimidation, blacks as organized through the Republican party remained a formidable electoral bloc in the mid-1880s. In September 1886, for example, all potential voters were required to reregister within a period of only six days. To the dismay of the political establishment, blacks still managed to register a considerably greater proportion of their numbers than whites.[9]

Two black Republican newspapers, the Virginia *Star* (1877–88) and the Richmond *Planet* (1883–), played an important role in the mobilization of black voters. The *Planet* was edited by John Mitchell, Jr., who had been born a slave in 1863. The young Mitchell turned to publishing after being dismissed with three other black school principals in the Democratic resurgence of 1883–84. The *Planet* quickly emerged as a beacon of proud, defiant black Republicanism, offering character sketches of leading citizens, boosting candidates and business enterprises, and even urging armed self-defense against racist lynchings. While a permanent if sizable political minority on its own, the black Republican presence in Richmond immediately threatened the ruling party in the event of a political split among white voters.[10]

Throughout the period the Republican party in Richmond was directed by white political managers in conjunction with a group of black officeholders. Local party boss John S. Wise, son of Governor Henry Wise and a lawyer with important northern business connections, had followed Mahone into the Readjuster movement in 1879. Mahone himself had impeccable credentials as a war hero and railroad tycoon and had been an early leader of the Conservative party. After Readjuster policies including abolition of the poll tax and increased educational spending for both races drew the reformers into open combat with Conservative party patriarchs, Wise with Mahone made the jump to take over the Republican machinery in 1883. The very respectability of the Readjuster-cum-Republican leaders lent them a basic self-confidence and even an air of scorn toward their opponents. John Wise, a man of intellectual bearing and literary bent, privately considered Fitzhugh Lee little more than a drunken "imbecile," and in familial correspondence he likewise referred to his cousin, Conservative Congressman George Wise as "one of the most despicable and ignorant and bad demagogues I know—without a spark of genuine affection or kind-heartedness to redeem him. . . . No tongue in all Virginia has dripped with the same venomous slander and traduction as his." Under Boss Wise a few other whites served as influential ward heelers within the black neighborhoods. Among these "grocers" (who ran grogshops that served as influential social and political centers) was James H. Bahen, an Irishman who had fought for the Union before settling in Richmond.[11]

For their part black Republicans dominated the party's municipal slates. The black officeholding group generally derived from the upper ranks of the black social ladder—the professional elite whose numbers could be counted on one hand, small businessmen (grocers, barbers, and contractors), and skilled artisans. Several men whose activism dated to the early days of Reconstruction like Joseph Farrar and Josiah Crump were still politically influential in the early 1880s.[12]

A querulous yet enduring unity prevailed between the black and white sections of the Republican party. As early as 1870 the Jackson Ward organization had protested an all-white ticket, and in 1880 it demanded that patronage be expanded beyond a narrow "Custom's House clique." Another controversy had divided blacks' loyal to the old local organization from the national Republicans anxious to do business with Mahone's Readjusters. Notwithstanding an internal tug-of-war for influence among various party factions, black political leaders and constituents remained solidly Republican. A Bahen-Mitchell axis with ties to John S. Wise effectively overcame all opposition for control of the party during the 1880s.[13]

Labor organization in Richmond had occurred in bursts of activity since the end of the war. A citywide alliance of white craft unions had formed around the carpenters as early as 1870. Even as the depression of the 1870s eroded the bargaining position of the skilled crafts, Richmond labor leaders were swept up in "independent" and "workingmen's" political challenges, which by 1878 tied into the national Greenback-Labor movement. Worker organization spread by the end of the decade to the more industrial cigarmakers and iron workers, including the employees of Tredegar Iron Works. By 1881 in unprecedented moves both the coopers and the Amalgamated Iron and Steel locals had strategically opened their doors to black as well as white workers. The organized strength that existed among Richmond workers was until the 1880s nevertheless an ephemeral phenomenon, repeatedly swept back to a marginal status in hard times. After defeat in an October 1882 strike at Tredegar, for example, both the black and white Amalgamated lodges disappeared.[14]

The return of prosperity following the recession in mid-1885 signaled another round of good news for workers in the city's basic industries and for all skilled tradesmen who would benefit from a general commercial expansion. More strikes occurred in Richmond in 1886 than in the previous five years. Of ten work stoppages in 1886–87, nine were offensive actions by craft workers for increased pay or reduced hours. Seven succeeded.[15]

Heightened confidence within the labor force spurred the growth of the Knights of Labor. A visit by Terence Powderly to Richmond in January 1885 touched off a wave of recruitment, expanding well beyond the original local chartered among telegraphers in 1882. Jubilant Richmond participants watched "hundreds flocking in" to join the "revival of the Knights of Labor" as early as June 1885. When the Order was opened to black recruits that summer, twelve "colored assemblies" formed in one two-week period alone. By the end of 1886, more than thirty-five local assemblies had been chartered in Richmond and Manchester (South Richmond). Contemporary estimates placed membership, arranged in two racially distinct district assemblies, at at least 7,000 with an overall distribution of four blacks to three whites. The preeminent leader of the Richmond Knights was William Mullen, a printer by trade and son of a Methodist temperance editor, who began publishing the weekly *Labor Herald* in 1885. The Order's white District Assembly (D.A.) 84 sent Mullen along with John M. Ryall, a tobacco engineer, and F. J. Reilly, cigar manufacturer, to national conventions in 1886. The distinct social as well as racial bases brought together in one organization was suggested by black D.A. 92's corresponding representation by Richard Thompson, a tobacco roller, and W. W. Fields, a porter, as well as the dairyman (not the editor) John Mitchell.[16]

By mid-1886 the Knights were a powerful local force in Richmond. A general boycott of convict-made barrels in January removed them from the local market; within weeks the very threat of a boycott speedily brought wholesalers of all other prison-made products into line. Granite cutters informed their bosses at the end of January that they would henceforth work but nine hours with an hour off for dinner. By the end of April painters, coopers, typographers, cotton compress workers, hod carriers, and foundry workers had all been swept up in a wave of strikes. Only one local cigar firm remained nonunion by mid-March, and manufacturers were preparing to market "Master Workman," "Unknown Knight," and "Mullen's Pets" brands. By May 1886 several large tobacco factories became "purely Knights of Labor." At least one granted the eight-hour day, and women cigarette-makers added the Progress Assembly to a list of six or seven other "ladies' locals." Other indications of the Order's local vitality included a lecture series and performances by their own dramatics company. The Knights also opened a cooperative soap factory and even laid plans for a cooperative building association and underwear factory.[17]

Perhaps most indicative of labor's spreading influence was the general caution with which leading local employers responded to the upheaval. The first attempt at a unified reaction by the business community did not come until February 1886. After a strike for union recognition at the Baughman Brothers printing company, the typographers union not only announced a boycott of the firm but also gained the support of the *Labor Herald* in circulating a "rat list" (or secondary boycott) of all Baughman patrons. A committee from the chamber of commerce quickly formed to negotiate with the labor forces. While the Knights and employers could easily agree to a first principle of future arbitration, the businessmen soon split among themselves on the issues at hand. The employers divided both over whether to draw the line of decency at the issue of the boycott or only the extended boycott and over the general tone that businessmen should adopt in relation to organized labor. The early fire-eaters among the businessmen's committee, who later pressed for an injunction against the boycott committee, were initially reprimanded and outvoted.[18]

By early spring of 1886 the Richmond labor movement prepared to test its new-found strength in the political arena. A series of lapses by conservative Democrats made the moment particularly auspicious. Perhaps lulled into somnolence by its usual electoral margins, the Ring had made few overtures to the new forces. Of twenty-six Democratic members of the common council elected in 1884, for example, one or two at most worked with his hands. More important, the construction of a new city hall, eagerly awaited by building craftsmen and day laborers alike, had languished for four years in Democratic wrangling over alternative proposals and contracts. On the state level, furthermore, the Democrats had failed to redeem election pledges with regard both to free school books and the perennial debt question.

The final chink in local conservative armor came over an unexpected issue. A coalition of Knights and Republicans seriously outfoxed the Conservative leadership in defeating a Democratic-sponsored prohibition referendum. By early March 1886 Republican boss Wise, who had followed labor's rise with intense interest, commented privately, "The Bourbons are in a sweet fix. . . . Our policy ought to be coalesce with any element to beat them. Here I am very hopeful we may combine with the liquor dealers and Knights of Labor and turn the Bourbons upside down." A personal letter from State Republican Chairman Mahone, "displayed where it would do the most good," helped in April to turn an estimated 95 percent of the black vote behind an overwhelming popular defense of local licensing. This victory of the "wet" constituency, ironically involving two organizations that were nationally associated with strong temperance (if not prohibitionist) positions, marked the first electoral setback for local Conservatives since the Civil War. The vulnerability of the city patriarchs was not lost on their enemies; the liquor referendum provided a direct stimulus to the Knights' effort a month later.[19]

In late April white Knights of Labor formally moved against the "edicts of ring rule" by separating themselves from the local machinery of the Democratic party. A convention of delegates from white District 84 authorized abstention from the April primary and fielded its own Reform slate of candidates for the May municipal election.[20]

The Reformers generally attacked the incumbent common council for addressing only the interests of the "wealthy class," "looking on those who earn their living by labor as secondary." Specifically, they demanded that the new city hall be built by Richmond mechanics on day labor with Virginia granite (the Knights had secured a foothold in the neighboring quarries), elimination of the contract system for city projects, and weekly cash payments to municipal employees. Condemning politically appointed supervisory personnel, the Reformers scored "those who are required to do comparatively nothing and whose time seems to be their own . . . while those who work hard and receive nothing are watched by paid overseers and docked for 10 minutes time lost." Only a "cleaning out of the legislative departments of our city government" could correct these "class and partisan" evils. Finally the opposition platform appealed for "a general understanding and cooperation of the toiling masses, irrespective of party color, or social standing."[21]

The workingmen's political movement, like its parent organization, the Knights of Labor, drew support from a broad social spectrum. Generally speaking, only the financial-industrial elite and the professional stratum were absent from Reform ranks. Workingmen's candidates for city council and board of aldermen were overwhelmingly skilled workers and small shopkeepers. Still, the Knights apparently weighed the sympathy and influence of their candidates as well as social position. Two iron manufacturers and a tobacco company manager, for example, were rewarded as "honorable" (compliant) employers with Reform endorsements. All but two of the Reform candidates had been long-time Democrats.[22]

If the white Reform movement drew a cross-section of the population for its support, its working-class core was itself heterogeneous. The prominence of names like Kaufman, Kaufeldt, Kelly, Lange, Molloy, Murphy, Parrish, and Pearce among the labor candidates suggest an ethnic as well as a class component to the disaffection from Bourbonism. To be sure, it is difficult to disentangle the immigrant from the rest of the white working people of Richmond. Although only 5 percent of the city's 1880 population was foreign-born, first- and second-generation immigrants composed one-fourth of skilled white artisans and nearly one-third of unskilled white laborers. During the 1880s the city supported two daily German-language newspapers as well as two branches of the Irish National League.[23]

Blacks in Richmond held the greatest significance for the white Reformers. No accidental flourish of egalitarian rhetoric accounted for the Reformers' address to men of a different "party, color, or social standing." Rather, it was a matter of political necessity. Before the spring elections Richmond's white insurgents had come to terms with the black Republicans. Reformers deferred to the Republican slate in Jackson Ward and in return secured a Republican endorsement of their ticket in the rest of the city.

The spring Reform campaign was capped by resounding victory. Workers trooped to the polls and carried all but one ward for the labor-Republican ticket. Reformers gained a clear majority of the city council and half the board of aldermen, as well as the post of city sergeant, the one contested executive office. On election day excitement ran high, fights broke out, and crowds paraded through the streets at midnight. Mahone received a gleeful Richmond report: "We had a slight volcanic eruption here on Thursday last . . . at which time all nature seemed convulsed. And all indications point to further upheavals during the year." The *Dispatch* referred to the city's "first disaster since Reconstruction days."[24]

But this initial success caused almost as much alarm within Reform ranks as among conservative Democrats. White workingmen had stepped outside the Democracy and extended a tentative hand to black Republicans to beat the Bourbons. How far should they carry this apostasy? Some of the Reformers began to take themselves seriously as an independent political force. Others balked at cutting themselves off from their traditional political guardians. Important differences of opinion also surfaced among Republicans. Mahone urged a delicate, cooperative stance toward the Reformers, but local party leaders, including John Wise, were more anxious to convert the Democratic loss to quick Republican gain. Black political leaders, in turn, took a wary *quid pro quo* attitude toward the Democrats-cum-insurgents. In a lead editorial entitled "What Will Be Done For Our People?" the *Planet* demanded immediate returns in the form of jobs at the colored almshouse, appointment of a black physician, and representation in all other areas of city employment. By the second meeting of the Reform caucus, twelve whites had withdrawn to protest the outspoken presence of the Jackson Ward councilmen who had taken up the *Planet*'s call.[25]

Black Republicans did not get their way with the caucus, but Wise more or less did. Wise had been careful not to show his hand too early: "I saw that [the Reformers] were without leadership, and wanted them to become thoroughly confused, knowing that when that occurred they would be grateful to any one who could pilot them, whereas an earlier interference might breed resistance or a feeling of resentment." The appropriate moment of chaos finally arrived among "Reformers" and "darkies." Wise then stepped between the feuding parties and quickly secured agreements from Mullen and Henry L. Carter, the coopers' leader, to a package of compromises on municipal appointments quite favorable to Republican interests.[26]

Unfortunately for the Reform strategists, by the time they settled down to business, they had lost their council majority. With astute diplomacy "straight-out" Democrats had met repentant insurgents in a "spirit of conciliation." In addition, the Regulars had not opposed the nomination of a Reformer for city council president, effectively encouraging him to act as a nonpartisan legislative steward. Finally, several Democratic officeholders had declined reappointment to allow loyal Knights of Labor to take their places. A Knights of Labor tinner thereby became fire department chief, and an Irishman nominated initially by the Reformers was unanimously supported for police court bailiff. But Reform choices generally were thwarted by successive twenty-nine to eighteen decisions of a joint meeting of the local legislative bodies. Four black members of the Reform coalition, which numbered twenty-two at full strength, withheld their votes from the caucus nominees in a pique. While Reformers still voted together more often than not, the record for the remainder of the year indicated that the initial frustrations had permanently wrecked caucus discipline.[27]

The postelection setbacks, however, only strengthened the independent political tendencies within the main body of the Knights. By August they were preparing to choose their own candidate for Congress. Not only had the Order been pushed further toward creation of an independent political party, but the momentum of events had strengthened ties between the politically minded white locals and the black district assembly. Unlike the white-organized April movement, all locals were now invited to join the Labor Reform Committee. Names submitted to the nominating convention included Mullen, Wise, Carter, and John Bethel, city council president. With 70 percent of his votes coming from blacks, Mullen easily captured the nomination. In a most significant parallel action, Republican Chairman Mahone's state committee unofficially endorsed the labor candidacy and agreed to make no Republican nomination in the third congressional district.[28]

Contemporaries disagreed about the character of William Mullen. A confident, thirty-six-year-old Virginian, he seemed equally dedicated to his ideals and his ambition. An admirer of Henry George, Mullen nevertheless had always toed a firm Democratic line in politics. He had derided alliance of Richmond workingmen with liquor dealers in 1877 but had overseen the creation of just such an alliance in 1886. On the race issue as well, Mullen's principles appeared sturdiest when coupled with self-fulfillment. In 1884 Mullen had sought a local patronage appointment from the Grover Cleveland administration; rumor had it that he had boasted at the time of turning "the d——d Republicans and d——d Negroes out." But, as a Knights' organizer, Mullen pressed vigorously for enrollment of blacks. Mullen did not appear uncomfortable with the Republican-abolitionist heritage of the national labor reform organization. Before the 1885 general assembly, he had presented Powderly with a gavel made of three symbolic pieces of wood. The first came from the hall of Patrick Henry's "Give me liberty" address; the second was cut from a tree at Yorktown, the scene of Cornwallis's surrender to Washington; the third derived from Old Libby prison, where "patriotic sons of our common country," as Mullen explained, "were confined . . . for being engaged in a struggle to liberate a race of people from the galling yoke of slavery." The Civil War, according to Mullen, had been America's "second Revolution"; he passed the gavel to "the chief of that grand army that is to work the third revolution," the liberation of "slaves of monopoly and oppression." The Order seemed to lift Mullen to his most generous sentiments and vision; for several years it practically consumed his attention. Powderly's choice of Richmond for the site of the Knights' Tenth General Assembly, scheduled for October 1886, represented, in part, a tribute to his southern field marshal.[29]

Mullen's nomination for Congress precipitated a major realignment within the city's opposition forces. The Jefferson Ward Tammany Reform Club spearheaded the Mullen campaign, arranging speakers, marches, and music. But seven anti-Mullen local assemblies, including the tinners' union, proclaimed themselves the "Democratic Knights of Labor." Two of the prominent figures in the Democratic Knights, both leaders of the typographers, had been indicted with Mullen and others in the Baughman Brothers boycott case. Although charges were dismissed following the election, it is possible that legal harassment or political plea-bargaining played some role in these defections from the independent ticket. Congressman George Wise, meanwhile, placated local granite workers by securing a day-labor clause in the contract for the federal customs house in Richmond.[30]

A more important dissenter from the labor candidacy was John S. Wise. From the beginning of his contact with the Knights, the Republican leader had expressed skepticism about their political potential: "they promise very bravely and then, when the fight comes, are whipped right back into Democratic traces." Disintegration of the Reform majority on the city council only confirmed his doubts. Disdaining personal interest in a labor nomination, Wise declared that Republicans should not go "whoring around after a lot of tramps who have no following and no principles." As a strong organization man, he spoke for the interests of a party that might count on an electoral majority in four of the six counties of the district. The rural party regulars, in particular, were not about to defer anonymously to an unknown political instrument and especially to a candidate who stirred their personal mistrust. "If coalition means only that the Republicans are to aid the Reformers whenever needed," Wise warned publicly in early September, "but the Reformers never to aid the Republicans, it is a one-sided affair that had better be abandoned at once." Resistance to Mahone's dictatorial control of party affairs also seems to have weighed heavily in the insistence of Wise and others to proceed as usual with their own district nominating convention.[31]

Approaching their October 2 conclave, Republicans split bitterly around the labor candidacy. Pro-Mullen Colored Independent Campaign Clubs opposed Regular Henrico County Republicans at each ward caucus. Anti-Mullen sentiment came from white Republicans looking to Wise for leadership, black postal and customs-house workers tied to federal patronage, and rural blacks untouched by the labor movement. Mullen's only reported white supporters within the party were Alderman Rowland Hill, a carpenter, and longtime labor leader and ship joiner, Dan Alley—undoubtedly both Knights of Labor. Mullen's twenty-odd black delegates included tobacco worker Ben Scott, an outspoken independent in Richmond black politics since 1867, and dry goods machinist J. T. Wilson. A carpenter, a blacksmith, a plasterer, a wood and coal merchant, a saloonkeeper, and a grocer combined with others identified in the city directory simply as "laborers" to make up the rest of Mullen's support.[32]

Even if less dramatically so than among the feuding white Democrats, class differences also divided the black Republicans. With one or two exceptions, the blacks now pushing for power within the Republican party were not people who had figured prominently in earlier political affairs. They did not come from the tiny professional group whose dependence on governmental favor encouraged their remaining stalwart party men. On the whole they did not meet James T. Moore's categorization of black politicians as the "emerging middle class" of the black community. Instead, it appears that the labor movement helped to prepare or embolden a new leadership group among some Richmond blacks. Such a group overlapped in social roots with the traditional leadership, but it also represented a shift in influence toward the laboring poor.[33]

Pro-Mullen Republicans, however, did not prevail over the party brass. Adverse rulings from the credentials committee and a hostile chair depleted the insurgents' strength, and after a spirited floor fight Judge Edmund Waddill, Jr., emerged as the Republican standard-bearer for November. County Sheriff J. W. Southward, presenting himself as a Knight of Labor who had "boycotted every one Mullen blacklisted even though he lived in the county," issued the official proscription of the labor candidate; the sheriff assailed the master workman for his temperance proclivities ("a milk and cider man"), for refusing to campaign openly for Republican favor, and for lack of commitment to "national issues," meaning that Mullen had not endorsed the high tariff.[34]

Despite the division in opposition ranks, no one yet counted Mullen out. The *Dispatch* accorded him good odds for election. Mahoneite Republicans, still trying to arrange a last-minute compromise with the labor men, were even more emphatic. They believed Wise and Waddill had committed "political suicide." A Republican paper in Petersburg warned, "The labor element will dominate *both* parties henceforth, and gentlemen who rashly incur the animosity of those elements may as well get out of politics as soon as possible."[35] Tensions mounted in Richmond with the approach of the federal election. Even the Democratic majority on the common council had accommodated itself to demands of the new political forces, and multiple signs of labor influence drew harsh reaction from the city's old guard. In early September "A Taxpayer" complained, "Will a man who is not a Knight of Labor be allowed to work on the City Hall?" A howl of disapproval followed news that public works employees had received a wage boost allegedly "50% above the market place."[36]

The shift in tone in the city's politics was most clearly illustrated by the deflated influence of the chamber of commerce. Holding a public meeting to aid the Charleston victims of the earthquake which struck the Southeast on August 31, the businessmen (apparently acting according to custom) decided on an appropriate amount for relief, determined that it must be taken from the public treasury ("the fairest and most equitable method"), and then approached the city government for ratification. The city council, approving its own contribution, refused even to consider the chamber's resolution. "As a representative of the people," Democrat Andrew Pizzini explained, "[he] did not require the Chamber of Commerce to tell him his duty."[37]

To its critics the reform movement had grown ominously larger than life. It no longer expressed particular grievances but seemed bent on a redistribution of political power. Conservatives worried that the Reformers "have become more partisan in the support of class doctrines and the demand for class legislation than they ever were as members of the Democratic and Republican parties." More disquieting still was the possibility that the Richmond movement was only a link in a chain of political and industrial insurrection slowly encircling the nation. With one eye on Henry George in New York and the other on Mullen at home, the *Whig* uncovered "socialistic and agrarian elements" threatening the "genius of our free institutions." In late September, a local merchant despaired of "this terrible social earthquake." Evoking "the scenes enacted at Pittsburg[h] in 1875 (or thereabouts)," he pointed to "what has actually been done in our own city during the past twelve months. I think of the boldness, the insolence, and some of the leaders of this fearful movement." By the time the general assembly of the Knights opened in Richmond even Democratic Governor Fitzhugh Lee was trying to steer the emerging southern labor movement into calmer waters. Addressing the first session of the Knights' convention on October 3, the governor expressed general agreement with the "original" aims of the Order. But, in pointed reference to events in the host city, he underscored General Master Workman Powderly's "assertion that the Knights of Labor would never be a political party" and insisted that "there has always been and always will be two great political parties. Room has never been found for a third. . . . Let us follow your chief's advice and keep politics out [of the Order]."[38]

The general assembly and its attendant racial events caught the political process in Richmond at both a revealing and decisive moment. To be brief, the events included a direct attack on the color line by D.A. 49 of New York and its black delegate Frank Ferrell. This pointed show of principle spread with the initial support of Powderly to encompass many other northerners among the 800 delegates. Virginians were shocked by the sight of Ferrell following Governor Lee to the podium to reaffirm the Order's commitment to the "abolition of distinctions maintained by creed and color," by interracial delegations inhabiting their hotels, and especially by the mixed company in public of men and women of the opposite race. The Bourbon press excoriated the Knights for their display of "social equality in its richest phrase."[39]

A showdown came midway through the convention. Invited by the visiting Shakespearean actor Daniel Bandmann to a performance of *Hamlet*, Ferrell and sixty other members of D.A. 49 took orchestra seats at the Mozart Academy. This breach of the traditional gallery-only restriction on blacks, coming as it did at the city's most fashionable concert hall, nearly led to violence. The next day, the local Law and Order League, formed to protect businesses from labor boycotts and containing "the best families in the city," had its members "armed and ready for bloodshed" in the event of further depredations of the city's cultural monuments. Shouts of "Coons and Forty Niners" were heard in the streets. Heeding the warnings of police chief Thomas Poe, Powderly quickly moved to avert calamity. The general master workman promised de facto compliance with the local social code and exacted a similar pledge from D.A. 49. An uneasy truce prevailed for the duration of the convention.[40]

The social equality issue pointed to the dilemma of the Knights of Labor in the South. Crusading egalitarianism mixed uneasily with practical considerations of the Order's survival and growth. Massachusetts delegate and labor editor Frank Foster reflected the ambivalence within the general assembly over how far to push an issue like racial equality. Foster believed that "perhaps a little too much of this color line question" had been agitated for the Order's own good: "Still, our southern brethren must learn."[41]

Southern white Knights of Labor greeted the practical application of equality doctrines by the general assembly with varying degrees of resentment. In Augusta the Richmond "events" set off "near panic" among striking Georgia textile workers, already aroused by rumors of the importation of black strikebreakers. In addition an Oxford, North Carolina, master workman reported that "disregard of the 'color line' " by the general assembly alongside local political gains by Republicans had set off a wave of recriminations against the Order: "They pointed at us with scorn and kept crying 'Nigger! Nigger!' until the two words 'nigger' and Knight became almost synonymous terms." That happened even though the Oxford mayor and ex-mayor were Knights; as a consequence the Order suffered a serious loss of support there. The reactions in Augusta and Oxford were admittedly extreme, but the likely fallout from the race issue was not lost on the southern convention delegates. White southerners successfully steered a resolution through the assembly specifying that the Order had no intention "to disrupt the social relations . . . in various parts of the country." At the last moment the Knights' executive board cancelled a fancy-dress ball in deference to southern opposition to mixed social gatherings. Local white Knights of Labor shared in the opposition to any attempt "to build a new social fabric during a two-week visit." While no mass exodus was recorded, a New York *Times* correspondent noted "a storm

of indignation and a new hesitancy by whites in their relation to the order."
One reporter heard that "a few" local Knights intended to quit the Order to
join the Law and Order League.[42]

A different response was accorded the gestures of the general assembly by
Richmond blacks. The white supremacy press turned up only a solitary black
voice, an unnamed out-of-town delegate, to protest the "stirring up of the
race issue at the convention." More typical reactions were readily apparent.
Local black families threw open their homes to mixed delegations of Knights
refused lodging at white-only hotels. Enthusiasm was undisguised. A wealthy
white woman complained nervously that since the convention had opened
"her colored cook and servant have been trifling and inclined to be impu-
dent." A labor parade and day of festivities heralded the mid-point of the
convention. White Richmond citizens pointedly avoided the activities, but
blacks turned out in force. One correspondent believed that "the entire colored population of Richmond" was present along the parade route, "including
a few colored women in carriages." Two blacks and a white served as the
parade marshals. The *Whig* found in the procession more than a good-humored
throng of 3,000 marchers: "It was a small army of workingmen, white and
black, animated by a common purpose, and marching under a common flag.
It was the outward manifestation of a great movement, yet in its incipiency
perhaps, the ultimate results of which only the revolving years can reveal."[43]

Richmond blacks reserved their boldest gestures for those most responsible
for the provocative racial events. As the general assembly neared its end, a
banquet was held in honor of D.A. 49 in the Negro hall above Harris's funeral
parlor. The occasion seemed to signal a semiofficial and nonpartisan expression of gratitude to the New Yorkers and their friends by leaders of the local
black community. Carefully tempering with words an act that doubtlessly
infuriated the city's patriarchs, "each one of the colored orators" dismissed
the social equality question "in good set terms." Said Republican District
Attorney Walter Scott, a Yale Law School graduate: "The only social equality
that had ever existed had been thrust upon them by whites." As if to underscore the refutation of any interest in racial amalgamation, black women did
not attend the banquet. While the blacks painstakingly tailored their public
words, the response to New York Socialist Victor Drury's address was uncen-
sored. Reported one newspaper: "He said that what Forty-Eight was to the
oppressed millions of Europe, it was hoped Forty-Nine might be to the struggling masses of Americans in this day, and this play upon words and reference
to a red-letter period of the revolutionary spirit nearly forty years ago abroad
were received with cheers."[44]

Cleavage between whites and blacks on the equality issue at the general
assembly created an immediate impact upon local politics. A Virginia organizer protested to Powderly that the racial events had done "great injury . . .
to our labor candidate for Congress." The southern version of the bloody

shirt, with its appeal to the deepest of racial loyalties, wreaked havoc on the independent campaign. In attempting to sidestep the race issue—appealing to both whites and blacks solely on class terms—Mullen himself permitted both of his opponents to cast him in the worst possible light. Ten days before the November election, Democrats revealed positive evidence of Mullen's sympathy "with what '49' had done." In the company of one black and one white campaign associate near the Goochland County courthouse, Mullen had sat down at the refreshment stand of Martha Cousins, "an old colored woman." When, according to custom, she refused to serve the mixed party at the same table, Mullen reportedly had risen and indignantly turned away with his friends, vowing to take his supper elsewhere. The Goochland courthouse incident soon was picked up by Republicans as well—only with a different twist. At a Waddill rally Wise claimed that the story had not ended with Mullen's declaration of principle. Rather, "half an hour afterwards Mullen shook his colored friend and sneaked back to the stand and bought a pie." Wise warned his audience, "You see how he went back on the negro there, don't you? And if you vote for him he will fool you."[45]

The campaign's direction pushed Mullen permanently onto the defensive. Democratic orators reviled Mullen as a secret Republican agent intent on the ruin of the South, while Democratic councilmen passed election-eve increases to selected city workers and Congressman Wise offered a smile of friendship to the general principles of Knights of Labor. The Republican campaign apparatus was also in high gear and operated smoothly above and below ground. Expecting whites to split their votes, Waddill promised a glorious victory if blacks remained solid. Meanwhile, organized disruptions made it increasingly difficult for Mullen to venture into Jackson Ward. The highlight of the labor campaign was a march and rally of 1,500 supporters, mostly blacks. But it was nearly broken up by black hecklers organized by Wise. By the end of October, both the *Dispatch* and the *Whig* were marveling at the Republicans' effectiveness: "Two or three weeks ago all the Negroes were said to be for Mullen. Today they are said to be for Waddill."[46]

The heated congressional campaign came to a quick and unexpected end. At the decision of his campaign committee, Mullen dropped out of the race and threw his support to the Democrat George Wise "to kill Waddill, [J. S.] Wise, and Co., the deadliest enemies of the Reform party." In a bitter message to his followers, the ex-candidate explained that the Republican county leaders had first induced him to run and then had "switched their minds and effectively sabotaged his campaign." In Mullen's mind both the party's chiefs and its rank and file bore the onus for his dashed hopes: "While this is slander on those of our colored brethren who have stood firm, a sufficient number have gone over to make our success doubtful. They have permitted themselves to be whipped into line by the party lash and are alone responsible for the defeat of the labor candidate." The mere likelihood of defeat, by transforming the independent third political alternative into a broker for one of the old parties, had created an impossible situation for the biracial ticket. "As workingmen," argued Mullen, "we cannot afford to assume . . . responsibility for taking a Democratic district and putting it in the hands of the Republican party."[47]

With only slightly less vituperation, Mahone Republicans concurred in the verdict of the labor leader. "Our friends ran the labor people back into the Democratic camp," C. C. Clarke wrote to Mahone. "I voted for Judge Waddill of course—through party fealty as well as personal friendship—but it was like casting the ballot in [the] James River—his defeat was a foregone conclusion after Mullen withdrew—and Mullen's withdrawal was also a foregone conclusion after they brought out a candidate against him and then abused him like a pickpocket." The black grocer, Colin Payne, who had resigned from the Republican city committee after Waddill's nomination, revealed that black Republicans were "very much divided" by the election. "The laboring men thinks it was done to defeat them and something have to be done to homonize [*sic*] our party."[48]

Republican strategy in the fall campaign was bitterly disputed for years afterward. John Wise would cling to the view that the party would have enjoyed a pure, uncompromised triumph had Mullen not hung on until he received an unspecified deal from the Democrats. Defeat in the congressional race stimulated an escalating disaffection between Wise and Mahone, leading to an open break in 1888. As late as 1890 Mullen's black aide, J. T. Wilson, was still fulminating against Wise as "a man who had come as a Moses and betrayed us." By the time Wilson spoke, Wise had already left town. Counsel for the first electric street railroad in Richmond, he moved to New York City to represent numerous urban transit interests.[49]

A period of demoralization, mistrust, and recrimination followed immediately upon the Mullen fiasco in labor circles. The campaign that had begun with such bright prospects "had not been advantageous to the order here," according to one Richmond Knight. Politically, the labor bubble had all but burst. On the common council, swing voters, recalculating where the political future lay, snuggled back among Conservative Democrats. In its first meeting since the election, the council excluded black mechanics from work on the city hall. Only a black councilman opposed the move. At the same time labor's bid to restrict the construction project to local workers and apprentices was rejected, and a city hall contract was given to a quarry being boycotted by the Knights. In April 1887 the council elected with labor votes heard a protest from Mullen and boilermaker J. P. Devine that workers who had shown "reform" sympathies on election day in 1886 had later been frozen out of city jobs. Collapse of labor's political power was evident in Devine's pleadings: "We didn't come here as a big railroad corporation, in royal array, we are but poor workingmen. I have just laid down my hammer. We represent the sons and daughters of men who are strewn over your battlefields." Within months of his aborted candidacy, Mullen was finding it difficult to get work. Within a year he had suspended publication of the *Labor Herald,* and in 1889 Powderly learned that Mullen had been dropped as master workman in an internal reorganization of the Richmond district.[50]

A last gasp of Reform activity in the fall of 1887 demonstrated both the electoral potential of interracial coalition and the deteriorating position of the labor movement. In this instance John Wise and General Mahone temporarily came to agreement in offering Republican support for a white workingmen's Reform state legislative ticket pledged to Mahone's senatorial reelection. The Reform party, again representing the Mullen wing of city council and labor circles, took as its keynote an attempt by the Law and Order League to transform the Democratic party into an overtly antilabor instrument. With a majority on the city's Democratic Central Committee, the leaguers had allegedly pressured city hall workers to renounce their union affiliations, conspired with the state legislature to pass a police commissioners' bill depriving local representatives of the selection of these officers, and engineered the creation of a new judgeship for a lower court judge who issued the Baughman boycott injunction. Meanwhile, the league had privately coordinated an employer offensive against all labor organizations including the launching of a boycott against union-made cigars and the breakup of a bricklayers' nine-hour strike in April 1887. Spending its efforts on wavering white Democrats and leaving to Wise and company the mobilization of Republican voters, the Reformers proclaimed that "with the support of the honest workingmen of this city and the help of God they will show the tyrannical faction which controls the Democratic party that the liberties of the people cannot be trampled down by unfeeling autocrats." This effort of united Richmond opposition forces still fell 600 votes short of victory and marked the last appearance of independent, labor-based political activity in Richmond.[51]

Fading even faster than insurgent political efforts in Richmond was the Knights' organization itself. With membership in both the white and black district assemblies dropping precipitously from the thousands to the hundreds, a white iron molder reported succinctly in March 1888 that "the order here is not holding its own." As aggressive, class-based organizations of workingmen fell away, a few, more conservative adaptations to the industrial order rose to take their place. In mid-1888, for example, the YMCA established an educational program aimed specifically at Tredegar iron workers. The same period marked the reappearance of the Colored Mercantile Association, a group set up to sell stock in land for homes and businesses "instead of allowing the best land . . . to pass into the hands of white foreigners." The *Dispatch* noted that the association had been founded "two or three years ago

. . . but just at that time the Knights of Labor excitement started. The originators decided to let this movement rest until the labor agitation quieted somewhat."[52]

Disappearance of an effective interracial political opposition ironically also appeared to soften elite concern about the maintenance of a strict social color line. With sardonic ill humor the *Labor Herald* (in one of its last issues) took note of a July 1888 dinner thrown at the Commercial Club by the Electric Street Railway Company for the city's most prominent gentlemen and public representatives. Included at the table were five black Republican leaders. Aside from the obvious power play for future political influence, the "electric gentlemen," in the *Herald*'s eye seemed to be directly contradicting the firm stand of the city's elite on the race issue: "We cannot fail to remember how severely these same gentlemen criticize our white working people about election times if they talk of coalescing with the colored workingman. . . . We also remember how severely the representatives of D.A. 49 were criticized for eating at the table of a restaurant kept by a colored man, while no voice of protest is raised against the representatives of our 'best people' for banqueting with colored men. . . . People who live in glass houses ought to be careful which way they throw rocks."[53]

For Richmond's blacks the late 1880s onward were increasingly desperate years politically. With a new vehemence, Bourbons preached total exclusion of blacks from public office. Facing additional impediments, nearly 2,000 fewer blacks in Richmond voted in Mahone's 1889 losing bid for governor than in the legislative election two years previously. In 1890, despite local black protest, the Republican party did not field a congressional candidate in the Third District. At the Colored Men's Convention of that year, after the final defeat in Washington of the Force Bill, J. T. Wilson raged, "We saved the National Government from dissolution to be treated as orphan children, apprenticed to the rice, cotton, and tobacco growers of the South." In 1896 the first all-white common council since the Civil War took office in Richmond, and the year 1902 witnessed the official disfranchisement of Virginia blacks.[54]

Nevertheless, even in this period of decline, there remained glimmerings of the common aspirations that had surfaced in 1886. George Duncan, a shoemaker by trade and new master workman of white D.A. 84, filed a complaint against harassment of Jackson Ward voters by Democratic poll-watchers in the fall of 1888. His petition led ultimately to the seating of the persistent Republican candidate, Edmund Waddill, by the U.S. Congress. A Knights' newspaper backed Mahone for governor in 1889. Three years later only fraud prevented a Populist victory in the Fourth Congressional District. In 1888 this same district had elected the black Republican John Mercer Langston to Congress. As late as 1895, Powderly received a letter from organizer W. T. Booze, asking him to allow ninety black men and women from Richmond to form a local. The evidence suggests that the core of the Knights that survived into the 1890s had finally moved into a close working relationship with the state Republican party. Only now the Order no longer represented a movement vying for power, but a lonely legion of dissenters.[55]

While unfolding in an intricate logic of their own, the Richmond events also formed a piece of the larger problem that the Knights of Labor encountered in trying to unify American workers. On the whole, it can be said that the Knights loomed in the mid-1880s as a beacon of racial enlightenment in a dark sea. In no other contemporary organization, it appears, was there such a quickening dynamic toward, rather than away from, race equality. Never, however, were the Knights so foolish as to think that the past had been overcome. The white master workman of Natchez, Mississippi, was hopeful of organizing women cotton operatives. He warned Powderly, nonetheless, that "the Colored race for the present at least had better be formed into separate assemblies." A black master workman from Montgomery, Alabama, delicately explained to the national leader, "As a general thing the colored people of the South cannot understand the whites and the white organizer cannot do just what is necessary for the up-building of the order." From Florence, South Carolina, the message was more blunt, "Our white Brothers down South is not eager to organize the Negro Race, thats why we appeal to you for a colored organizer."[56]

Blacks' embrace of the Knights of Labor in these circumstances was neither uncritical nor unlimited. The Washington *Bee*, for example, warned the Order to put its resolutions "into practical form before we would advise colored people to go too far." T. Thomas Fortune, the editor of the *Freeman* and a strong prolabor voice, chided Powderly for having pulled back on the race issue at the end of the general assembly "in craven deference to the yell of the Southern white press and the demands of Southern Knights of Labor."[57]

The record indicates that the Knights had not organized many blacks in the South; rather, blacks had adopted the Knights. No other conclusion makes sense given the lightninglike speed of formation of black assemblies in Richmond in 1885 and in other parts of the South. With black workers as with other groups in labor history, the image of movement from "the unorganized" to "the organized" may sometimes misrepresent the situation. Richmond black workers had organized as early as 1867 into benefit societies with names like the Stevedores and Waggoners Association, Baley factory hands, and Union Laboring Class. During the late 1860s and early 1870s organized strikes were conducted by black stevedores, coopers, railroad construction laborers, and waiters. Workingmen expressed themselves through various instruments. Thirty black laborers petitioned the federal government in 1885 for back pay due them in "services rendered" in 1865. Their agent of persuasion then was Mahone and the resources of the state Republican party. When black Richmond D.A. 92 was formed, one must suppose the reality to have been in part a shading of existing community organization into the new structure.[58]

If, when given the chance, black workers tended to organize en masse, or as a preexisting community, into the labor movement, the historian's questions shift to the southern white workingmen and their leaders. Why and how far were white workers willing to extend their areas of contact and cooperation with black labor? It would, of course, be naive to assume that the official equal-rights doctrines of the Knights of Labor alone converted the membership to take positive steps on the race issue. The calculation of Paul Chotier, Morgan City, Louisiana, master workman "that the Colored Laborers should be organized in this place as it will work detrimental to us if not taken in," for example, suggests that necessity was often the handmaiden of progress. C. Vann Woodward has offered an analytic framework for Chotier's opinion: "Two possible but contradictory policies could be used by the labor movement toward the Black worker: eliminate the Negro as a competitor by excluding him from the skilled trades either as an apprentice or as a worker, or take him in as an organized worker committed to the defense of a common standard of wages. Southern labor wavered between these antithetical policies from the seventies into the nineties, sometimes adopting one, sometimes the other."[59]

Accepting that Woodward's alternate poles of economic logic mark the long-term dilemma of the labor movement, one might question whether they describe the real options encountered at any particular moment in the late nineteenth century. The tentative, precarious relations of southern white and black workers assumed numerous intermediary positions, each with distinct degrees and limits of cooperation. If blacks and whites were not actively competing for the same jobs, choices might present themselves as other than full economic partnership or total exclusion. Within the Knights of Labor, generally speaking, black and white workers were together but not equal. Separate assemblies and the implicit acceptance of (or at least white disregard for) the inherited racial hierarchy of trades are signs that the movement represented only the first, tentative steps toward interracial trust and solidarity. Their very distance, both socially and economically, from the mass of black workers, however, presented southern white labor leaders with a strategic choice that stopped short of Woodward's ultimate economic polarities. A white Knights' organizer in the blackbelt Mississippi town of Wesson thus approached his task with a delicate combination of urgency and cautiousness:

Without their [i.e., black] organization the Order can effect next to nothing in any department of industry nor need we hope to accomplish anything by legislation till the masses of laborers of all colors and nationalities understand one another better, and more fully comprehend the mutual duties and reciprocal obligations between themselves and employers. Unless by means of organization we can be brought to cooperate, our case is lamentable, and will be perpetuated by the gross ignorance that pervades every nook and corner of our state. The old Bourbon element so long used to its almost unopposed labor, political, and pernicious system will not remain passive and indifferent while the masses are seeking to ameliorate their condition educationally, politically, morally and financially. Some of them are already imparting to us the purpose of inaugurating the social-equality principle, knowing that said principle is so odious to many of the white people that they will be deterred from the Order.[60]

In Richmond white Knights, in short, need not have greeted blacks directly as competitors or as brothers. The unskilled black laborer or factory operative posed little threat to the skilled white worker, especially during a period of local economic expansion. No self-interested white worker, for example, would have called for exclusion of blacks from the tobacco trade, the city's productive dynamo. The relative absence of direct economic friction left the course of race relations all the more open to political, cultural, and ideological influences. For whites a tug-of-war between traditional allegiances and fragile, new opportunities could therefore be played out on more neutral ground. For blacks the stakes were much higher. Were they really prepared to leave the Republican party? The party in the South had become a caste-confined institution, yet it remained the major protection of that caste. Should blacks desert the John Wises, Edmund Waddills, and James Bahens to join a fledgling reform movement of former Democrats? In the process, they would bear the double burden of race and class insurgency and risk what one skeptic called the jump "from the frying pan into the fire." In the end, black citizens, including many Knights, surrendered to the logic as well as the muscle of their local party leaders.[61]

In the circumstances the efforts of the Ben Scotts and J. T. Wilsons are more remarkable than their failures. Instead of retreating in the mid-1880s to weather a storm, they imagined a dramatically different scenario. Their perspective judged in the light of ultimate realities must appear illusory or at best utopian. But only in acknowledging their vision can one explain certain behavior, including the true ending—unacceptable to both Democratic and Republican chroniclers—of the Goochland courthouse story. According to the sworn affidavit of Martha Cousins, it was "the colored man [not Mullen] who remarked that if all of them could not sit together, no one of the three would eat at her table." A similar spirit was registered in Montgomery, Alabama, in April 1886. On the same day that Jefferson Davis was laying a cornerstone for a Confederate monument, a black man named W. J. Campbell arrived in town to begin organizing for the Knights of Labor. Elsewhere, the white master workman of an interracial Jackson, Mississippi, assembly declared his faith that "the clouds of superstition will gradually roll away and the destiny of man will be viewed in a new light. The relics of barbarism will tumble down and we can extend our hands clean across this broad land and know that we are Brothers in a common cause."[62]

Suggesting a radical shift both in the social distribution of power and in race relations, political reform efforts like the one in Richmond were seeds that did not germinate. The plowing under of such possibilities affected later southern and American political history. Defeats of attempted coalitions between skilled and unskilled workers in the late 1880s and early 1890s left a labor movement generally bereft of social initiative. Exclusionist trade unions, disfranchisement, a virulent Tom Watson, a more conservative T. Thomas Fortune, and the self-help ideology of a Booker T. Washington were mutually reinforcing, dominant strains by the turn of the century. In this sense, the Progressive Era inaugurated a social and political retreat for many Americans.

NOTES

1. Labor tickets appeared in Raleigh, Durham, Fayetteville, Oxford, Burlington, and Statesville, North Carolina; Key West and Jacksonville, Florida; Selma, Mobile, and Anniston, Alabama; Ft. Worth and Houston, Texas; Macon, Georgia; Hot Springs, Arkansas; Chattanooga, Tennessee; Vicksburg, Mississippi; and Lynchburg, Alexandria, West Point, Kanawha Falls, and Richmond, Virginia. No doubt these listings are incomplete.

2. U.S. Tenth Census, 1880, *Report on the Social Statistics of Cities* (Washington, 1887), Pt. 2, 85; U.S. Eleventh Census, 1890, *Report on the Population*, Pt. II (Washington, D.C., 1895), 128; U.S. Eleventh Census, 1890, *Report on Manufacturing Industries in the U.S.*, Pt. III (Washington, D.C., 1895), 385–88; B. W. Arnold, Jr., *History of the Tobacco Industry in Virginia from 1860 to 1894*, John Hopkins University Studies, Ser. 15, nos. 1–2 (Baltimore, 1897), 64–66; Trade Committee of the Chamber of Commerce, *Advantages of Richmond, Virginia as a Manufacturing and Trading Centre* (Richmond, 1882), 37–42; James P. Wood, *The Industries of Richmond . . .* (Richmond, 1886), 11–13.

3. Howard N. Rabinowitz, *Race Relations in the Urban South, 1865–1890* (New York, 1978), 98–99, 331–33.

4. Herbert G. Gutman, *The Black Family in Slavery and Freedom, 1750–1925* (New York, 1977), 479–81.

5. Testimony of Sir George Campbell reported in A. A. Taylor, *The Negro in the Reconstruction of Virginia* (Washington, D.C., 1926), 117.

6. *Ibid.*, 118; Charles B. Dew, *Ironmaker to the Confederacy: Joseph R. Anderson and the Tredegar Iron Works* (New Haven, 1966), 27, 28, 262.

7. U.S. Eleventh Census, 1890, *Report on Population*, 718–19. Figures for 1860 courtesy of Herbert G. Gutman; the 1860 census did not list occupations

of slaves, but Gutman has argued persuasively from other data that what little skilled work blacks performed was done by free blacks, not slaves. *Slavery and the Numbers Game: A Critique of* Time on the Cross (Urbana, Ill., 1975), 48–61.

8. Jack P. Maddex, Jr., *The Virginia Conservatives, 1867–1879: A Study in Reconstruction Politics* (Chapel Hill, N.C., 1970), xi-xv, 276–96, 55.

9. J. Morgan Kousser, *The Shaping of Southern Politics: Suffrage Restriction and the Establishment of the One-Party South, 1880–1910* (New Haven, 1974), 172; Richmond *Whig,* Sept. 26, 28, 30, 1886.

10. Statistics from the 1890 census (the first to break the populations of cities down into nativity groups) indicate that 8,308 Richmond black males, twenty and older, were outnumbered by 22,471 whites in the same age range. In this light a registered electorate 40 percent black in 1886 is all the more striking. Black voting strength at mid-decade was symbolized by the election in 1886 in neighboring Manchester of that town's first black councilman and justice of the peace. U.S. Eleventh Census, 1890, *Report on Population,* 128; cf. Charles Wynes, *Race Relations in Virginia, 1870–1902* (Charlottesville, Va., 1961), 34; Richmond *Planet,* Feb. 21, 1885, June 12, 1886, July 12, 1890. Only scattered issues of the black newspaper remain.

11. Ann F. Alexander, "Black Protest in the New South: John Mitchell, Jr. (1863–1929) and the Richmond *Planet"* (Ph.D. diss., Duke University, 1972), 72, 219–20, 223–24; John S. Wise to John James Henry Wise (cousin), Dec. 25, 1885, Mar. 6, 1886, Wise Family Papers, Virginia Historical Society, Richmond; Rabinowitz, *Race Relations,* 277, 284.

12. Luther Porter Jackson, *Negro Office-Holders in Virginia, 1865–1895* (Norfolk, Va., 1945), 57–58.

13. Rabinowitz, *Race Relations,* 282, 287; James T. Moore, "Black Militancy in Readjuster Virginia, 1879–1883," *Journal of Southern History,* 41 (1975), 172–75; Alexander, "Black Protest," 224.

14. Peter Rachleff, "Black, White and Gray: The Rise and Decline of Working Class Activity in Richmond, Virginia, 1865–1890" (M.A. thesis, University of Pittsburgh, 1976), 107, 147, 192–94, 239–44.

15. *John Swinton's Paper (*hereafter *JSP),* Mar. 21, 1886. See also Rendigs Fels, *American Business Cycles, 1865–1897* (Chapel Hill, N.C., 1959), 138; U.S. Commissioner of Labor, *Third Annual Report* (Washington, D.C., 1888), 588–95.

16. Rachleff, "Black, White and Gray," 266; *JSP,* June 21, 1885; Jonathan Garlock and N. C. Builder, "Knights of Labor Data Bank: Users Manual and Index to Local Assemblies" (1973), manuscript at the University of Rochester, Rochester, N.Y.; Richmond *Dispatch,* Sept. 30, Oct. 9, 1886; Knights of Labor, "Proceedings of the General Assembly, Richmond, 1886," Terence V. Powderly Papers, Catholic University, Washington, D.C.; Melton McLaurin, *The Knights of Labor in the South* (Westport, Conn., 1978), 171.

17. *JSP,* Jan. 24, Feb. 4, Mar. 7, May 23, 1886; Haverhill (Mass.) *Laborer,* Mar. 15, 1886. Richmond organizers appealed in vain against General Master Workman Powderly's forty-day freeze on new assemblies. Henry Trimble to Powderly, Mar. 5, 1886, Powderly Papers; *JSP,* Nov. 22, Dec. 13, 1885;

Journal of United Labor (hereafter *JUL*), Aug. 25, 1886; Raymond Pinch-beck, *The Virginia Artisan and Tradesman* (Richmond, 1926), 74; McLaurin, *Knights in the South,* 90.

18. Richmond *Dispatch,* Feb. 23, 1886, clipping in John S. Wise Scrap-book, Wise Family Papers.

19. Richmond city directory, 1885, New York Public Library; John S. Wise to John James Henry Wise, Mar. 6, 1886, Wise Family Papers; R. F. Walker to William Mahone, May 2, 1886, William Mahone Papers, Duke University, Durham, N.C.

20. Richmond *Dispatch,* May 2, 1886.

21. *Ibid.*

22. *Ibid.,* May 30, 1886; Richmond city directories, 1886–87, 1889.

23. Access to occupational breakdowns from the 1880 manuscript census courtesy of Herbert G. Gutman; Richmond city directory, 1889. The Irish presence within the southern Knights was apparent in a rumor circulated in Natchez, Mississippi, that the order admitted only Catholics. The Irish miner Nicholas Byrne Stack headed the organization in Alabama. John S. Power to Powderly, Apr. 12, 1886, Powderly Papers; *JUL,* June 16, 1888.

24. R. T. Hubbard to Mahone, June 1, 1886, Mahone Papers; Richmond *Dispatch,* May 28, 1886.

25. C. C. Clarke to Mahone, May 29, 1886, B. Taylor McCue to Mahone, July 17, 1886, R. F. Walker to Mahone, May 26, 1886, Wise to Mahone, July 2, 1886, Mahone Papers; Richmond *Planet,* June 12, 1886; Richmond *Dispatch,* June 23, 24, 30, July 1, 1886; whites like John S. Bethel and A. L. Owen who remained in the Reform caucus admitted their political debts to the blacks but still rejected black patronage demands on grounds that the present moment was "impolitic" for such advances, "as the movement is young and must be surrounded by every safeguard." *Ibid.,* June 30, 1886.

26. Wise to Mahone, June 25, 1886, Mahone Papers.

27. Richmond *Dispatch,* July 2, 1886; Richmond, Virginia, Common Council *Journal* (minutes), July 6, Aug. 2, 1886.

28. Richmond *Dispatch,* Sept. 11, 1886.

29. Mullen to Henry George, June 8, 1885, Henry George Papers, New York Public Library; Richmond *State,* Oct. 17, 1877 (courtesy of Peter Rach-leff). Mullen, who had come to Richmond as a young apprentice printer, had been active in the labor movement since the mid-1870s and had joined the Knights in 1884; Richmond *Whig,* Sept. 25, 1886; R. J. Steele to Powderly, Feb. 17, 1886, R. W. Cruse to Powderly, Apr. 28, 1886, Powderly Papers; *JUL,* Oct. 25, 1885 (quotation courtesy Peter Rachleff).

30. Richmond *Whig,* Oct. 6, 23, 1886; Richmond *Dispatch,* May 10, 1887; *Granite Cutters Journal,* Feb. 9, 1887.

31. John S. Wise to John James Henry Wise, Mar. 6, 1886, Wise Family Papers; John S. Wise to Mahone, Sept. 27, 1886, Mahone Papers. The pre-vious June an "understanding" between Wise and Reform leaders had entailed mutual acceptance of a "labor man" for Congress "who will agree to sustain the tariff policy, vote with the Republicans in organizing the House and not go into the Democratic caucus." At that time, however, Wise had personally

believed that "they will have no man" and eventually would have to turn to him to fulfill the bargain. Wise to Mahone, June 25, 1886, Mahone Papers.

32. Richmond *Dispatch*, Oct. 2, 9, 1886; Rabinowitz, *Race Relations,* 707–8, 736, 845–46. The tug of competing loyalties was suggested by the presence of W. W. Fields, an officer in black D.A. 92 of the Knights among the anti-Mullen delegates; one of the anti-Mullen black voices was that of Lewis Lindsay, long a Republican activist and customs-house janitor. As a slave Lindsay had been the "trusted body servant" of John Minor Botts, to whom Lindsay would later credit his considerable knowledge of constitutional law. In his political views Lindsay believed in recognizing the authority of "what he called the old aristocracy, of which he counted himself one," emphasizing the recruitment of respectable native white Virginians to the Republican party. He frequently reiterated his opinion that the " 'pore-whites' hated the blacks and that the gentlemen of the South were their best friends." John S. Wise's eulogy to Lindsay upon his death, Jan. 4, 1908, Wise Family Papers.

33. Jackson, *Negro Office-Holders*, 57–59; Moore, "Black Militancy," 172.

34. Richmond *Whig*, Oct. 3, 1886; Richmond *Dispatch*, Oct. 3, 1886.

35. *Valley Virginian*, Sept. 25, 1886; quotation from Petersburg *Index-Appeal* as cited in Richmond *Whig*, Oct. 10, 1886.

36. Quotations from Richmond *Whig*, Sept. 8, 12, 1886.

37. *Ibid.*, Sept. 8, 1886.

38. Quotations from *ibid.*, Sept. 18, 25, 1886; Lee's comments were reported in both the Richmond *Whig* and *Dispatch*, Oct. 5, 1886.

39. Quotations from Richmond *Dispatch*, Oct. 5, 12, 1886. Among incidents that the Bourbon press found repugnant were these. A black delegate from Baltimore was seen one morning in a Richmond hotel asking white delegates to join him for breakfast. Two white delegates from Boston reportedly stopped at the house of one of the most distinguished white residents in the city and asked to speak with "Miss ———." The lady of the house told them that there was "no one here by that name except our colored servant girl." "Lucy" then received the men in the servants' room, where she was given letters from a mutual acquaintance, "a colored gemmon" from Boston whom she had met several weeks before. Two white women delegates, strolling through the rotunda of the state capitol, stopped to chat with the black janitor and urged him to join the Knights. *Ibid.*, Oct. 7, 8, 1886; Richmond *Whig*, Oct. 10, 1886.

40. New York *Sun*, Oct. 7, 1886; Richmond *Dispatch*, Oct. 6, 7, 8, 1886. The leaders of the Law and Order League, as announced in the Sept. 10, 1887, Richmond *Dispatch*, included: Tazewell Ellett, attorney, L. L. Bass, president of the Richmond Elevator Company and a savings and loan bank, J. Taylor Ellyson, publisher, C. V. Meredith, city attorney, John B. Purcell, wholesale druggist, and N. V. Randolph, paper-box manufacturer; Burlington (Vt.) *Free Press*, Oct. 8, 1886. Bandmann had met Ferrell and company on the boat from New York to Richmond. Afterward, the actor continued to defend his action. "As an artist and a free-thinking American citizen I shall

be only too proud to play before so many colored people as the houses will hold." G. T. Stanes and J. T. Hamm, *Some Phases of Labor Relations in Virginia* (New York, 1934), 77; Trenton (N.J.) *Daily Gazette* as quoted in New York *Freeman,* Oct. 30, 1886. "Aristocratic" Richmonders had similarly picked up their guns to intimidate Mahoneite blacks on election day in 1883 (Moore, "Black Militancy," 185). Following the law-and-order outburst, Knights' leaders limited themselves to quieter demonstrations of their beliefs. Powderly and Thomas McGuire, master workman of D.A. 49, for example, attended mass at the city's black Catholic church (New York *Herald,* Oct. 11, 1886; Richmond *Dispatch,* Oct. 19, 1886). Police Chief Poe was a nephew of Edgar Allan Poe.

41. Haverhill *Laborer,* Oct. 16, 1886.

42. Melton McLaurin, *Paternalism and Protest: Southern Cotton Mill Workers and Organized Labor, 1875–1905* (Westport, Conn., 1971), 107, 116 (quotation); *JUL,* June 11, 1887; Richmond *Whig,* Oct. 17, 1886; Chicago *Tribune,* Oct. 12, 1886; Richmond *Dispatch,* Oct. 8, 1886 (statement of local Knight); New York *Times,* Oct. 7, 1886; Bay City (Mich.) *Evening Press,* Oct. 6, 1886.

43. Richmond *Dispatch,* Oct. 9, 1886; New York *Tribune,* Oct. 9, 1886; Richmond *Whig* comment on parade, Oct. 12, 1886. Frank Foster reported the turnout on parade day as "90 to 1" black (Haverhill *Laborer,* Oct. 23, 1886).

44. Pittsburgh *Dispatch* report as cited in Richmond *Dispatch,* Oct. 17, 1886.

45. R. J. Steele to Powderly, Oct. 21, 1886, Powderly Papers, Richmond *Dispatch,* Oct. 19, 23 (Democratic story), 24, 29 (Republican story), 1886.

46. Richmond *Whig,* Oct. 27, 30 (quotation), Nov. 2, 1886; Common Council *Journal,* Nov. 6, 1886; Richmond *Dispatch,* Oct. 31, 1886.

47. Richmond *Whig,* Nov. 2, 1886; Richmond *Dispatch,* Oct. 31, 1886.

48. Clarke to Mahone, Dec. 6, 1886, Payne to Mahone, Oct. 24, Nov. 3, 1886, Mahone Papers.

49. Richmond *Dispatch,* Apr. 7, 26, 1888. What deal Mullen might have arranged is difficult to surmise. Following the election he did, suggestively, switch his counsel in the Baughman case from John S. Wise to Congressman George D. Wise. But the next year both Mullen and George Wise were detained following a physical altercation shortly after the 1887 elections (Rachleff, "Black, White and Gray," 346, 363). As to the larger labor campaign committee, who reportedly instructed Mullen to withdraw in 1886, there is no sign of tangible reward garnered by them from the Democrats; Alexander, "Black Protest," 218–20; Richmond *Dispatch,* Apr. 24, 1888, Apr. 16, 1890.

50. *JSP,* Nov. 14, Dec. 12, 1886; Richmond *Dispatch,* Dec. 11, 24, 1886, Apr. 19, 1887 (quotation), Apr. 19, May 22, 25, 1888; Mullen to Powderly, Feb. 28, 1887, Powderly Papers.

51. Richmond *Evening Herald,* Oct. 3, 1887, clipping in John S. Wise Scrapbook, Wise Family Papers; Rachleff, "Black, White and Gray," 360.

52. C. E. Hills to Powderly, Mar. 23, 1888, Powderly Papers; Richmond

Dispatch, May 18, 1888. For the YMCA's role in socializing an industrial work force, see Gerd Korman, *Industrialization, Immigrants, and American-izers: The View from Milwaukee, 1866–1921* (Madison, Wis., 1967), 73–74, 89, 141–47; McLaurin, *Knights in the South,* 173, 178.

53. Richmond *Labor Herald,* July 28, 1888, clipping in John S. Wise Scrapbook, Wise Family Papers.

54. Rabinowitz, *Race Relations,* 791; Richmond *Dispatch,* Apr. 16, 1890; Alexander, "Black Protest," 192.

55. Richmond *Dispatch,* Nov. 25, 1888, Aug. 26, 1890; Carl N. Degler, *The Other South: Southern Dissenters in the Nineteenth Century* (New York, 1974), 333; William Dubose Sheldon, *Populism in the Old Dominion: Virginia Farm Politics, 1885–1900* (Princeton, 1935), 55, 92, 61, 102–3; Booze to Powderly, Aug. 12, 1895, Powderly Papers.

56. John L. Power to Powderly, Jan. 20, 1886, A. J. Loveless to Powderly, Apr. 1, 1887, S. T. S. Sweet to Powderly, Mar. 4, 1887, Powderly Papers. A Gadsden, Alabama, master workman confessed that "some of our brothers have misgivings about the Negro getting the same signs and Password as are in possession of white assemblies. Could the password given to them not be changed a little?" E. P. S. Dum to Powderly, Nov. 15, 1883, Powderly Papers. See Kenneth Kann, "The Knights of Labor and the Southern Black Worker," *Labor History,* 18 (Winter 1977), 49–70.

57. Washington *Bee,* Oct. 23, 1886; New York *Freeman,* Oct. 30, 1886; Pierre L. Van der Berghe, *Race and Racism, a Comparative Perspective* (New York, 1967), 15.

58. Records of the Freedmen's Savings Bank, Richmond, microfilm copy courtesy of John O'Brien, Dalhousie University, Halifax, Nova Scotia; Rabinowitz, *Race Relations,* 193–94; Israel Spotswood and John Booker to Mahone, May 18, 1885, Mahone Papers.

59. Chotier to Powderly, Mar. 6, 1886, Mahone Papers; C. Vann Wood-ward, *Origins of the New South, 1887–1913* (Baton Rouge, La., 1971), 229.

60. J. A. Belton to Powderly, Nov. 15, 1886, Powderly Papers. See the message to Powderly from the recording secretary of a Morgan City local assembly: "The colored laborers desire to be organized into a seperate assem-bly. In fact they have already two or three bodies that meet every week and are in every way prepared to be organized and admitted into our noble order." D. B. Allison to Powderly, July 7, 1886, Powderly Papers.

61. Staunton (Va.) *Critic,* Oct. 16, 1886.

62. Richmond *Whig,* Oct. 29, 1886; *JSP,* May 9, 1886; Phil Hammond to Powderly, Jan. 4, 1886, Powderly Papers.

7

Bullets and Ballots:
Worker Mobilization and the Path to Municipal Socialism, Milwaukee, Wisconsin

MILWAUKEE PROVIDES THE exceptional example of a successful third-party tradition stretching from the labor politics of the Knights of Labor era through the Great Depression of the 1930s. As the only major city in the country to be governed by a Socialist mayor for much of the twentieth century, Milwaukee, one might quickly surmise, must have been affected by a most particular and even peculiar set of local cicumstances. Of course, one focus for such an analysis is offered in the immigrant German-American political culture of this most foreign of large American cities. The city, which as early as the 1850s became known as the "Deutsche Athens," by 1890 contained a population in which nearly four out of every ten citizens were immigrants and nearly nine out of ten were of foreign parentage. Among the immigrants themselves, 70 percent came from Germany. From the vantage point of other Gilded Age communities, however, political developments in Milwaukee do not look so alien. The evolution of a third-party Socialist presence, in fact, appears to be a distinct form of a political process rooted in the social upheavel of the 1880s.[1]

The principal dilemma facing Gilded Age political radicals in Milwaukee as elsewhere in America was the organization and mobilization of a heterogenous and divided working class. The degree of success or failure on this score, while not dictating the exact contents of labor's political message, did at any given moment generally define the electoral options available to working-class political leaders. In Milwaukee this primary task was accomplished less as a function of the peculiar local political culture than as a consequence of the activity of the Knights of Labor as well as the public responses that their activity evoked. In subsequent years Socialist electoral advances coincided with the organizational consolidation of one part of the working-class community; at the same time the fragility of local Socialist rule may be traced to the fragmentation of a coalition first built in the 1880s. Throughout, the electoral fortunes of the party of the workers were intimately bound up with changing dimensions of workplace and community life in the city. Beginning with close attention to a series of pivotal events in 1886, this chapter takes the form of a selected structural analysis of Milwaukee politics over half a century. As such it is meant to sharpen our understanding of the active relationships in American history among industrial conflict, class formation and fragmentation, and political organization.

While Milwaukee could not really challenge Chicago's claim as "Queen City" of the Old Northwest in the 1870s, that decade nevertheless witnessed a critical expansion in the economic life of Wisconsin's urban center. Until the mid-1870s, Milwaukee acted as dispenser to the world's largest primary wheat market. But the combined influence of the 1873 price crash, poor harvests, and increased competition caused Wisconsin wheat production to slacken. Farmers turned to coarse grains (for malting and brewing) and to the production of dairy goods. Within the city flour-milling assumed a more modest position as one industry among several including meat-packing, tanning, brewing, and men's clothing. As an important early terminus for Minnesota ore and Pennsylvania soft coal, Milwaukee also developed into a center for the iron industry.[2]

The shift in investment from agriculture and railroads to diverse manufacturing marked Milwaukee's emergence as a modern industrial metropolis. Increase in the number of establishments between 1870 and 1880 was negligible, but a 147 percent jump in the number of wage earners over the same period indicated a growing concentration of industry. Population rose from 71,000 to 116,000 between 1870 and 1880 and reached 204,000 ten years later, making Milwaukee the nation's sixteenth city.[3]

Two key ingredients—metal and beer—paced the city's expansion through the century's last two decades. Milwaukee's metal and iron products rose in value from $402,000 in 1870 to $3.5 million in 1880 and to more than $14 million by 1900. When Edward Allis died in 1889, his Reliance Iron Works, purchased in 1857 for $31,000, returned $3 million annually. Although iron represented only half the value of beer as a product in 1885, the iron industry employed one and one-half as many workers as the city's breweries. Three thousand employees of the Milwaukee Iron Company and the North Chicago Rolling Mill made the South Side Milwaukee suburb of Bay View practically synonymous with iron-making.[4]

Not until the 1890s did such breweries as Schlitz, Pabst, and Blatz exploit the mass-marketing techniques that made them and their city nationally famous. But by the 1880s brewing had already matured from a household industry into a big business. Geoffrey Best (bought out by his son-in-law Captain Fred Papst in 1889), the biggest of the early brewers, had eight employees in 1860, 100 in 1870, and nearly 500 by 1886.[5]

In the 1880s the city's productive life was conducted primarily in foreign accents. Immigrants and their children comprised 90 percent of the work force in 1890 and only in the highest rungs of the occupational ladder did native-born Americans make up more than a quarter of the population. The working class of the city was not simply ethnic but overwhelmingly (65 percent) foreign-born; in general, the less skilled the position, the more likely it was to be filled by an immigrant. Three-quarters of Milwaukee general laborers, for example, were foreign-born (Table 15).

Since the 1840s only the Germans among the incoming groups had kept pace with the city's general expansion. By 1860, as Kathleen Neils Conzen has carefully documented, the Germans "were an occupationally stratified group fitting in, to a greater or lesser degree, at all levels of the city's economy." The relatively even occupational dispersion of the Germans was maintained through the following three decades, with new recruits continually resupplying the industrial sector even as others of their countrymen supplied the necessary internal services to the sprawling ethnic community. The German-born alone thus accounted for almost half of the city's wage-earning population. A typical advertisement in a local English-language newspaper ran, "Maidchen verlangt [Girls wanted] in der paper box factory." Certain industries, including brewing, carpentry and joining, cigarmaking, and tailoring, were essentially "German trades," with two-thirds to three-quarters of the work force of German origin. In 1890 only a few of the skilled trades (e.g., English iron workers, Irish railroad workers) still witnessed the concentrated presence of older, non-German immigrant groups.[6]

By the mid-1880s German-American workers had already exercised considerable influence over the institutional life of the city. As early as 1850, when the printers and typesetters of the radical *Banner und Volksfreund* brought Milwaukee its first legitimate theater, workers' organizations had formed an important cultural as well as political counterpoint to the roles of the Lutheran Synod and Catholic church among German-Americans. For years the councils of the carpenters, brewers, cigar-makers, and printers in the city's original "Germantown" district constituted a Socialist nucleus within which Lassalleans, Marxists, and anarcho-syndicalists vied for supremacy. Milwaukee was surely one of the few places in America, for example, where Lassallean Social Democrats in 1877 not only outpolled their Greenback-Labor rivals but also elected several men to local office. In the late 1870s and early 1880s a citywide trades assembly loosely coordinated the interests of some fourteen craft unions, including both German and English language printers, coopers, brewers, iron molders, railroad shopmen, building trades workers, cigar-makers, and a section of the Amalgamated Association of Iron and Steel

TABLE 15. Male Occupational Structure in Milwaukee, by Ethnic Group, 1890

Occupations	Native-Born, Native-Parents	Native-Born, Foreign-Parents	Foreign-Born	German-Born	Polish-Born[a]
Non–Wage Earners					
(N = 14,830)	18	40	42	28	6
Capitalists-professionals					
(N = 2,021)	28	34	38	26	4
Merchants (N = 6,312)	15	33	52	37	8
Salaried positions					
(N = 6,497)	17	50	33	21	3
Working Class					
(N = 38,608)	6	29	65	45	12
Skilled workers (carpenters, printers, etc.) (N = 15,455)	5	36	59	45	8.5
Industrial workers (machinists, iron and steel, brewers, railroad workers) (N = 10,333)	8	30	62	42	10
Unskilled workers (laborers, teamsters) (N = 12,820)	11	19	75	47	19
Total	(9%)	(33%)	(58%)	(40%)	(10%)
(N = 59,578[b])	5,667[c]	19,342	34,569	23,760	6,084

Source. U.S. Eleventh Census, 1890, *Population,* Pt. 2 (Washington, D.C., 1896), 692–93.
Note. All data are given as percentages, and are based on males, age ten and older.
[a]"Polish" is substituted here for the category "Other Countries" used in the 1890 census to describe immigrants other than those born in Germany, Ireland, Great Britain, Canada, Sweden, Norway, and Denmark. As such it undoubtedly includes some scattered non-Poles but is the closest approximation possible for 1890.
[b]Includes 6,140 individuals of unspecified occupation.
[c]Includes 206 persons of color (blacks, orientals).

Workers. When a fourteen-week lockout practically destroyed the cigar-makers' organization in 1881, the trades assembly with Democratic and Greenback-Labor backing carried its protest into the political arena and elected a sympathetic iron manufacturer as mayor on a labor slate.[7]

Neither the ideological third party nor the coalition of trades, however, proved a very durable political option. The trades assembly was, from the beginning, susceptible to downswings of the business cycle and only barely survived the recession of 1884–85; politically, it had no means to attract an electoral majority except by merger with one of the major parties. The labor-based third parties, for their part, similarly struggled against strong counter-currents. In the early 1880s, for example, much of their constituency was swallowed up by a swelling tide of German nationalism expressed in the mayoral campaigns of Emil Wallber. For despite their numbers Milwaukee Germans had long remained underrepresented in political affairs. With the state's dominant Republican party in the hands of pietistic temperance reformers and Americanizers inimical to both German-Lutheran and Catholic sentiments, the Germans had generally made the Democratic party their home. Yet even here the Germans served for years as troops behind a persistent old Irish general staff. Not until 1878, for example, did the editor of the Democratic Catholic *Seebote* become the city's first German-American Congressman. Of twenty-two state assembly positions chosen in Milwaukee County between 1879 and 1881, only four were filled by Germans or German-Americans. Thus, by 1883, pressure from the newly formed German Society spurred nomination by Republicans of Wallber, a Berlin-born lawyer, businessman, and president of the Turnverein for mayor. Narrowly defeated in his first attempt, this political moderate won the following year in a flush of cross-class ethnic feeling.[8]

The labor movement in Milwaukee was restricted not only by ready absorption into ethnic politics but also by the fact that the organized skilled trades ignored the increasing role that ethnic Poles played within the city's economic life. While their exact number remains difficult to fix (without a nation of their own the Poles were improperly enumerated in the state and federal census until after World War I), Polish laborers represented a significant minority presence within the manual working class by the 1880s. A few Polish settlers had arrived as early as the 1840s. The community that established a Polish parish on the South Side in 1866 grew to an estimated 1,000 members by 1880. During the ensuing decade, however, a mass emigration from the German Partition, spawned both by a crumbling agrarian order and Otto von Bismarck's *Kulturkampf,* had an immediate impact on Milwaukee. Milwaukee Poles likely exaggerated when they claimed 25,000 kinsmen (or nearly half the number of German-born) in the city in 1886 and 30,000 in 1890, but the 1890 federal census just as surely misidentified many Poles as Germans when it listed only 9,222 Polish residents. Scanty immigration data suggest that while most of the arriving Polish immigrants may have been of peasant origin, many undoubtedly had had firsthand experience with the industrial revolution in Germany. In Milwaukee the Polish immigrants overwhelmingly occupied the lowest rungs of manual labor. As late as 1895 the South Side Polish community included only nineteen contractors, two attorneys, and two physicians; similarly, there were twice as many Poles in unskilled jobs as in the skilled trades. Hundreds of Polish immigrants reportedly took the lowest-paid jobs in the Bay View iron mills.[9]

Despite the poverty and roughness of employment that they experienced in Milwaukee, the Poles quickly formed a tight, self-regulating community. According to Milwaukee police records, for example, the percentage of Poles arrested on all counts between 1884 and 1890 corresponded exactly to their proportion within the city's population, a remarkable fact given the Poles' low socioeconomic position (Table 16). A roster of male House of Correction inhabitants confirms the impression of internal community discipline; of 1,500 inmates in 1885, only ten were of Polish birth.[10]

This is not to say, however, that the new Polish immigrants generally found life to their liking, even as compared to the Old Country. A recent survey of letters written back to Europe in this period stresses the ambivalence of reactions to new conditions, including a sense of bitter disappointment that there was "no freedom in America." Such feelings, no doubt, contributed to a little-studied wave of industrial rebellion from 1882 to 1887 in the form of Polish mobs or crowd action in Detroit, Cleveland, South Bend, and Michigan's Saginaw Valley as well as in Milwaukee.[11]

Initial neglect of the exploding Polish laboring community by the established German radical and trade union organizations was quite predictable. A history of national enmities combined with conflicting cultural and immediate economic interests tended to keep the two groups apart. Milwaukee's secular-minded German trade unionists and Socialists, for example, contrasted with a Polish laboring community that in its struggle for survival had

TABLE 16. A Comparison between Crime and Nativity in Milwaukee, 1884–90

Place of Birth	Number of Arrests	Percentage of Arrests	Percentage of Population[a]	Arrest Index[b]
United States (white)	11,049	51	61	0.84
Germany	6,171	28	27	1.04
Ireland	1,825	8	8	4.00
Poland	831	4	4	1.00
Other	1,870	9	6	1.50
Total	21,746	100	100	1.00

Source. Annual Reports of Chief of Police, Milwaukee, 1884–85, 1886–87, 1887–88, 1888–89, 1889–90, New York Public Library.
[a]Based on figures from the U.S. Eleventh Census, 1890. As explained in the text, the census estimate of Polish population is probably low; correspondingly, the number of Poles arrested is probably underestimated. This table assumes that the key relationship—i.e., the comparison of percentage arrested to pecentage in the population—should therefore remain constant.
[b]Arrest index computed as: percentage arrested/percentage of population.

remained closely tied to the Catholic church. Aside from ideology the rules and regulations of the trades assembly themselves intrinsically operated to exclude the lesser-skilled newcomers. A craft union like the Amalgamated Association of Iron and Steel Workers, locked as it was in a far-flung battle for control of the new industrial technology, tended to view the immigrants as willing tools of the employers. When in 1876 some Milwaukee Poles were recruited to break a coal-handlers' strike, the incident reinforced suspicions on both sides. The labor movement, therefore, had little to do with the Poles' first assertive steps into the city's political affairs. When August Rudzinski took office as city supervisor in 1878, he became the city's first elected Pole. An emigre from Russia in 1859, Rudzinski had set up a tailoring shop and made army uniforms during the Civil War. By 1880 Rudzinski's Hall, doubling as saloon and meeting room, was a center of political life in what would become the Polish fourteenth ward. Rudzinski had also played a leading role in establishing the city's first of three Polish parishes and in organizing the Kosciusko Guards, a company of the state militia, to which prominent members of the Polish-American community might be honored with an appointment as captain. Attorney Francis Borchardt, chief officer of the guard, was elected as the state's first Polish assemblyman in 1882. The following year Rudzinski's twenty-six-year-old son Theodore, who ran a travel agency featuring rips to Hamburg, was elected Milwaukee's first Polish alderman. Both Borchardt and Rudzinski's successes came in the face of the trades assembly tickets that had failed to include any Polish candidates.[12]

The growth of the Knights of Labor in Milwaukee accentuated many tendencies evident in the Order nationwide. After a slow beginning the Knights grew in exponential fashion. From early spring 1885 to late spring a year later, a single mixed assembly composed mostly of German printers who had affiliated in 1878 exploded into forty-two assemblies representing some 12,000 members. Initially the Knights' strength and numbers rested squarely on those sections of Milwaukee's working class with a history of labor organization. The universalism of the Knights' message, however, combined with the self-activity of the formerly unorganized quickly intensified the scope of the campaign. The resulting movement within a movement touched off a polarizing confrontation with local industrialists and state authorities. The rise of a sturdy third-party tradition in Milwaukee, ultimately under Socialist direction, may be traced directly to the tumult of the Knights' era. The very strength of the Milwaukee Knights as a social movement, in short, carried a lasting structural impact on local political affairs.

There is no underestimating the Knights' reliance on craft organization in the initial months of their expansion in Milwaukee. Of twenty-six assemblies formed by March 1886, seventeen officially represented specific trades. In addition, some of the other mixed assemblies were, in fact, aggregations of craftsmen like the feeders, heaters, rollers, molders, and nailers who formed a mixed metal trades assembly. Some of the sudden surge to the Knights may be attributed to skilled workplace groups who reorganized at a propitious moment. The cigar-makers' union, for example, had dwindled to forty members by January 1886. In mid-March Knights' initiatives had so revitalized their movement that the Progressive Cigarmakers' secured an eight-hour day with increased pay, plus a prohibition on lower-paid female and child employment as long as unionized men were out of work. The predominant ethnic make-up of the Order also suggests its strong ties to the city's skilled work force; an Irish Knight of Labor complained that at least eleven assemblies conducted business only in German.[13]

Like the Order's advance elsewhere, the Knights' growth in Milwaukee was experienced as a spiraling momentum, wherein a victory for one group of workers seemed to carry ramifications for all. By October 1885, for example, the Knights were reportedly "whooping things up," alternating weekly enrollment ceremonies with "amusements—readings, recitations, songs, jigs and clog dancing," and discussions of the relations between "capital and labor." When a jeweler marketed nonunion, officially boycotted watches in December, he experienced the Order's power. "Mystic marks were made on the sidewalk and street. His store was full of people that night [with] hundreds standing outside. But not a sale did he make. No one spoke to him or his clerks. Next morning he decamped." In February 1886 a week-long boot-and-shoe strike secured Knights' workers their requested new scale. During the same month the popular German *Herold* caved in to Knights' demands for a union shop. The collective power of the Order was such that the *Herold*'s capitulation was due not so much to demands of its own printers but to pressure from striking carpenters upset at its editorial policy. Economic influence also translated into political currency. Seeking to head off the possibility of another independent labor challenge, Mayor Wallber met with Knights' leaders in February 1886 and endorsed their demands for an eight-hour day for city workers. A month later the demand passed the common council with only one dissenting vote. A few days before the April balloting, the mayor helped assure his reelection by his conspicuous appearance at a comic opera benefit performance for the Knights' Agitation Fund.[14]

The political portraits of two key figures in the Milwaukee Knights, state organizer Robert Schilling and future political representative Henry Smith, suggest that one key to a movement that would combine native-Americans with Irish, German, and ultimately also Polish immigrants was an ideological common-denominational Americanism. Robert S. Schilling, brought to the United States from Germany as a young boy, had already established himself as one of America's most influential labor reformers when he became state organizer for the Knights in 1881. He grew up in St. Louis, served an enlistment in the wartime Union Army, trained as an apprentice cooper, and joined the Coopers' Union in 1863. In 1871 the Coopers' International (CIU) elected him its first vice-president, and he moved to Cleveland to edit the union's German-language paper. The coopers' involvement in the late 1860s with the cooperative movement and the National Labor Union (NLU) acquainted Schilling with the world of labor reform. When a few leaders of suffering national trade unions came together in 1874 to create a successor to the NLU, Schilling succeeded to the presidency of the new Industrial Brotherhood. The preamble of this short-lived organization, as drafted by Schilling, became a tenet of faith for both the Knights of Labor and the Populists in later years. It was in the brotherhood that Schilling first met Terence Powderly, five years before Powderly became the Knights' grand master workman. Schilling reportedly joined the Knights himself in 1875, the same year he was elected president of the CIU. Like other early leaders of the Knights, Schilling jumped enthusiastically into Greenback-Labor politics, serving as Ohio state chairman of the new party until his 1880 move to Milwaukee, where he launched two German-language papers, *Der Reformer* and *Volksblatt*. While attempting to dislodge the national Greenback party from its agrarian and entreprenurial moorings, Schilling showed more interest in results than in consistent political doctrine. The *Volksblatt,* for example, was friendly both to Karl Marx and Henry George.[15]

Henry Smith likewise established links between an older reform tradition of democratic-minded artisans and manufacturers and the new movement of industrial workers. Smith, as his son would write in 1916, was "pre-eminently a self-made man." Born in Baltimore, Maryland, in 1838, Henry moved with his German-born parents first to Stark County, Ohio, and then to Milwaukee in 1844. By age ten he had already worked summers as a cattle guard and helper in a tobacco factory. Although his "scholastic training" ended in 1850 after four years in the public schools, Smith loved to read and "oftimes would pick up scraps of newspapers from the street." In later years he became a student of the Bible ("but no believer"), world history, political economy, and scientific subjects. Smith began his apprenticeship as a bookbinder in 1851 but turned for health reasons to the trade of millwright. By the early 1860s the firm of Smith Brothers, Millwrights, was constructing most of the state's flour mills and many of its tanneries, grain elevators, and malt houses. Together, Henry and his three brothers added numerous improvements to agricultural and industrial machinery, including the roller flour-mill system, pneumatic malting, and the installation of the state's first turbine water wheel.[16]

Smith also applied his mechanical ingenuity to local government. From his election to the city council in 1868, he took the greatest interest in the details of a city waterworks and sewerage system and even invented a special metal cover for sewerage catch-basins. In 1871 he convinced the council to build the city's first iron bridge and thus avoid the continuing repair bills incident to wooden construction. He also expedited the preparation of the Milwaukee

River for docking by persuading his father to turn over to the city land use rights around the family flour mill. Elected state assemblyman in 1877 with the support of the Social Democrats (he later claimed he was an independent, not a Socialist), Smith took a leading role in securing Milwaukee's municipal library. A few years later he cooperated with Edward Allis in getting municipal title to a dam for river flushing and port development. By the mid-1880s Henry Smith (elected alderman in 1880, city comptroller in 1882, and re-elected alderman in 1884) was one of the city's most experienced municipal architects. During his term as city comptroller, Smith so advanced the system of municipal bookkeeping that even financier and railroad owner Alexander Mitchell begged the trades' assembly representative to seek reelection.[17]

Smith's guiding star from the late 1860s onward was the philosophy of radical Greenbackism. To the disbelieving eyes of this young Douglas Democrat, the "demonetization act" first proposed in 1869 inflicted "more misery" on "the farmer and laboring man and small businessman . . . than the civil war." Together with the centralizing 1863 National Banking Act, demonetization constituted "the most stupendous piece of class legislation ever perpetrated upon the people"; "it made me a bitter enemy of both the Republican and Democratic parties and I cannot get over that feeling." Starting in the 1870s, Smith always ran on an independent or third-party ticket. He dutifully supported the national candidacies of Peter Cooper, James Weaver, and Ben Butler. In 1885 the radical manufacturer joined a mixed assembly of the Knights of Labor because "its Declaration of Principles coincided with my views as a greenbacker." With their appeal to significant numbers of their fellow German-Americans, the political philosophies of both Schilling and Smith may offer a particular labor variant of Conzen's thesis that "ethnicity for Milwaukee's Germans" "accompanied rather than precluded Americanization."[18]

As with other social movements the development of the Milwaukee Knights of Labor depended both upon an internal dynamic and the intervention of outside circumstances. By the beginning of 1886 the organization that Schilling led and Smith joined had substantially consolidated and revitalized the traditional roots of trade union strength within the city. Moreover, it was also making gains in places previously ignored by every labor organization. As early as July 1885, Milwaukee District Master Workman and iron molder Timothy Cruise had pointed to "the great army of unskilled labor" as the Order's next target. Formation of two women's assemblies (including one of tailoresses) provided one indication of the important change. Another was evident in the Reliance assembly's admission of predominantly unskilled Polish workers; 618 men joined the Order in a single day. By mid-March 1886 the Reliance's 1,600 workers formed the country's largest Knights' assembly, part of a 3,000-man Milwaukee contingent of organized metal trades workers. In addition, 1,000 Polish workers, drawn mostly from Bay View plants, had joined the Polonia assembly. The crucial opening for the less skilled iron workers seems to have been stimulated by the stalemated end of a nine-month strike and lockout of Bay View nailers in February, a struggle that graphically demonstrated the weaknesses of skilled Amalgamated iron workers acting alone. Labor's 1885–86 expansion thus ultimately depended on lowering the tailgate to the Knights' bandwagon.[19]

Acceptance of the Knights by Polish workers, in particular, was aided by the efforts of a group of liberal Polish nationalists associated with the weekly *Krytyka*. The newspaper was an early manifestation of what would become by the early 1900s a bitter dispute within the Polish-American middle class over the hegemony of the Catholic church hierarchy in the affairs of Polonia. The activities of *Krytyka* publisher Michael Kruszka and editor Anton Parysso suggest the degree to which American domestic issues shaped the positions of lay leaders, whose efforts have usually been defined in relation to the struggle for restoration of the European homeland or to resentment against Irish (and in Milwaukee, German) control of the American Catholic church. Kruszka had emigrated to New Jersey in 1880 at age twenty from an uncommonly well-educated family of landholding peasants. Already something of a rebel in German Posen, he had been disciplined in school for insisting on speaking Polish. After working in a sewing machine factory in Elizabeth, New Jersey, and trying his luck as an insurance agent in Bayonne, Kruszka moved to Milwaukee in 1883 to set type in a small print shop. Parysso was a man of middle-class family and considerable education. With a background as a revolutionary "nihilist," he appeared, even to friends, as "occasionally indiscreet in his utterances respecting the Church and labor organization." It was no accident that *Krytyka* spread to 3,500 Polish readers in the same period that the Knights of Labor were themselves attracting Polish workers. From the beginning, Parysso served as a paid Knights' organizer. Kruszka, too, soon became an officer of the Polonia assembly. As early as 1886 *Krytyka* was known as the official "organ of the Polish Knights of Labor."[20]

The very growth of the Knights raised the stakes for future actions. Across the country active workers took advantage of their newfound collective strength to press their gains or to resist employer-backed initiatives. In large cities like Boston, Baltimore, New York, and Chicago, skilled workers, whether through their Knights' trade assemblies or national craft locals and central labor unions, embarked upon a coordinated campaign for the eight-hour day. At the national level Terence Powderly and the general executive board, panicking over their inability to control the growing wave of strikes, boycotts, and calls for solidarity, pointedly disassociated the Order from the shorter-hours campaign in a secret circular. This directive, however, had an irregular impact at the local level, and in Milwaukee, most notably, it was effectively ignored.

It was the spring 1886 eight-hour campaign, in fact, which proved to be the ultimate catalyst for the organization and mobilization of Milwaukee workers. Strategically, it had the advantage of simultaneous appeal to Milwaukee's varied working class—skilled and unskilled, Germans and Poles, Socialists and Catholics. The state labor commissioner subsequently noted that the eight-hour movement "was *the* topic of conversation in the shop, on the street, at the family table, at the bar, in the counting rooms, and subject of numerous able sermons from the pulpit." For reasons later to be explored the eight-hour struggle also prepared the way for its strategic mirror-opposite, the political campaign.[21]

Milwaukee's Eight Hour League took shape in February 1886, the result of a tenuous and strained alliance between Robert Schilling's Knights of Labor and the craft-based Central Labor Union led by Socialist Paul Grottkau. The league supported the demands of different trades for new contract terms, encouraged mass agitation, and coordinated political pressure that centered on the threat of a general strike unless the demands were accepted by May 1. By officially acting through the Eight Hour League, to which each assembly or affiliated trade union sent three delegates, Schilling neatly sidestepped the official proscription on Knights' sponsorship.[22]

Schilling himself had been won over to this neosyndicalist strategy following his own experience in upstate Wisconsin in the wake of Michigan's Saginaw Valley ten-hour strikes in 1885. At that time he had been able to settle a dispute among Menominee River sawmill workers to the immense benefit of the Order's numbers and influence. As early as November 1885, Schilling, therefore, laid plans through the *Volksblatt* for a Milwaukee-based campaign the following spring.[23]

Paul Grottkau led the left-wing of the Milwaukee eight-hour movement. A Berliner by birth, Grottkau had fled Bismarck's anti-Socialist laws and arrived in Chicago in 1878. Opposing the local political alliance between Social Democrats and Greenbackers, he became associated with August Spies and the left-wing anarchism of the Black International (International Working People's Association). As editor of the Chicago *Arbeiter Zeitung* in 1880, however, Grottkau appeared more concerned with strengthening workers' organization than with fomenting insurrection. In 1879 he had joined demonstrations for an eight-hour day; soon his support for trade unionism would lead to an open break with the anarchists. In 1885 the wholesale confectioner, Valentine Blatz, invited Grottkau to take over Milwaukee's Socialist *Arminia* (renamed the *Arbeiter Zeitung*) from an editor who had grown more attached to an anticlerical sheet called *Lucifer*.[24]

Grottkau and the hundred-odd members of Milwaukee's Socialist Labor party sharply distinguished themselves from the native-American reform ideology of the Schilling-led movement. For Schilling the class question had been provoked by the specific abuses of men with power to wield. The

Volksblatt applied the demeaning term "capitalist" only to those representatives of "unprincipled corporations and monopolies" who refused to negotiate with the leaders of the "producing classes." The *Arbeiter Zeitung*, on the other hand, spoke of an inevitable struggle between a "capitalist ruling class" or "bourgeoisie" and the "proletariat." Similarly Grottkau's journal would attack grand juries as "capitalist inquisition-tribunals" that "everywhere" preserved the "capitalist interest." Schilling, offering a less systematic critique of political institutions, argued for "simplification of the laws so that lawyers might not continue to dominate the courts."[25]

Grottkau soon articulated the feelings of a bloc of a few thousand German craft workers already disgruntled with the Knights of Labor. Whether because of Powderly's tactical conservatism or internal jurisdictional feuding between trade unions and the Knights' district assemblies, carpenters and joiners, custom tailors, International Cigar-makers, and others in March 1886 had, under Grottkau's command, formed the Central Labor Union (CLU), which sent delegates of its own to the Eight Hour League.[26]

The shorter-hours campaign brought astonishing results. By the end of April, twenty-one firms, in addition to the municipal government, had acceded to the eight-hour demand. By the evening of May 1, 10,000 workers were on strike or were idle because their employers had shut down to avoid trouble. They reportedly included 3,000 brewers, 3,000 shop tailors, 1,200 cabinet makers and carpenters, 600 coal yard hands, 500 cigar-makers, 150 brick yard men, 200 slaughterhouse workers, 150 Allis plant men, 120 German bakers, and 100 broom-makers.[27]

The militancy of the city's brewery workers suggested how fast events had moved in a month's time. Captain Best prided himself on a personal, conciliatory approach to his relatively highly paid employees, who ranged downward from the malthouse men at the top of a work force hierarchy to the tight-barrel coopers, firemen, washhouse brewers, and cellar men and then to the unskilled washhouse men and teamsters at the bottom. When his maltsters joined the Knights in March, Best quickly extended recognition and abolished Sunday work. His employees publicly expressed their gratitude. But a month later Gambrinius assembly had organized not only the maltsters but also Best's semiskilled brewery workers as well. Together they demanded a Knights' shop, an eight-hour day, time-and-a-half for overtime, and a guarantee of the traditional right to free beer for all brewers. On Monday, May 3, the Milwaukee Knights' executive board ordered all the city's breweries shut tight.[28]

Even as the eight-hour drive brought different sectors of Milwaukee's work force into common struggle, it did not eliminate the tensions that had previously separated the participants. Political divisions among the Eight Hour League's leaders were apparent from the beginning. Local Knights' leaders, for their part, adopted a cautious attitude toward a coordinated May Day work stoppage. They took pains to avoid confrontation with the law and any appearance of insurrection. Schilling hastened to dismiss as "bosh" daily press rumors that armed revolutionaries had camped in the city. As public tensions mounted before May 1, the Knights encouraged negotiation of grievances on an industry-by-industry basis, a policy Schilling later justified by saying: "One must not shoot cannon at sparrows, therefore not strike and boycott equally against every rascal." In general, the Knights used the eight-hour issue as a negotiating tool, winning the demand for those workers in strong bargaining positions but trading it for union recognition or other advances where workers had less leverage. Schilling's temporizing brought him into increasing conflict with the head of the CLU. When Schilling, for example, pressured a committee of shop tailoresses to settle, regardless of the demands made by male tailors, Grottkau openly rebuked the Knights for "selling out." The rift between the two organizations led to official Knights' withdrawal from a scheduled demonstration on Sunday, May 2, when Schilling learned that the CLU would receive half the proceeds from a fund-raising picnic following the march. With red flags waving, some 2,500 workers including CLU crafts and German Socialist factions of the Knights belied business warnings of violence and peacefully paraded through the streets on Sunday, neither stopping traffic nor coercing bystanders. Notwithstanding their militant rhetoric, the Socialists, in common with the Knights, believed in a disciplined, orderly approach to labor protest.[29]

The split in labor's ranks not only reflected ideological and organizational differences but also revealed the conflicting interests among the eight-hour movement's basic constituencies. By no means did the events of this period result, as historians of quite different perspectives have suggested, in "the obliteration, apparently complete, of all lines that divide the laboring class, whether geographic or trade." Indeed, a close examination of the Milwaukee events suggests that the very tension (rather than all-out cooperation) between skilled and semiskilled workers, Germans and Poles, lay behind the spread of the mass work stoppages.[30]

Skilled trade unionists dominated Milwaukee's first eight-hour strikes. Surveying the constituent groups of the May 2nd demonstration, the Democratic Milwaukee *Journal* counseled calm, "[There] are too many homeowners for a riot." Some of these striking skilled workers, moreover, showed an inclination to settle at the expense of less skilled workers in the same plant. Reliance metal workers were a case in point. Owner E. P. Allis, who had run for governor on the Greenback ticket in 1878 and considered himself a prudent reformer, sidetracked labor's offensive in the early spring. When the Knights started to agitate in his plant, Allis unveiled his Mutual Aid Society, a "cooperative" plan that offered matching company grants to an employee fund for capital investment. Allis responded promptly to the shorter-hours movement. On April 3 he reached agreement with the Eight Hour League for an eight-hour day, but at reduced pay—a settlement that only the most skilled and highly paid workers could have afforded to regard as a victory. The success of Allis's approach was apparent in the presence of only 150 found-rymen at the initial eight-hour demonstrations. Similarly, the St. Paul railroad shop skilled workers continued to work as did Amalgamated men at the North Chicago rolling mill. Owing to the conciliation of most skilled craft workers, the city's largest industrial establishments appeared to have protected success-fully what Allis called "our inalienable rights—my right to run my works and your right to sell me your labor."[31]

Signs of employer resistance and conservatism among the skilled workers, however, only unleashed a new and more militant phase of the popular move-ment. On Monday, May 3, 300 to 400 "Polish laborers" marched toward West Milwaukee's St. Paul yards carrying tricolor eight-hour flags and "armed with clubs and some knives." They first marched onto the railroad tracks and disengaged shovelers from their labors. The crowd gained the support of yard laborers and then invaded the shops, interrupted the molders, and "hustled and yelled" until the machinists also laid down their tools. In one swoop between 1,500 to 1,800 additional men had been added to those out of work. From the railroad yards the enlarged assembly headed for the Allis shops, where loyal Reliance employees icily greeted them, "armed with hammers, clubs and three lines of fire hose." Unsuccessful in their first assault, the crowd hurled rocks at a score of policemen drawn up around the plant. "The police captured five of their assailants, but their friends [re-]captured all but one." Allis closed the plant indefinitely, citing inadequate police protection. Heretofore sympathetic toward the Knights, the *Journal* now condemned the unskilled workers: "The driving out of one set of laborers who have gained a point by those who have failed is the work of crazed men."[32]

The *Journal*'s opprobrium failed to impress the strikers. The next day, a crowd that included members of Polonia assembly collected at St. Stanislaus Church and marched out of the Polish district making a "brr" sound with swinging clubs as they headed toward Bay View. By the time the marchers reached the rolling mills, their numbers had reached 2,000. Meanwhile, on the northwest side of town, a group of German trade unionists leaving a rally chaired by Grottkau called out the Brandt and Company stove molders. These two actions aroused Republican Governor Jeremiah Rusk to ignore the cau-tions of Milwaukee's mayor, sheriff, and police chief and to order several militia companies, already on alert and bivouacked in the city, to show their colors at Bay View. The Kosciusko company was among those units of the National Guard that had been specifically primed in the expected event of urban riots to put down the "dregs [on] whom it might be a municipal blessing to fire." As the all-Polish unit wheeled in front of the giant industrial plant on May 4, their countrymen in the crowd "set up a cry of 'Rats' and 'Scabs' . . . punctuating their epithets with well-aimed sticks and stones." Several guardsmen turned impulsively and fired into the air, temporarily driving the demonstrators back.[33]

The crowd's actions beginning on May 3 changed the balance of forces within the labor movement. Once it had ignited the eight-hour campaign, the Order proved incapable of confining activity to the respectable limits preferred by its leaders. The least political of the city's workers had forced the order into direct confrontation with governmental authority. Knights' leaders faced an unwanted and unexpected situation but one they could not ignore. By the evening of May 4, more than half of 14,000 unemployed Milwaukee workers belonged to the Knights. The leadership's predicament became apparent during the morning's rolling mill demonstrations. When a crowd threatened to storm the plant, Schilling along with Polonia assembly Master Workman Andrew Boncel rushed there and agreed to enter the factory to ascertain the conditions and desires of its workers. After an hour's conference, the leaders returned to report that local plant officials had no authority to change working hours and had to await word from company headquarters in Chicago. Schilling and Boncel preserved order. But when they asked for a vote of confidence for their negotiating efforts, the crowd roared back in Polish and German, "Eight Hours!"[34]

The militia's arrival at Bay View placed the Knights' officers in an even more difficult position. Along the lines of the successful settlement at Saginaw, Michigan, the year before, Schilling proposed that the Knights act as special police to restore order on condition the militia were recalled. The government turned him down. The Knights nevertheless cooperated with civil authorities by requesting that members remain at work or at home and keep away from public meetings. Laborers who remained camped outside the Bay View mills spoke bitterly of leaders who "made terms with the capitalists." Would-be peacemakers in the Polish community also encountered resistance from their own rank and file. The Polonia assembly, for example, rented Rudzinski's hall the night of May 4 to dampen South Side passions. Alderman Rudzinski later testified regarding the meeting: "The hall was crowded, and I could not get far into the doorway, hearing many parties dissatisfied with the remarks of the master mechanic of the Polish assembly, and many threats against the militia; cries of burning the mills and urging the men to go to the mills, and that the speaker was not with them, and they wanted others to lead them on. . . . When I counseled with them to refrain from . . . violence, I was cooly informed . . . that I was also bought up."[35]

The Socialists also were unprepared for the turn of events. Addressing German cabinet-makers on May 4, Grottkau unveiled his plan for dealing with the volatile situation. Union leaders would negotiate with employers, strikers would be urged to stay off the streets, and the governor would withdraw the guardsmen. His advice went unheeded on all sides. Debated for

years in assemblies of the best-educated of German workers, syndicalist battle
plans suddenly had been rendered academic (although by no means forgotten
by anti-Socialists) by the altered terms of real-life action.[36]

An angry crowd reassembled along the road to Bay View during the early
morning of May 5. A Knights' officer later privately commented that "it can
be proved that Polonia Assembly or members of it were the ringleaders and
the greater part of the mob." This time, acting under explicit orders from the
governor, battalion commander Major George P. Traeumer did not wait to be
provoked. With the marchers still 200 yards from the plant, a coordinated
burst of fire rang out and killed five demonstrators and injured another dozen.
A child who had joined the parade on his way to school and an old man (the
only non-Polish casualty) who had been standing in his garden were among
the dead. Hours later, other troops threatening to shoot broke up a Socialist
rally called to reinvigorate the eight-hour drive. Bay View had followed Haymarket by less than a day, and hysterical fears of a dynamite plot spread
through the city. Arrests and recriminations followed. The authorities had
great difficulty identifying individuals among the unruly Poles, but the Socialist and anarchist agitators were well known. Grottkau and nineteen of his
followers were rounded up within hours.[37]

Arrests and prosecutions did not end there. Judge James A. Mallory charged
a grand jury quickly empanelled by the county sheriff with jurisdiction over
all earlier illegal acts, including peaceful boycotts, which may have contributed to the May violence. The judge's charge led to the arraignment and arrest
of the entire district executive board of the Knights of Labor. Denied reduced
bail, Robert Schilling in early June stepped hesitantly into the same cell with
anarchist Frank Hirth and other Socialists who had already accused him of
abetting their original arrests.[38]

The Polish community was singled out for special reprisals. Individuals
linked to the crowd, like Master Workman Boncel, were arrested, and Polish
workers were dismissed en masse from the city's industries. Three hundred
lost their jobs at the St. Paul shops. In many cases Poles later had to get
specific clearances from the Kosciusko Guards to regain employment. Those
who had lent support to the workers also came under fire. His appearance at
the May 4 tavern meeting along with his critical remarks about the governor's
actions throughout the crisis led to Theodore Rudzinski's impeachment by a
common council investigating committee. He was accused of "inciting to
riot" and, following a vote of censure, barely permitted to retain his seat.
Governor Rusk stripped Rudzinski of his notary public. The Catholic church
joined in the assault on the secular leadership of the working-class Poles.
Father A. J. Decker pointed to the Rudzinski family saloon as the source of
the city's troubles. Newspapers over the entire state heaped abuse upon the
"mob-loving Polacks of Milwaukee." In addition, a special coroner's jury
exonerated the militia of wrongdoing in the "accidental" killings. Lauded

nationally for his actions, Rusk staked his reelection chances for the fall on his tough law-and-order Bay View stance.[39]

Bay View's hail of bullets ended one phase of the labor movement in Milwaukee but just as surely began another. The repression directed at organized labor in the aftermath of the shootings brought the eight-hour drive to an abrupt halt. Within a week of the shootings, Allis's Reliance plant and the North Chicago Rolling Mill reopened after "amicable" settlements with their employees. When Allis agreed to reinstate 100 Knights of Labor and magnanimously offered to chair future grievance sessions himself, the Reliance assembly accepted the old terms of ten hours' pay for ten hours' work. In ordering the rolling mill workers back to work, district leaders of the Knights accepted an employer-laden panel of three arbitrators—the superintendent of the Allis works, the former superintendent of the West Milwaukee railroad shops, and an engineer. An October settlement boosted the pay but did not reduce the hours of non-Amalgamated iron workers. Brewers likewise received a pay increase but went back to work after May 5 with neither a union shop nor an eight-hour day. Other Milwaukee factories in this period posted signs: "Knights of Labor need not apply." Some employers fixed political tests and oaths. By the last week in May, the number of Milwaukee strikers had fallen from 16,000 to 2,000. Few had attained their goal. Those still voluntarily out of work were limited to select trades such as the tailors, hod carriers, cabinet-makers, and planing mill workers. The boycott also fell victim to the Bay View Massacre. In the face of legal attacks on this special brand of protest, the Knights practically gave it up as a weapon.[40]

At first local political officials lined up loyally behind the governor's actions. Within the common council, only assemblyman and Knight Henry Smith voiced opposition to a public resolution of gratitude to the state's chief executive. Despite a general ban on public meetings, Judge Mallory chaired a meeting at which local businessmen heard the state's militia commandant call for more dollars and equipment for domestic military purposes. Mayor Wallber, who only months' previously had been elected with labor votes, took cover during the storm. Abstaining from the resolution to the governor, he won respect from no one. Just how far the political pendulum had swung was revealed in an overwhelming repudiation—ostensibly on cost-cutting grounds—of the municipal eight-hour law. By July city workers again labored from seven in the morning until six at night.[41]

Slowly, Milwaukee's Knights attempted to reassemble their forces. In the worst of these times a hard core of their wide-ranging community support held solid. Of twenty-three bondsmen who came to the aid of the Order's arrested leaders, for example, most were middle-class or self-employed Germans, including a hotel proprietor, a real estate agent, a billiard table company foreman, a peddler, and a music teacher. The industrial regiments also regrouped. More than 5,000 strong with twelve brass bands and a drum corps, the Knights of Labor marched through the heart of the city on May 20, defying business protests. The tone of the demonstration was one of forbearance, not advance. Marshals permitted only American flags to be carried. The tricolor eight-hour emblem as well as the Socialist red banner were forbidden. As if to reassure a city poised on the brink of further violence, the *Volksblatt* afterward stressed the disciplined "clockwork" of the marchers: "every assembly knew its place." While the Knights had survived Bay View in somewhat battered form, the CLU was less fortunate. Without Grottkau's leadership or an expanding mass movement that might sustain their left-wing critique of the Knights, membership fell off "to a corporal's guard," and the organization disbanded in January 1887.[42]

Notwithstanding their defensive posture, the city's labor chieftains were by no means resigned to defeat. In a slap at official harassment, the Knights filed suits against local coal and transportation companies charging monopolistic restraints of trade. Privately, the Order's executive board counseled jittery assembly leaders that the Bay View reaction would "blow over after a while." And, indeed, some citizens who had initially supported repressive actions soon protested that the all-out judicial assault on organized labor had "overshot the mark." "The Knights of Labor," warned the *Journal*, "are the largest, most respectable and representative labor organization in this labor city. In striking at this body the grand jury at once divides the community and arraigns class against class." Robert Schilling's first public statement on the Bay View events seemed to confirm the *Journal*'s fears. He called the shootings "cowardly, premediated murder." "The most guilty," he charged, "is Old Know-Nothing Jerry Rusk." Preparing for trial, the Knights' leader still called for the "hanging" of the man responsible for sending in the troops. Schilling's counsel, N. S. Murphey, addressed a polarized public as much as the jury in his closing argument: "The fight between capital and labor will go on. . . . I would rather be Schilling in jail than a free man who sent him there."[43]

Schilling's trial ended in a hung jury. Within days of the verdict, this political veteran announced his aim to "gain revenge—by the ballot." Together with the mayor of LaCrosse, Frank "White Beaver" Powell, patent medicine salesman and an alleged former prairie bandit, Schilling crafted the Wisconsin People's party. Particularly in the cities, the new political creature provided only the thinnest veneer for the Knights of Labor. Master workmen and district executive board members of the Order dominated party councils from the beginning. Seeking to attract farmers, Schilling chose the head of the state Grange as gubernatorial candidate. In Milwaukee County Henry Smith ran for Congress and Newell Daniels, a former Knights of St. Crispin leader, was proposed for sheriff.[44] The People's party offered Henry Smith in particular a thoroughly comfortable political home. The party platform included such staples of Greenback dogma as government control of money, land, and all means of transportation, communication, and public improvements; direct legislation and simplification of the laws; a graduated income tax; and abundant issue of legal tender. To underscore the episode that had precipitated this latest resurrection of the radical banner, Schilling, Smith, and their supporters also demanded the "abolition of the use of violence in labor disputes."[45]

The shadow of Bay View dominated Wisconsin's fall campaign. Republican state convention delegates in October sang new verses to the tune of "Rally Round the Flag," recomposed as "Down with the Red Flag, Up with the Stars." But the cry of anarchy with which Governor Rusk stumped the state made little impression in the city of record. Indeed, the People's party benefited from a protective local pride turned against the governor's attacks. Addressing scores of rallies, Schilling played up and ridiculed the insults of outsiders on the honor of the city and its working people. Scoffing at Republican talk of the "red flag at Bay View" in one campaign debate, Schilling yelled out, "Here it is!" "He then unrolled a package and showed a red, white, and blue banner bearing the words 'Eight Hours' and the design of a clock. This caused the wildest sensation, the audience cheering themselves hoarse. 'That is the flag they called red. Here are the bullet-holes.' " Milwaukee Republicans soon deemphasized the riot as a campaign issue. Unable or unwilling to combine with the Democrats against the labor party as the governor had urged them to do, local Republicans fell to bickering with their usual partisan opponents.[46]

The Democrats had even more to lose by the polarization of sentiments around the labor movement. Nowhere was this clearer than in the usually Democratic pocket of the Polish South Side. Within the Polish neighborhoods spontaneous protest had quickly given way to an organized vengeance against all those connected with the fatal shootings. A communitywide boycott hit businesses owned by members of the Kosciusko Guard. A week after the shootings the Milwaukee merchants' association entertained motions to subsidize five Guard grocers who acknowledged an 80 percent drop in sales. Captain Francis Borchardt, whose house had reportedly been attacked after the tragedy, subsequently confessed that his legal practice had fallen off severely. Critics of the labor movement within the Polish district like Alderman Stanislaus Hanizaewski also suffered abuse. Alderman Rudzinski, on the other hand, had been hoisted onto the People's party ticket for state assemblyman. The new political magnet also attracted a few others from the Polish middle class, including furniture dealer John Czerwinski, the first Pole ever nominated for county coroner.[47]

Older guides to Polish political conduct recognized that abrupt changes were taking place. The Catholic church did its best to stem the tide of immigrant political radicalism. The influential South Side priest, the Reverend

Hyacinth Gulski, scored Henry Smith's state assembly vote for taxation of church property and urged Polonia assembly members to steer clear of the People's party. A week before the election, however, the Democratic *Journal* worried openly that the Poles were slipping out of their natural political orbit, throwing the outcome in doubt: "[It] is apparent that their pastors have not inherited the sceptre of the czars over them. . . . As Democrats they are safe and law-abiding citizens, but lectured to by socialists, they are in danger of their lives."[48]

The People's party carried practically its entire Milwaukee County slate in the November election, causing the *Journal* to pronounce the election, "An Earthquake—The Charleston Shake Reaches Milwaukee." Henry Smith was elected to Congress over his two opponents by more than 3,000 votes. Labor men like Sheriff Daniels and Coroner Czerwinski succeeded to the county government. One state senator and six assemblymen (five skilled German craftsmen and Theodore Rudzinski) were sent to Madison. No mystery surrounded the key to the election's outcome. The political clout of the Knights was recognized instantly when the newly elected district attorney dropped boycott-related charges against Schilling and the Knights' district officers.[49]

A ward-by-ward breakdown of the 1886 election returns confirms the city-wide social polarization that characterized the campaign. Simply put, Milwaukee's working-class immigrant communities carried the new party. Smith lost in only four wards, including three with the city's highest Yankee concentration which went Republican and one Irish-weighted ward which went Democratic. In general, Smith and the labor ticket captured old German areas with healthy pluralities. But it was in the new immigrant or first-generation American wards—the heart of the city's wage-earning industrial population—that the People's party registered its most smashing successes. In the tenth and thirteenth (German), twelfth (German and Polish), and fourteenth (Polish) wards Smith won overwhelming majorities. In the fourteenth ward, a district populated by many "Polish laborers in small frame dwellings," the old Greenbacker received no less than 80 percent of the vote. Ironically, the neosyndicalist Milwaukee eight-hour movement had in the end enfranchised and galvanized a powerful new political coalition.[50]

The election also demonstrated the limits of the People's party as a strictly urban industrial phenomenon with little appeal to other social bases. The new party did relatively well in other Knights' centers, such as Marinette, La Crosse, and Racine, but all the rural areas demonstrated strong approval of Governor Rusk and the law-and-order Republicans. On balance, the labor party seemed to have secured the allegiance only of those most aroused by the shorter-hours campaign. Even Henry Smith's 12,000 votes barely reached the number of strikers and demonstrators reportedly in the streets a few months earlier.[51]

The history of Milwaukee workers between the years 1886 and 1910 will only be sketched in summary forms. At the industrial level it was a period of retrenchment for organized labor, evident in the precipitous decline of the Knights of Labor followed a few years later by a revival of federated craft unionism under the new banner of the AFL. Disintegration of the working-class movement of the mid-1880s was accompanied by a renewed emphasis upon social organization geared to interethnic rivalries and indeed to conflicts internal to specific ethnic communities. In politics a shifting radical reform alliance first exhausted the potential direct legacy of the Knights' buildup, then faded before a revived two-party partisanship, and finally resurfaced through the skillful efforts of a new group of Milwaukee radicals, the Social Democrats.

Among the organizations, the Milwaukee Knights of Labor never recovered from the defensive position that they were placed in after the Bay View massacre. Internal division as well as employer hostility slowly sapped the Order's strength from mid-1886 to early 1888 from which point one observes a truly abrupt decline. As early as 1887 local trade unions had begun to defect from the Knights to the Federated Trades Council (FTC), which would shortly become Milwaukee's AFL affiliate. Although trade union disaffection from the Knights was a nationwide phenomenon, certain decisions of the Order's national executive board had a particularly destructive impact in Milwaukee. The entire Milwaukee brewers' section, for example, departed from the Order en masse in the summer of 1887 following Powderly's edict banning beer at Knights' picnics. Tight-barrel coopers, who derived their living from the same industry, quickly followed suit. There is a hint that some of Powderly's advisers had come to view Wisconsin's politically minded leaders as a threat to their own stewardship of the Order. In May 1887 Robert Schilling fumed to the General Master Workman that his newspapers had suffered a "serious loss" from being left off an approved list of publications in the official *Journal of United Labor*.[52]

Whatever the organizational rubric, it would take years before Milwaukee workers regained the initiative lost in the aftermath of May 1886. At the level of the workplace the years 1887–89 offered organized labor bleak returns. Of twenty-five strikes waged during the period, twelve were defensive, and more than half were unsuccessful. A few of the building trades showed continued strength, but in none of the mass-production industries—such as the railroads, brewing, metal trades, or cigar-making—did workers demonstrate signs of progress. The 1888 state labor commissioner's report summed up prospects at the workplace exactly at the moment of decline of labor's political effort: "Everywhere the life and spirit of 1886 have departed."[53]

Not until 1890 did the labor movement again stir itself to action. A second, more modest, eight-hour campaign received the support of both the Knights and the FTC; in April 1890 the common council again approved an eight-hour ordinance. Following the severe depression of the 1890s, the FTC mushroomed, claiming forty-six organized trades in 1896 and 20,000 affiliated members by 1899. Nothing, however, averted the collapse of the Knights of Labor; no public sign of the Order appeared after 1896.[54]

For a short time, it seems, the city's labor strategists were able to make up in influence at the ballot box what they were losing on the shop floor. But unable to assume power and obtain a tangible reward from political office, labor's foray soon collapsed. The spring municipal elections of 1887, for example, still depended on unshaken memories of the previous year. When the Union Labor party (ULP), into which the People's party had merged, nominated for municipal judgeship two lawyers active in the post–Bay View defense, the city's political establishment responded with uncharacteristic unity. While the Democratic *Journal* spoke of an "imminent danger to the state," the Republican *Sentinel* concentrated on the "alien" character of a party composed of "Rudzinski's and other ski's . . . and only one of the family of Smiths [and this one] spelled 'Schmidt' by his father."[55]

The leaders of the major parties reached a bipartisan accommodation. Headed by an illustrious Citizens' Committee chaired by Judge Mallory, a new Fusion party took aim against the labor menace with the slogan "No Class Rule." The committee's most significant work was carried out among the settled German population, where its persuasive spokesman was the lawyer F. W. von Cotzhausen. Referred to by Schillings's *Der Reformer* as "the leading politician of the parties of order," von Cotzhausen already had proven himself a formidable political presence. As strategist for the Personal Liberty League in 1873, he engineered the defeat of a Republican prohibition governor. A few years later he laid the groundwork for a new German immigrant aid society. In 1890 he would again effectively marshall German national and parochial interests against the state's Bennett Law, which recognized only English-language instruction in the public schools. Working to defeat the ULP in 1887, von Cotzhausen crafted his political appeal to a peculiarly German, prolabor audience. Drawing around him old Forty-Eighters and Free Soilers like realtor Louis Auer, he declared himself a "socialist," but one who had learned that there was no place for class struggle in the United States.[56]

The labor party carried the city of Milwaukee but lost the election of 1887 on the adverse vote of the surrounding county districts. In addition, a reduction in the number of aldermen up for election together with the bunching of ULP strength in the 1886 strongholds secured the new party only five of thirty-four positions on the common council. Despite the lack of leverage over the administration of government, political prospects for the labor movement were still by no means entirely pessimistic. While the ULP in 1887 fell 100 votes shy of Smith's 1886 performance, the tally of labor's opponents plummeted by about 4,000 votes. In addition, labor had won a symbolic victory in the elevation of assemblyman and ex–notary public Rudzinski to justice of the peace.[57]

For another year Milwaukee's labor movement appeared solvent. Both Henry George and Father Edward McGlynn paid visits during 1887 to a city hailed as the mecca of labor reform. Huge crowds still attended the Knights' annual Fourth of July celebration presided over by the new state master workman, Congressman Henry Smith. Taking advantage of a printers' strike against the major dailies, W. H. Park expanded the readership of his weekly *Labor Review* and also launched a successful daily labor newspaper. Within the pages of the *Daily Review* individual merchants made certain that the consuming public understood their political sympathies. One advertisement editorialized about the lengthening of terms and reduction in size of the common council: "The new aldermanic law . . . is an outrage upon the voters of this city, and was framed by the so-called 'upperclass' citizens to defraud the people out of their right of suffrage, but the people have the right to judge, by their vote, which is right or wrong. The people have long since judged the Light-Running 'Domestic' as the best sewing machine on the market. For sale by Messrs Gregg and Warner, 129 Grand Ave."[58]

The citywide labor constituency again outpolled the opposition Citizens' slate in the 1888 spring municipal elections. This time, however, it was old divisions within labor's house which denied ULP mayoral candidate Herman Kroeger the taste of victory. While Kroeger, a German-Catholic clothier, gathered 15,033 votes, labor's highest total to that date, he ended second by 945 ballots. A splinter Socialist Labor party (SLP) challenger spelled the difference with 964 votes. The SLP, initially cooperative toward the People's party, had assumed nationally a combative stance toward the "backward," "capitalistic," agrarian-centered ULP. Personal relations between the ULP's Schilling and SLP leader Paul Grottkau only embittered the situation. Even with an SLP endorsement in 1887, Schilling had refused to share a platform with Grottkau. For his part the *Arbeiter Zeitung* editor kept up a steady attack on Schilling as an "informer" and "leader of deception." Calling out the name "Schilling" in a public address, Grottkau immediately added, "Give us a spittoon." In Grottkau's eyes, Schilling was ultimately responsible for the fact that Milwaukee's district attorney had pursued 1886–related charges against the Socialists long after he had disposed of the cases of Knights' leaders. For two years Grottkau had fought a one-year sentence for incitement to riot; before the spring 1888 election, in fact, he awaited final judgment from the appeals court. Although he had established a photography shop in Chicago while out on bail, Grottkau managed to return to Milwaukee to campaign with sufficient sting to provoke the pro-ULP prosecutor to file libel charges against the Socialist newspaper that printed Grottkau's remarks. The Socialist leader was, in any case, soon rewarded by authorities who had never before shown him much sympathy.

Judge A. Scott Sloan, assuming jurisdiction in the Bay View cases from Judge Mallory, did not overturn the original verdict against Grottkau but urged the governor to pardon him on account of "the great good he has done to the people of Wisconsin in the last election." Six weeks later Grottkau was released from prison on a legal technicality.[59]

Although the labor party carried eight council seats in 1888, the frustration of the second near-miss coupled with the decline of an organized labor constituency seemed to debilitate the losers. By November, ULP politics in Milwaukee—the direct legacy of the 1886 working-class mobilization—was in tatters. While A. J. Streeter, the ULP presidential candidate, showed more strength in Milwaukee than in any other large American city, his 5,000 votes, 10 percent of the total cast in the county, represented only one-third of the party's spring constituency. Even a special fusion effort of Democrats and Union Labor men on behalf of Henry Smith—itself taken as a sign of weakness for a party previously pledged to electoral "independence"—could not boost the incumbent over his Republican congressional opponent.[60]

Drastic slippage in the fall elections tangibly measured the deterioration of a once-imposing popular movement into a back-biting claque of reform politicians. Well before the popular vote was in, signs had surfaced that the Knights could no longer control their heterogeneous following. As early as October 1887 Sheriff Newell Daniels had alienated himself from the rest of the labor team by refusing to pay the heavy assessment levied on ULP officials to keep the official Knights' newspapers afloat. Responding to criticism, Daniels charged labor editor Schilling with pressuring him to appoint personal friends and incompetents to his department.[61]

More important fissures among labor's friends developed in the Polish community. Early in 1887 publisher Michael Kruszka quarreled with ex-editor Anton Parysso's "instigations against the Polish priests." Kruszka attributed blanket attacks on the clergy to "insanity or a scheme to bust the Polish assemblies." Since "almost all Polanders [were] solid Catholics," he had tried to conciliate a hostile church by pointing to "the fact that two of my brothers are Catholic priests." The conflict resulted in Parysso's temporary suspension from the Knights despite a defense of the admittedly "impetuous" agitator by Henry Smith. Suspension of *Krytyka* and its fledgling offspring, *Dziennik Polski,* in the spring of 1888 represented a further splintering of the Polish labor-liberal alliance. Kruszka's new paper, the daily *Kuryer Polski,* promised to restrict itself to "Polish news" and "Polish affairs." Political "polemics" henceforth would be conducted in a "decent," noninflammatory manner. In effect, the *Kuryer* spoke for liberals disaffected from the more independent and anticlerical political path of Parysso and Rudzinski. Henceforth, the great issue for Michael and his younger brother, the Reverend Wacław Kruszka, would be Polish representation in the Roman Catholic hierarchy, which ultimately provoked as much heat in Polonia as had the

Knights of Labor. Calling for the November 1888 election of all "reliable" Democrats, the *Kuryer* backed grocery clerk Ignatz Czerwinski for county register of deeds over "the career politician" Rudzinski. For its part the Union Labor camp seized on Czerwinski's position as financial secretary of the Kosciusko Guards to try to stir old embers. A Polish Union Labor orator from La Crosse feigned incredulity that the Democrat had "the nerve to run against Rudzinski who suffered for the Poles like Jesus."[62]

The image of Bay View, however, no longer rallied the troops for the third party. While Smith's fusion candidacy still ran well in the Polish areas ("Polanders stood by me but many Germans did not"), Rudzinski and others running on a separate slate had no chance.[63] Even the Republican candidate outpolled Rudzinski's 255 votes in the fourteenth ward, while Czerwinski amassed a commanding thousand-plus votes in refashioning Democratic loyalties among the Poles.

In the absence of a mass working-class movement, ethnic partisanship and patronage, pumped by two energetically open parties, returned to the political center stage. By the end of the 1880s, German candidates dominated Milwaukee municipal tickets, while an increasing number of Polish names also appeared on the major party slates. Michael Kruszka, for example, was elected to the state assembly as a Democrat in 1890, although he later supported the Robert La Follette Progressive Republicans. Andrew Boncel, apparently frozen out of Democratic support, went looking elsewhere and in 1892 ran for alderman as an independent with Republican backing. Three years later, he, too, had made his peace with the Democratic party and defeated a Populist opponent for a seat in the state legislature. Self-conscious class identity simultaneously receded in importance as an influence on political behavior. The highest praise that the *Kuryer* paid Czerwinski in 1888 was to picture him as "a great Polish patriot and dedicated Catholic even though he works in a German store."[64]

Union Labor strategists responded to the shrinkage of the labor movement by turning to new sources of potential support. Nomination of a Citizens ticket in 1890—the ULP in new guise—suggested that Schilling, always the political innovator, was looking to capture the progressive middle class as a fulcrum of political power. A new Schilling enterprise, the *Advance,* played down industrial conflict, dedicating itself to city ownership of utilities and transportation. The Citizens' campaign was the first in Milwaukee—and probably one of the first in the country—to combine a long-standing radical reform program with an appeal to efficient, businesslike administration of government: "What Milwaukee needs above all things is cheaper fuel and light and lower taxes." In its orientation it foreshadowed much of the Progressive impulse at the turn of the century. This early effort, however, failed miserably, and the ever-hopeful Schilling turned to another will-o'-the-wisp.[65]

This time Schilling anticipated the ultimate political merger of the Knights with the National Farmers' Alliance in the Populist movement. In 1891 he became first national secretary of the People's party. But no matter what he called his following and no matter with whom he allied, Schilling could not uncover a new majority. Wisconsin's Populist vote "remained exclusively urban"; within Milwaukee it drew its support from familiar districts. The Populist gubernatorial candidate of 1892 received over 100 votes only in the "new German" ninth, tenth, and thirteenth wards. Between 1894 and 1896 trade union support produced a temporary resurgence of strength for the Schilling-directed forces, and the Populist candidate for governor in 1894 garnered about 9,000 votes, eight times as many as in the previous election. Henry Smith repeated this rather solid 20 percent of the vote in his Populist run for mayor in 1896. Nevertheless, the returns indicated that the People's party had succeeded only in partially reigniting the city's old Knights' base. In the 1894 race, for example, the Populist candidate again did best in the German immigrant wards. The curve of Populist strength generally followed that of the original (1886) People's party with the significant exception of the Polish wards. The fourteenth ward, for example, contributed only 22 percent of its vote to the third party in 1894, no more than the citywide average. At the same time it contributed more votes than any other ward to the Democrats. Thus, while the Populists were able to take advantage of a partially reconstituted trade union constituency, they had evidently lost the support of a large section of once-unionized industrial workers.[66]

It was a new group of Socialists rather than Schilling's urban populists who garnered the fruits of labor's renewed standing at the turn of the century. Their success was particularly striking, given the fact that as late as April 1888 fewer than a thousand citizens had cast votes for the Socialist ticket identified with Paul Grottkau and what remained of the Central Labor Union. How was it, then, that the next labor-elected Congressman after Henry Smith was the Socialist Victor Berger and that labor's first successful mayoral candidacy ever in Milwaukee was Socialist Emil Seidel's run in 1910? The answers imply more about the evolution of labor and political organization in the city than any radical shift in political ideology.

Beginning in 1892 Milwaukee Socialism came under the influence of Austrian-born Victor Berger. A local schoolteacher since 1880, Berger had taken over the *Arbeiter Zeitung,* renamed it the *Vorwarts* after the organ of the parliamentarian German Social–Democratic party, and enunciated a new pragmatic Socialist outlook. "Nothing more ought to be demanded," he explained in 1893, "than is attainable at a given time and under given circumstances." Living in uneasy alliance for a few years with both the Populists and Socialist Labor supporters, the Berger-led Socialists secured a vehicle more to their liking in 1897 in Branch One of Eugene Victor Debs's Social

Democracy of America (the forerunner to the Socialist party of America), or, as it soon became known locally, the Social Democratic party. The new party did not enjoy immediate success, receiving only 2,500 votes in its 1898 premiere performance. But its leaders worked skillfully to improve its position.[67]

Under Berger's tutelage the Social Democrats first closed ranks with the city's craft unions. Schilling's acquiescence in the 1896 Populist fusion with William Jennings Bryan Democrats had loosened his hold on the independent-minded forces within the FTC. Frank J. Weber proved the crucial link between the old Knights of Labor-ULP-Populist labor network and the Social Democrats. A sailor, teacher, and ship carpenter in his early years, Weber had joined the Knights and helped lead the carpenters' 1886 eight-hour strike. During the early 1890s as the FTC's chief officer, he had given crucial assistance to the People's party. But for the next three decades, both as FTC secretary and legislative lobbyist for the state federation of labor, Weber was the single most important advocate of the Social Democratic party. Socialists won control of the FTC's executive committee in December 1899. The next year the labor federation emerged as the organizational backbone of the new party. Berger's Social Democratic *Herald* became the FTC's official newspaper in 1901.[68]

The Social Democrats' relation to the city's trade union movement has appropriately been defined by Marvin Wachman as an "interlocking directorate." In 1900 sixty-seven of 147 party convention delegates were trade union representatives; what was more, only trade union members were eligible for nomination to public office. Of twelve Socialist assemblymen in 1912, eight were trade union leaders—drawn from the bakers, glassblowers, cigar-makers, house painters, seamen, molders, and machinists. Old class-conscious militants who had once rallied around Grottkau still formed an important wedge of Social Democratic influence within the unions. Grottkau himself periodically returned to the local hustings from his position as the AFL's national eight-hour organizer.[69]

Adroit seizure of the municipal reform issue provided a second critical ingredient for Socialist success. During the steady growth of Social Democratic organization between 1898 and 1908, the city was in the hands of five-time Democratic mayor, David G. Rose. Elected with reform pretensions on the "Popocratic" ticket of 1898, Rose substituted an elaborate personal appeal for programmatic commitments. With a flair for dramatic appearances and extravagant attire, and with the active support of the Polish clergy, "All-the-time-Rosy" campaigned for "Personal Liberty" and triumphed again and again over business-oriented Republicans who sermonized in vain about a local explosion of gambling, prostitution, and corruption. Exposés of his subversion of civil service commissions and collusion with street railway companies (which Rose had first promised to transfer to city ownership) failed to diminish the mayor's popularity.[70]

Turning Rose's abuses into Socialist capital, Berger attracted many middle-class citizens affected by the contemporary municipal reform enthusiasm. The historian Bayrd Still thus attributes Social Democratic victory in 1910 less to Socialist ideology than "exasperation with the existing incompetence, not to say corruption of the old-line parties." Virulent in its hostility to the 1886 eight-hour campaign, the Milwaukee *Journal* endorsed the Socialist ticket as early as 1908 on the anticorruption issue. Preelection commendation of Socialist aldermen by the city's Voters' League in 1910 also tends to confirm Still's assessment. The league's leading figures were corporation attorneys and capitalists, including representatives of Milwaukee's oldest and wealthiest families. Throughout their tenure of office, the Social Democrats committed themselves to graft-free administration, municipal budgeting, public safety, and law enforcement. They not only effected a working alliance with Progressives in the state legislature but also, with the help of the city's small Fabian society, steered native-American, middle-class members of the Municipal League and Good Government Clubs into the ranks of municipal Socialism. Even anti-Socialist Reformers found extensive ground for cooperation. Professor John R. Commons, for example, no ideological radical, headed Mayor Seidel's bureau of economy and efficiency. When Democrats tried to topple Mayor Daniel Hoan with their old standby David Rose in 1924, it was not altogether surprising that a section of Protestant clergy, particularly the upper-class Episcopalians, rallied to the Socialists' defense. Reminiscent of, only more durable than, Tom Johnson's Cleveland or Samuel Jones's Toledo, Milwaukee's Socialist regimes astutely combined strong party organization, administrative efficiency, and reform fervor.[71]

With one significant alteration, Socialist strength in Milwaukee generally followed the electoral pattern established after Bay View by the Knights of Labor–based People's Party (Figure 1). German working-class areas remained the bulwark of third-party strength. New German or first-generation-dominated areas, presumably both out of occupational configuration and exposure to Old Country Social Democracy, provided the party its single most loyal ethnic constituency. Indeed, even in the infant campaign in 1898, where the Milwaukee Social Democrats made little real impact, they still outpolled the Populists in three immigrant German wards. Strong, if somewhat less dramatic, showings for the Socialists came in older German-American wards. Least susceptible to Socialist influence, just as they had been to the People's and Union Labor parties, were the native-American wards, along with one old pocket of Irish residency in the city. Three-fifths the size of the German-born population by 1920, Milwaukee Poles provided a crucial swing constituency for the Socialists. While never as congenial to the third party as they had been in the 1880s, the Polish districts might yet occasionally be wrested from Democratic hands. In 1910 an all-out effort complete with Polish-language newspapers and a speaking tour by a sympathetic priest imported for the

FIGURE 1. Comparative Ethnic Support for Third-Party Candidacies, Milwaukee, 1877–1924

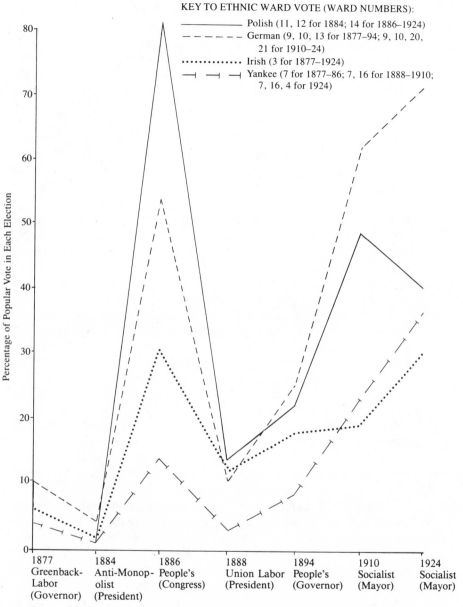

KEY TO ETHNIC WARD VOTE (WARD NUMBERS):

——————— Polish (11, 12 for 1884; 14 for 1886–1924)
— — — — — German (9, 10, 13 for 1877–94; 9, 10, 20, 21 for 1910–24)
••••••••••••• Irish (3 for 1877–1924)
⊢ ⊢ ⊣ Yankee (7 for 1877–86; 7, 16 for 1888–1910; 7, 16, 4 for 1924)

Percentage of Popular Vote in Each Election

1877	1884	1886	1888	1894	1910	1924
Greenback-	Anti-Monop-	People's	Union Labor	People's	Socialist	Socialist
Labor	olist	(Congress)	(President)	(Governor)	(Mayor)	(Mayor)
(Governor)	(President)					

Source. Election results compiled from Milwaukee *Journal* and Wisconsin *Blue Book*. Ethnic wards selected from data compiled in Jensen, *The Winning of the Midwest,* 128; Wisconsin State Census, 1896; U.S. Eleventh Census, 1890, *Population,* Pt. 1, 558; *Report on Vital and Social Statistics,* Pt. 2, 258–67; U.S. Twelfth Census, 1900, *Population,* Pt. 1, 684; U.S. Thirteenth Census, 1910, *Population,* Vol. 3, 1062; U.S. Fourteenth Census, 1920, *State Compendium, Wisconsin* 49–50.

occasion tipped the fourteenth ward to Seidel. Hoan repeated the feat in 1916. Hostility between Poles (who rallied to Woodrow Wilson's support for an independent Poland) and Germans (who rallied to the Socialists' antiwar position) during World War I permanently accentuated the already apparent imbalance in ethnic support for the Social Democrats. Henceforth, the Socialist mayor was obliged to work with Polish aldermen interested in specific reform legislation but always elected on Democratic slates. When Rose made his unsuccessful comeback bid in 1924, he trounced Hoan by 700 votes in the bellwether fourteenth ward.[72]

Electoral base was not the only point of comparison between the labor politics of the 1880s and that of the first three decades of the twentieth century. Although he may never have reconciled himself to Socialism (he dropped out of politics after Bryan's defeat to devote himself to spiritualism and the nursing milk industry), Schilling could not have complained much about Social Democratic municipal goals. Municipal ownership of utilities—blocked in any case for both Knights and Socialists by long-term private contracts and a hostile city council—remained platform priorities from the 1888 ULP candidacy through Mayor Hoan's long tenure. The conditions of city workers (Socialist influence safeguarded the eight-hour day and Hoan even argued for six hours) and the neutral dispatch of police power motivated labor's interest in independent politics in both periods. Indeed, the most controversial, if never activated, piece of Socialist legislation was the mid-1930s ordinance introduced by alderman Frank Boncel that empowered the city administration to shut down a firm operating during a union-authorized strike. Boncel, born in Milwaukee in 1881, was most likely at least a distant cousin of the Knights' leader Andrew Boncel. Extension of state services to the poor and working classes also formed part of a common political agenda. In 1888 Schilling and the ULP had proposed public bathhouses, free textbooks, public works for the unemployed, and public pawn shops. Socialists had soon imaginatively added to these a call for free legal and medical service for the needy, city condemnation of slum properties, the after-hour openings of schools as social centers, expansion of public parks, and at least one symphony concert a month at a nominal fee. Finally, both parties had capitalized on the issue of honest and open government, backing such measures as direct election and home rule bills. Henry Smith's public career, which spanned several political eras, testified to the common denominator of pre-Socialist and Social Democratic approaches to government. Although he served as an "independent" (not a Socialist) alderman in the twentieth century, the veteran reformer worked closely with Socialist leaders in his last years.[73]

While it is difficult to isolate specifically Socialist contributions to municipal reform realized or even proposed by Milwaukee's Social Democrats, some noteworthy distinctions between the pre-Socialist and Socialist movements in Milwaukee do suggest themselves. The first, and perhaps most obvious, difference is that politics and political administration itself had become recognized as more substantial and more important arenas of maneuver. Both the Knights and their left-wing anarcho-syndicalist rivals of the 1880s initially rested their strategies on the education, organization, and mobilization of workers who would themselves put their ideas into practice. They saw the beginnings of a future social order in the values and practice of their own brotherhood, in vivid contrast to the order of the "monopolists" and "plutocrats." The effect was to create an oppositional movement—manifest in cooperatives, boycotts, and shorter-hours struggles—that had to grow and succeed or expire. Knights' electoral strategy sprang up primarily as a rejoinder to attacks leveled at the labor movement by the opposing order. Parties like Milwaukee's early People's party and the ULP were only as strong as the organizational influence of the Knights of Labor within the community. As the Knights' membership fell off, the new party's political hold on the working class everywhere fell off, too. Indeed, when electoral politics dominated the Order's activity, as it did in Milwaukee from the fall of 1886 onward, it was a sure sign of the deceleration of the movement. At most, Knights' entry into politics represented the admission within its vision of a positive yet still limited role for government. Election of Henry Smith to Congress did not rest on the persuasiveness of a list of electoral demands but on class alignments already polarizing the city in the aftermath of the eight-hour crusade. By organizing workers into one big union, the Knights catalyzed a social process; People's party or Union Labor politics merely reaped a few of its early fruits.

By the late 1890s the world view of American labor leaders had already shifted considerably. Application of state power to crush labor militancy had driven some like Samuel Gompers toward an incremental strategy eschewing grand industrial and political designs. More visionary leaders attempted variously to escape the implications of state power, as in Debs's original cooperative colony plan, or to concentrate totally on state power as in the Socialist party's electoral strategy. In either of the dominant early twentieth-century working-class strategies, the labor movement itself no longer assumed the role of incubator of the new society. Rules beyond the worker's (as well as the individual good or bad employer's) control now seemed to govern the development of the marketplace. Many now accepted the capitalist's historically progressive role, with his concentration of industry seen as an inevitable step preparing the way for the ultimate efficiency of Socialist planning. In this light Berger and others welcomed the trusts, predicting that at some future moment Socialism would be realized in a shadowy shift of the industrial empire from private to public hands. Faith in a Socialist future, however distant, undoubtedly conveyed an important moral legitimacy to the painstaking incrementalism of the Milwaukee Social Democrats. Convinced of the rightness of their course they would defend ground already won by the trade unions while cautiously expanding democratic claims on the public sector.

On balance, Social Democratic tenure in Milwaukee showed that organized workers could have class consciousness and more at the same time.[74]

Berger's Socialism, however, offered less certain benefits to the unorganized and unskilled workers of the city. Intimate ties with the FTC empowered the Social Democrats but also cast them as defenders of the existing craft union structure rather than allowing the Socialists to impose a direction of their own on the labor movement. Socialist successes thus occurred unaccompanied by visibly increased cohesion among the city's working-class population. The FTC did not admit a Polish-language affiliate until 1905. The labor movement in the city was no larger in 1930 than it had been in 1900. Labor-management relations, historian Thomas Gavett concluded, thus were hardly affected by the Socialists' presence. Given the lack of a complementary workplace organizing strategy, the success of the Social Democrats in the early twentieth century in retaining at least a sizable fraction of the Polish vote, for example, was a remarkable accomplishment.[75]

The very autonomy of Milwaukee's municipal Socialists in the end proved their undoing. Lacking a mass labor electoral base as well as ties to a party with federal influence, the Social Democrats were inevitably superceded by a New Deal-CIO-Democratic coalition that could out-promise even the Socialists in delivering favors to working people. Loss of FTC support, as the new industrial unions looked to national connections for sustenance, was one critical blow to independent labor politics. Overwhelming endorsement of the Democrats by less-skilled and less-unionized working-class voters in the Franklin D. Roosevelt years was another, leading to the defeat and disintegration of the Hoan administration in 1940.[76]

Comparatively speaking, early twentieth-century Milwaukee proved an exceptional but not an outlandish example of contemporary political developments. In most American cities one of the major parties (usually the Democrats) functioned as the municipal agent for the labor unions. Particularly if a politician combined the freewheeling insouciance of an "All-the-time-Rosy" with tangible concessions to union leaders, he might expect support both from organized workers and from the poorer, generally unorganized and unskilled immigrant community. In Milwaukee, however, the political education of the Germans together with astute Socialist leadership fashioned an alternative progressive coalition, supplanting both conservative business Republicanism and corrupt Democratic bossism.

Ethnic brokerism generally served as the twentieth-century American substitute for a mass party of the urban working class. The case of Milwaukee modified but did not directly challenge this rule. Organized labor in the city formed an insufficient numerical base for a party. And the craft union structure discouraged a disciplined, collective political viewpoint. Nevertheless, by keeping fences mended at once with the trade unions, ethnic community leaders, and middle-class reformers, Socialist politicians not only earned themselves a long life but also provided a model of honesty and creativity in local government.

Both Knights of Labor and Socialist leaders, it should be noted, encountered the difficulty of harmonizing the dynamic of popular mobilization with the year-in-year-out persistence required to gain political power. From this perspective Milwaukee's Social Democrats may in retrospect be judged at once more effective and more conservative than their pre-Socialist forebears. The Knights of Labor was like a locomotive whose coals had been stoked too high for its engineers to keep it on the track. On the other hand, it might be said of the Social Democrats that they never raised sufficient fire to travel more than a short way down their projected path. In an important sense, room for the Socialists to maneuver had been severely limited by the very dispersion of that uncertain behemoth, the Knights of Labor, which had preceded them. For without organization of the working class it proved impossible to create and sustain a working-class party. Following a similar line of logic in 1913, a young and impatient Walter Lippman expressed his frustration with the municipal Socialist regime in Schenectady, New York: "Political action in order to be effective must represent a power in the community behind it. That power is built out of economic forces made intelligent by conviction. Votes must represent the size of that power: all other votes are a menace."[77]

NOTES

1. Socialist mayors included Emil Seidel, 1910–12, Daniel Hoan, 1916–40, and Frank P. Zeidler, 1948–60. Mayor Zeidler's tenure occurred through a Socialist-Democratic coalition, rather than an independent Socialist organization. As such it is not treated in this chapter, although reasons for Socialist absorption into the party of the New Deal may be inferred from the last section; Bayrd Still, *Milwaukee: The History of a City* (Madison, Wis., 1965), 258, 265–66, U.S. Eleventh Census, 1890, *Compendium of the Eleventh Census*, Pt. 2 (Washington, D.C., 1897), 680–82.

2. Still, *Milwaukee*, 323–27.

3. *Ibid.*, 257, 325; U.S. Tenth Census, 1880, *Report on the Social Statistics of Cities*, Pt. 2 (Washington, D.C., 1887), 676–77.

4. Still, *Milwaukee*, 335–39; Wisconsin State Department, *Tabular Statement of the Census Enumeration*, 1855 (Madison, 1906), 702–3; U.S. Eleventh Census, 1890, *Report of Manufacturing Industries in the United States*, Pt. 2 (Washington, D.C., 1895), 334–43.

5. Thomas C. Cochran, *The Pabst Brewing Company: The History of an American Business* (New York, 1948), 271–72.

6. Kathleen Neils Conzen, *Immigrant Milwaukee, 1836–1860: Accommodation and Community in a Frontier City* (Cambridge, Mass., 1976), 124–25; Milwaukee *Journal*, Mar. 31, 1886; Gerd Korman, *Industrialization,*

Immigrants, and Americanizers: The View from Milwaukee, 1866–1921 (Madison, Wis., 1967), 16, 27, 36. When John Jarrett, president of the Amalgamated, delivered a protariff speech in the city in 1888, his remarks included the comment that he was ashamed of being born an Englishman. The Acorn Lodge of the Sons of St. George, composed largely of English-born workingmen, expressed outrage at the slur on their heritage. Besides the Germans and Poles, foreign-born groups in Milwaukee according to the 1890 census included the Irish (3,436), the English (2,409), and the Norwegians (1,821).

7. John A. Hawgood, *The Tragedy of German America* (New York, 1970), 202–6; Robert C. Nesbit, *Wisconsin, a History* (Madison, Wis., 1973), 155–56, 242–43; Still, *Milwaukee,* 115–25; Wilhelm Hense-Jensen and Ernst Bruncken, "Wisconsin's German-Americans until the End of the Nineteenth Century," esp. 5–6, 11, manuscript at the Wisconsin State Historical Society, Madison, hereafter WSHS; Thomas W. Gavett, *Development of the Labor Movement in Milwaukee* (Milwaukee, Wis., 1965), 33, 40–46, 51–53.

8. Still, *Milwaukee,* 151–63; Richard Jensen, *The Winning of the Midwest; Social and Political Conflict 1888–1896* (Chicago, 1971), esp. 55–88, 122; Wisconsin, *Blue Book, 1879–1883;* Milwaukee *Volksblatt,* Apr, 8, 1883; Milwaukee *Trades Assembly Bulletin,* Apr. 1, 1882.

9. Still, *Milwaukee,* 268–69; Paul Fox, *The Poles in America* (New York, 1970), 58–59; interview by telephone with Mrs. Celia Orzelska Wong, Aug. 11, 1975. The Orzelska family moved to Milwaukee from Kujany, Poland, in 1904 when Celia was still an infant. Mrs. Wong remembers her father trying to get his Polish neighbors to register as Poles, not Germans, during the census count of 1920. Milwaukee *Journal,* Mar. 30, 1886; U.S. Eleventh Census, 1890, *Compendium of the Eleventh Census,* Pt. 2, 604–11. The state census count of 659 Poles in Milwaukee in 1895 was ridiculously low. *Wisconsin State Census, 1895* (Madison, 1895–96), 88–89; Still, *Milwaukee,* 273.

10. Milwaukee *Journal,* May 17, 1886.

11. Jerzy Jedlicki, "Land of Hope, Land of Despair: Polish Scholarship and American Immigration," *Reviews in American History,* 3 (Mar. 1975), 87–94; reference to Detroit in Rutland (Vt.) *Herald,* Mar. 21, 1887; for Cleveland see Henry B. Leonard, "Ethnic Cleavage and Industrial Conflict in Late 19th Century America: the Cleveland Rolling Mill Company Strikes of 1882 and 1885," *Labor History,* 20 (Fall 1979), 524–48; knowledge of Saginaw Valley drawn from Saginaw *Courier* and Bay City *Evening Press,* 1885.

12. Fox, *Poles,* 78–79; Korman, *Industrialization, Immigrants, and Americanizers,* 51–52; Still, *Milwaukee,* 269–72; Francis Bolek, ed., *Who's Who in Polish America* (New York, 1943); *Kuryer Polski,* July 14, 1888; *Volksblatt,* Apr. 8, 1883.

13. Jonathon Garlock and N. C. Builder, "Knights of Labor Data Bank: Users Manual and Index to Local Assemblies" (1973), manuscript at the University of Rochester, Rochester, N.Y. Two other early Knights' assemblies, including one of telegraphers, collapsed before the period of sustained

growth; see Gavett, *Development of the Labor Movement,* 50–53. The Order probably possessed 12,000–15,000 members at its peak in May 1886. Gavett's figure is corroborated by Henry Smith's recollection: "Reminiscences of My Political Life" (1912), 15, Henry Smith's Papers, WSHS; D. L. Galehey to Powderly, May 22, 1886, Terence V. Powderly Papers, Catholic University, Washington, D.C.; Milwaukee *Journal,* Mar. 19, 1886.

14. *John Swinton's Papers* (hereafter JSP), Oct. 1, 8, 1885, Dec. 20, 1885; the reference to "Schwarze Liste" is in Milwaukee *Boycott-Post,* Mar. 6, 1886; Milwaukee *Journal,* Feb. 18, 20, 23, 26, Mar. 3, 16, 19, Apr. 4, 7, 1886.

15. Gary M. Fink, ed., *Biographical Dictionary of American Labor Leaders* (Westport, Conn., 1974), 319; Norman Ware, *The Labor Movement in the United States, 1860–1895* (New York, 1929), 11–18; Milton Small, "Robert Schilling and the Origins of Populism in Wisconsin" (1950), 3, manuscript at WSHS; *Volksblatt,* Apr. 8, 1883.

16. Charles R. Smith, "Outline of the Life of Henry Smith, Public Servant, 1838–1916" (1916), 1–3, Henry Smith Papers.

17. Henry Smith, "My Official Life" (1912), 7, 9, 14–31, Henry Smith Papers.

18. Henry Smith, "Why I Became a Greenbacker in Politics" (n.d.), 8, 10, 12–13, Henry Smith Papers, and "Reminiscences of My Political Life," 14; Conzen, *Immigrant Milwaukee,* 227.

19. Milwaukee *Journal,* July 6, 1885; Gavett, *Development of the Labor Movement,* 58; Garlock and Builder, "Knights of Labor Data Bank"; given the overlap of Poles and ironworkers and the large memberships of both the all-Polish and ironworkers assemblies, it seems possible that some Poles belonged to two assemblies, one for their trade and one for their nationality.

20. Victor Greene, *For God and Country: The Rise of Polish and Lithuanian Ethnic Consciousness in America* (Madison, Wis., 1975), 66–69, quotation, 67; Polish Academy of Learning, *Polski Slownik Biograficzny,* 15 (Poland, 1970), as translated by Mrs. Celia Wong. Michael Kruszka's younger brother, Wacław, who did not arrive in the United States until 1893, became a prominent advocate for the recognition of ethnic pluralism and Polish rights within the Roman Catholic church. A generally liberal and reform-minded priest, the Reverend Kruszka was the first to install a playground in a Milwaukee parish school. Some parishioners were "shocked to see him ice-skating with children in the yard." Greene, *For God and Country,* 132–34; interview with Mrs. Wong, Sept. 12, 1975. See also the Reverend Alexander Syski, "The Nestor of Polish Historians in America: Reverend Wacław Kruzska," *Bulletin of the Polish Institute of Arts and Sciences of America,* 3 (Oct. 1944), 102–11; Milwaukee *Journal,* Oct. 15, 1886; Henry Smith to Powderly, Mar. 2, 1887, M. S. Cyborowski to Powderly, Jan. 24, 1887, Michael Kruzska to Powderly, Jan. 31, 1887, Powderly Papers.

21. Quoted in Jeremy Brecher, *Strike!* (San Francisco, 1972), 40, see also 37–38.

22. Gavett, *Development of the Labor Movement,* 56–57. For Powderly's account of his role in the eight-hour movement, see his *Thirty Years of Labor,*

1859–1889 (New York, 1967), 253–58. See also Brecher, *Strike,* 25. For comparative statistics on strikes, see Florence Peterson, *Strikes in the U.S., 1880–1930,* U.S. Department of Labor, Bureau of Labor Statistics, Bulletin no. 651 (Washington, D.C., 1938), 29, and Gavett, *Development of the Labor Movement,* 34, 56–57.

23. Milton Small, "The Biography of Robert Schilling" (M.A. thesis, University of Wisconsin, 1953), 192–95.

24. Gavett, *Development of the Labor Movement,* 34, 56–57. Information regarding the confectioner (*not* the brewer) Blatz courtesy of Neil Basen.

25. *Volksblatt,* Apr. 8, 1883; *Arbeiter Zeitung,* May 29, 1886.

26. Gavett, *Development of the Labor Movement,* 56.

27. Milwaukee *Journal,* May 1, 1886. Discrepancy between these strike figures (e.g., 3,000 brewers) and the census occupational figures (e.g., 1,000 plus brewers in 1890) probably reflects a mixture of journalistic exaggeration and the fact that the census did not include bottom-rung laborers within the specific industry.

28. *Ibid.;* Cochran, *Pabst,* 274–80; Small, "Biography of Robert Schilling," 26.

29. Milwaukee *Journal,* Apr. 28, 30, May 3, 1886; *Arbeiter Zeitung,* May 4, 1886; *Volksblatt,* May 29, 1886; Small, "Biography of Robert Schilling," 26.

30. John R. Commons's description was assimilated uncritically by Brecher, *Strike,* 26.

31. Milwaukee *Journal,* Apr. 7, 14, May 1, 1886; E. P. Allis to Horace A. Tenney, June 29, 1878, Oct. 9, 1879, Horace A. Tenney Papers, WSHS; Gavett, *Development of the Labor Movement,* 38; Small, "Biography of Robert Schilling," 35. Compare Allis's response to that of a Saginaw mill-owner in 1885 who stated that "it was not at the present time a question of hours or wages. It was whether property owners had the right to manage their own business affairs." Saginaw *Courier,* Aug. 6, 1885.

32. Gavett, *Development of the Labor Movement,* 60–61; Milwaukee *Journal,* May 3, 4 (special ed.), 1886; Brecher, *Strike,* 40; Small, "Biography of Robert Schilling," 27–28.

33. Small, "Biography of Robert Schilling," 30; Milwaukee *Journal,* June 2, 1886; see esp. Jerry M. Cooper, "The Wisconsin National Guard in the Milwaukee Riots of 1886," *Wisconsin Magazine of History,* 55 (Autumn 1871), 31–48, quotation, 35.

34. Small, "Biography of Robert Schilling," 26, 28. Alderman Rudzinski would later say of the demonstrators, "They were Poles without exception, not socialists or anarchists." See Milwaukee *Journal,* May 8, 1886.

35. *Ibid.,* 22; Milwaukee *Journal,* May 4, 5, 1886; "Proceedings of the Milwaukee Common Council," May 10, 24, 1886, WSHS.

36. Gavett, *Development of the Labor Movement,* 63.

37. Milwaukee *Journal,* May 6, 16, 1886.

38. *Ibid.,* May 12, June 5, 1886.

39. Gavett, *Development of the Labor Movement,* 67; *Common Council*

Proceedings, May 10, 24, 1886; Milwaukee *Journal,* May 14, 16 (quoting Racine *Times*), 1886.

40. Milwaukee *Journal,* May 19, 26, June 7, Oct. 26, Nov. 1, 1886; Still, *Milwaukee,* 294; Gavett, *Development of the Labor Movement,* 66; Cochran, *Pabst,* 262; Small, "Biography of Robert Schilling," 40.

41. Milwaukee *Journal,* May 26, June 2, 1886; Gavett, *Development of the Labor Movement,* 66.

42. Milwaukee *Journal,* May 20, 21, June 19, 1886; *Volksblatt,* May 29, 1886; Small, "Biography of Robert Schilling," 38; Gavett, *Development of the Labor Movement,* 76–77.

43. Milwaukee *Journal,* May 20, June 3, 5, 30, 1886.

44. Small, "Robert Schilling and the Origins of Populism," 1; Milwaukee *Journal,* June 15, 1886.

45. Small, "Robert Schilling and the Origins of Populism," 3.

46. Milwaukee *Journal,* Oct. 4, 6, 9, 22, 1886.

47. Wyandott (Kans.) *Gazette,* May 7, 1886; Gavett, *Development of the Labor Movement,* 65; Milwaukee *Daily Review,* Mar. 22, 1887.

48. Milwaukee *Journal,* Oct. 9, 26, 1886.

49. Small, "Robert Schilling and the Origins of Populism," 4. Following the election, John Thompson, a Chicago Knight of Labor, wrote a poem entitled "Hail Milwaukee":

> A Bethlehem star shines out from the north,
> O'er the city by Michigan's waters,
> And a conquering shout from out Labor's clean swarth,
> Where the vanguard of truth the enemy slaughters,
> Milwaukee Advance! Your place is in front,
> The birthplace of freedom's success,
> And eyes of glad labor looks up to the font,
> The baptismal place of freemen's redress.
>
> . . . .
>
> Oh! Shout the glad tidings of hope to men,
> Shout; for the corpse of the beast lies burned,
> And through all the great fight was Milwaukee the van,
> Where in charging the beast, the ranks were so served,
> So served! ho! Magna Carta again!
> From barons of monopoly's fraud,
> Oh! Swell the glad tidings that's embossed in the name,
> "Milwaukee!" Shibboleth; thanks unto God!
>
> —Chicago *Knight of Labor,* Dec. 4, 1886.

50. Milwaukee *Journal,* Nov. 2, 3, 1886; ward characterizations by ethnicity determined from Jensen, *Winning of the Midwest,* 128; *Wisconsin State Census, 1895;* U.S. Eleventh Census, 1890, *Population,* Pt. 1 (Washington, D.C., 1895), 558.

51. Milwaukee *Journal*, Nov. 3, 1886. Governor Rusk would become the nation's first secretary of agriculture in 1889.

52. Gavett, *Development of the Labor Movement*, 77, 79; Garlock and Builder, "Knights of Labor Data Base"; Cochran, *Pabst*, 282–83; Schilling to Powderly, May 24, 1887, Powderly Papers. Schilling's complaints were directed at Charles H. Litchman, secretary of the Order: "I shall do what I can to have the *Journal of United Labor* done away with altogether, as long as it is to be used to advance the personal aggrandizement of C.H.L."

53. U.S. Commissioner of Labor, *Tenth Annual Report* (Washington, D.C., 1896), 1218–61; Gavett, *Development of the Labor Movement*, 7.

54. Gavett, *Development of the Labor Movement*, 80–82, 114; Garlock and Builder, "Knights of Labor Data Base"; Milwaukee city directories, 1888–98, WSHS.

55. Milwaukee *Journal*, Mar. 8, 12, 18, 24, 1887; Milwaukee *Sentinel*, Mar. 24, 1887.

56. Hense-Jensen and Bruncken, "Wisconsin's German-Americans," ch. VII, 10, 12; file of "Biographical Sketches," WSHS.

57. Gavett, *Development of the Labor Movement*, 73; Small, "Biography of Robert Schilling," 9.

58. Gavett, *Development of the Labor Movement*, 78–79; *Daily Review*, Mar. 3, Apr. 5, 1887.

59. Milwaukee *Journal*, Apr. 4, Oct. 26, 1888; *Kuryer Polski*, July 3, 9, 1888; *Arbeiter Zeitung*, May 4, Dec. 28, 1886; Small, "Robert Schilling and the Origins of Populism," 7; Gavett, *Development of the Labor Movement*, 75.

60. Gavett, *Development of the Labor Movement*, 76; Small, "Robert Schilling and the Origins of Populism," 9.

61. Daniels to Powderly, Oct. 28, 1887, Powderly Papers.

62. *Kuryer Polski*, June 23, Oct. 3, 8, 13, 1888. Not that news from Poland did not intersect with labor news as in the case of the strike of bakers' apprentices in Lwowie. *Ibid.*, July 24, 1888.

63. Milwaukee *Journal*, Nov. 7, 1888.

64. Wisconsin *Blue Book*, 1891; Milwaukee *Journal*, Apr. 6, 1892, Nov. 1, 7, 1894; Still, *Milwaukee*, 296–97; *Kuryer Polski*, Oct. 13, 1888.

65. Milwaukee *Advance*, Feb. 2, Mar. 22, 1890; Small, "Robert Schilling and the Origins of Populism," 11–12.

66. Small, "Robert Schilling and the Origins of Populism," 13–14. Paul Kleppner's earlier analysis of the 1893–94 Populist vote in Milwaukee, treating it as a sudden outcropping of the 1890s depression, i.e., as a protest vote against the depression-saddled Democrats and the too-pietistic Republicans, misses entirely the Populists' organic relation to the labor movement and preceeding political polarization. *The Cross of Culture: A Social Analysis of Midwestern Politics, 1850–1900* (New York, 1970), 251–61.

67. Marvin Wachman, *History of the Social-Democratic Party of Milwaukee, 1897–1910* (Urbana, Ill., 1945), 11; Still, *Milwaukee*, 529–30; Gavett, *Development of the Labor Movement*, 92–96.

68. Wachman, *Social-Democratic Party,* 11, 12; Gavett, *Development of the Labor Movement,* 89.

69. Still, *Milwaukee,* 304–5; Wachman, *Social-Democratic Party,* 39–40; Gavett, *Development of the Labor Movement,* 80–82; Wisconsin *Blue Book,* 1911; city directory, 1896.

70. Still, *Milwaukee,* 307–9.

71. *Ibid.,* 318, 516; Wachman, *Social-Democratic Party,* 106–13; Milwaukee *Journal,* Apr. 6, 1910.

72. U.S. Fourteenth Census, 1920, *Wisconsin State Compendium* (Washington, D.C., 1925), 49–50; Still, *Milwaukee,* 528. See, generally, the excellent overview by Donald Pienkos, "Politics, Religion, and Change in Polish Milwaukee, 1900–1930," *Wisconsin Magazine of History,* 61 (Spring 1978), 179–209.

73. Fink, ed., *Biographical Dictionary of Labor Leaders,* 319; Still, *Milwaukee,* 285, 302, 305; Frederick C. Howe, "Milwaukee, a Socialist City," *Outlook,* 95 (June 25, 1910), 420–21. Hoan's administration produced remarkable calm between police and striking workers. Minimum picket lines and noncooperation by constabulary authorities with strikebreakers went hand in hand. Still, *Milwaukee,* 500, 529; Gavett, *Development of the Labor Movement,* 147.

74. Sally A. Miller, *Victor Berger and the Promise of Constructive Socialism, 1910–1920* (Westport, Conn., 1973), 25–31; David Montgomery, "The 'New Unionism' and the Transformation of Workers' Consciousness in America, 1909–1922," *Journal of Social History,* 7 (Summer 1974), 509–29. In 1909 the Social Democrats declared their party "the American expression of the international movement of modern wage-workers for better food, better houses, sufficient sleep, more leisure, more education, and more culture." Still, *Milwaukee,* 316; also see Andrew Dawson, "The Paradox of Dynamic Technological Change and the Labor Aristocracy in the U.S., 1880–1914," *Labor History,* 20 (Summer 1979), 325–51. In private correspondence David Montgomery has drawn my attention to Robert Hunter, *Violence and the Labor Movement* (New York, 1914), esp 229–75. Written by an ally of Berger's within the leadership of the American Socialist party, this antianarchist, antisyndicalist tract offers dramatic testimony of the changes in radical thinking since 1886. Here, the conflict among radicals is portrayed entirely within the framework of being pro- or antistate. Appealing entirely to a legislative strategy ("the more property the State owns, the fewer will be the number of capitalists to be dealt with and the easier it will be eventually to introduce socialism"), Hunter implicitly deprecates all forms of workers' direct action as either inherently reformist (i.e., trade union action) or "a fantastic dream" (i.e., syndicalist mass strikes).

75. Gavett, *Development of the Labor Movement,* 117, 137; Korman, *Industrialization, Immigrants, and Americanizers,* 52; Pienkos, "Politics, Religion, and Change in Polish Milwaukee," 185–88.

76. Gavett, *Development of the Labor Movement,* 146–51, 171–75. Construction unions, affiliated to the local Building Trades Council, had already

broken off and formed an anti-Socialist bloc early in the twentieth century. Roosevelt's support within the Polish wards was as follows: in 1932, he carried the city by 67 percent, Polish wards by 75 percent; in 1936, the figures were 78 percent and 84 percent, respectively; in 1940, the figures were 64 percent and 76 percent, respectively; by this time the Socialist party was effectively dead as a political force.

77. Lippmann to Carl D. Thompson, Oct. 29, 1913, reprinted in Bruce M. Stave, ed., *Socialism and the Cities* (Port Washington, N.Y., 1975), 195–96.

8
Labor, Party Politics, and
American Exceptionalism

WHAT KIND OF MOVEMENT was the Knights of Labor? How do its achievements as well as its ultimate political failure fit into a larger picture of American institutional development? These questions quickly propel us from the distinctiveness, even the relative autonomy, of local events toward larger patterns within the nation. Their answers also collide with certain general interpretations of the American past.

From a late twentieth-century American perspective, what is perhaps most striking about the political tumult of the 1880s is the centrality of worker organization to both the structure and outcome of the contests. In each of the communities under study a radical political realignment reflected the social conflict between the Knights of Labor and their antagonists. In each community claims to authority by workers at the workplace and in the public realm effectively reoriented local political geography along a new axis. In this era at least union organization and labor politics were not juxtaposed to an alternating economic current; rather the industrial struggle was the generator of political action. As such, the battles described here, in which immediate economic antagonisms curled around wider frameworks of political meaning, might best be considered a form of class conflict as Edward Thompson has defined it: "When some men, as a result of common experiences (inherited or shared), feel and articulate the identity of their interests as between themselves, and as against other men whose interests are different from (and usually opposed to) theirs."[1]

Certainly such a definition of these events rings truer than the body of literature on the nineteenth century that subordinates contemporary social divisions to the "stresses of modernization" or the "coming of industrialism." The towns examined here were not "island communities" protesting the construction of a bridge to the bureaucratic-industrial mainland. Those links had been forged well before the Great Upheaval of the 1880s. Indeed, the early years of factory-building, quarrying, and railroad construction had been marked by a relative consensus of civic boosterism and popular expectation that would reward an Edwin Wallace with public office and see an Edward Allis make common political cause with Milwaukee mechanics. When the break did come, it did not pit an older community against a single new capitalist intruder nor an earlier code of social relationships against a sudden imposition of one from above. The workingmen's movement challenged the very pillars of the old community, or at least that local community with which the workers themselves had had direct experience.[2]

Throughout this study the community and cultural roots of Knights' organization have been stressed. While this formulation is obviously at odds with the immiserization-alienation view of popular mobilization common to classical Marxism, it also takes issue with views that tend to subordinate the creative political dimension of social movements to cultural resistance. The recent hypothesis, for example, that "most commonly, popular movements arise as efforts to *resist* threats to established patterns of everyday life" overstates the purely defensive aspects of movement building, at least as applied to the Knights. A similar inference based on the current writing in social history that "people draw on a range of ethnic, kinship, religious, and other traditional relations in fighting back and in developing a collective consciousness" is likewise limited by a failure to distinguish between the traditions upon which a movement draws and traditionalism itself. After taking account of the social and ideological wellsprings of American radicalism, it is also important to emphasize the break with the past made by American workers in 1886. In their patterns of unionism, political loyalty, and to some extent even in their circles of personal association, the swelling ranks of the Knights of Labor signified and defined a conscious revolt from a social order that they as individuals had previously tolerated. The shock of established authority at their presumption, evident in editorials, sermons, and official governmental pronouncements, should not be taken as counterfeit. Fear of the disordering implications of the workers' actions was real.[3]

If a modified class conflict model provides an indispensable framework for understanding the events of the 1880s, other indices of social identity are also necessary to penetrate the inner life of the workingmen's movement. One is the category of "peoplehood" that Harry Boyte has proposed to define the inherited, subjective set of ties among a particular group; both in reference to the nation as a whole and in reference to smaller communities of locale, craft, and ethnicity, the concept has relevance here.[4]

The national peoplehood, of course, was neither an ancient nor, given the transfusions of immigration, a wholly organic growth. As a product of what Eric Hobsbawn called the "dual revolution" of capitalistic and democratic developments, the national culture of the United States confidently anticipated both material progress and protection of the public good. The class critique of the Knights and other American radicals of the late nineteenth century began, as demonstrated in Chapter 1, with the disparity between national ideological expectations and material realities. The Populist alternative, like subsequent Socialist blueprints for a new society, preserved both sides of this original national promise of democratic abundance. The last thing the Knights of Labor had in mind was to move backward toward some preindustrial arcadia. While supporting nationalization of the railroads, telephones, and telegraph and introducing legislation to reserve to the public title all iron and coal on federal lands, Milwaukee Congressman and millwright Henry Smith also defended the installation of labor-saving plate-printers at the treasury department, even though it displeased some of the employees. "I can not go back on one-third of a century of practical experience of the progress of my country." Rutland Knights showed a similar American fascination with new technology in their support for the acquisition of a stone crusher for road work. Only when improvement threatened acute distress did the Gilded Age labor parties temper their modernizing instincts. T. H. Brown's veto of wire fences to replace the wooden ones whose maintenance occupied the unemployed during the winter represented the exception rather than the rule.[5]

Within the larger national identity, a variety of discrete communities, notably those based upon work and ethnicity, helped to define the character of the workingmen's movement. One basis of internal aggregation was occupation and skill, as evidenced both by the important role of trades assemblies within the Knights of Labor and by the later splintering off of the skilled membership when the Knights no longer met their needs. The settings examined here suggest that skilled trade unionists played a vanguard role in the rise of the Order. Wherever the Order achieved political successes, it did so by linking semiskilled and unskilled industrial workers including blacks, new immigrants, and women with this leadership sector. To some degree this alliance also represented an admixture of generations, the transference of the accumulated wisdom of older craftsmen to younger workers entering the factories (Table 17).[6]

As emphasized throughout this work, the Knights' coalition of trades and occupations also critically depended on the cooperation of diverse racial and ethnic communities. The mobilization of these communities within and alongside the labor movement raises problems for those conversant only with a conceptual antipathy between class and ethnic consciousness or with an alternating identity theory wherein the subjectivities instead of directly fighting it out with each other enjoy separate seasons of development. To be sure, there are moments in the foregoing study—Polish priests attacking Henry Smith, a F. W. von Cotzhausen explicitly appealing to German as opposed to labor loyalties—where such conventional wisdom seems to fit. Generally, however, the attempt (most recently by quantitative historians) to isolate socioeconomic (or class) influences on political behavior from sociocultural (or ethnic) ones

TABLE 17. Comparative Ages of Preindustrial and Industrial Workers

Category of Work	Percentage Under Thirty Years of Age	Percentage Under Forty Years of Age
Preindustrial		
Skilled artisans	35	56
Rutland	39	57
Richmond—whites	36	56
Kansas City	31	55
Unskilled laborers	39	62
Rutland	39	57
Richmond—whites	40	62
Richmond—blacks	33	55
Kansas City—whites	46	83
Kansas City—blacks	36	55
Industrial		
Skilled craft workers	48	73
Rutland scale workers	52	86
Rutland machinists/ironworkers	39	67
Richmond machinists (white)	51	70
Kansas City railroad shop workers	48	68
Semiskilled factory, mill, and quarry workers	58	79
Rochester shoeworkers	51	80
Rutland marble workers	55	75
Richmond tobacco workers—white	84	94
Richmond tobacco workers—black	61	71
Kansas City packinghouse workers	39	76

Source. U.S. Tenth Census, 1880, population manuscript. Richmond data courtesy of Herbert Gutman. Calculation of workers' ages drawn from a sample of 20 percent or more of the population in each occupational category. In the case of Richmond, Gutman's figures covered the total population.

seems particularly misguided. Were the black workers of Richmond more affected by racial or class consciousness? Did economic situation or national origin motivate the votes of Rutland marble workers? And how does one apportion the identity of the Milwaukee Socialist who, when arrested while waving a stick in the street after the Bay View murders, was reportedly yelling, "We will show the bloodhounds what German blood can do"?[7]

There are three points to be made here. One is that class and ethnicity were not only coincident characteristics of these communities; they sometimes were asserted simultaneously into political life. Second, even when one of these aspects of social identity was politically dominant, some version of the other was still contained within it. Thus, the style, organization, and personnel of Milwaukee Socialism were unmistakably German. But a distinct, if alternative, economic rationale also contributed to the politics of ethnic factionalism that reigned in Milwaukee after the demise of the People's party and in Kansas City at the end of the Hannan regime. Third, social class and ethnic identity had evolving historical meanings. For example, being an iron worker or a member of St. Hyacinth's parish carried a different cultural as well as political significance after the Bay View massacre.[8]

One other aspect of community affecting the workingmen's political movement deserves comment. That is the influential role played by certain middle-class sympathizers of friends of the workingmen such as George L. Hayes, James F. Hogan, Thomas Hannan, J. T. Wilson, E. B. Moore, and Theodore Rudzinski. To a considerable extent this significant cross-class undercurrent in the labor movement was obviously related to its ethnicity, i.e., to the opportunity for advancement that the movement provided to those groups on the margins of American economic and political life. Ethnic newspaper editors and shopkeepers were often neither physically nor experientially far removed from the working poor. As such they may be seen in part as educated and sympathetic mediaries between their working-class neighbors and the larger community, perhaps even within Antonio Gramsci's sense of "organic intellectuals."[9] The political mobilization of the laboring masses, furthermore, offered local ethnic leaders potential leverage within the larger community that they had never possessed before. The labor movement therefore either swept up a group's traditional middle-class leaders as in the case of C. H. J. "Alley" Taylor, J. T. Wilson, or Theodore Rudzinski or brushed them aside as it did Francis Borchardt and John D. Spellman, replacing them with more appropriate spokesmen like Horatio Cate, Thomas Brown, and Andrew Boncel.

The participation of such nonworkers in labor's cause ought more generally to be related to the comparative porousness of American economic life in the communities examined during the late nineteenth century. No great cleavages of education, economic inheritance, or residential segregation separated foremen, shopkeepers, and in some cases even entrepreneurs from employees. Some of the early literature on the Knights of Labor pointed just to this petit bourgeois presence as a source of weakness in the Order; subsequent AFL unionism seems more thoroughly proletarian. The opposite may well have been the case. The presence of the small town or ethnic middle class within the Order not only lent the movement articulate and influential support but also reflected its drive on the centers of power within the larger community. It was a sign not of its backwardness or ideological confusion (that case must be made on its own merits) but of the movement's ambitious purpose to transform society, not just to improve the standing of one trade or another, that accounts for the blurring within it of sociologically determined class lines.

In this sense the structural similarity between the Knights and subsequent powerful voices of radical reform in American history can be noted. In the early twentieth century the Socialist party scored its greatest successes in the rural Southwest and Midwest industrial and mining towns, where, one may presume, a working notion of the producing classes still bound people together. Elsewhere, the Socialists drew support only from urban ethnic communities (Jews, Germans, Finns), where displaced intellectuals and professionals provided an important stimulus. The revival of American labor in the CIO period also depended to an important degree on the political coming of age of the southern and eastern European immigrant (as well as displaced Appalachian) communities. This same quality of community solidarity gave strength to the civil rights movement of the 1960s, where the southern black church leaders provided a crucial link between local rank and file and outside power centers.[10]

Some of the very strengths of the Knights of Labor as a social movement were also the sources of its greatest weaknesses. First, the Knights' self-appointed role as a responsible intermediary offering a sane and progressive solution to industrial conflict could work only under certain circumstances. It required both a local contingent of workers strong and disciplined enough to pick and sustain their own fight (since the Order's national financial and tactical resourses were minimal) and a decisive third force (e.g., public sympathy or supportive political officials) to legitimize the Knights in this role. When such conditions did not apply, as they did not in national confrontations with steel, railroad, and packinghouse bosses as well as in unincorporated areas or company mill towns, the Knights of Labor were poorly situated for battle. The very local and community-based power of the Knights thus possessed its own intrinsic drawbacks, as the members of national trade unions discovered all too soon. Chronic leadership problems in which mutual recrimination and bad faith among officers and organizers reached titanic levels may also have reflected certain qualities of the laboring community. Just as the rank and file combined an emotional nationalism with a day-to-day preoccupation with more local matters, so, too, did they both enshrine and ignore their own national executive officers. Scorn for the professional partisan politician also all too often easily overlapped into suspicion of any comparatively detached decision-maker. Fears surrounding what appeared to be a power-hungry and overly intellectual Home Club within District Assembly 49 of New York City were probably of such vintage. Finally, the national republican political heritage, which provided the Knights with a forceful and effective critique of corporate capitalism, led them to their most deplorable social-political position. As members of an ethnically, racially, and sexually integrated movement, the Knights fell victim to hatred of the un-American

Chinese and sometimes to an unflattering condescension toward southern European immigrants.[11]

When political conflict means what it says, parties fall into disrepute.
—Giovanni Sartori

Labor's political campaigns cast a revealing light not only on the movement and communities of the workingmen but also on the political system that the movement both entered and engaged. As the hypothesis of political sociologist Giovanni Sartori suggests, the very dissolution of normal party structures in dozens of Gilded Age communities itself signaled an unusual, crisis-ridden moment for the American political culture.[12] In each community conventional political organization suddenly and dramatically gave way in the mid-1880s to a new sociopolitical alignment. Informal factions and cleavages between Democrats and Republicans were replaced by the more self-consciously class-oriented competition between Workingmen (People's or United Labor) and Citizens (Nonpartisan) organizations. In each case a subculture of political opposition—rooted in local assemblies and craft locals but hosted as well by labor cooperatives, reading rooms, dramatic clubs, and workingmen's lodges and nourished at labor holidays, picnics, and fairs—had grown strong and distinctive enough to define its own political vehicle. In so doing the labor movement either simply overwhelmed the traditional ethnocultural partisanship of its rank and file (e.g., Milwaukee's Polish-Catholic Democrats) or effectively accommodated those older loyalties (e.g., Rutland's Irish-Democrats, Kansas City's black Republicans) within a new political home.

Of course, there were many places where the workingmen's movement did not crack open the party system or bring forth a political option of its own. Curiously, one difference between those communities that experienced a significant independent labor politics and those that did not would appear to be size. Of all the major urban-industrial centers in the country, only Chicago, Cincinnati, and Milwaukee produced successful labor tickets (see Table 1); several dozen smaller towns were successful, however. The line of division, indeed, recalls that one drawn by Herbert Gutman for the 1870s, although not on the basis he then implied—that the large cities were comparatively "more often hostile toward workers." Cities such as Philadelphia, Boston, Pittsburgh, Baltimore, San Francisco, and Detroit were certainly not weak labor centers; on the contrary both the Knights of Labor and the craft unions were well established in all of them. The distinction lies rather in the specific relation of the local labor movement to the political party system. One of two situations seems, according to this study, to have characterized those centers of active labor political upheaval: either workers had achieved negligible political influence by 1886 or what leverage they had gained was rendered meaningless by the dramatic industrial confrontations of that year. Smaller manufacturing centers—with the exception of coal and iron towns swept by an earlier upheaval in the 1870s—were more likely than big cities to meet the first criterion. The personalism of traditional social relations in a Rochester or Rutland promoted deference both at work and at the ballot box, while in Richmond a special legacy of racial paternalism inhibited class-wide politics. In Kansas City and Milwaukee, on the other hand, the dominant party apparatus had been irreversibly tainted by complicity of party officials with the state repression of industrial protest. Chicago's Haymarket affair and the dispatch of troops to Cincinnati's streets carried similar repercussions. In such communities the industrial polarization of the period was accentuated by a crisis of political legitimacy, as an aggrieved new majority swept its enemies from their public offices.[13]

The situation was different in the big cities. There the labor unions (as well as the working-class ethnic communities) had already fought their way into a give-and-take relationship within the major parties. As such, industrial conflict did not so neatly challenge a clear class allegiance of the local political administration. In Pittsburgh, for example, Frank Couvares has convincingly argued that frustration with earlier Labor Reform and Greenback-Labor experiences combined with the "lure of office" available to labor leaders through major-party machine connections effectively blunted the appeal of independent labor politics after 1882. Recent studies of Boston, Toronto, and San Francisco point in a similar direction. In the latter case Chris "Blind Boss" Buckley advanced in 1881 to control of a rejuvenated Democratic party by borrowing organizational principles as well as the constituency of Dennis Kearney's fading Workingmen's party of California.[14]

The American political party system thus bent, but only so far, before the rise of the Gilded Age labor movement. In areas of the greatest social polarization or weakest party organization, the Great Upheaval, at least temporarily, dislodged existing political elites; where the party elites had previously met and contained a pluralistic constituency, on the other hand, party hegemony held firm. In either case the dominant two parties emerged from this period with a stronger grip than ever on the working class. Ironically, a movement that began by defying the contemporary party system may in the end have left workers even more firmly within its confines. The testing time, to be sure, was ever so brief, as the main body of the labor movement, battered in its industrial confrontations, fell back from the messianic mood of the 1880s to a self-protecting incrementalism. Strategic retreat into defensive assemblages of automonous craft units limited both its constituency and its capacity to carry out any but the most modest of electoral strategies. The "reward our friends, punish our enemies" invocation of political faith by Samuel Gompers in 1906 confessed realistically to labor's inability to control the agenda or structures of the political world around it.[15]

Despite labor's limited power, urban politics continued to owe something to the late nineteenth-century social settlement. Contests outwardly fought between party bosses and party reformers during the first third of the twentieth century had to take into account demands arising from ethnic and working-class constituents. Exploitative and unprincipled as they were, the big-city political machines, as John D. Buenker has demonstrated, sometimes engaged labor support with liberal stands on interurban transit and tax and utility rates as well as specific labor legislation. Party machines, in short, were as shameless in adapting to selective working–class-based reform issues as they were to the shifting ethnocultural demography of a given city. Unable to achieve its own ends, the workingmen's political movement had at least raised a critique of corporate power and an affirmation of popular rights that would play an abiding role in the political culture.[16]

From a structural point of view, city government in the period between 1890 and 1930 appears as a kind of politician's state, an untidy social compromise enervating to both working-class radicalism and to a business-oriented efficiency in government. On the one hand, active contention among antagonistic social groups supported the stage that the urban politico would dominate in the early twentieth century; on the other hand, the very weakness of social organization from below and fragmentation among constituency groups made him less a representative than an entrepreneur. As such, local party politics appeared parasitic and destructive of the public good alike to Socialists, Progressives, and genteel reformers. Variants of structural reform (e.g., the city commission system, proportional representation, civil service extension, budgetary modernization) aimed at the laxity of urban political administration drew support not only from an efficiency-minded middle class but also from labor radicals working in Progressive coalitions or even heading Socialist tickets.[17]

Perhaps the sharpest contrast to the party-dominated pluralism in most industrial cities was provided by the urban South in the same period. With an occasional exception like Memphis or New Orleans, civic-commercial elites, not party machines, ran southern cities. Such undiluted rule by one social estate was possible only because of the near-total suppression of the southern labor movement and disfranchisement of its black citizens. The more characteristic urban political forms of the early twentieth century—two-party competition or a one-party boss system playing off diverse interests—drew on the reverberations of social conflict and political revolt, even as they minimized the chances for radical renewal.[18]

The murkiness of urban politics touched off a growing mistrust of local democratic institutions by business reformers and sections of the middle class. The Law and Order Leagues of the 1880s, which sought to impose an authority outside normal political processes, were an early symbol of antiplebeian reaction. Industrial relations by injunction and use of the state militia, jury qualification laws, and police consolidation measures all suggested that elected local officials were too unpredictable to preside over the disputes of civil society. City manager and commission forms of government offered one means of sanitizing local affairs; divesting economic decision-making from locally elected officials to appointed bodies (e.g., planning boards, zoning commissions, or insurance and banking commissions) and to the courts offered another remedy. Gabriel Kolko has identified the parallel trend at the federal level. The dramatic national decline in voter turnout beginning in the 1890s is likely related to this tendency toward depoliticizing reform from above—as is, perhaps, the modern stereotype of the working-class voter as a truculent nay-sayer to progress.[19]

The Knights of Labor envisioned a kind of workingmen's democracy. The organized power of labor was capable of revitalizing democratic citizenship and safeguarding the public good within a regulated marketplace economy. Through vigilant shop committees and demands such as the eight-hour day, organized workers—both men and women—would ensure minimal standards of safety and health at the industrial workplace, even as they surrounded the dominant corporate organizational model of business with cooperative models of their own.[20] A pride in honest and useful work, rational education, and personal virtue would be nurtured through a rich associational life spread out from the workplace to meeting hall to the hearth and home. Finally, the integrity of public institutions would be vouchsafed by the workingmen in politics. Purifying government of party parasitism and corruption, cutting off the access to power that allowed antilabor employers to bring the state apparatus to their side in industrial disputes, improving and widening the scope of vital public services, and even contemplating the takeover of economic enterprises that had passed irreversibly into monopoly hands—by these means worker-citizens would lay active claim to a republican heritage.

The dream was not to be. At the workplace management seized the initiative toward the future design and control of work. A managerial revolution overcoming the tenacious defenses of the craft unions transferred autonomy over such matters as productivity and skill from custom and negotiation to the realm of corporate planning. Except for the garment trades and the mines, the national trade unions had generally retreated from the country's industrial heartland by 1920. In the local community as well, the differences, even antagonisms, among workers often stood out more than did the similarities. Segmentation of labor markets, urban ethnic and socioeconomic residential segregation, cultural as well as a protectionist economic disdain for the new immigrants, and the depoliticization of leisure time (i.e., the decline of associational life sponsored by labor organizations) all contributed toward a process of social fragmentation. In such circumstances working–class political cooperation proved impossible. The Socialist party and the Progressive slates could make little more than a dent in the hold of the two increasingly conservative national parties over the electorate. Only with the repolarization of political life beginning in 1928 and culminating in the New Deal was the relation of labor and the party system again transformed. By the late 1930s and 1940s a revived labor movement was beginning, with mixed success, to play the role of a leading interest group and reform conscience within the Democratic party.[21]

This impressionistic overview permits one further observation of a quite general nature. One of the favorite tasks of American historians has been to explain why the United States, alone among the nations of the Western world, passed through the industrial revolution without the establishment of a class consciousness and an independent working-class political movement. Cheap land, the cult of individualism, a heterogeneous labor force, social mobility, and the federal separation of powers comprise several of the numerous explanations that have been offered. While not directly denying the importance of any of the factors listed above, this study implicitly suggests a different approach to the problem of American exceptionalism.

The answer appears to lie less in a permanent structural determinism—whether the analytic brace be political, economic, or ideological—than in a dynamic and indeed somewhat fortuitous convergence of events. To understand the vicissitudes of urban politics, we have had to keep in mind the action on at least three levels: the level of working-class social organization (i.e., the nature and strength of the labor movement), the level of business response, and the level of governmental response. During the Gilded Age each of these areas took an incendiary turn, but only briefly and irregularly and most rarely at the same moment. The 1880s, as R. Laurence Moore has recently reiterated, were the international seedtime for the strong European working-class parties of the twentieth century. In America, too, the momentum in the 1880s was great. Indeed, examined both at the level of working-class organization and industrial militancy, a European visitor might understandably have expected the most to happen here first. At the political level, as well, American workers were in certain respects relatively advanced. In the 1870s and in the 1880s they established independently organized local labor regimes well before the famous French Roubaix or English West Ham labor-Socialist town councils of the 1890s. Then, a combination of forces in the United States shifted radically away from the possibilities outlined in the 1880s. The labor movement fragmented, business reorganized, and the political parties helped to pick up the pieces. The initiatives from without directed at the American working class from the mid-1890s through the mid-1920s—part repression, part reform, part assimilation, and part recruitment of a new labor force—at an internationally critical period in the gestation of working-class movements may mark the most telling exceptionalism about American developments.[22]

It would in any case be years before the necessary conditions again converged and labor rose from the discredited icons of pre-Depression America with a new and powerful political message. Workplace, community, and ballot box would all once again be harnessed to a great social movement. But no two actors are ever in quite the same space at the same time. The choices open to the CIO, it is fair to say, were undoubtedly influenced both by the achievement and failure of their counterparts a half-century earlier.

NOTES

1. E. P. Thompson, *The Making of the English Working Class* (New York, 1964), 9. A classic formulation of the politics versus trade unionism thesis is found in Selig Perlman, *A History of Trade Unionism in the United States* (New York, 1923). Perlman describes events during the "long depression" of 1837–62 as follows: "With industry disorganized, trade unionism, or the effort to protect the standard of living by means of strikes, was out of the question. As the prospect for immediate amelioration became dimmed by circumstances, an opportunity arrived for theories and philosophies of radical social reform. Once the sun with its life-giving heat has set, one begins to see the cold and distant stars" (p. 29).

2. For good examples of the application of a modernization framework, see Robert H. Wiebe, *The Search for Order, 1877–1920* (New York, 1967), and Samuel P. Hayes, *The Response to Industrialism, 1885–1914* (Chicago, 1957). Implicitly, the preindustrial/industrial dichotomy projected in Herbert Gutman's *Work, Culture, and Society in Industrializing America, 1815–1919* (New York, 1977), 3–78, leaves itself open to a similar interpretation.

3. Richard Flacks, "Making History vs. Making Life," *Working Papers for a New Society,* 2 (Summer 1974), 60; Harry C. Boyte, "Populism and the Left," *democracy,* 1 (Apr. 1981), 58, also quotes Flacks uncritically. Leon Fink, "Class Conflict in the Gilded Age: The Figure and the Phantom," *Radical History Review,* 3 (Fall-Winter, 1975), 56–73, falls into the same exaggeration (58–59).

4. Boyte, "Populism and the Left," 60–61.

5. Eric Hobsbawm, *The Age of Revolution, 1789–1848* (New York, 1962). For a thorough explication of the radical Populist faith, see Bruce Palmer, *"Man Over Money": The Southern Populist Critique of American Capitalism* (Chapel Hill, N.C., 1980). See also Gerald N. Grob, *Workers and Utopia: A Study of Ideological Conflict in the American Labor Movement, 1865–1900* (Evanston, Ill., 1961), 38, 58–59; Henry Smith, "My Official Life" (1912), 39–40, and Charles R. Smith, "Outline of the Life of Henry Smith, Public Servant, 1838–1916" (1916?) 38–39, both manuscripts at the Wisconsin State Historical Society, Madison.

6. The figures in Table 17 suggest that by 1880 younger workers were entering the expanding industrial enterprises and older workers were disproportionately rooted in preindustrial crafts and general labor. More precisely, 56 percent of workers in preindustrial trades were under forty years of age; the figures for skilled and semiskilled industrial workers jumped to 73 percent

and 79 percent, respectively. Local, ethnic, and racial differences may, of course, modify this general tendency. The youth of the Kansas City white unskilled laborers, for example, may have to do with specific patterns of recent migration to a young city from surrounding agricultural districts. The table also detects a discrepancy throughout between white and black workers, with blacks in a given category of unskilled or semiskilled work consistently older than whites. The gap likely reflects the greater chances for whites to achieve occupational mobility as they grew older. There is also a hint, however, that the black work force, as a whole, in these cities was older than the white work force. If so, that fact provides one of several starting points for more systematic demographic and social analysis of the working-class population.

7. Milwaukee *Journal,* May 17, 1886.

8. David A. Shannon quotes the story of the Milwaukee Socialist "who was explaining the failure of a Socialist candidate with a Polish name to win an election. 'If we had had someone with a good American name like Schemmelpfennig we could have won.' " *The Socialist Party of America* (New York, 1955), 23–24. A sophisticated restatement of contemporary political identities by one of the leading historians of American voting behavior still does not do justice to the relation of class and ethnicity. Paul Kleppner, *The Third Electoral System, 1853–1892* (Chapel Hill, N.C., 1979), 364, concludes: "In the political universe of the late nineteenth century, fundamental and irreconcilable belief system differences between distinguishable clusters of ethnoreligious groups *primarily* structured partisan cleavage among the mass electorate. . . . The operative word, of course is *primarily.* And that word should not be construed to imply either *exclusively* or *invariably,* for other social attributes also played roles. . . . And just as American society was composed of a kaleidoscopic mix of contexts and experiences, so it reflected no monolithic uniformity in the ways in which, nor the relative weights with which, social determinants combined to shape mass partisan identifications." The problem here (and I think for the quantitative approach to politics more generally) is that "social determinants" like class and ethnoreligious groups, no matter how qualified in their relative importance, remain themselves unchanging, ahistorical categories. Within Kleppner's metaphor they are flecks of indissoluble social identity, more visible and prominent at some moments than others, but each of fixed and distinct substance.

9. John M. Cammett, *Antonio Gramsci and the Origins of Italian Communism* (Stanford, 1967), 201–64.

10. See James R. Green, *Grass-Roots Socialism: Radical Movements in the Southwest, 1895–1943* (Baton Rouge, La., 1977); James Weinstein, *The Decline in Socialism in America, 1912–1925* (New York, 1967); Samuel Lubell, *The Future of American Politics* (New York, 1952), 28–57; see also Arno J. Mayer, "The Lower Middle Class as Historical Problem," *Journal of Modern History,* 47 (Sept. 1975), 409–36.

11. On the shadowy Home Club, see Norman J. Ware, *The Labor Movement in the United States, 1860–1895: A Study in Democracy* (New York, 1929), 111–15; Carlos A. Schwantes, "Race and Radicalism: The Legacy of

the Knights of Labor in the Pacific Northwest," paper presented at the 1979 Knights of Labor Symposium, Newberry Library, Chicago; see also Alexander Saxton, *The Indispensable Enemy: Labor and the Anti-Chinese Movement in California* (Berkeley, 1971).

12. Giovanni Sartori, *Parties and Party Systems, a Framework for Analysis* (Cambridge, 1976), 16.

13. Herbert G. Gutman, "The Worker's Search for Power: Labor in the Gilded Age," in H. Wayne Morgan, ed., *The Gilded Age, a Reappraisal* (Syracuse, N.Y., 1963), 41; Steven J. Ross, "Strikes, Knights, and Political Fights: The May Day Strikes . . . and Rise of the United Labor Party in 19th Century Cincinnati," paper presented at the 1979 Knights of Labor Symposium.

14. Frank G. Couvares, "Work, Leisure, and Reform in Pittsburgh: The Transformation of an Urban Culture, 1860–1920" (Ph.D. diss., University of Michigan, 1980), 127–29; Jama Lazerow, "The Knights of Labor: Boston as a Case Study," paper presented at the 1979 Knights of Labor Symposium; Gregory S. Kealey, *Toronto Workers Respond to Industrial Capitalism, 1867–1892* (Toronto, 1980), esp. 216–53; William A. Bullough, *The Blind Boss and His City: Christopher Augustine Buckley and Nineteenth-Century San Francisco* (Berkeley, 1979), 48–71. New York City, it must be noted, does not neatly fit the model proposed here. While no adequate study of the subject yet exists, labor politics there, as expressed through the 1886 Henry George campaign, must take into account grievances with the party system, the extraordinary strength of the Central Labor Union, and George's personal magnetism.

15. David Brody, *Workers in Industrial America: Essays on the 20th Century Struggle* (New York, 1980), 28.

16. John D. Buenker, *Urban Liberalism and Progressive Reform* (New York, 1973); see also Clifton K. Yearley, *The Money Machines: The Breakdown and Reform of Governmental and Party Finance in the North, 1860–1920* (Albany, N.Y., 1970), esp. 253–79; see also Roger W. Lotchin, "Power and Policy: American City Politics between the Two World Wars," in Scott Greer, ed., *Ethnic Machines and the American Urban Future,* forthcoming.

17. Lotchin, "Power and Policy"; in making this characterization I have also been influenced obliquely by the analysis of Theda Scocpol, "Political Response to Capitalist Crisis: Neo-Marxist Theories of the State and the Case of the New Deal," *Politics and Society,* 10 (1980), 155–201.

18. Blaine A. Brownell, *The Urban Ethos in the South, 1920–1930* (Baton Rouge, La., 1975), esp. 125–55. Southern business leaders, notes Brownell, tried "to guide their cities into a metropolitan world while retaining control of that world" (126–27).

19. The presence of Law and Order Leagues has also been noted in Pittsburgh, Cincinnati, Detroit, and Troy, New York. On the role of lawyers and the courts, see Morton Keller, *Affairs of State: Public Life in Late Nineteenth-Century America* (Cambridge, Mass., 1977), 345–50, 405. On the implications of structural political reforms at the turn of the century, see Samuel P. Hays's seminal essays: "The Changing Political Structure of the City in Industrial America," *Journal of Urban History,* 1 (Nov. 1974), 6–38, and

"The Politics of Reform in Municipal Government in the Progressive Era," *Pacific Northwest Quarterly,* 55 (Oct. 1964), 157–69; Gabriel Kolko, *The Triumph of Conservatism, a Reinterpretation of American History, 1900–1961* (Chicago, 1960); on voter turnout, see Robert D. Marcus, *Grand Old Party: Political Structure in the Gilded Age, 1880–1896* (New York, 1971), 251–65.

20. Paul Buhle, "The Knights of Labor in Rhode Island," *Radical History Review,* 5 (Spring 1978), 39–73.

21. Richard Edwards, *Contested Terrain: The Transformation of the Workplace in the Twentieth Century* (New York, 1979), esp. 90–110, 163–83; David Montgomery, *Workers' Control in America* (New York, 1980), esp. 113–38; Brody, *Workers in Industrial America,* 3–81; John T. Cumbler, *Working-Class Community in Industrial America: Leisure and Struggle in Two Industrial Cities, 1880–1930* (Westport, Conn., 1979), esp. 41, 126, 161; Gareth Stedman Jones, "Working-Class Culture and Working-Class Politics in London, 1870–1900," *Journal of Social History,* 7 (Summer 1974), 460–508; Lubell, *Future of American Politics.* Lotchin, "Power and Policy," notes that the rise of the new unions in the 1930s also sparked serious challenges to machine politics in Memphis, Jersey City, and Chicago.

22. R. Laurence Moore, *European Socialists and the American Promised Land* (New York 1970) xv; Joan Wallach Scott, "Social History and the History of Socialism: French Socialist Municipalities in the 1890s," *Le Mouvement Social,* 3 (1980), 145–55; Leon Fink, "Socialism in One Borough: West Ham Politics and Political Culture 1898–1900" (M.A. thesis, University of Rochester, 1972); James Holt, "Trade Unionism in the British and U.S. Steel Industries, 1888–1912: A Comparative Study," *Labor History* 18 (Winter 1977), 5–35.

Selected Bibliography:
Primary Sources

NEWSPAPERS AND JOURNALS

American NonConformist and Kansas Industrial Liberator. Winfield, Kans. 1886–89.
Argentine, later Kansas City (Kans.) *Labor Review,* 1890–92.
Bay City (Mich.) *Evening Press.* 1885–86.
Boston *Labor Leader.* 1887–97.
Burlington (Vt.) *Free Press,* 1886–88.
Chicago *Knight of Labor.* 1886–89.
Chicago *Tribune,* 1886.
Concord (N.H.) *Evening Monitor.* 1886–88.
Concord (N.H.) *People and New Hampshire Patriot.* 1886–90.
Granite Cutters Journal. Philadelphia, 1885–87.
Granite State Free Press, Lebanon, N.H., 1886–88.
Haverhill (Mass.) *Laborer.* 1884–87.
John Swinton's Paper. New York, 1883–87.
Journal of United Labor. Philadelphia, 1880–90.
Kansas City (Kans.) *American Citizen.* 1889–92.
Kansas City (Mo.) *Boycotter.* 1886.
Kansas City (Kans.) *Labor Record.* 1894–95.
Kansas City (Mo.) *Pioneer.* 1878–79.
Kansas City (Mo.) *Star.* 1885–88.
Kansas City (Kans.) *Sun.* 1891–96.
Kansas Cyclone. Kansas City, Kans., 1887–88.
Kansas Pioneer. Wyandotte, 1885–89.
Manchester (N.H.) *Union.* 1886–88.
Milwaukee *Advance.* 1890.
Milwaukee *Arbeiter Zeitung.* 1886.
Milwaukee *Boycott-Post.* 1886.
Milwaukee *Daily Review.* 1887–88.
Milwaukee *Daily Journal.* 1883–96, 1910, 1916.
Milwaukee *Kuryer Polski.* 1888.
Milwaukee *Labor Review.* 1887–88.
Milwaukee *Sentinel.* 1886–87.
Milwaukee *Trades Assembly Bulletin.* 1882–83.

Milwaukee *Volksblatt*. 1883–88.
National Labor Tribune. Pittsburgh, 1884–86.
New York *Freeman*. 1886.
New York *Sun*. 1886.
New York *Times*. 1886.
New York *Tribune*. 1886.
New York *World*. 1886.
Quincy (Mass.) *Monitor*. 1886–89.
Quincy (Mass.) *Patriot*. 1885–87.
Richmond *Daily Whig*. 1885–88.
Richmond *Dispatch*. 1884–90.
Richmond *Planet* [1885–90; run incomplete].
Rochester (N.H.) *Anti-Monopolist and Local Record* (later the *Strafford County Record*). 1878–90.
Rochester (N.H.) *Courier*. 1884–90.
Rutland *Herald*. 1878–1904.
Saginaw (Mich.) *Courier*. 1885–86.
Staunton (Va.) *Critic*. 1886.
Valley Virginian. Staunton, 1886.
Washington, D.C., *Bee*, 1886.
Wyandotte (Kans.) *Gazette* (became Kansas City *Gazette* in 1888). 1878–96.
Wyandotte (Kans.) *Herald*. 1885–96.

MANUSCRIPTS

Bishop Louis M. Fink Papers. Benedictine College, Atchison, Kans.
Henry George Papers. New York Public Library, New York City.
John W. Hayes Papers. Catholic University, Washington, D.C.
Wilhelm Hense-Jensen and Ernst Bruncken. "Wisconsin's German-Americans until the End of the Nineteenth Century," tr. Joseph C. Shafer, 1900–1902. Wisconsin State Historical Society, Madison.
Knights of Labor. "Proceedings of the General Assembly," 1884–96, in Powderly Papers.
William Mahone Papers. Duke University, Durham, N.C.
Governor John A. Martin Papers. Kansas State Historical Society, Topeka.
Frank C. Partridge. "The Vermont Marble Company, Its Past and Future," address given at a general conference in Proctor, Vt. December 28–31, 1920.
Terence V. Powderly Papers. Catholic University, Washington, D.C.
Proctor Family Papers. Proctor Free Library, Proctor, Vt.
Proctoriana Collection. Vermont State Library, Montpelier.
Charles Smith, "Outline of the Life of Henry Smith," 1916. Wisconsin State Historical Society, Madison.
Henry Smith Papers. Wisconsin State Historical Society, Madison.
Edward Love Temple. "Old Rutland—Sidelights on Her Honorable and Notable Story, 1761–1922," n.d. Local Archives, New York Public Library.

Horace A. Tenney Papers. Wisconsin State Historical Society, Madison.
Wise Family Papers. Virginia Historical Society, Richmond.

GOVERNMENT RECORDS

Kansas Bureau of Labor and Industrial Statistics. *Annual Reports.* Topeka, 1885–95.

Kansas State Board of Agriculture. *Fifth Biennial Report including the Decennial Census for 1885.* Topeka, 1887.

Milwaukee, Wis. "Proceedings of the Common Council," 1885–90.

Richmond, Va. *Common Council Journal,* 1886–92.

———. *Records of the Freedmen's Savings Bank, 1867–72.*

Rochester, N.H., School Board. *Annual Report, including List of Vital Statistics.* Rochester, 1887, 1891.

U.S. Tenth Census, 1880. *Report on the Building Stones of the U.S. and Statistics of the Quarry Industry,* Vol. X. Washington, D.C.: Government Printing Office, 1885.

———. *Report on Manufactures of the United States.* Washington, D.C.: Government Printing Office, n.d.

———. *Report on the Social Statistics of Cities.* Washington, D.C.: Government Printing Office, 1887.

———. *Statistics of the Population,* I. Washington, D.C.: Government Printing Office, 1883.

U.S. Tenth Census, 1880. Population manuscripts, Strafford County, N.H.; Rutland County, Vt.; Wyandotte County, Kans., U.S. National Archives microforms.

U.S. Eleventh Census, 1890. *Compendium of the Eleventh Census, Population.* Washington, D.C.: Government Printing Office, 1892.

———. *Report on Manufacturing Industries in the U.S.* Washington, D.C.: Government Printing Office, 1895.

———. *Report on the Population.* Washington, D.C.: Government Printing Office, 1895.

U.S. Thirteenth Census, 1910. *Population, Occupation Statistics.* Washington, D.C.: Government Printing Office, 1914.

U.S. Fourteenth Census, 1920. *Wisconsin State Compendium.* Washington, D.C.: Government Printing Office, 1925.

U.S. Labor Bureau. *Annual Report of the Commissioner, Third and Tenth.* Washington, D.C.: Government Printing Office, 1888, 1896.

U.S. Congress, House of Representatives. *Investigation of Labor Troubles in Missouri, Arkansas, Texas, and Illinois.* 49th Cong., 2d sess., 1887, H.R. 4174. Washington, D.C.: Government Printing Office, 1887.

———, U.S. Senate. *Report of the Committee of the Senate upon the Relations between Labor and Capital,* 3 vols. Washington, D.C.: Government Printing Office, 1885.

West Rutland, Vt. (Town). *Annual Reports of the Board of Officers,* 1885–90.

————. *Minutes of the Selectmen,* 1887–96.
State of Wisconsin. *Blue Book,* 1879–1916.
State of Wisconsin. *Wisconsin State Census,* 1895. Madison, 1895–96.
————. *Tabular Statement of the Census Enumeration, 1885.* Madison, 1906.

PUBLISHED ARTICLES BOOKS AND PAMPHLETS

Adams, Charles Francis. *Three Episodes of Massachusetts History,* 2 vols. Cambridge, Mass., 1894.
Appleton's Annual Cyclopaedia, 1881. New York, 1882.
Book of Biographies, Biographical Sketches of Leading Citizens of Rutland County, Vermont. Buffalo, N.Y., 1899.
Carleton, Hiram. *Genealogical and Family History of the State of Vermont.* New York, 1903.
Crockett, Walter H. *Vermont, the Green Mountain State,* 5 vols. New York, 1921.
Davison, F. E. *Historical Rutland, an Illustrated History of Rutland Vermont, from the Granting of the Charter in 1761 to 1911.* Rutland, 1911.
Deatherage, Charles P. *Early History of Greater Kansas City, Missouri and Kansas, 1492–1870.* Kansas City, Mo., 1927.
Fogg, Alonzo J. *The Statistics and Gazetteer of New Hampshire.* Concord, N.H., 1874.
Gale, David C. *Proctor, the Story of a Marble Town.* Brattleboro, 1922.
Howe, Frederic C. "Milwaukee, a Socialist City." *Outlook,* 95 (1910), 411–21.
Hurd, D. H. *History of Rockingham and Strafford Counties.* Philadelphia, 1882.
"Kansas City in 1879": Sketches of the Trade, Manufacture & Progress of the City. Kansas City, Mo., 1879.
Kent, Dorman B. E. *One Thousand Men.* Montpelier, Vt., 1915.
McDuffee, Franklin. *History of the Town of Rochester from 1722 to 1890,* 2 vols. Manchester, N.H., 1892.
McNeill, George. *The Labor Movement: The Problem of Today.* Boston, 1887.
Morgan, Perl W. *History of Wyandotte County and Its People,* 2 vols. Chicago, 1911.
Powderly, Terence V. *The Path I Trod: The Autobiography of Terence V. Powderly.* New York, 1940.
————. *Thirty Years of Labor, 1859–1889.* Columbus, Ohio, 1889.
Richmond Chamber of Commerce. *Advantages of Richmond, Virginia, as a Manufacturing and Trading Centre.* Richmond, 1882.
Rutland County Gazetteer and Business Directory, 1881–1882. Syracuse, N.Y., 1881.
Scales, John. *History of Strafford County, New Hampshire, and Representative Citizens.* Chicago, 1914.

Smith, H.P., and W.S. Rann, eds. *History of Rutland County*. Syracuse, 1886.
Ullery, Jacob G. *Men of Vermont, an Illustrated Biographical History of Vermonters and Sons of Vermont*. Brattleboro, Vt., 1894.
Vermont Historical Gazetteer. Claremont, N.H., 1877.
Wood, James P. *The Industries of Richmond*. Richmond, Va., 1886.

Index

Abraham, A. H., 87
Adams, Charles Francis, 2, 38, 39, 73
Advance, 203
Afro-Americans. *See* Blacks
Age: of workers, 222, 230–31
Alley, Dan, 160
Alliancemen: in Kansas, 112
Allis, Edward, 179, 187, 195, 220;
    and Eight Hour League, 191–92
Amalgamated Association of Iron and
    Steel Workers, 180, 184
American Citizen, 128, 142
American Federation of Labor, 133,
    199
American NonConformist, 136, 139
American Railway Union, 137, 147
Anderson, Rev. Charles, 139
Anderson, Joseph T., 149, 152
Anthony, George T., 124
Anti-Monopolist, 47, 48, 52, 56
Argentine, Kans., 134, 135, 146
Argersinger, Peter H., 148
Armstrong, Henry J., 122
Armstrong, Russell D., 114
Armstrong, Samuel, 113
Armstrong, Silas, 114
Associationalism, 35–36
Atlanta, Ga., 11
Auer, Louis, 200
Augusta, Ga., 163
Austin, Joseph, 91
Aveling, Edward, 6

Bahen, James H., 153, 171
Baker, Joel, 70, 71, 110
Bandmann, Daniel, 163, 175
Banner und Volksfreund, 180
Baptists: in Rochester, 46

Barrett, J. C., 106
Barry, Thomas B., 5, 12
Bass, L. L., 175
Battle, James, 99
Baughman Brothers printing co.:
    boycott, 155, 160, 167, 176
Baxter, Hugh Henry, 70
Baxter, John, 83, 106
Bay View Massacre, 30, 193–95
Beard, Charles, 140
Beaumont, Ralph, 5, 27
Bellamy, Edward, 140
Berger, Victor, 204, 205, 206, 210,
    217
Berry, Frank P., 48
Berry, George G., 47, 49
Berry, Mrs. George G., 49
Best, Geoffrey, 180, 190
Bethel, John, 159, 174
Betton, F. H., 119
Beyond Equality, 20–21
Birnbaum, Norman, 3
Bishop, C. C., 137
Bismarck, Otto von, 182
Blacks: in Kansas City, 115, 116–17,
    128–29; and politics in Kansas, 141–
    42; in Richmond, 150–52, 157, 164,
    168
Blair, Sen. Henry, 8
Blanqui, Louis Auguste, 22
Blatz, Valentine, 189
Bliss, Rev. W. D. P., 140
Bohl, Charles, 124, 129
Boncel, Andrew, 192, 194, 203, 208,
    223
Boncel, Frank, 208
Booze, W. T., 168
Borchardt, Francis, 184, 197, 223

Boritt, S. G., 12
Boston *Labor Leader,* 59; on the Knights, 14
Botts, John Minor, 175
Bourbon press, 175
Boyte, Harry, 220
Brandt and Co., 192
Breidenthal, John W., 13, 135
Breweries: in Milwaukee, 179–80
Brock, S. W., 59
Brown, Mrs. Henry, 103
Brown, John, 152
Brown, Thomas H., 77, 89, 90, 91, 96, 99, 100, 101, 110, 221; on Hogan, 81; and Henry George, 94; and Powderly, 97; and social mobility, 102-3
Browne, Thomas H. *See* Brown, Thomas H.
Brundage, David, 12
Bryan, William Jennings, 135, 205
Buchan, Sen. William J., 119, 122, 126, 127, 134, 136
Buckley, Chris, 226
Buenker, John D., 227
Buhle, Mari Jo, 139
Business: and labor rule in Rutland, 92
Butler, Ben, 140, 187

Cable, Judge R. E., 117
Cambridge, Mass.: streetcar workers protest, 95
Campbell, W. J., 171
Cannon, M. W., 86, 87
Carder, J. S., 94, 99, 104
Carlton, A. A., 94
Carson, Kit, 113
Carter, Henry L., 158, 159
Cate, Horatio, 55, 56, 223
Catholic church: in Rutland, 77, 99; in Milwaukee, 183; and Bay View incident, 194
Central Labor Union, 189
Central Trades and Labor Council, 99
Chamberlain, Clarence, 55
Chesley, Fred, 60
Chessman, John, 49
Chicago: meatpacking firms, 5; packers and Powderly, 133; and workingmen's movement, 225

Chicago *Arbeiter Zeitung,* 189
Chicago *Times,* 6
Chicago *Tribune,* 37
Chotier, Paul, 170
Cincinnati: and workingmen's movement, 225, 226
Citizens' Alliance: Kansas City, 137; Kansas, 147-48
Citizens' Committee: in Milwaukee, 200
Citizens party: in Rutland, 96–98
Clarke, C. C., 166
Class: conflict in Gilded Age, 4–5; boundaries, 9–10; and Knights' values, 12–13; conflict and Knights, 219–20
Clement, Charles, 67, 68, 83, 106
Clement family, 70, 104
Clement, Percival W., 101, 102
Cleveland, Grover, 87, 103, 159
Clow, William, 124
Cogswell, Col. Charles, 53
Colored Mercantile Association, Richmond, 167
Commons, John R., 206
Community, 39; and workingmen's movement, 221–24
Comparative ages of preindustrial and industrial workers, 222, 230–31
Concord *Evening Monitor,* 53, 54
Congress of Industrial Organizations, xiii, 35, 230
Conzen, Kathleen Neils, 180
Cooperation: and Knights, 7
"Cooperative commonwealth," 16
Cooper, Peter, 187
Coopers' International, 186
Copps, Bridget Maloney, 74
Copps, Edward, 74–75
"Corbin's chattel," 5
Corrigan Cable Car Co., 124
Cougher, John, 119, 120
Cousins, Martha, 165, 171
Couvares, Frank, 226
Coy, William A., 134
Craft organization: in Milwaukee, 184–85
Cramton, John W., 69
Cree, Nathan, 127, 132
Creed, James, 96
Crocker, Fred, 55

Cromwell, Mark, 130
Cruise, Timothy, 187
Crump, Josiah, 154
Cultural imperatives: and Knights, 8–13
Czerwinski, Ignatz, 203
Czerwinski, John, 197, 198

Daniels, Sheriff Newell, 196, 198, 202
Debs, Eugene V., 137, 204, 209
Decateur, Frank, 60
Decker, Father A. J., 194
Declaration of Principles, 23
DeLeon, David, 21
Democratic party: and Germans in Milwaukee, 182; in Milwaukee and labor movement, 197
Devine, J. P., 166
Diggs, Annie, 139
"The Dignity of Labor from a Bible Standpoint," 139
Domestic: work in Rochester, N.H., 42; servants in Rochester, 61–62; servants in Rutland, 106–7
Donnergan, P. J., 83–84
Dorr, Julia Caroline Ripley, 70
Dover Cocheco Woolen Co., 41
Drake, Lydia, 14–15
Drury, Victor, 164
Ducharme, Megloire, 80
Duncan, George, 168
Duntley, J. L., 45
Dunton, Judge Walter C., 67, 78, 83, 96, 106
Dziennik Polski, 202

Edmunds, George F., 79
Education: in Rutland, 91–92
Edwards, Richard, 120
Eight-hour campaign, 188–95
Eight Hour League, Milwaukee, 190, 191–92
Electric Street Railway Co., Richmond, 168
Ellett, Tazewell, 175
Ellyson, Henry K., 152
Ellyson, J. Taylor, 175
Ely, Vt., 68
Engels, Friedrich, 6, 21
English: in Rochester, 44; in Kansas City, 115, 116

Episcopal church: in Rochester, 46
Ethnic groups: in Kansas City, 115–17
Ethnicity, 221; and class in Rutland, 72–75
Evans, Anna, 46
Evans, Edward E., 46
"Exodusters," 116–17

Fall River, Mass., 10
Family life, 11–12
Farmers' Alliance. *See* National Farmers' Alliance
Farrar, Joseph, 154
Fay, James J., 76, 83, 88, 89, 92, 93, 94, 96, 102, 103
Federated Trades Council, 199
Ferguson, Charles, 64
Ferguson, Sheriff James, 120
Ferrell, Frank, 162, 175–76
Fields, W. W., 155, 175
Fink, Bishop Louis M., 134
Flanders, Benjamin M., 60
Fletcher, William, 120, 126, 128, 137
Fogg and Vinal company, 58
Folsom, Charles W., 46
Fortune, T. Thomas, 169, 172
Fort Worth, Tex., 26, 121
Foss, James F., 65
Foster, Frank, 11, 163
Foster, Mayor T. C., 119, 123, 128
Fourier, François, 22
Fowler, George, 130
Freeman, 169
Fremont, John C., 113
French-Canadians: in Rochester, 42, 44, 49–50, 55; in Rutland, 72, 74, 90
Friends' Society: in Rochester, 46
Frisbee, Barnes, 38
Frisch, Michael, 39, 58
Funston, E. H. "Farmer," 119
Furlong, Thomas, 125, 126
F. W. Breed company, 58

Gadsden, Ala., 177
Gardiner, Me., 26
Garrisonians, 21
Gaskill, Col. V. A., 92
Gavett, Thomas, 210
George, Henry, 6, 32, 80, 84, 99, 162; single tax, 7; and New York City

George, Henry (*cont.*)
  mayorality, 26, 75; and politics, 27; and Hayes, 57; and Rutland, 76; and T. H. Brown, 94; and Kansas City, 131; and Mullen, 159; and *Volksblatt*, 186; and Milwaukee, 201; 1886 campaign, 232
Georgeite Anti-Poverty Society, Rutland, 94
Germans: in Kansas City, 115, 116; in Milwaukee, 178, 180–82; and Milwaukee Socialism, 223
Gilded Age: political and social change in, xi–xiv; working-class radicalism in, 3–17
Gillespie, James, 79–80
Gilson and Woodfin, 68
Gilson, E. P., 68, 69, 70
Gilson family, 71
Gompers, Samuel, 4, 209, 226
Gonic Woolen Mills, 40
Goochland courthouse story, 171
Goodman, Paul, 21
Gould, Jay, xii, xiii, 9, 67, 112, 119–20, 121, 142
Gould strikers, 77
Gramsci, Antonio, 223
Granger, L. H., 83
Grangers: in Kansas, 112
Great Lake Seamen's Union, 11
Great Southwest Strike. *See* Southwest Strike
Great Upheaval, 32, 33, 226
Greenback-Labor party, 7, 39; failure of in 1870s, 24; in Rochester, 47–50, 56; in Rutland, 108; in Kansas, 112, 147; in Richmond, 154; in Milwaukee, 180–81; and Schilling, 186; and Henry Smith, 187
Grob, Gerald, 18, 19, 20, 21
Grottkau, Paul, 189–90, 191, 192, 193, 194, 196, 201–2, 204, 205
Gulski, Rev. Hyacinth, 197–98
Gutman, Herbert G., 31, 150, 172–73, 174, 225

"Hail Milwaukee," 215
Hamilton, George, 125, 126, 127, 131
Hanizaewski, Stanislaus, 197
Hanna, Mark, 3
Hannan, Mayor Thomas, 31, 113, 118,

123–26, 127–28, 129–35, 141, 145, 222, 223; and social reform, 131–32; third administration of, 134–35
Hanrahan, Dr. J. D., 71, 79
Harper, Col. Jesse, 139
Harris, Joel, 106
Harrison, Benjamin, 3, 68
Hartigan, Patrick H., 65
Haskell, Brunette G., 140
Hayes, George L., 53, 60, 223
Hayes, George P., 57
Hayes, John, 135
Hayes, Rutherford, 3
Hayes, S. O., 46
Haymarket affair, 25, 31, 57, 121, 226
Herold, 185
Hewitt, Abram, 26
Hill, Rowland, 160
Hilliker, Robert W., 119, 120, 123, 127, 129, 130, 132
Hinton, Richard J., 4
Hirth, Frank, 194
Hoan, Maj. Daniel, 206, 208, 210, 211, 217
Hobsbawn, Eric, 220
Hogan, James F., 80–81, 82, 83, 109, 223
Hogan, Mrs. James, 94
Holli, Melvin G., 132, 138
Holy Cross College, 80
Homo faber ideal, 3
Horn, I. M., 56
Horne, Albert M., 47
House Labor Committee, 119
Howard, Robert, 10
Howe Scale Co., 78, 101, 109
Hoxie, R. M., 120
Huffmire, John, 88, 93, 96
Hunter, Robert, 217
Hussey, Silas, 45, 63–64

Immigrants: in Rochester, 42; in Kansas City, 115–17; in Kansas, 142–43; in Milwaukee, 178, 179–84, 212
Industrial capitalism: social implications of, xiii
Industrialization: and social change, 38–40, 44
Ingalls, Sen. John J., 135
Ingersoll, Robert G., xiii, 57

Intellectual development, 10–11
International Workers of the World, 35
International Working People's
    Association, 189
Irish: in Rochester, 44, 55; and labor
    movement, 52; in Rutland, 72–75,
    90, 99; in Kansas City, 115, 116;
    and Knights in South, 174
Irons, Martin, 121, 122

Jackson, Miss., 172
Jackson, Professor J. H., 129
Jackson Ward, Richmond, 150, 152,
    154, 157, 158, 165, 168
James, Edward T., 56
Jarrett, John, 212
Jefferson Ward, Richmond, 160
Johnson, Charles P., 126–27
Johnson, Tom, 206
John Swinton's Paper, 27, 54, 57
Jones, Samuel, 206
Jones, Walter, 50
Journal of United Labor, 25, 199
"Justitia," 78

Kalakaua, King, xiii
Kansas: politics, 1880s, 112–13; and
    WCTU, 139
Kansas City *Boycotter,* 121; and Law
    and Order League, 122–23
Kansas City *Gazette,* 118, 119; and
    Hannan, 123, 125, 126, 127, 128,
    131, 138; and Coy, 134
Kansas City, Kans., 112–48; and
    police, 31, 144; history of, 113–15;
    ethnic distribution within
    occupational groups, 1880, 115;
    blacks in, 115, 116–17, 128–29;
    ethnic groups in, 115–17;
    immigrants in, 115–17; occuptional
    structure by ethnic groups, 1880,
    116; residential patterns in, 117;
    politics in, 118–42; and Populists,
    135–39
Kansas City, Mo., 114; *Journal,* 121
Kansas City *Weekly Sun,* 138
Kansas Cyclone, 130, 131, 134
Kansas-Nebraska Act of 1854, 113
Kansas Pioneer, 134
Kearney, Dennis, 226

Keene, N.H.: Knights of Labor song,
    54
Kelley, Henry M., 48
Kelloggism, 7
Keogh, John, 10
Keyes, E. D., 83
King, Edward, 11
Kingsley, Gen. Levi, 70, 79, 97, 102
King, S. S., 138
Kleppner, Paul, 216, 231
Knights of Labor: and cultural
    imperatives, 8–13; and temperance,
    12; and women, 12; values of and
    class, 12–13; use of the past, 13;
    membership of, 13–15; and politics,
    18–37; Declaration of Principles, 23;
    political tickets, by state or territory,
    1885–88, 28–29; and the Irish, 52;
    and lodges, 64; growth of in
    Rutland, 75–77; and division
    question in Rutland, 83–84; and
    politics in Rutland, 88–89; and Jay
    Gould, 119–20, 121; in Kansas City,
    119–22, 133, 136; and Hannan,
    123–24; in Kansas and Populism,
    141; in Richmond, 154–55, 156–57,
    162–63; decline in Richmond, 167–
    68; and racial equality, 169–72; in
    Milwaukee, 184–96, 199;
    achievements and failures of, 219–
    29; membership and skill and
    ethnicity, 221; vision of, 228
Knights of St. Crispin, 50
Kolko, Gabriel, 228
Kosciusko Guards, 184, 192, 194, 197
Kroeger, Herman, 201
Kruszka, Michael, 188, 202, 203, 213
Kruszka, Rev. Waclaw, 202, 213
Krytyka, 188, 202
Kulturkampf, 182
Kuryer, 203

Labadie, Joseph, 7
Labor: and politics, xiii–xiv, 20, 113
Labor Herald, 155
Labor movement: and class conflict, 4–
    5; in Richmond, 154–56, 168; in
    Milwaukee, 182
Labor Review, 137
La Follette, Robert, 203
Lane, V. J., 123, 130

Langston, John Mercer, 168
Lassalle, Ferdinand, 22
Lassallean Social Democrats, 180
Lasters' Protective Union, 50
Law and Order League(s), 122, 227;
  Kansas City, 130; Kansas, 139;
  Richmond, 163, 167, 175
Lawyers: and Knights, 24
Layton, Robert, 11
Lease, Mary E., 139
Lee, Gen. Fitzhugh, 152, 162
Leroy, N.Y., 26
Levine, Susan, 12
Lillis, James, 146
Lindsay, Lewis, 175
Lippman, Walter, 211
Lucifer, 189
Lynn, Mass., 59

McAlpine, Nicholas, 127, 142
McDuffee family, 46
McDuffee, Mrs. Frank, 49
McDuffee, John, 40, 62
McGlynn, Father Edward, 77, 201
McGuire, Thomas B., 11, 25, 176
McGuirk, John, 100
McKinley, William, xi, 103
McKinney, Rev. Luther F., 53, 60
McNeill, George, 63
Mahone, Gen. William, 152, 153, 154,
  156, 158, 159, 160, 166, 167, 168
Mallory, Judge James A., 194, 195,
  200, 202
Maloney, Father, 75
Maloney, Thomas W., 75, 96
Manchester *Union,* 52
Manning, Michael J., 131, 137
Marble business: in Rutland, 67–68
Marx, Eleanor, 6
Marx, Karl, xiii, 20, 21, 22, 186
Marxists, 180
Martin, Dr. J. C., 119, 121, 122, 127
Material progress, 220
Mead, John A., 69
Meldon, P. M., 102
Melvin, John, 140
Membership: of Knights, 13–15
Meredith, C. V., 175
Merrill, James, 88, 96
Methodism: and Wyandots, 142
Meyerhoffer, V. C., 76, 89, 93

Middle class: in Rochester, 55–56; in
  Rutland, 94; and workingmen's
  movement, 223
Milwaukee *Arbeiter Zeitung,* 189, 190,
  201, 204
Milwaukee *Daily Review,* 201
Milwaukee *Herald,* 205
Milwaukee Iron Co., 179
Milwaukee *Journal,* 200; and Knights,
  192, 196; and Socialists, 206
Milwaukee *Labor Review,* 201
Milwaukee *Sentinel,* 200
Milwaukee, Wis., 178–218;
  immigrants in, 178, 179–84, 212; in
  1870s, 179; male occupational
  structure by ethnic group, 1890,
  181; labor movement in, 182;
  Germans in and Democratic party,
  182; a comparison between crime
  and nativity, 1884–90, 183; Knights
  in, 184–96, 199; and eight-hour
  campaign, 188–95; politics in, 196–
  210; and Socialists, 204–10;
  comparative ethnic support for third-
  party candidacies, 207; contributions
  of Socialists in, 208–10; poem "Hail
  Milwaukee," 215; and
  workingmen's movement, 225, 226
Missouri Pacific Railroad, 125
Mitchell, John (dairyman), 155
Mitchell, John, Jr. (editor), 153
Montgomery, Ala., 171
Montgomery, C. F., 64–65
Montgomery, David, 20–21, 101
Moore, Edgar B., 80, 88, 92, 93, 96,
  102, 103, 223
Moore, James T., 161
Moore, R. Laurence, 229
Morrison, John, 11
Mullen, William, 155, 158, 159-61,
  162, 165–66, 174, 176
Murphey, N. S., 196

National Farmers' Alliance, 27, 32–33,
  136, 204
National Labor Union, 186
National Union Labor party. *See* Union
  Labor party
Newburyport, 75
New York *Times,* 163–64
Nicholson, Judge David, 83

North Chicago Rolling Mill, 179, 195
Northrup, Hiram M., 142
Northwestern Confederacy of Indian
    Tribes, 113
Northwestern Railroad, 124
Norway Plains company, 41
Nugent, Owen, 143

Odd Fellows, 62, 64
Orcutt, A. A., 76
O'Reilly, Rev. Charles, 77
Orzelska family, 212
Owen, A. L., 174

Packinghouse workers, 146
Page, John B., 106
Page, W. R., 69
Papst, Capt. Fred, 180
Paris Commune, 22, 33, 36–37
Park, W. H., 201
Parshley, A. S., 46
Parsons, Albert, 140
Parsons, Kans., 121, 144, 147
Partyism: and Knights, 32
Parysso, Anton, 188, 202
Patterson, Corvine, 117, 127, 134, 141
Payne, Colin, 166
Peabody, Mass., 26
"Peoplehood," 220
People's Journal, 89
People's party, 32; Kansas City, 135;
    Wisconsin, 196–98; in Milwaukee,
    198; and Schilling, 204
Perlman, Selig, 18, 19, 230
Petersburg, Va., streetcar workers, 10
Philadelphia: shoe manufacturers in,
    59
Phillips Exeter Academy, 40
Phillips, James, 120, 130
Piatt, Donn, 5
Picard, Father, 77
Pingree, Hazen S., 132, 145
Pingree, John H., 55, 60
Pinkerton agents, 5
Pioneer, 129–30, 131
Pittsburgh, 226
Pixley, Frank M., 36–37
Pizzini, Andrew, 162
Poem: "Hail Milwaukee," 215
Poe, Police Chief Thomas, 163, 176
Police: in Kansas, 144

Polish: in Milwaukee, 182–84
Political parties: in Gilded Age, xi-xii;
    and workingmen's movement, 226–
    27
Political power: uses of, 30–32
Politics: and labor issues, xiii–xiv; and
    labor, nineteenth century, 20; and
    workers', song, 26–27; and Knights,
    18–37; in Rochester, 44–50; in
    Rutland, 70–71, 75–85, 88–104; in
    Kansas City, 118–42; in Richmond,
    152–72; in Milwaukee, 196–210;
    and workingmen's movement, 225–
    28
Polonia assembly, 192, 194
Populists, xi, 27; and Knights, 19; in
    Kansas, 112, 138–40, 141; in
    Kansas City, 135–39; in Milwaukee,
    204
"Powderly pledge," 12
Powderly, Terence, xiii, 6, 9, 13, 164,
    177; and temperance, 12; and
    politics, 24; and political parties, 27;
    and Rochester Knights, 57; and
    shoeworkers, 59; and Willard, 62;
    and Brown, 97, 103; and Kansas
    City, 120; and Hannan, 123; and
    Fletcher, 126; and Chicago packers,
    133; and Richmond, 154, 162, 163,
    168, 176; and Mullen, 159, 167; and
    Fortune, 169; and Schilling, 186;
    and eight-hour campaign, 188; and
    Milwaukee, 199
Powell, Frank "White Beaver," 196
Powers, Richard, 11
Proctor family, 68–69
Proctor, Fletcher, 68, 82
Proctor Free Library, 70
Proctor papers, 61
Proctor, Redfield, 68–70, 89, 91, 105,
    108; on marble prices, 78; and
    Proctor, Vt., 79, 85–86; and United
    Labor party, 81; and Rutland
    division, 82–83; and servants, 106
Proctor, Vt., 68, 79; creation of, 84;
    YMCA, 111
Producers' Marble Co., 68
Prohibitionists: in Rochester, 47; in
    N.H., 62; in Kansas, 112, 143; in
    Kansas City, 138
Protestant tradition: in Kansas, 139–40

Prout, John, 70
Public good, 220
Pullman, Ill., 92
Purcell, John B., 175
Putnam, Jonas, 89

Quincy, Mass., 31, 38, 39
Quincy *Monitor:* quoted, 2

Rabinowitz, Howard, 150
Racial equality: and Knights in
    Richmond, 169–72
Radicalism: working-class, 3–17
Railroads: and Rutland, 67
Railroad strikes, xi, 112
Randolph, N. V., 175
Reading rooms, 11
Readjuster movement, 152, 153, 154
Redington family, 71
Redington, L. W., 71, 87
Red Wing, Minn., 26
Der Reformer, 186, 200
Reilly, F. J., 155
Reliance Iron Works, 179, 195; metal
    workers, 191
Rendville, Ohio, 26
Republicanism: and American radicals,
    21
Republicans: and labor rule in Rutland,
    95
Residential patterns: in Kansas City,
    117
Richmond *Dispatch,* 152–53, 158,
    165; and Mullen, 161
Richmond *Labor Herald,* 166, 168
Richmond *Planet,* 153, 158
Richmond, Va., 30, 149–77; Knights
    in, 31, 154–55, 156–57; women in,
    150–51; blacks in, 150–52, 164;
    female occupational structure, 1890,
    151; male occupational structure,
    1890, 151; politics in, 152–72; labor
    movement in, 154–56, 168; 1890
    census, 173
Richmond *Whig,* 6, 165
Ripley and Sons, 68
Ripley, E. H., 109
Ripley, E. W., 70
Ripley family, 71
Ripley, Gen., 78
Ripley, William, 106

Ripley, W. Y., 68
Ripley, Zilma Delacy Thomas, 70
Rochester *Courier,* 41, 46
Rochester *Leader,* 52
Rochester, N.H., 4, 38–65; town
    meeting, 1886, 30, 31–32, 52–53;
    women in, 41–42, 43; male
    occupational structure, 1880, 42;
    female occupational structure, 1880,
    43; women's employment, 1880, 43;
    social structure, 1880, 44; politics
    in, 44–50; occupational structure by
    ethnic groups, 1880, 45;
    shoeworkers in, 50–51; occupations
    of shoeworkers' fathers, 1880, 51;
    exercise of power by Knights, 57–
    58; servants in, 61–62
Rochester Savings Bank, 41
Roosevelt, Franklin D., 210, 218
Roosevelt, Theodore, 26, 99
Rose, David G., 205, 206, 208
Rosenthal, Louis, 130
Rudzinski, August, 184, 193
Rudzinski, Theodore, 184, 194, 197,
    198, 203, 223
Rusk, Gov. Jeremiah, 192, 194, 195,
    196, 197, 198
Rutland *Evening Telegram,* 98
Rutland *Herald,* 79; and Tuttle family,
    69; and Knights, 75–76, 89; and
    division, 83, 84, 85; and labor rule,
    93, 95, 96; and Citizens party, 97,
    98
Rutland Marble Co., 68, 105
Rutland Shirt Co., 96
Rutland, Vt., 31, 32, 34, 38, 39, 66–
    111; town meeting, 30; and
    railroads, 67; and marble-quarrying,
    67–68; social elite in, 69–70;
    politics in, 70–71, 75–85, 88–104;
    public office and social prestige, 71;
    ethnicity and class, 72–75; native
    and immigrant components of the
    occupational structure, 1880, 73;
    occupational structure by ethnic
    groups, 1880, 74; women in, 78,
    106; division of, 79, 82–87; after
    division, 88–104; first- and second-
    generation components within the
    Irish-American working class, 90;
    education in, 91–92; labor rule in,

Rutland, Vt. (*cont.*)
91–101; labor rule and self-improvement, 94; Citizens party in, 96–98; politics after 1888, 99–103; results of workingmen's movement, 101–4; servants in, 106–7; Greenback-Labor party in, 108. *See also* West Rutland
Ryall, John, M., 155
Ryan, Richard, 96, 99
Ryegate conspiracy case, 110

Salvation Army: in Rutland, 93
Sartori, Giovanni, 225
Sawyer, Charles H., 53
Schenectady, N.Y.: Socialists in, 211
Schilling, Robert, 30, 185–86, 189, 190, 199, 200, 201, 202; and eight-hour campaign, 191, 193, 194; and Bay View events, 196, 197; in 1890s, 203–4; and Socialism, 208
Scots: in Rochester, 44; in Kansas City, 115, 116
Scott, Ben, 160, 171
Scott, Attorney Walter, 164
Sedalia, Mo., 122
Seebote, 182
Seidel, Emil, 204, 206, 208, 211
Senate Committee on Labor and Capital, 8; and Keogh, 10; and McQuire, 25
Shannon, David A., 231
Sheldon, Charles, 68, 106
Sheldon family, 71, 79
Sheldon, John A., 70
Sheldon Marble Co., 87
Sherman, Porter, 137, 138
Shoeworkers: in Rochester, 50–51, 58–59; in Maine, 63
Skilled trade unionists, 221
Skilled workers: and eight-hour strikes in Milwaukee, 191
Sloan, Judge A. Scott, 201–2
Smith Brothers, Millwrights, 186
Smith, Henry, 185, 186–87, 195, 196–98, 201, 202, 221; and 1886 election, 198; and Populists, 204; and Socialists, 208, 209
Smith, Hiram, 81
Smith, J. Gregory, 70
Smith, Page, 39

Social change: in Gilded Age, xii; and industrialization, 38–40; in Rochester, 44
Social conflict: and Knights, 219
Social Democratic party, 205
Social elite: in Rutland, 69–71
Social equality: and Richmond, 163–64
Socialism, 7, 34; in Milwaukee, 178–79, 204–10, 223; and Schilling, 208
Socialist Labor party: in Milwaukee, 189, 201
Socialists: and eight-hour movement, 193–94
South, the, 149–77
South Ryegate, Vt., 97
Southward, Sheriff J. W., 161
Southwest Strike, xiii, 25, 31, 112, 120–22, 125, 126, 133
Spellman, John D., 79, 81, 83, 85, 96, 98, 100, 223
Spies, August, 189
Splitlog, Mathias, 113
Springfield, George, 45
Stack, Nicholas Byrne, 174
Stafford County Improved Peat Co., 41
Still, Bayrd, 206
St. John, John P., 116–17
"Stonepeggers," 73, 83
Stout, J. C., 134
Strasser, Adolph, 8
Streeter, A. J., 59, 202
Stromquist, Shelton, 147
Sumner, William Graham, 4
Sutherland Falls Marble Co., 68
Swedes: in Kansas City, 115
Swinton, John, xiii; quoted, 26, 27

Tarschys, Daniel, 21–22
Taxpayers' League, Kansas City, 137
Taylor, C. H. J. "Alley," 128–29, 134, 135, 141–42, 223
Taylor, Edwin, 136
Temperance, 12; and Rochester, 46, 47; in N.H., 62
Thernstrom, Stephan, 39, 75
Third party: in Milwaukee, 178–79
Tholfson, Trygve R., 3–4
Thompson, Edward, 219
Thompson, John, 215
Thompson, Richard, 155
Thrall, William B., 106

Town meeting: in New England, 39
Tredagar Iron Works, 149, 152, 154, 167
Trades assembly: in Milwaukee, 181–82
Traeumer, Maj. George P., 194
Trevellick, Richard, 11–12
Tuttle family, 69
Tuttle, Harley C., 83
Twiss, George J., 138
Twist, W. S., 137

Union Labor party, 13, 27, 32; in Rochester, 53; in Kansas, 136, 147; in Milwaukee, 200, 201
United Boot and Shoe Workers National Trade Assembly, 59
United Labor party, 32; in Chicago, 26, 36; in Rochester, 53; in Rutland, 80–81, 88
Universalists: in Rochester, 46
Urban centers: and workingmen's movement, 225
Urban workers, 112–48

Values, 8–13
Vanderbilt, Cornelius, 9
Varney, Philander, 45
Veazey, Judge Walter G., 96
Veazey, Judge Wheelock G., 79
Vemont Central Railroad, 70, 104
Vermont Marble Co., 74, 79, 85, 105, 109
Vickery, Fanny Randolph, 139
Vincent, Henry, 136
Virginia *Star*, 153
Volksblatt, 186, 189, 190, 196
von Cotzhausen, F. W., 200, 221
Vorhees, J. W., 141
Vorwarts, 204
Vossen, William, 126
Vrooman, Frank, 140
Vrooman, Harry, 140
Vrooman, Hiram Perkins, 138, 140
Vrooman, Walter, 140–41, 148

Wachman, Marvin, 205
Waddill, Edmund, 161, 165, 168, 171
Wage slavery, 7

Walker, Joel, 113, 142
Walker, Samuel, 7
Walker, William, 113
Wallace, Albert, 41
Wallace, Anthony, 49
Wallace company, 58, 59
Wallace, Ebenezer, 40–41, 47
Wallace, Edwin, 40–41, 49, 62, 220
Wallace family, 46; and shoeworkers, 50, 51
Wallace, Sumner, 60
Wallber, Emil, 182, 185, 195
Waller, John L., 121
Wardwell, George J., 68, 81–82
Wardwell channeler, 105
Ware, Norman, 18, 19, 20, 59
Warner, Maj. William, 126
Washington *Bee*, 169
Washington, Booker T., 172
Waterloo, Ia., 26
Watson, Tom, 172
Weaver, James, 187
Weber, Frank J., 205
Weil, Louis, 129–30
Wentworth, Russell, 45
Wesson, Miss., 170–71
West Rutland, Vt., 73; and Knights' growth, 77; and division, 83, 84; new town of, 86–87
Wiebe, Robert H., 107
Willard, Francis, 62, 141
Williams, William Appleman, 31
Wilson, J. T., 161, 166, 168, 171, 223
Wise, George, 152, 153, 160, 165, 176
Wise, Henry, 152, 153
Wise, John, 153, 154, 156, 158, 159, 160, 161, 165, 166, 167, 171, 174–75, 176
Wobblies, 21, 34
Wolf, Simon, 58, 65
Women: and Knights, 12; in Rochester, 41–42, 43: in Rutland, 78, 106; in Kansas City, 148; in Richmond, 150–51; and Knights in Milwaukee, 187
Women's Christian Temperance Union: in Kansas, 139
Women's Exchange, Rutland, 100
Women's rights activists: in Kansas, 112

Women's suffrage advocates: in Kansas City, 138–39
Wong, Mrs. Celia, 212, 213
Woodfin, Charles, 106
Woodward, C. Vann, 170
Work ethic, 9
Working class: in Rutland, 72–75
Workingmen's Convention, 36
Workingmen's movement: results in Rutland, 101–4; and community, 221–24; and urban centers, 225; and politics, 225–28; and political parties, 226–27
Wright, Carroll D., xi
Wyandot Indians, 113–14, 142
Wyandotte *Gazette,* 114
Wyandotte *Herald,* 123
Wyandotte, Kans., 114–15

Zeidler, Frank P., 211

A Note on the Author

Leon Fink is a member of the department of history at the University of North Carolina at Chapel Hill. He received his bachelor's degree from Harvard University (1970) and his master's degree and Ph.D. from the University of Rochester (1971 and 1977, respectively). His articles and essay-reviews have appeared in *Labor History, Social History, Labour le Travailleur, International Labor and Working Class History, Radical History Review,* and *Social Education.* He has also contributed to anthologies on *The Southern Common People: Studies in Nineteenth-Century Social History, Health Care in America: Essays in Social History,* and *Working-Class America: Essays on Labor, Community, and American Society.* Currently Mr. Fink is at work with Brian Greenberg on a study of labor organizations in American hospitals.

Books in the Series
The Working Class in American History

Worker City, Company Town: Iron and Cotton-Worker Protest in Troy
and Cohoes, New York, 1855–84
DANIEL J. WALKOWITZ

Life, Work, and Rebellion in the Coal Fields: The Southern
West Virginia Miners, 1880–1922
DAVID ALAN CORBIN

Women and American Socialism, 1870–1920
MARI JO BUHLE

Lives of Their Own: Blacks, Italians, and Poles in Pittsburgh, 1900–1960
JOHN BODNAR, ROGER SIMON, AND MICHAEL P. WEBER

Working-Class America: Essays on Labor, Community, and American Society
EDITED BY MICHAEL H. FRISCH AND DANIEL J. WALKOWITZ

Eugene V. Debs: Citizen and Socialist
NICK SALVATORE

American Labor and Immigration History: 1877–1920s:
Recent European Research
EDITED BY DIRK HOERDER

Workingmen's Democracy: The Knights of Labor and American Politics
LEON FINK

Electrical Workers: A History of Labor at General Electric
and Westinghouse, 1923–60
RONALD W. SCHATZ

The Mechanics of Baltimore: Workers and Politics in
the Age of Revolution, 1763–1812
CHARLES G. STEFFEN

The Practice of Solidarity: American Hat Finishers
in the Nineteenth Century
DAVID BENSMAN

The Labor History Reader
EDITED BY DANIEL J. LEAB

Solidarity and Fragmentation: Working People and Class
Consciousness in Detroit, 1875–1900
RICHARD OESTREICHER

Counter Cultures: Saleswomen, Managers, and Customers in
American Department Stores, 1890–1940
SUSAN PORTER BENSON